LAND TENURE AND TENEMENTS LEGISLATION

SECOND EDITION

Annotated by

Professor Robert Renn

Professor of Conveyan
Partner, He

THOMSON

™

W. GREEN

First published in 2003

Published in 2005 by

W. Green & Son Ltd
21 Alva Street
Edinburgh EH2 4PS

www.wgreen.thomson.com

Typeset by YHT Ltd, London

*Printed in Great Britain by Athenaeum Press Ltd.,
Gateshead, Tyne & Wear*

No natural forests were destroyed to make this product;
Only farmed timber was used and replanted

A CIP catalogue record for this book is available from the British Library

ISBN 0 414 016 130

Annotations © W. Green & Son Ltd 2005

CONTENTS

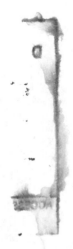

TABLE OF CASES

Table of Cases

TABLE OF STATUTES

TABLE OF STATUTORY INSTRUMENTS

[1] ABOLITION OF FEUDAL TENURE ETC. (SCOTLAND) ACT 2000

(asp 5)

[JUNE 9, 2000]

NOTE

1. The sections which came into force on Royal Assent (June 9, 2000) are specified in s.77 of this Act. The remaining sections have all now been brought into force by the Abolition of Feudal Tenure etc. (Scotland) Act 2000 (Commencement No.1) Order 2003 (SSI 2003/455) (effective November 1, 2003), Abolition of Feudal Tenure etc. (Scotland) Act 2000 (Commencement No.2) (Appointed Day) Order 2003 (SSI 2003/456) (effective November 28, 2004), and Abolition of Feudal Tenure etc. (Scotland) Act 2000 (Commencement No.3) Order 2003 (SSI 2003/620) (effective November 28, 2004), Abolition of Feudal Tenure etc. (Scotland) 2000 (Prescribed Periods) Order 2004 (SSI 2004/478) (effective November 28, 2004).

PART 4

REAL BURDENS

Extinction of superior's rights

Reallotment etc.

Conservation burdens

Compensation

Miscellaneous

Interpretation

An Act of the Scottish Parliament to abolish the feudal system of land tenure; to abolish a related system of land tenure; to make new provision as respects the ownership of land; to make consequential provision for the extinction and recovery of feuduties and of certain other perpetual periodical payments and for the extinction by prescription of any obligation to pay redemption money under the Land Tenure Reform (Scotland) Act 1974; to make further provision as respects real burdens affecting land; to provide for the disentailment of land; to discharge all rights of irritancy held by superiors; to abolish the obligation of thirlage; to prohibit with certain exceptions the granting of leases over land for periods exceeding 175 years; to make new provision as respects conveyancing; to enable firms with separate personality to own land; and for connected purposes. [June 9, 2000]

INTRODUCTION AND GENERAL NOTE

The Scottish Law Commission have been looking at the abolition of the feudal system since 1990. It would be fair to say however that they are not the first body to have looked at this particular question. Indeed the framers of the Land Tenure Reform (Scotland) Act 1974 had the view that on the passing of the Act the feudal system would wither on the vine. That theory was based on the premise that no new feus would be granted if there was no feuduty. That hope proved to be false. The Scottish Law Commission published an initial discussion paper entitled *Property Law Abolition of the Feudal System* in July 1991 (Scot. Law Com. No. 93). Comments were invited at the time. Anyone who reads the initial discussion paper will marvel at what little resemblance there is between the original proposals and the eventual legislation. The Act deals only with the feudal system, although there are certain miscellaneous provisions. In reality this Act is only the first half of a fundamental legislative change in the law of heritable property. The Title Conditions (Scotland) Act 2003 is the second half and is based on the Scottish Law Commission have produced a report in relation to title conditions and real burdens (*Real Burdens*, Scot. Law Com. No. 181, October 2000).

The Act deals with the abolition of the feudal system, land transfers, feu duties, real burdens in feudal writs, conservation burdens, limited compensation for superiors in relation to development values, entails and various other miscellaneous matters such as the abolition of the superior's right of irritancy, the prohibition of leases in excess of 175 years, the abolition of odd forms of tenure such as the Kings Kindly Tenants of Lochmaben and the removal of the difficulty in relation to descriptions in standard securities created by the Beneficial Bank cases (*Bennett v Beneficial Bank plc*, 1995 S.L.T. 1105; *Beneficial Bank plc v McConnachie*, 1996 S.C. 119; *Beneficial Bank plc v Wardle*, 1996 G.W.D. 30-1825). The main point of the Act is, of course, to abolish the entire system of feudal tenure. The abolition provisions came into effect on the appointed day (November 28, 2004) as did the Title Conditions (Scotland) Act 2003 and the Tenements (Scotland) Act 2004. Certain notices which could be served to reallot or preserve burdens had to be recorded before November 28, 2004. Some of the provisions of the Act, however, came into force on Royal Assent on June 9, 2000. These provisions came into effect for convenience or to prevent steps being taken to preserve some sort of tenure structure akin to the feudal system. The prohibition of the creation of leases (for any type of property) in excess of 175 years, (s.67) abolition of superior's right of irritancy (s.53) and the Beneficial Bank reform (Sch.12 para.30(23)(a)) all came into effect on June 9, 2000.

One may be forgiven for coming to the conclusion that although there are certain rights given to the former superior, the Act itself is fundamentally anti-superior. One may also conjecture as to whether or not the provisions which at first glance appear to be in favour of the superior, have been inserted purely from the point of view of human rights. The superiority title is a form of ownership and Article 1 of Protocol 1 to the European Convention on Human Rights does provide that every natural or legal person is entitled to the peaceful enjoyment of his possessions subject to the right of a state to interfere in the public interest (Human Rights Act 1998, Sch.1, Part II, art. 1). Even the provisions for compensation in respect of reserved development value, where a superior may be said to have feued out land for no consideration or for a reduced consideration because of a restriction placed on the title, are not likely to produce vast amounts of compensation for superiors. Moreover, the steps which a superior will have to take to attempt to claim compensation for such a reserved development value are complicated and may well put off many superiors (ss.33–40). Edward I prohibited further sub-infeudation in England and Wales in the 13th century. No steps were, however, taken to prevent the proliferation of leasehold tenure. It is presumably for this reason, therefore, that there is a prohibition of leases for over 175 years. This will create a significant difference between Scotland and England, where there is no such restriction. It is thought, however, that a term of 175 years will be long enough for commercial development purposes and that the restriction will not act as a disincentive to development north of the border.

The Act is in seven parts and consists of 77 sections and 13 schedules.

PART 1

ABOLITION OF FEUDAL TENURE

Abolition on appointed day

1.—The feudal system of land tenure, that is to say the entire system whereby land is held by a vassal on perpetual tenure from a superior is, on the appointed day, abolished.

GENERAL NOTE

The opening words of the first section are nothing if not dramatic. It is striking to note that the entire system of land tenure is abolished in two lines. The framers of the Act are to be congratulated for achieving this in such short compass. What is made clear is that it is the system whereby a party holds land of a superior on perpetual tenure which ceases to exist. The feudal system is essentially a contract between superior and vassal which is renewable by tenure, and that system, and with it the perpetually renewable contract, are abolished on the appointed day.

Consequences of abolition

2.—(1) An estate of dominium utile of land shall, on the appointed day, cease to exist as a feudal estate but shall forthwith become the ownership of the land and, in so far as is consistent with the provisions of this Act, the land shall be subject to the same subordinate real rights and other encumbrances as was the estate of dominium utile.

(2) Every other feudal estate in land shall, on that day, cease to exist.

(3) It shall, on that day, cease to be possible to create a feudal estate in land.

GENERAL NOTE
This section makes it clear that an existing estate of *dominium utile* shall, on the appointed day, become simple or absolute ownership of the land, subject to any burdens and incumbrances which survive abolition. Where a property is subject to a standard security, that standard security will remain as an incumbrance on that property notwithstanding the fact that the title ceases to be feudal. Similarly, any non-feudal burdens which are applicable and enforceable will remain as burdens on the property. If the superior has been able to reallot a feudal burden, that reallotted burden will remain a burden on the property. It is not just the immediate superiority which is extinguished. Section 2(2) makes it clear that every other feudal estate in land shall cease to exist on the appointed day. In effect, the system will collapse in on itself from the paramount superiority of the Crown downwards. Section 58 of the Act provides that, so far as property rights are concerned, the Act binds the Crown and the Prince and Steward of Scotland. As the Bill was going through its parliamentary stages, there was a suggestion that the paramount superiority of the Crown and the Prince and Steward should be retained. This suggestion was prompted by fears of the concept of absolute and unfettered ownership. The proposal was, however, not accepted. To have retained a paramount superiority would have retained a feudal system. Section 2(3) provides that on the appointed day it will not be possible to create any new feudal estate by any means.

Amendment of Land Registration (Scotland) Act 1979

3.—The Land Registration (Scotland) Act 1979 (c.33) shall be amended as follows—

(a) in section 4(2) (applications for registration which are not to be accepted by the Keeper of the Registers of Scotland), after paragraph (a) there shall be inserted—

"(aa) it relates in whole or in part to an interest in land which by, under or by virtue of any provision of the Abolition of Feudal Tenure etc. (Scotland) Act 2000 (asp 5) is an interest which has ceased to exist;";

(b) in section 9 (rectification of Land Register of Scotland)—

(i) in subsection (3), at the beginning insert "Subject to subsection (3B) below,"; and

(ii) after subsection (3A) insert—

"(3B) Subject to subsection (3C) below, rectification (whether requisite or in exercise of the Keeper's discretion) to take account of, or of anything done (or purportedly done) under or by virtue of, any provision of the Abolition of Feudal Tenure etc. (Scotland) Act 2000 (asp 5), other than section 4 or 65, shall, for the purposes of subsection (3) above (and of section 12(3)(cc) of this Act), be deemed not to prejudice a proprietor in possession.

(3C) For the purposes of subsection (3B) above, rectification does not include entering or reinstating in a title sheet a real burden or a condition affecting an interest in land."; and

(c) in section 12(3) (circumstances in which there is no entitlement to be indemnified by the Keeper), after paragraph (c) insert—

"(cc) the loss arises in consequence of—

(i) a rectification which; or

(ii) there being, in the register, an inaccuracy the rectification of which,

were there a proprietor in possession, would be deemed, by subsection (3B) of section 9 of this Act, not to prejudice that proprietor;".

GENERAL NOTE
The abolition of feudal tenure has many consequences. This section amends the Land Registration (Scotland) Act 1979 in relation to the type of deed which the Keeper must reject, the powers the Keeper has to rectify the title sheet, and the liability that the Keeper may have to pay indemnity. An extra sub-paragraph is inserted in s.4(2) of the 1979 Act. The effect of this is that the Keeper will not be able to accept any application for registration where it relates to an

interest in land which has been abolished by virtue of the Abolition of Feudal Tenure etc. (Scotland) Act 2000. So far as rectification is concerned, the general thrust of the 1979 Act is that the Keeper cannot rectify to the prejudice of a proprietor in possession. Section 3(b) of the 2000 Act provides that any rectification to take account of anything done by virtue of the Act shall be deemed not to prejudice a proprietor in possession. The Keeper will therefore be able to delete superiority titles from the Land Register altogether, although he may have to split off titles to minerals where these are reserved to the superior. Similarly, the indemnity provisions contained in s.12 of the 1979 Act are amended. Section 3(c) inserts a new statutory exclusion of indemnity where a loss arises in consequence of a rectification which is made to take account of the abolition of the feudal system.

PART 2

LAND TRANSFERS ETC. ON AND AFTER APPOINTED DAY

Ownership of land

4.—(1) Ownership of land shall pass—
(a) in a case where a transfer is registrable under section 2 of the Land Registration (Scotland) Act 1979 (c.33), on registration in the Land Register of Scotland;
(b) in any other case, on recording of a conveyance of the land in the Register of Sasines.
(2) This section is without prejudice to any other enactment, or rule of law, by or under which ownership of land may pass.
(3) In subsection (1) above—
(a) conveyance includes;
   (i) conveyance by, or under, any enactment, rule of law or decree; and
   (ii) a notice of title deducing title through a conveyance; and
(b) "registrable" and "registration" have the meanings respectively assigned to those expressions by section 1(3) of the Land Registration (Scotland) Act 1979 (c.33).

GENERAL NOTE
There are no dramatic changes to the method of transfer of heritable property. Section 4(1) does, however, provide that ownership of heritable property shall pass on registration in the Land Register or in the Register of Sasines. This principle was re-affirmed by the Inner House of the Court of Session in *Sharp v Thomson*, 1995 S.L.T. 837. The decision of the House of Lords in *Sharp v Thomson*, 1997 S.L.T. 636, is largely an interpretation of company insolvency law and not one of property law. The decision of the Inner House in *Sharp* has been reaffirmed by the House of Lords in *Burnett's Trustee v Grainger*, 2004 S.L.T. 513. Nevertheless, s.4(2) states that the general rule is without prejudice to any other enactment or rule of law by which ownership of land may pass. One suspects that what is envisaged here is something like the automatic vesting provisions for *ex officio* trustees (Titles to Land Consolidation (Scotland) Act 1868, s.26; Conveyancing (Scotland) Act 1874, s.45). What will be transferred after the appointed day is simple or absolute ownership.

Form of application for recording deed in Register of Sasines

5.—(1) Any application for the recording of a deed in the Register of Sasines shall be made by, or on behalf of, the person in whose favour the deed is granted; and it shall not be necessary to endorse on any deed a warrant of registration.
(2) The Scottish Ministers may, after consultation with the Lord President of the Court of Session, make rules—
(a) prescribing the form to be used for the purposes of subsection (1) above; and
(b) regulating the procedure relating to applications for recording.

GENERAL NOTE

This is a formal section. Warrants of registration will no longer be required where deeds are sent to the Register of Sasines. This will mean a dramatic decrease in the Keeper's workload. Much time is taken up in returning deeds because of defective or unsigned warrants. Section 5(2) allows the Scottish Ministers, after consultation with the Lord President, to make rules relating to forms and procedures for recording. If any other rules are required, primary legislation will not be necessary.

Deduction of title for unregistered land etc.

6.—In respect of any land—

(a) a real right in which has never been registered in the Land Register of Scotland; and

(b) title to which has never been constituted by the recording of a deed in the Register of Sasines,

title may be deduced from any person having ownership of the land.

GENERAL NOTE

Clauses of deduction of title are not required where the title is registered in the Land Register. A deduction of title is required where the title is to be registered in the Sasine Register. There are, however, some titles which pre-date the Registration Act 1617. This section makes it clear that for unrecorded or unregistered titles a deduction of title will still be competent.

PART 3

FEUDUTIES

Extinction of feuduties

Extinction on appointed day

7.—Without prejudice to section 13 of this Act, any feuduty which has not been extinguished before the appointed day is extinguished on that day; and accordingly no payment shall be exigible, in respect of feuduty, for that day or for any period after that day.

GENERAL NOTE

Feuduty was an integral part of the feudal system. There had to be a return or *reddendo* to the superior. Formerly, these returns would have been by way of military service or the supply of commodities. Eventually all these returns were commuted into a money payment. The Land Tenure Reform (Scotland) Act 1974 contained provisions for the voluntary and compulsory redemption of feuduty (ss.4, 5 and 6). Despite this, many feu duties were still being collected. Worse still, there were many feu duties which had not been redeemed but which were not collected. Difficulties have also been caused in some cases because the superior simply could not be traced. This section makes it clear that any remaining feu duties will be extinguished on the appointed day.

Requiring compensatory payment

8.—(1) Where a feuduty is extinguished by section 7 of this Act, the person who was the superior in relation to the feu (that person being in the following provisions of this Part of this Act referred to as the "former superior") may, within two years after the appointed day, duly serve on the person who was the vassal in relation to the feu (that person being in those provisions referred to as the "former vassal") notice requiring that a payment specified in the notice (being a payment calculated in accordance with section 9 of this Act) be made to him by the former vassal; and any such payment is referred to in this Act as a "compensatory payment".

(2) In its application to a feuduty which was, at extinction, a cumulo feuduty, subsection (1) above shall be construed as relating to separate notice being duly served on each former vassal from whom payment is

sought; and in that application, notice under that subsection shall be in (or as nearly as may be in) the form, with its Appendix, contained in schedule 1 to this Act.

(3) Except in the application mentioned in subsection (2) above, notice under subsection (1) above shall be in (or as nearly as may be in) the form contained in schedule 2 to this Act.

(4) To any notice served under subsection (1) above shall be attached a copy of the explanatory note which immediately follows, as the case may be—

(a) the Appendix to the form in schedule 1; or

(b) the form in schedule 2,

to this Act.

(5) Subject to section 10 of this Act, if subsections (1) to (4) above are complied with, then within 56 days after due service on him a former vassal shall make the compensatory payment.

(6) The reference in subsection (1) above to a notice being duly served shall be construed in accordance with section 11 of this Act.

GENERAL NOTE

'Where a feuduty has been extinguished, a compensatory payment requires to be made to the former superior. However, whereas the obligation was firmly placed on the vassal to redeem in terms of the Land Tenure Reform (Scotland) Act 1974, the obligation in terms of s.8 is placed firmly on the former superior. The former superior may, within two years of the appointed day, serve a notice on the former vassal requiring a compensatory payment. Where a *cumulo* feuduty has been informally apportioned among various properties, the superior must send a separate notice to each vassal liable for the *cumulo*. The forms of notice are set out in Scheds 1 and 2. The notices must be sent with the appropriate explanatory note. The amount of the compensatory payment must be inserted. The former vassal must make the compensatory payment within 56 days after due service of the notice.

Calculation of amount of compensatory payment

9.—(1) In calculating the compensatory payment in respect of which notice may be served under section 8(1) of this Act, there shall first be determined the sum of money which would, if invested in two and a half per cent. Consolidated Stock at the middle market price at the close of business last preceding the appointed day, produce an annual sum equal to the feuduty.

(2) Unless the feuduty was, at extinction, a cumulo feuduty the sum so determined shall be the compensatory payment.

(3) If the feuduty was, at extinction, a cumulo feuduty the former superior shall, after determining that sum, allocate it among the former vassals in such proportions as are reasonable in all the circumstances; and an amount which is so allocated to a former vassal shall be the compensatory payment for that former vassal.

(4) If the feuduty was, at extinction, a cumulo feuduty wholly or partly apportioned among the former vassals, then for the purposes of subsection (3) above the proportions of an allocation shall be presumed reasonable in so far as they accord with that apportionment.

GENERAL NOTE

The calculation of the compensatory payment is based on the formula already set out in the Land Tenure Reform (Scotland) Act 1974. The sum to be paid is the sum which would, if invested in two and a half per cent Consolidated Stock at the middle market price at the close of business last preceding the appointed day, produce an annual sum equal to the feuduty. In the case of *cumulo* feu duties, the former superior has the task of allocating the compensatory payment among the former vassals in such proportions as are reasonable. Where the *cumulo* has already been apportioned in a disposition or other deed, that allocation will be deemed to be reasonable.

Making compensatory payment by instalments

10.—(1) Where notice under subsection (1) of section 8 of this Act requires from a former vassal a compensatory payment of not less than £50, the former superior shall serve with it a filled out document (in this section referred to as an "instalment document"), in (or as nearly as may be in) the form contained in schedule 3 to this Act, for signature and dating by the former vassal (there being appended to the document so sent a copy of the explanatory note which immediately follows that form in the schedule); and if the former superior does not do so then no requirement to make the compensatory payment shall arise under subsection (5) of that section by virtue of that notice.

(2) Subject to subsection (3) below, a former vassal on whom an instalment document is served shall obtain the option of making the compensatory payment by instalments if (and only if)—

(a) he signs, dates and returns the document within the period which (but for this section) is allowed for making that payment by section 8(5) of this Act; and

(b) when so returning the document, he pays to the former superior an amount equivalent to one tenth of the compensatory payment (being an amount thus payable in addition to the compensatory payment and irrespective of how or when the compensatory payment is subsequently made).

(3) If on or after the date on which an instalment document is served on a former vassal he ceases by virtue of a sale, or transfer for valuable consideration, to have right to the land in respect of which the feuduty was payable or any part of that land (that land or any part of it being in this section referred to as "the land") then—

(a) where he has obtained the option mentioned in subsection (2) above, he shall lose that option; and

(b) where he has not obtained that option, he shall lose the right to obtain it.

(4) Where the option of making the compensatory payment by instalments is obtained, those instalments shall be equal instalments payable where—

(a) the compensatory payment is £500 or less, on each of the five;

(b) it is more than £500 but not more than £1,000, on each of the ten;

(c) it is more than £1,000 but not more than £1,500, on each of the fifteen; and

(d) it is more than £1,500, on each of the twenty, term days of Whitsunday or Martinmas which then next follow; except that—

(i) in a case where any such instalment remains unpaid for forty-two days after falling due, the outstanding balance of the entire compensatory payment shall immediately fall due;

(ii) in a case where, by virtue of subsection (3)(a) above, the option is lost, that outstanding balance shall fall due on the seventh day after the day on which the former vassal ceases to have right to the land; and

(iii) in any other case, the former vassal may pay that outstanding balance at any time.

(5) In a case where, by virtue of subsection (3)(b) above, the right to obtain the option of making the compensatory payment by instalments is lost, section 8(5) of this Act shall apply accordingly.

GENERAL NOTE

If the compensatory payment is not less than £50, the former superior must advise the former vassal of his or her right to pay by instalments. In these cases, the notice must be accompanied by an instalment document in the form contained in Sch.3. The former vassal then has the option of making the compensatory payment by instalments if he or she signs, dates and returns the instalment document. The instalment document must be returned within the 56 day period and it must be accompanied by a payment equivalent to one tenth of the compensatory payment. This initial payment is in addition to the total compensatory payment which will be due. If the former vassal ceases to be the owner, he loses the option in terms of s.10(3) and must then pay the outstanding balance 7 days after he or she ceases to have right to the land. The timing of the payment of the instalments depends on the amount of the compensatory payment and this is set out in s.10(4). If an instalment is unpaid for 42 days, the balance of the entire compensatory payment immediately falls due. The former vassal may pay the outstanding balance at any time.

Service under section 8(1)

11.—(1) Due service under section 8(1) of this Act is effected by delivering the documents in question to the former vassal or by sending them by registered post, or the recorded delivery service, addressed to him at an appropriate place.

(2) An acknowledgement, signed by the former vassal, which conforms to Form A of schedule 4 to this Act, or as the case may be a certificate which conforms to Form B of that schedule and is accompanied by the postal receipt, shall be sufficient evidence of such due service; and if the packet containing the documents in question is, under subsection (1) above, sent by post but is returned to the former superior with an intimation that it could not be delivered, the packet may be delivered or sent by post, with that intimation, to the Extractor of the Court of Session, the delivering or sending to the Extractor being taken to be equivalent to the service of those documents on the former vassal.

(3) For the purposes of subsection (2) above, an acknowledgement of receipt by the Extractor on a copy of those documents shall be sufficient evidence of their receipt by him.

(4) The date on which notice under section 8(1) of this Act is served on a former vassal is the date of delivery, or as the case may be of posting, in compliance with subsection (1) or (2) above.

(5) A reference in this section to an "appropriate place" is, for any former vassal, to be construed as a reference to—

(a) his place of residence;
(b) his place of business; or
(c) a postal address which he ordinarily uses,

or, if none of those is known at the time of delivery or posting, as a reference to whatever place is at that time his most recently known place of residence or place of business or postal address which he ordinarily used.

GENERAL NOTE
Service is by delivery, registered post or recorded delivery. The former vassal may sign an acknowledgement in the style of Form A of Sch.4. Alternatively, a certificate of posting in terms of Form B of Sch.4 is evidence of service. In the event that a notice is returned by the postal authorities, service may be made on the Extractor of the Court of Session. Service should be on the former vassal at his or her place of residence, place of business or some other postal address which the vassal ordinarily uses, or failing all these at the former vassals most recently known place of residence or business or the most recently known postal address.

Extinction by prescription of requirement to make compensatory payment

12.—In Schedule 1 to the Prescription and Limitation (Scotland) Act 1973 (c.52) (which specifies obligations affected by prescriptive periods of five years under section 6 of that Act)—

(a) in paragraph 1, after sub-paragraph (a) there shall be inserted—
"(aa) to any obligation to make a compensatory payment ("compensatory payment" being construed in accordance with section 8(1) of the Abolition of Feudal Tenure etc.

(Scotland) Act 2000 (asp 5), including that section as read with section 56 of that Act);"; and
(b) in paragraph 2(e), after the words "paragraph 1(a)" there shall be inserted "or (aa)".

GENERAL NOTE

The obligation to make a compensatory payment will be subject to the short negative prescription of 5 years.

Arrears

Arrears of feuduty etc.

13.—(1) Feuduty shall continue to be exigible for any period before the appointed day; and if (in so far as so exigible) it has not fallen due before that day, it shall fall due on that day.

(2) On the appointed day feuduty shall cease to constitute a debitum fundi as shall any amount secured, in favour of a superior, by virtue of section 5 of the Land Tenure Reform (Scotland) Act 1974 (c.38) (redemption on transfer of land).

(3) The superior's hypothec is, on the appointed day, abolished.

(4) Subsections (2) and (3) above are without prejudice to any—
(a) action—
    (i) founded on a debitum fundi or superior's hypothec; and
    (ii) commenced before the appointed day; or
(b) right or preference—
    (i) so founded; and
    (ii) claimed in a sequestration, or in some other process in which there is ranking, commenced before that day.

GENERAL NOTE

Although arrears of feuduty will continue to be due, the feuduty and the arrears will, on the appointed day, cease to be real burdens on the land itself. This will remove much of the difficulty which surrounds sales of heritable property where the superior cannot be traced and there appears to be an outstanding feuduty. Purchasers of property will not need to have any regard to the provisions relating to compensatory payments to the former superior. These will simply be matters between the seller and the former superior. There will be no need for purchasers to demand to see evidence of payment of any compensatory amount. The hypothec of the superior will be abolished on the appointed day, without prejudice to any action commenced before the appointed day or any right in preference arising before the appointed day, including ranking in any sequestration.

Disclosure

Duty of collecting third party to disclose information

14.—For the purposes of section 8(1) of this Act, a superior (or, on or after the appointed day, a former superior) who receives, or has at any time received, from a third party an amount collected in respect of feuduty from and remitted to the superior (or former superior) on behalf of a vassal (or, on or after the appointed day, a former vassal) may require the third party to disclose the identity and address of the vassal (or former vassal) and, in the case of remission as a part of a feuduty, the amount so collected from the vassal (or former vassal); and the third party shall, in so far as it is practicable for him to do so, forthwith comply with that requirement.

GENERAL NOTE

In many cases, unallocated proportions of *cumulo* feuduties are collected by a factor or one proprietor in a tenement who then accounts to the superior. One concession made to superiors is that factors or collectors will require to disclose the names and addresses of the parties who are liable to pay. This will enable the former superior to serve the appropriate notice in terms of s.8(2).

Duty to disclose identity etc. of former vassal

15.—Where the former superior purports duly to serve notice under section 8(1) of this Act but the person on whom it is served, being a person who had right to the feu before the appointed day, is not the former vassal because, immediately before the appointed day, some other person and not he had right to the feu, he shall forthwith disclose to the former superior—

(a) the identity and address of that other person; or

(b) (if he cannot do that) such other information as he has which might enable the former superior to discover that identity and address.

GENERAL NOTE

If a superior serves notice on a party he regards as the former vassal but that party has immediately before the appointed day transferred the property to someone else then the party on whom the notice is served must disclose the identity of the true former vassal or alternatively give such information as may allow the former superior to trace the former vassal.

Interpretation

Interpretation of Part 3

16.—(1) In this Part of this Act, unless the context otherwise requires—
"compensatory payment" shall be construed in accordance with section 8(1) of this Act; "feuduty" includes blench duty; "superior", in relation to a feu, means the person who, immediately before the appointed day, has right to the immediate superiority, whether or not he has completed title (and if more than one person comes within that description, then the person who has most recently acquired such right); and "former superior" shall be construed in accordance with section 8(1) of this Act; and "vassal", in relation to a feu, means the person who, immediately before the appointed day, has right to the feu, whether or not he has completed title (and if more than one person comes within that description, then the person who has most recently acquired such right); and "former vassal" shall be construed in accordance with section 8(1) of this Act.

(2) Where a feu comprises parts each held by a separate vassal, being parts upon which feuduty has not been allocated, the whole of any feuduty exigible in respect of the parts so held is in this Part of this Act referred to as a "cumulo feuduty"; and any reference in this Part of this Act to a feu is to be construed, in relation to the parts so held, as a reference to those parts collectively.

(3) Any reference in this Part of this Act to a feu is to be construed as including a reference to any part of a feu if it is a part upon which feuduty has been allocated.

(4) Where, immediately before the appointed day a feu, or any part of a feu, is held by two or more vassals as common property—

(a) they shall be severally liable to make any compensatory payment (but as between, or as the case may be among, themselves they shall be liable in the proportions in which they hold the feu); and

(b) subject to section 11 of this Act they shall together be treated for the purposes of this Act as being a single vassal.

GENERAL NOTE

This is a special definition section for this part of the Act. Interestingly enough, feuduty is stated to include blench duty, although a blench duty is normally of a nominal amount. It is unlikely that a former superior will want to be bothered claiming a compensatory payment in respect of a blench duty. It will not matter for the purposes of the compensatory payment whether the former superior or former vassal has actually completed title. *Cumulo* feuduty is given the appropriate definition and allocated feuduties will be treated as separate feuduties. Where the former vassals own the property in common, the liability to make the compensatory payment will be joint and several so far as the superior is concerned. As between the common owners, liability will depend on the proportions in which the title is held. Where there is a liability to disclose information such as an address, the obligation shall apply to each common owner.

PART 4

REAL BURDENS

Extinction of superior's rights

Extinction of superior's rights

[1] **17.**—(1) Subject to sections 18 to 18C, 19, 20, 27, 27A, 28, 28A and 60 of this Act and to sections 52 to 56 (which make provision as to common schemes, facility burdens and service burdens) and 63 (which makes provision as to manager burdens) of the Title Conditions (Scotland) Act 2003 (asp 9)—

(a) a real burden which, immediately before the appointed day, is enforceable by, and only by, a superior shall on that day be extinguished; and

(b) any other real burden shall, on and after that day, not be enforceable by a former superior other than in that person's capacity as owner of land or as holder of a conservation burden, health care burden or economic development burden.

(2) Subject to subsection (3) below and to the provision made by section 20 of this Act for there to be a transitional period during which a real burden shall yet be enforceable—

(a) on or after the appointed day, no proceedings for such enforcement shall be commenced;

(b) any proceedings already commenced for such enforcement shall be deemed to have been abandoned on that day and may, without further process and without any requirement that full judicial expenses shall have been paid by the pursuer, be dismissed accordingly; and

(c) any decree or interlocutor already pronounced in proceedings for such enforcement shall be deemed to have been reduced, or as the case may be recalled, on that day.

(3) Subsection (2) above shall not affect any proceedings, decree or interlocutor in relation to—

(a) a right of irritancy held by a superior; or

[2] (aa) a right of enforcement held by virtue of any of the provisions mentioned in subsection (1) above;

(b) a right to recover damages or to the payment of money.

AMENDMENT

1. As amended by the Title Conditions (Scotland) Act 2003 (asp 9), Sch.13, para.2 and Sch.15 (effective April 4, 2003).

2. Inserted by the Title Conditions (Scotland) Act 2003 (asp 9), Sch.13, para.2 (effective April 4, 2003).

GENERAL NOTE

This Act deals with feudal burdens only. The Title Conditions (Scotland) Act deals with real burdens and conditions after abolition of the feudal system. Burdens which are purely feudal in the sense of being enforceable only by the superior, will be extinguished on the appointed day. In many ways this is the whole point of abolition of the feudal system. Superiors will no longer be able to extract payments for waivers of real burdens and conditions. In cases where a burden is enforceable by the superior and another party such as a co-feuar by virtue of an *ius quaesitum tertio*, the burden will remain enforceable by that other party. No proceedings for enforcement of a burden by a former superior shall be competent after the appointed day and any proceedings already commenced shall be deemed to be abandoned without expenses. Even any decree or interlocutor already pronounced in enforcement proceedings shall be deemed to be reduced or recalled. The only exceptions to this are in relation to a right of irritancy held by a superior or a right to recover damages or the payment of money. Presumably, therefore, subs.(2) will only apply to declaratory actions, whereby a vassal is ordained to do something, or interdicts, where a vassal is restrained from doing something. Irritancies are also dealt with in s.53. Extinction is subject to the reallotment and preservation provisions in the Act and in the Title Conditions (Scotland) Act 2003.

Reallotment etc.

Reallotment of real burden by nomination of new dominant tenement

¹ **18.**—(1) Without prejudice to sections 18A to 18C of this Act, where—

(a) a feudal estate of dominium utile of land is subject to a real burden enforceable by a superior of the feu or which would be so enforceable were the person in question to complete title to the dominium directum; and

(b) at least one of the conditions set out in subsection (7) below is met,

the superior may, before the appointed day, prospectively nominate other land (being land of which he has right to the sole dominium utile or sole allodial ownership), or any part of that other land, as a dominant tenement by duly executing and registering a notice in, or as nearly as may be in, the form contained in schedule 5 to this Act.

(2) The notice shall—

(a) set out the title of the superior;

(b) describe, sufficiently to enable identification by reference to the Ordnance Map, both the land the dominium utile of which is subject to the real burden (or any part of that land) and the land (or part) nominated;

(c) specify which of the conditions set out in subsection (7) below is (or are) met;

(d) set out the terms of the real burden; and

(e) set out the terms of any counter-obligation to the real burden if it is a counter-obligation enforceable against the superior.

(3) For the purposes of subsection (1) above a notice is duly registered only when registered against both tenements described in pursuance of subsection (2)(b) above.

(4) Before submitting any notice for registration under this section, the superior shall swear or affirm before a notary public that to the best of the knowledge and belief of the superior all the information contained in the notice is true.

(5) For the purposes of subsection (4) above, if the superior is—

(a) an individual unable by reason of legal disability, or incapacity, to swear or affirm as mentioned in that subsection, then a legal representative of the superior may swear or affirm;

(b) not an individual, then any person authorised to sign documents on its behalf may swear or affirm;

and any reference in that subsection to a superior shall be construed accordingly.

(6) Subject to subsection (6A) below, if subsections (1) to (5) above are complied with and immediately before the appointed day the real burden is still enforceable by the superior (or by his successor) or would be so enforceable, or still so enforceable, were the person in question to complete title to the dominium directum then, on that day—

(a) the land (or part) nominated shall become a dominant tenement; and

(b) the land the dominium utile of which was subject to the real burden (or if part only of that land is described in pursuance of subsection (2)(b) above, that part) shall be the servient tenement.

² (6A) Such compliance as is mentioned in subsection (6) above shall not

15

be effective to preserve any right to enforce a manager burden ("manager burden" being construed in accordance with section 63(1) of the Title Conditions (Scotland) Act 2003 (asp 9)).

(7) The conditions are—

(a) that the land which by virtue of this section would become the dominant tenement has on it a permanent building which is in use wholly or mainly as a place of human—

  (i) habitation; or

  (ii) resort

and that building is, at some point, within one hundred metres (measuring along a horizontal plane) of the land which would be the servient tenement;

(b) that the real burden comprises—

  (i) a right (other than any sporting rights, as defined by section 65A(9) of this Act) to enter, or otherwise make use of, the servient tenement; or

  (ii) a right of pre-emption or of redemption; or

(c) that the land which by virtue of this section would become the dominant tenement comprises—

  (i) minerals; or

  (ii) salmon fishings or some other incorporeal property,

and it is apparent from the terms of the real burden that it was created for the benefit of such land.

(8) This section is subject to sections 41 and 42 of this Act.

AMENDMENT

1. As amended by the Title Conditions (Scotland) Act 2003 (asp 9), Sch.13, para.3 (effective April 4, 2003).

2. Inserted by the Title Conditions (Scotland) Act 2003 (asp 9), Sch.13, para.3 (effective April 4, 2003).

GENERAL NOTE

It was felt that there might be situations where it would be unfair to remove the right of the former superior to enforce a real burden contained in a feu. The correct legal advice to have given the seller of property where it was intended to burden that property with various conditions and prohibitions would, until a few years ago, have been to feu the ground rather than dispone it. The superior's title would have been obvious; it was the superiority title itself. Moreover, the interest of a superior to enforce a burden was always presumed, at least in the first instance (*Earl of Zetland v Hislop* (1882) 9 R. (H.L.) 40). On the other hand, where a real burden or condition is inserted in a disposition, although that burden can be enforced between the original disponer and disponee as a matter of contract (*Scottish Co-operative Wholesale Society v Finnie*, 1937 S.C. 835), questions of enforcement by singular successors of the original disponer have always been more difficult, especially where the disposition creating the burden does not specify that the burden is to be enforceable by the disponer and his or her successors as owners of identifiable land. The reallotment provisions are designed to cater for cases where it would have been reasonable to impose a burden. An obvious case would be where someone (perhaps a widow) had decided that the garden ground was too much work and, having obtained planning permission for the erection of a bungalow in the lower part of the garden, feued that part in return for payment of a purchase price, subject to strict conditions as to the height and maintenance of walls and fences and the height of the bungalow, with prohibitions against the keeping of powerboats or against the carrying on of any trade, business or profession, and the like. On the appointed day the widow, still living in the original house, would lose all right to enforce these burdens. Section 18 allows such a superior to reallot the right to enforce the burden from the superiority title of the part of the garden feued to the ordinary *dominium utile* of the ground remaining with the original house. Given the fact that it has been decided that real burdens and conditions are to remain a feature of the land tenure system in Scotland, the provisions of s.18 are reasonable. The superior must take certain steps before the appointed day to reallot the burden and some might argue that these steps are quite complicated. If the superior fails to take these steps then, no matter what amenity considerations there may be, the right to enforce the burdens will be extinguished along with the superiority itself. There are three situations in which the superior can reallot the burden in terms of this section and the superior must, prior to submitting any notice of reallotment to the

Land Register or Register of Sasine, serve a copy of the notice and an explanatory note on the vassal unless it is not reasonably practicable to do (s.41).

Subs.(1)

The superior need not have a completed title to the superiority but must, before the appointed day, nominate other land in his or her ownership as the dominant land for the purpose of enforcing the former feudal burden. This is done by executing and registering a notice in the form contained in Sch.5. A superiority title on its own cannot be a dominant tenement for the purposes of reallotment.

Subs.(2)

This subsection sets out what must be contained in the notice. The land which is subject to the burden, and the new land which is to be the dominant tenement for enforcement in the future, must both be described in the notice so that they can be identified on the ordnance map. The burden itself must be set out, along with any counter-obligation on the part of the superior. The notice must also state on which of the three grounds the superior considers he or she has the right to reallot.

Subs.(3)

The notice is not effective until it is registered against both the burdened property and the nominated property which is to be the dominant tenement for enforcement in the future. This provision (and others like it in the Act) recognises one of the main difficulties of the existing system of real burdens, namely that it is often impossible to ascertain who can enforce the burden. One of the benefits of the feudal system was that the superior provided a focus for enforcement. In fact many solicitors simply ignored the law of *ius quaesitum tertio* and were satisfied with a waiver or consent from a superior alone. The law of *ius quaesitum tertio* is notoriously complicated and confusing, and where burdens are created in a disposition the granter of that disposition may have sold his or her remaining lands in lots so that the original dominant land may have sub-divided, with perhaps 20 or more people possibly entitled to enforce the original burden. In such a case, of course, it is unlikely that all of these 20 people would have any interest. This subsection will ensure greater clarity in relation to enforcement rights where a burden is reallotted.

Subs.(4)

A superior will not be entitled to register a notice of reallotment without the matter being given some serious consideration. One would not want a situation to arise where superiors issued notices against all their vassals simply in the hope of preserving the right to enforce burdens. The superior must therefor swear or affirm before a notary public that to the best of his or her knowledge and belief the information contained in the notice is true.

Subs.(5)

A legal representative of the superior, or a director or other officer authorised to sign documents in the case of a corporate superior, may swear or affirm.

Subs.(6)

The process had to be completed before the appointed day, although it does not matter that the superior does not have a completed title. Where the reallotment procedure has been properly complied with, the nominated land (or whichever part is appropriate) becomes a dominant tenement for the purpose of enforcement of the burden and the burdened land remains as a servient tenement. The terminology used in the Act is taken from the law of servitudes but emphasises that a burden, to be real, must be praedial both in relation to the burdened land and the land entitled to enforce. It is the fact of ownership of the dominant land which gives the right to enforce.

Subs.(6A)

Manager burdens are dealt with separately in the Title Conditions (Scotland) Act 2003.

Subs.(7)

This is in many ways the most important provision in this section. A reallotment notice could only be registered in three situations. Firstly, it could be registered if the land nominated as the dominant land had on it a permanent building in use wholly or mainly as a place of human habitation or resort and that building (not the land) was at some point within 100 metres, measuring along a horizontal plane, of the burdened land. This caters for the situation described above in the general note. It should be noted that the measurement of 100 metres is taken from the building and not the boundary of the proposed dominant land. It should also be noted that the building had to be permanent. This presumably excludes caravans and other mobile homes. Although the situation in which this is most likely to arise will involve an ordinary residential dwellinghouse, the building needed only be wholly or mainly used as a place of human resort. This would include, for example, public houses, hotels, theatres, shops, factories and other places of employment. It is difficult to envisage a building which might not be a place of human resort. Even a crematorium might qualify. It should also be noted that the building need only be used "mainly" as a place of human habitation or resort. It need not be exclusively so used. Secondly, reallotment was possible where the real burden comprises a right to enter or otherwise make use of the burdened property, or a right of pre-emption or redemption. The superior might have reserved some access or other right over the burdened property which benefits not just the superiority title but also some other adjoining land. Reallotment of the burden to that adjoining land would be reasonable. There is no distance qualification. Similarly, rights of pre-emption or redemption might be attached to superiority titles. If the superior wished to retain these then he or she required to take the necessary steps to reallot these real rights on other land owned by the superior. Again there is no distance qualification. Thirdly, reallotment was possible where the land which would become the dominant tenement for enforcement purposes comprised minerals, salmon fishings or some other incorporeal property and it was apparent from the terms of the real burden that it was created for such land. It is common to find reservations of minerals in the titles to most properties. Often the ancillary rights to work the minerals are reserved, but in some cases these ancillary rights may be enshrined in real burdens on the surface of the land. There may, for example, be a prohibition of building or of building without taking certain steps to reinforce the foundations against subsidence. It should be apparent from such a burden that it was created for the benefit of the mineral title. Accordingly, it was reasonable to allow such a burden to be reallotted to the mineral title and away from the superiority. Similarly, there may be burdens placed on the title to land bounded by a river where the salmon fishings themselves are separately owned. The enforcement of these burdens may be vital to the proper enjoyment of the salmon fishings and accordingly,where the superior owns the salmon fishings and superiority of adjoining land, it was appropriate to allow reallotment of the burden from the superiority title to the salmon fishings title itself.

Personal pre-emption burdens and personal redemption burden

[1] **18A.**—(1) Without prejudice to section 18 of this Act, where a feudal estate of *dominium utile* of land is subject to a real burden which comprises a right of pre-emption or redemption and is enforceable by a superior of the feu or would be so enforceable were the person in question to complete title to the *dominium directum* the superior may, before the appointed day, by duly executing and registering against the *dominium utile* a notice in, or as nearly as may be in, the form contained in schedule 5A to this Act, prospectively convert that burden into a personal pre-emption burden or as the case may be into a personal redemption burden.

(2) The notice shall—

(a) set out the title of the superior;

(b) describe, sufficiently to enable identification by reference to the Ordnance Map, the land the *dominium utile* of which is subject to the real burden (or any part of that land);

(c) set out the terms of the real burden; and

(d) set out the terms of any counter-obligation to the real burden if it is a counter-obligation enforceable against the superior.

(3) Before submitting any notice for registration under this section, the superior shall swear or affirm as is mentioned in subsection (4) of section 18 of this Act.

(4) Subsection (5) of that section applies for the purposes of subsection (3) above as it applies for the purposes of subsection (4) of that section.

(5) If subsections (1) to (3) above are, with subsection (4) of that section, complied with and immediately before the appointed day the real burden is still enforceable by the superior (or his successor) or would be so enforceable, or still so enforceable, were the person in question to complete title to the *dominium directum* then, on that day—

(a) the real burden shall be converted into a real burden in favour of that person, to be known as a "personal pre-emption burden" or as the case may be as a "personal redemption burden"; and

(b) the land the *dominium utile* of which was subject to the real burden (or if part only of that land is described in pursuance of subsection (2)(b) above, that part) shall become the servient tenement.

(6) Title to enforce the burden against the land to which the notice relates shall be subject to any such counter-obligation as was set out by virtue of subsection (2)(d) above.

(7) The right to a personal pre-emption burden or personal redemption burden may be assigned or otherwise transferred to any person; and any such assignation or transfer shall take effect on registration.

(8) Where the holder of a personal pre-emption burden or personal redemption burden does not have a completed title—

(a) title may be completed by the holder registering a notice of title; or

(b) without completing title, the holder may grant a deed—

　　(i) assigning the right to; or

　　(ii) discharging, in whole or in part,

the burden; but unless the deed is one to which section 15(3) of the Land Registration (Scotland) Act 1979 (c.33) (circumstances where unnecessary to deduce title) applies, it shall be necessary, in the deed, to deduce title to the burden through the midcouples linking the holder to the person who had the last completed title.

(9) This section is subject to sections 41 and 42 of this Act.

AMENDMENT
　1. Inserted by the Title Conditions (Scotland) Act 2003 (asp 9), s.114 (effective April 4, 2003).

GENERAL NOTE
　Section 18 of the 2000 Act allowed a superior to re-allot a pre-emption or redemption to specific land owned by the superior as a new benefited property. There were cases of course where the superior did not own any other land. Section 18A allowed a superior to convert a pre-emption or redemption into a personal right, subject to the same provisions in relation to notice, the swearing of oaths and other matters. The right to the personal pre-emption or redemption burden may be assigned and any such assignation takes effect on registration. This creates the rather odd situation of personal burdens which are not praedial in so far as the benefit is concerned, but yet require registration either of a notice or assignation.

Conversion into economic development burden

　¹ **18B.**—(1) Without prejudice to section 18 of this Act, where a feudal estate of *dominium utile* of land is subject to a real burden which is imposed for the purpose of promoting economic development and is enforceable by the Scottish Ministers or a local authority, being in either case the superior of the feu, or would be so enforceable were the Scottish Ministers or as the case may be the local authority to complete title to the *dominium directum*, the superior may, before the appointed day, by duly executing and registering against the *dominium utile* a notice in, or as nearly as may be in, the form contained in schedule 5B to this Act, prospectively convert that burden into an economic development burden.

(2) The notice shall—

(a) set out the title of the superior;

(b) describe, sufficiently to enable identification by reference to the Ordnance Map, the land the *dominium utile* of which is subject to the real burden (or any part of that land);

(c) set out the terms of the real burden;

(d) set out the terms of any counter-obligation to the real burden if it is a counter-obligation enforceable against the superior; and

(e) state that the burden was imposed for the purpose of promoting economic development and provide information in support of that statement.

(3) If subsections (1) and (2) above are complied with and immediately before the appointed day the real burden is still enforceable by the superior or would be so enforceable were the Scottish Ministers or as the case may be the local authority to complete title to the *dominium directum* then on that day the real burden shall be converted into an economic development burden and on and after that day the Scottish Ministers or, as the case may be, the authority, shall—

(a) have title to enforce the burden against the land to which the notice relates; and

(b) be presumed to have an interest to enforce it.

(4) Title to enforce the burden against the land to which the notice relates shall be subject to any such counter-obligation as was set out by virtue of subsection (2)(d) above.

(5) This section is subject to sections 41 and 42 of this Act.

AMENDMENT

1. Inserted by the Title Conditions (Scotland) Act 2003 (asp 9), s.114 (effective April 4, 2003).

GENERAL NOTE

Economic development burdens in respect of claw-back obligations to local authorities or Scottish Ministers are introduced by s.45 of the Title Conditions (Scotland) Act 2003. New s.18B in the 2000 Act allowed Scottish Ministers or a local authority to convert existing feudal burdens into economic development burdens. Again it was not be necessary to re-allot to land. The form of notice is contained in Sch.5B. The local authority or Scottish Ministers will have title to enforce the burden and be presumed to have an interest in it.

Conversion into health care burden

[1] **18C.**—(1) Without prejudice to section 18 of this Act, where a feudal estate of *dominium utile* of land is subject to a real burden which is imposed for the purpose of promoting the provision of facilities for health care and is enforceable by a National Health Service trust or the Scottish Ministers, being in either case the superior of the feu, or would be so enforceable were the trust or as the case may be the Scottish Ministers to complete title to the *dominium directum*, the superior may, before the appointed day, by duly executing and registering against the *dominium utile* a notice in, or as nearly as may be in, the form contained in schedule 5C to this Act, prospectively convert that burden into a health care burden.

(2) The notice shall—

(a) set out the title of the superior;

(b) describe, sufficiently to enable identification by reference to the Ordnance Map, the land the *dominium utile* of which is subject to the real burden (or any part of that land);

(c) set out the terms of the real burden;

(d) set out the terms of any counter-obligation to the real burden if it is a counter-obligation enforceable against the superior; and

(e) state that the burden was imposed for the purpose of promoting the provision of facilities for health care and provide information in support of that statement.

(3) If subsections (1) and (2) are complied with and immediately before the appointed day the real burden is still enforceable by the superior or would be so enforceable were the trust or as the case may be the Scottish Ministers to complete title to the *dominium directum* then on that day the real burden shall be converted into a health care burden and on and after that day the trust or, as the case may be, the Scottish Ministers, shall—

(a) have title to enforce the burden against the land to which the notice in question relates; and

(b) be presumed to have an interest to enforce it.

(4) Title to enforce the burden against the land to which the notice relates shall be subject to any such counter-obligation as was set out by virtue of subsection (2)(d) above.

(5) In subsections (1) and (2) above, "facilities for health care" includes facilities ancillary to health care; as for example (but without prejudice to that generality) accommodation for staff employed to provide health care.

(6) This section is subject to sections 41 and 42 of this Act.

AMENDMENT
  1. Inserted by the Title Conditions (Scotland) Act 2003 (asp 9), s.114 (effective April 4, 2003).

GENERAL NOTE
  This allowed a feudal superior (a National Health Service Trust or Scottish Ministers) to convert a burden for the provision of facilities for healthcare into a healthcare burden notwithstanding the fact there was no other land to which the burden could be re-allotted. Provisions are set out for notification and registration. Title and interest are presumed.

Reallotment of real burden by agreement

19.—(1) Where a feudal estate of dominium utile of land is subject to a real burden enforceable by a superior of the feu or which would be so enforceable were the person in question to complete title to the dominium directum the superior may, before the appointed day—

(a) serve notice in, or as nearly as may be in, the form contained in schedule 6 to this Act, on the person who has right to the feu that he seeks to enter into an agreement with that person under this section prospectively nominating other land (being land of which the superior has right to the sole dominium utile or sole allodial ownership), or any part of that other land, as a dominant tenement;

(b) enter into such an agreement with that person; and

(c) duly register that agreement;

but if they think fit they may, by the agreement, modify the real burden or any counter-obligation to the real burden if it is a counter-obligation enforceable against the superior (or both the real burden and any such counter-obligation).

(2) The notice shall—

(a) set out the title of the superior;

(b) describe both the land the dominium utile of which is subject to the real burden (or any part of that land) and the land (or part) nominated;

(c) set out the terms of the real burden; and

(d) set out the terms of any such counter-obligation as is mentioned in subsection (1) above.

(3) An agreement such as is mentioned in paragraph (b) of subsection (1) above shall be a written agreement—

(a) which expressly states that it is made under this section; and

(b) which includes all the information, other than that relating to service, required to be set out in completing the notice the form of which is contained in schedule 6 to this Act.

(4) For the purposes of subsection (1)(c) above an agreement is duly registered only when registered against both tenements described in pursuance of subsection (2)(b) above.

(5) If subsections(1)(b) and (c), (3) and (4) above are complied with and immediately before the appointed day the real burden is still enforceable by the superior (or by his successor) or would be so enforceable, or still so enforceable, were the person in question to complete title to the dominium directum then on that day—

(a) the land (or part) nominated shall become a dominant tenement; and

(b) the land the dominium utile of which was subject to the real burden (or if part only of that land is described in pursuance of subsection(2)(b) above, that part) shall be the servient tenement.

(6) A person may enter into an agreement under this section even if he has not completed title to the dominium utile of the land subject to the real burden, or as the case may be title to the dominium directum of that land or to the dominium utile of the land nominated (or, if the land nominated is allodial land, to the land nominated), provided that, in any case to which section 15(3) of the Land Registration (Scotland) Act 1979 (c.33) (simplification of deeds relating to registered interests) does not apply, he deduces title, in the agreement, from the person who appears in the Register of Sasines as having the last recorded title to the interest in question.

(7) This section is subject to section 42 of this Act.

GENERAL NOTE

The suggestion that a former vassal might have been prepared to sign an agreement whereby the right to enforce a burden was transferred from a superiority to other land owned by the former superior is, at first glance, odd. Presumably most former vassals will be glad to be free of feudal restriction. One suspects, therefore, that this section may have been inserted with a view to compliance with Article 1 of Protocol 1 to the European Convention on Human Rights. It is possible, however, that a reverse waiver situation might arise and a former superior might pay a former vassal a lump sum as a consideration for allowing the burden to remain.

Subs.(1)

It was up to the superior to invite the vassal to enter into an agreement by serving on the vassal before the appointed day a notice in the form contained in Sch.6. The notice was merely a request, but if the vassal agreed then the agreement was completed and registered. The agreement may modify the burden.

Subs.(2)

The notice had to set out the title of the superior and describe both the burdened land and the land nominated as the dominant land for enforcement of the burden in the future. The terms of the burden and any counter-obligation must be set out.

Subs.(3)

The agreement had to be in writing and must state expressly that it is made under s.19. The agreement must include all the information contained in the Sch.6 notice.

Subs.(4)

Following the pattern of the Act, the agreement had to be registered against the titles of both the burdened land and the dominant land.

Subs.(5)

Once the agreement was registered prior to the appointed day, the nominated land became the dominant land for enforcement of the burden. It should be noted, however, that entering an agreement in terms of s.19 will not make a burden real and enforceable if it was not real and enforceable by the superior prior to the date and registration of the agreement.

Subs.(6)

It does not matter that title to the superiority, the burdened land, or indeed the nominated land, has been completed as long as the parties entering the agreement have right. Allodial land is included.

Subs.(7)

Section 42 relates to various reallotment sections but *inter alia* provides that once an agreement has been registered, a further agreement cannot be registered in relation to the same burden unless the first agreement is discharged.

Reallotment of real burden by order of Lands Tribunal

20.—[1] (1) Where but for paragraph (b) of subsection (1) of section 18 of this Act a superior could proceed under that subsection prospectively to nominate land (in this section referred to as the "prospective dominant tenement") he may, provided that he has first, in pursuance of section 19 of this Act, attempted to reach agreement as respects the real burden in question with the person who has right to the feu, apply to the Lands Tribunal for an order under subsection (7) of this section; but such an application is competent only if made before the appointed day.

(2) An applicant under subsection (1) above shall include in his application a description of the requisite attempt to reach agreement.

[2] (3) After sending or delivering to the Lands Tribunal an application under subsection (1) above, the superior may, within—
42 days; or such longer period of days (being a period which ends before the appointed day) as the Lands Tribunal may allow if it is satisfied that there is good cause for so allowing, duly execute and register a notice in, or as nearly as may be in, the form contained in schedule 7 to this Act.

(4) The notice shall—

(a) set out the title of the superior;

(b) describe, sufficiently to enable identification by reference to the Ordnance Map, both the land the dominium utile of which is subject to the real burden (or any part of that land) and the prospective dominant tenement;

(c) set out the terms of the real burden; and

(d) set out the terms of any counter-obligation to the real burden if it is a counter-obligation enforceable against the superior.

(5) For the purposes of this section, a notice is duly registered only when registered against both tenements described in pursuance of subsection (4)(b) above; and if it is so registered and immediately before the appointed day—

(a) the real burden is still enforceable by the superior (or by his successor) or would be so enforceable, or still so enforceable, were the person in question to complete title to the dominium directum; and

(b) no order under subsection (7) below has been registered under subsection (11) below in respect of the application,

then on that day the prospective dominant tenement shall, for the transitional period, become the dominant tenement and the land the dominium utile of which is subject to the real burden (or, if part only of that land is described under paragraph (b) of subsection (4) above, that part) shall, for the transitional period, be the servient tenement.

(6) The reference in subsection (5) above to the transitional period is to the period beginning on the appointed day and ending on—

(a) the day on which an order under subsection (7) below is registered under subsection (11) below in respect of the application; or

(b) if no such order is so registered, such day later than the appointed day as the Scottish Ministers may by order specify (that later day being in this Act referred to as the "specified day").

[2] (7) If, on an application under subsection (1) above as respects which a notice has been duly registered—

[1] (a) the Lands Tribunal is satisfied that, were the real burden to be extinguished, there would be material detriment to the value or enjoyment of the applicant's ownership (taking him to have owner-ship) of the dominant tenement, the Tribunal may order that, subject to subsection (9) of this section—

(i) if the order can be and is registered before the appointed day, then on that day the prospective dominant tenement shall become the dominant tenement and the land the dominium utile of which is subject to the real burden (or, if part only of that land is described under paragraph (b) of subsection (4) above, that part) shall be the servient tenement; or

(ii) the dominant tenement for the transitional period shall, after that period, continue to be the dominant tenement and the

23

servient tenement for the transitional period shall, after that period, continue to be the servient tenement; or

(b) the Lands Tribunal is not so satisfied, it may make an order refusing the application.

(8) Where in respect of the application—

(a) an order under paragraph (a) of subsection (7) above is registered—

(i) before the appointed day and immediately before that day the real burden is still enforceable by the superior (or by his successor) or would be so enforceable, or still so enforceable, were the person in question to complete title to the dominium directum, then on that day; or

(ii) on or after the appointed day and immediately before the day of registration the real burden is still enforceable by the former superior (or by his successor) or would be so enforceable, or still so enforceable, as mentioned in sub-paragraph (i) above, then on the day of registration,

the prospective dominant tenement shall become the dominant tenement and the land the dominium utile of which was subject to the real burden (or, if part only of that land is described under paragraph (b) of subsection (4) above, that part) shall be the servient tenement;

(b)–(c) [*Repealed by the Title Conditions (Scotland) Act 2003 (asp 9), Sch.15, (effective April 4, 2003*]

(9) An order under subsection (7)(a) above may modify the real burden or any counter-obligation to the real burden if it is a counter-obligation enforceable against the applicant (or both the real burden and any such counter-obligation).

(10) The decision of the Lands Tribunal on an application under subsection (1) above shall be final.

(11) An order under subsection (7) above shall forthwith be extracted and registered by the Lands Tribunal against both tenements described in pursuance of subsection (4)(b) above; and the expenses of registration shall be borne by the applicant.

(12) Subsections (2) and (3) of section 17 of this Act shall apply in relation to real burdens extinguished or rendered unenforceable by virtue of this section as they apply in relation to real burdens extinguished or so rendered by subsection (1) of that section with the substitution, if the extinction or rendering is after the appointed day, for each reference in them to that day, of a reference to the day which ends the transitional period.

(13) A person opposing an application made under subsection (1) above incurs no liability, unless in the opinion of the Lands Tribunal his actings are vexatious or frivolous, in respect of expenses incurred by the applicant.

(14) This section is subject to sections 41 and 42 of this Act.

(15) Before submitting any notice for registration under this section, the superior shall swear or affirm before a notary public that to the best of the knowledge and belief of the superior all the information contained in the notice is true.

(16) For the purposes of subsection (15) above, if the superior is—

(a) an individual unable by reason of legal disability, or incapacity, to swear or affirm as mentioned in that subsection, then a legal representative of the superior may swear or affirm;

(b) not an individual, then any person authorised to sign documents on its behalf may swear or affirm;

and the references in that subsection to the superior shall be construed accordingly.

<small>AMENDMENTS</small>

1. As amended by the Title Conditions (Scotland) Act 2003 (asp 9), Sch.13, para.4 (effective April 4, 2003).

2. As amended by the Title Conditions (Scotland) Act 2003 (Consequential Provisions) Order (SSI 2003/503), art.2, Sch.1, para.4 (effective October 22, 2003).

GENERAL NOTE

It has been recognised that there will be circumstances where the superior cannot register a notice of reallotment under s.18 because none of the three conditions for reallotment apply. In such a situation, the superior may seek to enter into a voluntary agreement with the vassal in terms of s.19. If the vassal refuses to enter into an agreement, the superior could as a last resort apply to the Lands Tribunal.

Subs.(1)

An application to the tribunal had to be made within a period prescribed by Scottish Ministers and that period ended before the appointed day. The thrust of the legislation in relation to feudal burdens is that all matters of reallotment should be decided before the appointed day so that it is clear which burdens still apply.

Subs.(2)

Any application had to contain a description of the attempt to reach agreement. Presumably that would involve indicating when the notice in terms of s.19(1)(a) was served and any response thereto. Applicants would be well advised to send copies of all notices and correspondence to the Lands Tribunal with the application.

Subs.(3)

In many ways this was a controversial provision because it allowed the superior within a set period to execute and register a notice in the form contained in Sch.7 to the Act, which virtually kept the burden alive even after the appointed day until the matter has been disposed of by the Tribunal. The Land or Sasine Register will therefore indicate that the burden still applies and one could envisage situations where transactions which contravened or potentially contravene the burden will be held up. In such a situation, the parties may agree a commercial consideration for the withdrawal of the application.

Subs.(4)

In this case, the notice must set out the title of the superior and describe both the burdened land and the prospective dominant land to enable both to be identified with reference to the ordnance map. The notice must set out the terms of the real burden and any counter, obligation.

Subs.(5)

The notice must be registered against the titles of both the burdened land and the nominated dominant land, and for a transitional period the burden will still apply.

Subs.(6)

The transitional period begins on the appointed day and ends either when an order of the Lands Tribunal is registered or if an order is not registered on a day specified by Scottish Ministers after the appointed day. Orders by the Tribunal may be in favour of the burden being retained, or against it. In either case, there is the possibility that the parties will not register the order. Accordingly the burden will cease to be enforceable at the end of a specified period if there is no registration.

Subs.(7)

If the Lands Tribunal is satisfied that, if the real burden was extinguished, there would be substantial loss or disadvantage to the applicant as owner of the proposed dominant land, the Tribunal may order that the nominated land will become the dominant land for enforcement of the burden in the future. It will not matter that the order is registered before or after the appointed day for abolition. If the Lands Tribunal is not so satisfied, it will order the real burden to be extinguished. It should be noted that the question of material detriment to the applicant relates to the applicant's ownership of the proposed new dominant land and not to the applicants position as a superior. There may be cases where a superior owns land adjoining the burdened land but cannot satisfy one of the conditions in s.18(7). The adjoining land owned by the superior may not have a permanent building as a place of human habitation or resort within 100 metres, but there could still be disadvantage to a superior as owner of the adjoining land if a burden is extinguished.

Subs.(8)

The effect of an order will be either that the burden remains enforceable by the former superior as proprietor of a new dominant area of land or that the burden shall be extinguished on the appointed day. If the negative order is issued after the appointed day then the burden shall be extinguished on registration of the order. If no order has been made and registered after the time limit set out in subs.(6) then the burden shall be extinguished on the expiry of that time limit.

Subs.(9)

There may be circumstances in which the Tribunal feels that it would be wrong to extinguish the burden altogether and that there is some merit in the superior's arguments. In such a case, it will be open to the tribunal to modify the burden, in which event the modified burden shall be enforceable for the future. This is of course in line with the general jurisdiction of the Lands Tribunal to modify real burdens as opposed to discharging them. (Conveyancing and Feudal Reform (Scotland) Act 1970, ss.1 and 2). A counter-obligation may also be varied.

Subs.(10)

There will be no appeal from a decision of the Lands Tribunal under this section. It is plain that the right to apply to the Tribunal is grudgingly given. The legislation recognises, however, that a former superior's human rights may be infringed if a burden is wiped out without some right of appeal. However, the question which the Lands Tribunal will have to decide is not a legal one. There is therefore no need for any appeal to the courts.

Subs.(11)

Any order must be registered against both the burdened land and the nominated dominant land.

Subs.(12)

This simply makes it clear that the transitional provisions set out in s.17(2) and (3) will apply notwithstanding any application to the Tribunal, but where an application has been made and where the burden is extinguished or rendered unenforceable after the appointed day, it will be the day which ends with the transitional period which matters rather than the appointed day.

Subs.(13)

One suspects that this provision is to deter superiors from attempting to retain real burdens by default. A vassal may be concerned at the expense involved in opposing an application. This provision makes it clear that there will be no liability for expenses unless the vassal's actings are deemed to be vexatious or frivolous. It is difficult to see a situation where this could arise.

Subs.(14)

This provision makes it clear that the whole of s.20 is subject to the provisions of ss.41 and 42 which relate to service of notices, duplication of notices etc.

Subs.(15)

Before the superior submits a notice under this section for registration, he or she must swear or affirm before a notary public that to the best of his or her knowledge and belief all the information in the notice is true. However, the affidavit is not to the effect that the superior believes that there would be substantial loss or disadvantage where the burden to be extinguished. The affidavit only covers the actual contents of the notice in terms of Sch.7.

Subs.(16)

The legal representative of a superior, or an authorised person of a corporate entity, may swear or affirm.

Manner of dealing with application under section 20

21.—(1) On receiving an application under section 20 of this Act the Lands Tribunal shall give such notice of that application, whether by way of advertisement or otherwise, as may be prescribed for the purposes of that section by the Scottish Ministers by rules under section 3 of the Lands Tribunal Act 1949 (c.42) to any person who has right to the feu which is subject to the real burden in question and, if the Lands Tribunal thinks fit, to any other person.

(2) Any person who, whether or not he has received notice under subsection (1) above, has right to the feu which is subject to the real burden in question (or as the case may be has right to the servient tenement) or is affected by that real burden or by its proposed reallotment shall be entitled, within such time as may be so prescribed, to oppose or make representations in relation to the application; and the Lands Tribunal shall allow any such person, and may allow any other person who appears to it to be affected by that real burden or by its proposed reallotment, to be heard in relation to the application.

(3) Without prejudice to subsections (1) and (2) above, the Scottish Ministers may, in rules under the said section 3, make special provision in relation to any matter pertaining to proceedings in applications under section 20 of this Act (or in any class of such applications).

GENERAL NOTE
This section deals with procedure at the Lands Tribunal. The Lands Tribunal may give notice of the application by way of advertisement or otherwise, not only to the vassal but also to any other person who may be affected by the burden or by its proposed reallotment.

Amendment of Tribunals and Inquiries Act 1992

22.—In section 11 (proceedings in relation to which there is no appeal from the decision of the Lands Tribunal) of the Tribunals and Inquiries Act 1992 (c.53), in subsection (2)—
(a) the words after "in relation to" shall be paragraph (a); and
(b) after that paragraph there shall be inserted "; or
proceedings under section 20 of the Abolition of Feudal Tenure etc. (Scotland) Act 2000 (asp 5) (reallotment of real burden)".

GENERAL NOTE
This is a consequential amendment.

Reallotment of real burden affecting facility of benefit to other land etc.

23. [*Repealed by the Title Conditions (Scotland) Act 2003 (asp 9), Sch.15, (effective April 4, 2003)*]

Interest to enforce real burden

[1] **24.**—Sections 18 to 20 of this Act are without prejudice to any requirement that a dominant proprietor have an interest to enforce a real burden (and such interest shall not be presumed).

AMENDMENT
1. Amended by the Title Conditions (Scotland) Act 2003 (asp 9), Sch.15, (effective April 4, 2003).

GENERAL NOTE
For a party to be able to enforce a real burden it has always been necessary for that party to have both title and interest to enforce. So far as interest is concerned, in feudal theory at least, the superior's interest was presumed to exist (*Earl of Zetland v Hislop* (1882) 9 R. (H.L.) 40). It is accepted that the interest must be a praedial or patrimonial interest rather than a personal one. Where superiors were concerned, it would have been difficult in some cases to show just how a bare superiority title could ever give rise to a praedial or patrimonial interest which was not intensely personal. For many superiors the main interest in enforcing a real burden was simply to obtain payment for a waiver (see the excellent discussion of the nature of the superior's interest in Reid, *The Law of Property in Scotland* para.408). This provision preserves the rule that interest must exist, but reverses the rule that interest to enforce a burden will be presumed. This is a vitally important section. No one should assume that merely because a burden has be reallotted to a new dominant land that this implies that the burden has in some way been reinvented or created real of new. If the burden is not a real burden then no amount of notices or agreements will make it real. Even if a burden is a real burden and is successfully reallotted, the party

enforcing will still have to show an interest. The section does not indicate what sort of interest will be required, but presumably the law has not been changed and the interest will require to be praedial or patrimonial. This means that the benefit must be to the new dominant land rather than the owner of that land personally. Of course, for a burden to be real in the first place it must be praedial (*Tailors Of Aberdeen v Coutts* (1840) 1 Rob.App 296, 306 and 307; Reid, *The Law of Property in Scotland* para.407). In most cases, it may be relatively easy to prove interest, especially where the burden relates to the erection or non erection of buildings or the use of the burdened land (see *MacDonald v Douglas*, 1963 S.C. 374; *Howard de Walden Estates Ltd v Bowmaker Ltd*, 1965 S.C. 163). There has, however, always been a difficulty in relation to benefits which are perceived to be commercial, especially where the burden is apparently conceived in favour of the proprietor of other land which is used for a competing business. (See *Aberdeen Varieties Ltd v James F Donald (Aberdeen Cinemas) Ltd*, 1939 S.C. 788; 1940 S.C.(H.L.) 52). It is often difficult to disentangle commercial interests from praedial ones. On the one hand, one could argue that to protect a commercial business is not the function of a real burden. On the other hand, one could argue that the value of buildings used as a public house could be adversely affected if another public house were to open two doors down in the same street (see *Co-operative Wholesale Society v Ushers Brewery* 1975 S.L.T. (Lands Tr 9). Professor Reid suggests that the distance between the two properties may be important in deciding whether the burden is purely commercial or partly commercial and partly praedial or patrimonial (Reid, *The Law of Property in Scotland* para.407; see *Phillips v Lavery* 1962 S.L.T. (Sh. Ct) 57). Presumably, so far as a reallotted burden is concerned, the former superior will be in the same position as a disponer. As between the original disponer and disponee a burden is always enforceable as a matter of personal contract (*Scottish Co-operative Wholesale Society v Finnie* 1937 S.C. 835). However, reallotment as such will not mean that there is some new personal contract between the owner of the burdened land and the owner of the nominated land. If the parties are singular successors then the question of interest will become critical. Although where singular successors are concerned it will be up to the owner of the nominated dominant land to prove interest (*Aberdeen Varieties Ltd v James F Donald (Aberdeen Cinemas) Ltd, supra*), where the properties are close together it may be relatively easy to prove interest in respect of some burden which prohibits or restricts some use of the burdened land. The big difference, however, is that the party seeking to enforce will certainly require to consider the question of interest more carefully than a feudal superior would have had to do (for further discussion on the question of interest see Halliday, *Conveyancing Law and Practice* 2nd ed. 34–42 *et seq*; Reid, *The Law of Property in Scotland* para.407 *et seq*; Gordon, *Scottish Land Law* 2nd ed. 22–32, 22–66, 23–15). Interest to enforce is now defined in the Title Conditions) Scotland) Act 2003, s.8(3).

Counter-obligations on reallotment

[1] **25.**—Where a real burden is reallotted under section 18, 19 or 20 of this Act or under section 56 or 63 of the Title Conditions (Scotland) Act 2003 (asp 9) (which make provision, respectively, as to facility burdens and service burdens and as to manager burdens), the right to enforce the burden shall be subject to any counter-obligation (modified as the case may be by the agreement or by the order of the Lands Tribunal) enforceable against the superior immediately before reallotment is effected.

AMENDMENT

1. As amended by the Title Conditions (Scotland) Act 2003 (asp 9), Sch.13, para.5, (effective April 4, 2003).

GENERAL NOTE

If a burden which is reallotted is subject to a counter-obligation on the part of the former superior, the reallotment will have the effect of making the nominated dominant land the burdened land insofar as the counter-obligation is concerned.

Conservation burdens

Conservation bodies

26. [*Repealed by the Title Conditions (Scotland) Act 2003 (asp 9), Sch.15, (effective April 4, 2003).*]

Notice preserving right to enforce conservation burden

[1] **27.**—(1) Where a conservation body has, or the Scottish Ministers have, the right as superior to enforce a real burden of the class described in subsection (2) below or would have that right were it or they to complete title to the dominium directum, it or they may, before the appointed day, preserve for the benefit of the public the right to enforce the burden in question after that day by executing and registering against the dominium utile of the land subject to the burden a notice in, or as nearly as may be in, the form contained in schedule 8 to this Act; and, without prejudice to section 27A(1) of this Act, any burden as respects which such a right is so preserved shall, on and after the appointed day, be known as a "conservation burden".

(2) The class is those real burdens which are enforceable against a feudal estate of dominium utile of land for the purpose of preserving, or protecting—

(a) the architectural or historical characteristics of the land; or
(b) any other special characteristics of the land (including, without prejudice to the generality of this paragraph, a special characteristic derived from the flora, fauna or general appearance of the land).

(3) The notice shall—

(a) state that the superior is a conservation body by virtue of section 38 of the Title Conditions (Scotland) Act 2003 (asp 9) (which makes provision generally as respects conservation burdens) or that the superior is the Scottish Ministers;
(b) set out the title of the superior;
(c) describe, sufficiently to enable identification by reference to the Ordnance Map, the land subject to the real burden (or any part of that land);
(d) set out the terms of the real burden; and
(e) set out the terms of any counter-obligation to the real burden if it is a counter-obligation enforceable against the superior.

(4) This section is subject to sections 41 and 42 of this Act.

AMENDMENT
  1. Amended in part by the Title Conditions (Scotland) Act 2003 (asp 9), Sch.13, para.6, (effective April 4, 2003).

GENERAL NOTE
  It was recognised that conservation bodies would have granted feus prior to the appointed day, or indeed the date of Royal Assent, laying down very strict conditions in respect of particular buildings or land which have special characteristics. The function of these burdens will have been, in part at least, to protect these characteristics for the benefit of the public. An obvious example would be where the National Trust for Scotland or a similar body undertake the renovation of old cottages (possibly with the aid of public money) and then grant feus to individuals. On the appointed day the superiority title held by that body ceased to exist. Moreover, there will be little opportunity to reallot the burdens unless the body in question happens to own neighbouring land. Accordingly, if the body is a designated conservation body it could, prior to the appointed day, preserve the right to enforce the burden for the benefit of the public by executing and registering against the burdened land a notice in the form of Sch.8. Henceforth a burden so preserved is known as a conservation burden. The notice must state that the superior is a conservation body or alternatively that the superior is the Scottish Ministers. The notice must describe the burdened land, or that part subject to the burden, sufficiently to identify it by reference to the ordnance map and it must also set out the terms of the burden and any counter-obligation. As it is for s.20, this section is subject to ss.41 and 42. There is no requirement for an officer of the conservation body to swear any affidavit. A conservation burden is a new creation. The concept flies in the face of one of the most basic principles of the law relating to real burdens, namely that the burden is enforceable by a party by virtue of that party's ownership of other land. A conservation burden is not praedial so far as enforcement is concerned. There was a view that the regulation of properties in the public interest might be best left to the planning and other public authorities. However, it was

recognised that real burdens might have a role to play and that they had been used in the past by public or quasi public bodies to better protect special features of certain property. Conservation bodies are now defined in s.38 of the Title Conditions (Scotland) Act 2003.

Nomination of conservation body or Scottish Ministers to have title to enforce conservation burden

[1] **27A.**—(1) Where a person other than a conservation body or the Scottish Ministers has the right as superior to enforce a real burden of the class described in section 27(2) of this Act or would have that right were he to complete title to the *dominium directum*, he may, subject to subsection (2) below, before the appointed day nominate for the benefit of the public, by executing and registering against the *dominium utile* of the land subject to the burden a notice in, or as nearly as may be in, the form contained in schedule 8A to this Act, a conservation body or the Scottish Ministers to have title on or after that day to enforce the burden against that land; and, without prejudice to section 27(1) of this Act, any burden as respects which such title to enforce is by virtue of this subsection so obtained shall, on and after the appointed day, be known as a "conservation burden".

(2) Subsection (1) above applies only where the consent of the nominee to being so nominated is obtained—

(a) in a case where sending a copy of the notice, in compliance with section 41(3) of this Act, is reasonably practicable, before that copy is so sent; and

(b) in any other case, before the notice is executed.

(3) The notice shall—

(a) state that the nominee is a conservation body (identifying it) or the Scottish Ministers, as the case may be; and

(b) do as mentioned in paragraphs (b) to (e) of section 27(3) of this Act.

(4) This section is subject to sections 41 and 42 of this Act except that, in the application of subsection (1)(i) of section 42 for the purposes of this subsection, such discharge as is mentioned in that subsection shall be taken to require the consent of the nominated person.

GENERAL NOTE

Originally the 2000 Act allowed conservation bodies to preserve burdens of a conservation type where these had been created in feudal writs. The new section allowed a superior which is not a conservation body to execute and register a notice against the burdened land in terms of Sch.8A to the 2000 Act to the effect that an actual conservation body or Scottish Ministers will have title to enforce the burden. The conservation body or Scottish Ministers who are to take responsibility for enforcement must consent. The existing provisions in relation notice apply.

Enforcement of conservation burden

28.—[1] (1) If a notice has been executed and registered in accordance with section 27 of this Act and, immediately before the appointed day, the burden to which the notice relates is still enforceable by the conservation body or the Scottish Ministers as superior or would be so enforceable, or still so enforceable, were the body in question or they to complete title to the dominium directum then, on and after the appointed day, the conservation body or as the case may be the Scottish Ministers shall—

(a) subject to any counter-obligation, have title to enforce the burden against the land to which the notice in question relates; and

(b) be presumed to have an interest to enforce that burden.

(2) The references in subsection (1) above to—

(a) the conservation body include references to—

(i) any conservation body which is; or

(ii) the Scottish Ministers where they are,
its successor as superior;
    (b) the Scottish Ministers include references to a conservation body
which is their successor as superior.

AMENDMENT
1. As amended by the Title Conditions (Scotland) Act 2003 (asp 9), Sch.15, (effective April 4, 2003).

GENERAL NOTE
Obviously a conservation body would have a difficulty, after abolition, in showing some sort of praedial or patrimonial interest to enforce a burden which was not actually in their favour as owner of land. Accordingly, conservation bodies are presumed to have an interest to enforce conservation burdens, although the nature of that interest is not further specified. On the notice being registered, the burden will remain enforceable by the conservation body or Scottish Ministers as the case may be, purely by virtue of their status.

Effect of section 27A nomination

[1] **28A.**—If a notice has been executed and registered in accordance with section 27A of this Act and, immediately before the appointed day, the burden to which the notice relates is still enforceable by the nominating person as superior (or by such person as is his successor) or would be so enforceable, or still so enforceable, were the person in question to complete title to the *dominium directum* then, on and after the appointed day, the conservation body or as the case may be the Scottish Ministers shall—
    (a) subject to any counter-obligation, have title to enforce the burden against the land to which the notice in question relates; and
    (b) be presumed to have an interest to enforce that burden.

AMENDMENT
1. Inserted by the Title Conditions (Scotland) Act 2003 (asp 9), s.114 (effective April 4, 2003).

GENERAL NOTE
Subs.(4)
Effect of s.27A nomination
The title and interest of the conservation body or Scottish Ministers taking over the enforcement rights in respect of a conservation burden and the interest to enforce that burden are presumed.

29.—32. [*Repealed by the Title Conditions (Scotland) Act 2003 (asp 9), Sch.15, (effective April 4, 2003).*]

Compensation

Notice reserving right to claim compensation where land subject to development value burden

33.—(1) Where—
    (a) before the appointed day, land was feued subject to a real burden enforceable by a superior (or so enforceable if the person in question were to complete title to the dominium directum) which reserved for the superior the benefit (whether wholly or in part) of any development value of the land (such a real burden being referred to in this Part of this Act as a "development value burden"); and
    (b) either—
        (i) the consideration paid, or payable, under the grant in feu was significantly lower than it would have been had the feu not been subject to the real burden; or
        (ii) no consideration was paid, or payable, under the grant in feu,

the superior may, before that day, reserve the right to claim (in accordance with section 35 of this Act) compensation by executing and registering against the dominium utile of the land subject to the burden a notice in, or as nearly as may be in, the form contained in schedule 9 to this Act.

(2) A notice under this section shall—

(a) set out the title of the superior;

(b) describe, sufficiently to enable identification by reference to the Ordnance Map, the land the dominium utile of which is subject to the development value burden;

(c) set out the terms of the burden;

(d) state that the burden reserves development value and set out any information relevant to that statement;

(e) set out, to the best of the superior's knowledge and belief, the amount by which the consideration was reduced because of the imposition of the burden; and

(f) state that the superior reserves the right to claim compensation in accordance with section 35 of this Act.

(3) Before submitting any notice for registration under this section, the superior shall swear or affirm before a notary public that to the best of the knowledge and belief of the superior all the information contained in the notice is true.

(4) For the purposes of subsection (3) above, if the superior is—

(a) an individual unable by reason of legal disability, or incapacity, to swear or affirm as mentioned in that subsection, then a legal representative of the superior may swear or affirm;

(b) not an individual, then any person authorised to sign documents on its behalf may swear or affirm;

and any reference in that subsection to a superior shall be construed accordingly.

(5) In this Part of this Act, "development value" (except in the expression "development value burden") means any significant increase in the value of the land arising as a result of the land becoming free to be used, or dealt with, in some way not permitted under the grant in feu.

(6) This section is subject to sections 41 and 42 of this Act.

GENERAL NOTE

The abolition of the feudal system on the appointed day meant that superiority titles will on that day ceased to exist as rights of property. Despite the rather clear terms of Article 1 of Protocol 1 to the European Convention on Human Rights, no compensation is payable to former superiors for the loss of this property right. The Scottish Executive feel that they can rely on the general public interest exception in Article 1 and cases already decided would indicate that this view is correct (*Sporrong and Lonnroth v Sweden* (1983) 5 E.H.R.R. 35, E.C.H.R., para.61; *James v United Kingdom* (1986) 8 E.H.R.R. 123, E.C.H.R., para.50). Nevertheless it was recognised that in some cases a superior might have granted a feu of land for no consideration or a reduced consideration because of the existence of a particular burden. The most obvious case would be where a local landowner was prevailed upon to provide land for some sort of public or quasi public use like, for example, a park. Having been so prevailed upon, the superior grants a feu to the local authority subject to a burden that the ground will never be used for anything other than a public park. No price is paid and the feuduty is nominal. On the appointed day, the superiority title was extinguished and with it the right to enforce the burden. The successors of the original local authority are desperate for cash and they agree to sell the park to a firm of developers for millions of pounds. The original superior (after whom the park is named) is long dead but his family are naturally aggrieved. Their grief, however, can be assuaged by base coin. Sections 33 to 40 are an attempt to provide limited compensation to former superiors in these circumstances. The operative word is "limited".

Subs.(1)

A superior might, before the appointed day, reserve a right to claim compensation if land had been feued subject to a burden which can be said to have reserved some sort of development value to the superior and either there was no consideration or a reduced consideration because of the existence of the burden. The superior reserved the right to claim development value by executing and registering against the burdened property a notice in the form set out in Sch.9.

Subs.(2)

The notice must set out the title of the superior, describe the burdened land so that it can be identified by reference to the ordnance map, set out the terms of the burden, and state specifically that the burden does reserve development value. The notice must also set out any information which justifies that statement and, to the best of superior's knowledge and belief, the amount by which the original consideration was reduced because of the burden.

Subs.(3)

It should be noted that the superior had to swear not only that the formal parts of the notice are accurate but also that a development value was reserved and that the price was reduced by a specific amount because of the burden. The superior also had to swear or affirm as to the information relevant to the assertion that development value has been reserved.

Subs.(4)

A legal representative or officer of a corporate body may swear or affirm.

Subs.(5)

"Development value" is given a specific definition. It is any significant increase in the value of the land which would arise as a result of the burden not being applicable. This, however, is subject to s.37. The amount of compensation which can actually be claimed is not the total development value as defined in subs.(5).

Subs.(6)

The right to register a notice claiming development value is subject to the service and other provisions in ss.41 and 42.

Transmissibility of right to claim compensation

34.—A right to claim compensation reserved in accordance with section 33 of this Act is transmissible.

General Note

A right to claim compensation can be transmitted by will or in accordance with the laws of intestate succession.

Claiming compensation

35.—(1) Where the conditions mentioned in subsection (2) below are satisfied, any person who has, by or by virtue of a notice executed and registered in accordance with section 33 of this Act, a reserved right to claim compensation shall be entitled, subject to any order under section 44(2) of this Act, to compensation from the person who is the owner.

(2) The conditions are that—

(a) the real burden set out in the notice was, immediately before the appointed day, enforceable by the superior or would have been so enforceable immediately before that day had the person in question completed title to the dominium directum;

(b) on that day the burden, or as the case may be any right (or right on completion of title) of the superior to enforce the burden, was extinguished, or rendered unenforceable, by section 17(1) of this Act; and

(c) at any time—

(i) during the period of five years ending immediately before the appointed day, there was a breach of the burden; or

(ii) during the period of twenty years beginning with the appointed day, there was an occurrence, which, but for the burden becoming extinct, or unenforceable, as mentioned in paragraph (b) above, would have been a breach of the burden.

(3) Where a person is entitled, by virtue of subsection (1) above, to

compensation, he shall make any claim for such compensation by notice in writing duly served on the owner; and any such notice shall specify, in accordance with section 37 of this Act, the amount of compensation claimed.

(4) Where, in relation to a claim made under subsection (3) above, the condition mentioned in—

(a) sub-paragraph (i) of subsection (2)(c) above applies, any such claim may not be made more than three years after the appointed day;

(b) sub-paragraph (ii) of subsection (2)(c) above applies, any such claim may not be made more than three years after the date of the occurrence.

(5) For the purposes of this section, if a breach, or occurrence, such as is mentioned in subsection (2)(c) above is continuing, the breach or, as the case may be, occurrence shall be taken to occur when it first happens.

(6) The reference in subsection (3) above to a notice being duly served shall be construed in accordance with section 36 of this Act.

GENERAL NOTE

The registration of a notice did not of itself entitle the former superior to claim compensation from the unfortunate person who happens to be the vassal at that time. For a claim to compensation to arise, the real burden must have been enforceable prior to the appointed day and extinguished in accordance with the abolition provisions. More importantly, however, the burden in question must have been contravened either during the period 5 years prior to the appointed day or in the period 20 years after the appointed day. Accordingly, it is the breach of the burden which gives rise to the claim for compensation and only within a set time frame. In the example quoted, if the local authority hold on to the park and maintain it as a park for a period in excess of 20 years after the appointed day then no claim for compensation will be competent even although the council then sell the land for development. Similarly, if the land was sold for development 6 years prior to the appointed day and the superior did nothing no claim will arise for compensation. Where a former superior is entitled to compensation a notice must be served on the vassal specifying the amount of compensation which is claimed in terms of s.37. Where the breach pre-dates the appointed day, the claim cannot be made more than 3 years after the appointed day. Where the breach post-dates the appointed day, the claim cannot be made more than 3 years after the date of the breach. Where a breach may be regarded as a continuing matter then the breach or occurrence shall be taken to occur when it first happens.

Service under section 35(3)

36.—(1) Due service under section 35(3) of this Act is effected by delivering the notice in question to the owner or by sending it by registered post, or the recorded delivery service, addressed to him at an appropriate place.

(2) An acknowledgement, signed by the owner, which conforms to Form A of schedule 10 to this Act, or as the case may be a certificate which conforms to Form B of that schedule and is accompanied by the postal receipt, shall be sufficient evidence of such due service; and if the notice in question is, under subsection (1) above, sent by post but is returned to the person who is entitled to compensation with an intimation that it could not be delivered, the notice may be delivered or sent by post, with that intimation, to the Extractor of the Court of Session, the delivery or sending to the Extractor being taken to be equivalent to the service of that notice on the owner.

(3) For the purposes of subsection (2) above, an acknowledgement of receipt by the Extractor on a copy of that notice shall be sufficient evidence of its receipt by him.

(4) The date on which notice under section 35(3) of this Act is served on an owner is the date of delivery, or as the case may be of posting, in compliance with subsection (1) or (2) above.

(5) A reference in this section to an "appropriate place" is, for any owner, to be construed as a reference to—

(a) his place of residence;
(b) his place of business; or
(c) a postal address which he ordinarily uses,

or, if none of those is known at the time of delivery or posting, as a reference to whatever place is at that time his most recently known place of residence or place of business or postal address which he ordinarily used.

GENERAL NOTE

A notice claiming compensation is served by delivery, registered post or recorded delivery. There is provision for the former vassal to sign an acknowledgement conform to Form A of Sch.10 or for the former superior to produce a certificate of posting conform to Form B of that Schedule. There is also provision for service on the Extract or of the Court of Session where service on the former vassal has been ineffective. The notice should be served at the former vassal's place of residence, place of business or a postal address ordinarily used or the most recently known place in these categories.

Amount of compensation

37.—(1) The amount of any compensation payable on a claim made under section 35(3) of this Act shall, subject to subsections (2) and (3) below, be such sum as represents, at the time of the breach or occurrence in question, any development value which would have accrued to the owner had the burden been modified to the extent necessary to permit the land to be used, or dealt with, in the way that constituted the breach or, as the case may be, occurrence on which the claim is based.

(2) The amount payable as compensation (or, where more than one claim is made in relation to the same development value burden, the total compensation payable) under subsection (1) above shall not exceed such sum as will make up for any effect which the burden produced, at the time when it was imposed, in reducing the consideration then paid or made payable for the feu.

(3) In assessing for the purposes of subsection (1) above an amount of compensation payable—

(a) any entitlement of the claimant to recover any part of the development value of the land subject to the development value burden shall be taken into account; and

(b) a claimant to whom the reserved right was assigned or otherwise transferred shall be entitled to no greater sum than the former superior would have been had there been no such assignation or transfer.

(4) The reference in subsection (1) above to a burden shall, in relation to an occurrence, be construed as a reference to the burden which would have been breached but for its becoming, by section 17(1) of this Act, extinct or unenforceable.

GENERAL NOTE

It might be thought that if land was feued in 1970 for £500 under a burden that it be used as a public park and is then sold in 2005 to developers for £1.2m, the amount of compensation payable would be the difference between these two figures, or a similar calculation taking account of inflation since 1970. However, the amount of compensation is restricted to such a sum which does not exceed the reduction in price which the burden produced at the time it was imposed. Accordingly, if the appropriate market price for the land when feued would have been £2,500 if there had been no burden, the amount of development value compensation is restricted to £2,000, the original consideration being £500. It does not matter that the local authority have been able to sell the former park for £1.2m. Former superiors will no doubt feel that this compensation is derisory in these circumstances but for the purposes of Article 1 of Protocol 1 of the European Convention on Human Rights the compensation need not represent the actual loss. In human rights matters relating to property, the principle of proportionality comes into play. This is a delicate balancing act between the rights of the individual and the rights of the public or the state in general (see *H.M. Advocate v McSalley*, 2000 S.L.T. 1235). If the former superior is entitled to claim development value in some other way, as, for example, where a right to participate in increased development value is preserved by a back agreement and standard security, this will be taken into account in assessing any compensation in terms of s.37. If the right to development value compensation has been assigned, the assignee will have no greater rights to compensation than the former superior. It is unlikely that inflation will be taken into account or that interest will be payable.

Duty to disclose identity of owner

38.—Where a person ("the claimant") purports duly to serve notice under section 35(3) of this Act and the person on whom it is served, being a person who had right, before the time of the breach (or, as the case may be, occurrence) founded on by the claimant, to the dominium utile (or the ownership) of the land, is not the owner, that person shall forthwith disclose to the claimant—

    (a) the identity and address of the owner; or

    (b) (if he cannot do that) such other information as he has that might enable the claimant to discover the identity and address;

and the notice shall refer to that requirement for disclosure.

GENERAL NOTE

If a notice claiming compensation under s.35(3) is served on a person who is a former owner then that party must disclose to the former superior the identity and address of the current owner or such other information as will enable the current owner to be traced.

The expression "owner" for purposes of sections 35 to 38

39.—(1) In sections 35 to 38 of this Act, "owner" means the person who, at the time of the breach or, as the case may be, occurrence, mentioned in section 35(2)(c) of this Act, has right to—

    (a) the dominium utile; or

    (b) the ownership,

of the land which, immediately before the appointed day, was subject to the development value burden, whether or not he has completed title; and if more than one person comes within that description, then the owner is the person who has most recently acquired such right.

(2) Where the land in question is held by two or more such owners as common property, they shall be severally liable to make any compensatory payment (but as between, or as the case may be among, themselves they shall be liable in the proportions in which they hold the land).

GENERAL NOTE

The owner or former vassal need not have completed a title, and if two or more persons own the burdened property liability for the compensatory payment shall be joint and several, although there will be a right of relief between the parties themselves depending on the proportions in which they hold title.

Assignation, discharge, or restriction, of reserved right to claim compensation

40.—A reserved right to claim, in accordance with section 35 of this Act, compensation may be—

    (a) assigned, whether wholly or to such extent (expressed as a percentage of each claim which may come to be made) as may be specified in the assignation; or

    (b) discharged or restricted,

by execution and registration of an assignation, or as the case may be a discharge, or restriction, in the form, or as nearly as may be in the form, contained in schedule 11 to this Act.

GENERAL NOTE

Where a right to claim development value compensation has been reserved it may be assigned or it may be discharged or restricted. A composite form is provided in Sch.11.

Miscellaneous

Notices: pre-registration requirements etc.

41.—(1) This section applies in relation to any notice which is to be submitted for registration under this Act.

(2) It shall not be necessary to endorse on the notice a warrant of registration.

(3) Except where it is not reasonably practicable to do so, a superior shall, before he executes the notice, send by post to the person who has the estate of dominium utile of the land to which the burden relates (addressed to "The Proprietor" where the name of that person is not known) a copy of—

    (a) the notice; and

    (b) the explanatory note set out in whichever schedule to this Act relates to the notice.

(4) A superior shall, in the notice, state either—

    (a) that a copy of the notice has been sent in accordance with subsection (3) above; or

    (b) that it was not reasonably practicable for such a copy to be sent.

GENERAL NOTE

This section made general provision in respect of all notices which are sent for registration. No registration warrants were required, but before the superior executed the notice he or she had, unless it is not reasonably practicable to do so, to intimate the notice to the vassal including whichever explanatory note was appropriate. When the superior executed and forwards the notice for registration, the superior was required to state that appropriate service had been made or that it was not reasonably practicable for a copy to be sent to the former vassal. There is no guidance given in relation to the definition of the words "reasonably practicable". Presumably a superior would require to make some sort of enquiry by way of a search or otherwise into the identity of the current vassal. There may, however, be cases where the vassal cannot be traced. Presumably a superior would not require to go to inordinate expense, but there might, for example, be a requirement to advertise in a local paper before coming to the view that it was not reasonably practicable to serve the notice on the vassal.

Further provision as respects sections 18 to 20, 27 and 33

¹ **42.**—(1) Where—

    (a) a notice relating to a real burden has been registered under section 18, 18A, 18B, 18C, 20, 27, 27A or 33 of this Act; or

    (b) an agreement relating to a real burden has been registered under section 19 of this Act,

against the dominium utile of any land which is subject to the burden, it shall not be competent to register under any of those sections against that dominium utile another such notice or agreement relating to the same real burden; but nothing in this subsection shall prevent registration where—

    (i) the discharge of any earlier such notice has been registered by the person who registered that notice (or by his successor); or

    (ii) as the case may be, the discharge of any earlier such agreement has been registered, jointly, by the parties to that agreement (or by their successors).

(2) Where the dominium utile of any land comprises parts each held by a separate vassal, each part shall be taken to be a separate feudal estate of dominium utile.

(3) Where more than one feudal estate of dominium utile is subject to the same real burden enforceable by a superior of the feu, he shall, if he wishes to execute and register a notice under section 18, 18A, 18B, 18C, 20, 27, 27A or 33 of this Act against those feudal estates in respect of that real burden, require to do so against each separately.

(4) Where a feudal estate of dominium utile is subject to more than one real burden enforceable by a superior of the feu, he may if he wishes to—

(a) execute and register a notice under section 18, 18, 18A, 18B, 18C, 20, 27, 27A or 33 of this Act against that feudal estate in respect of those real burdens, do so by a single notice; or

(b) enter into and register an agreement under section 19 of this Act against that feudal estate in respect of those real burdens, do so by a single agreement.

[2] (5) Nothing in this Part requires registration against land prospectively nominated as a dominant tenement but outwith Scotland.

AMENDMENTS
1. As amended by the Title Conditions (Scotland) Act 2003 (asp 9), Sch.13, para.7, (effective April 4, 2003).
2. Inserted by the Title Conditions (Scotland) Act 2003 (asp 9), Sch.13, para.7, (effective April 4, 2003).

GENERAL NOTE
Where a notice or agreement is registered against the vassal's title, it is not competent to register any other notice or agreement in respect of the same real burden, although notices can be discharged by the former superior and agreements may be discharged by both parties. In such cases a fresh notice or agreement will be possible. In many cases the burdened land will have been sub-divided many times. The superior will have to deal with each vassal separately if he wishes to maintain or reallot the burden or reserve a development value against the whole of the original *dominium utile*. Similarly, if the superior has granted individual feus subject to the same burdens, he will still require to deal with each individual vassal separately in relation to any notices. If more than one burden is being reallotted, either by notice or agreement, this can be done in one notice or agreement.

Notices and agreements under certain sections: extent of Keeper's duty

[1] **43.**—(1) In relation to any notice submitted for registration under section 18, 18A, 18B, 18C, 20, 27, 27A or 33 of this Act, the Keeper of the Registers of Scotland shall not be required to determine whether the superior has complied with the terms of section 41(3) of this Act.

(2) In relation to any notice, or as the case may be any agreement, submitted for registration under—

(a) section 18, 18A, 18B, 18C, 19, 20, 27, 27A or 33 of this Act, the Keeper shall not be required to determine whether, for the purposes of subsection (1) of the section in question, a real burden is enforceable by a superior;

(b) section 18 of this Act, the Keeper shall not be required to determine, where, in pursuance of subsection (2)(c) of that section, the condition specified is that mentioned in subsection (7)(a) of that section, whether the terms of that condition are satisfied;

[2] (bb) section 18B or 18C of this Act, the Keeper shall not be required to determine whether—

(i) the requirements of subsection (1) of the section are satisfied: or

(ii) the statement made in pursuance of subsection (2)(e) of the section in question is correct;

(c) paragraph (c) of subsection (1) of section 19 of this Act, the Keeper shall not be required to determine whether the requirements of paragraph (a) of that subsection are satisfied;

(d) section 20 of this Act, the Keeper shall not be required to determine—

(i) whether the description provided in pursuance of subsection (2) of that section is correct;

(ii) whether the notice has been executed, and is being registered, timeously; or

(iii) any matter as to which the Lands Tribunal must be satisfied before making an order under that section;

(e) section 33 of this Act, the Keeper shall not be required to determine whether—

    (i) the requirements of subsection (1)(a) and (b) of that section are satisfied; or

   (ii) the statements made or information provided, in pursuance of subsection (2)(d) or (e) of that section, are correct.

(3) The Keeper shall not be required to determine—

(a) for the purposes of section 18(6), 18A(5), 18B(3), 18C(3), 19(5), 20(5) or (8)(a)(i), 28, 28A or 60(1) of this Act, whether immediately before the appointed day a real burden is, or is still, enforceable, or by whom; or

(b) for the purposes of subsection (8)(a)(ii) of section 20 of this Act, whether immediately before the day of registration of an order of the Lands Tribunal under subsection (7) of that section a real burden is, or is still, enforceable, or by whom.

AMENDMENTS

  1. As amended by the Title Conditions (Scotland) Act 2003 (asp 9), Sch.13, para.8, (effective April 4, 2003).

  2. Inserted by the Title Conditions (Scotland) Act 2003 (asp 9), Sch.13, para.8, (effective April 4, 2003).

GENERAL NOTE

It was thought that if superiors attempted to reallot, preserve or reserve development values in terms of the Act then notices might come flooding in to the Keeper. This has not proved to be the case as at June 2004. It is clear that once notices or indeed anything is registered in one of the registers, it takes on the appearance, at least, of validity. Indeed, once the registration process is completed in the Land Register, the Keeper normally grants indemnity in relation to the registered interest. However, s.43 severely curtails the role of the Keeper in relation to notices. In the first place, the Keeper is not required to verify that the superior has indeed attempted to serve a copy of the notice on the vassal in terms of s.41(3). Similarly, the Keeper is not required to take a view on whether, prior to the notice, the burden in question is actually enforceable. Where reallotment is under s.18, the Keeper will have no duty to determine whether or not there is in terms of s.18(7)(a) a permanent building on the dominant tenement wholly or mainly used as a place of habitation or resort within the 100 metre limit. Where a superior has attempted to reallot by agreement in terms of s.19, the Keeper will not be bound to verify that the superior served the appropriate notice under s.19(1)(a) and Sch.6. The Keeper will not be required to determine whether or not an applicant for reallotment by the Lands Tribunal in terms of s.20 did attempt to reach agreement with the vassal, whether the description is correct, whether the notice has been executed and is being registered timeously or indeed any matter as to which the Land Tribunal have to be satisfied before making their order. Where reserved development values are concerned, the Keeper shall not be required to determine whether the original price did indicate a reserved development value or whether statements made by the superior in relation to development value and the amount of development value are in any way accurate. The general thrust of the legislation in relation to notices is therefore that the Keeper will be entitled to take them at face value and register them on that basis. The Keeper's position is, of course, that he does not have the resource to attempt to verify the accuracy of the notices or anything stated therein.

Referral to Lands Tribunal of notice dispute

44.—(1) Any dispute arising in relation to a notice registered under this Act may be referred to the Lands Tribunal; and, in determining the dispute, the Tribunal may make such order as it thinks fit discharging or, to such extent as may be specified in the order, restricting the notice in question.

(2) Any dispute arising in relation to a claim made under section 35(3) of this Act may be referred to the Lands Tribunal; and, in determining the dispute, the Tribunal may make such order as it thinks fit (including an order fixing the amount of any compensation payable under the claim in question).

(3) In any referral under subsection (1) or (2) above, the burden of proving any disputed question of fact shall be on the person relying on the notice or, as the case may be, making the claim.

(4) An extract of any order made under subsection (1) or (2) above may be registered and the order shall take effect as respects third parties on such registration.

GENERAL NOTE
Obviously a vassal may feel aggrieved at a notice being registered against the title to his or her property. Accordingly, any dispute arising in relation to a notice may be referred to the Lands Tribunal. It will be for them to make enquiry in relation to the procedures and they will be entitled to discharge or restrict any notice if they are not satisfied. Even a claim to development value compensation may be referred to the Tribunal and they may fix the amount of compensation. Presumably they would require some evidence from surveyors or valuers. The burden of proof in relation to any disputed question of fact relating to notices is firmly on the person who relies on the notice or who makes the claim to development value compensation. Any order made by the Tribunal may be registered and will take effect as regards third parties on registration.

Circumstances where certain notices may be registered after appointed day

45.—(1) Subject to subsection (2) below, where—
(a) a notice submitted, before the appointed day, for registration under this Act, or an agreement so submitted for registration under section 19 of this Act, is rejected by the Keeper of the Registers of Scotland; but
(b) a court or the Lands Tribunal then determines that the notice or agreement is registrable,
the notice or agreement may, if not registered before the appointed day, be registered—
      (i) within two months after the determination is made; but
      (ii) before such date after the appointed day as the Scottish Ministers may by order prescribe,
and any notice or agreement registered under this subsection on or after the appointed day shall be treated as if it had been registered before that day.

(2) For the purposes of subsection (1) above, the application to the court, or to the Lands Tribunal, which has resulted in the determination shall require to have been made within such period as the Scottish Ministers may by order prescribe.

(3) In subsection (1)(b) above, "court" means any court having jurisdiction in questions of heritable right or title.

GENERAL NOTE
If the Keeper rejects a notice or agreement but a court or the Lands Tribunal determines that the notice or agreement should have been registered, then it may be registered after the appointed day provided that is within two months after the determination by the Tribunal or court is made. Nevertheless, there will still be a prescribed date beyond which a notice or agreement cannot be registered.

Duties of Keeper: amendments relating to the extinction of certain real burdens

46.—[1] (1) The Keeper of the Registers of Scotland shall not be required to remove from the Land Register of Scotland a real burden extinguished by section 17(1)(a) of this Act unless—
(a) subject to subsection (3) below, he is requested to do so in an application for registration or rectification; or
(b) he is, under section 9(1) of the Land Registration (Scotland) Act 1979 (c.33) (rectification of the register), ordered, subject to subsection (3) below, to do so by the court or the Lands Tribunal;
and no such request or order shall be competent during a period which commences with the appointed day and is of such number of years as the Scottish Ministers may by order prescribe.

² (2) During the period mentioned in subsection (1) above a real burden, notwithstanding that it has been so extinguished, may at the discretion of the Keeper, for the purposes of section 6(1)(e) of that Act of 1979 (entering subsisting real right in title sheet), be taken to subsist; but this subsection is without prejudice to subsection (3) below.

(3) The Keeper shall not, before the date mentioned in subsection (4) below, remove from the Land Register of Scotland a real burden which is the subject of a notice or agreement in respect of which application had been made for a determination by—

(a) a court; or
(b) the Lands Tribunal,

under section 45(1)(b) of this Act.

(4) The date is whichever is the earlier of—

(a) that two months after the final decision on the application; and
(b) that prescribed under section 45(1)(ii) of this Act.

AMENDMENTS

1. As amended by the Title Conditions (Scotland) Act 2003 (asp 9), Sch.15, (effective April 4, 2003).
2. As amended by the Title Conditions (Scotland) Act 2003 (asp 9), Sch.13, para.9, (effective April 4, 2003).

GENERAL NOTE

One of the difficulties relating to conveyancing practice is that a property may appear to be subject to a vast array of burdens and conditions contained in a series of ancient writs, some of which relate to vast tracts of land and not just to the particular plot or dwellinghouse. Even when a title to property is registered in the Land Register, the burdens section is almost bound to contain a whole host of burdens and conditions, some or even the vast majority of which have no application. Now that the feudal system has been abolished, a large number of strictly feudal burdens enforceable only by a superior will be extinguished. The hope had been expressed that this would allow the Keeper to cleanse the title sheets in the Land Register of feudal burdens. It was, however, recognised that the Keeper would not have the resource to carry out such an exercise on his own initiative. It was suggested, therefore, that the Keeper would have a duty to cleanse the burdens section of a title sheet on the occurrence of the next dealing after the appointed day or on a special application being made by the registered proprietor. Section 46 provides that the Keeper will not be required to cleanse the burdens sections of title sheets in the Land Register unless requested to do so in an application for registration or rectification, or on being ordered to do so in a rectification matter. However, no such request or order shall be competent for some time. The period is 10 years from the appointed day (Abolition of Feudal Tenure etc. (Scotland) Act 2000 (Prescribed Periods) Order 2004 (SSI 2004/478)). Section 6(1)(e) of the Land Registration (Scotland) Act 1979 places a duty on the Keeper to insert subsisting real burdens in a title sheet. Subsection (2) of s.46 of the 2000 Act makes it clear that, even although a burden has been extinguished, the Keeper will still be able to repeat it in the burdens section even although it may not be said to subsist legally. Burdens which are still the subject of notices or applications will also require to remain on the Register until these matters are finally determined by a court or the Lands Tribunal. The Keeper will, however, be able to remove such burdens two months after the final decision (if the burden is to be extinguished) or after the time limit prescribed under s.45(1)(ii) of the Act, whichever is the earlier.

Extinction of counter-obligation

47.—Without prejudice to any other way in which a counter-obligation to a real burden may be extinguished, any such counter-obligation is extinguished on the extinction of the real burden.

GENERAL NOTE

If a real burden is extinguished then any counter-obligation on the former superior is also extinguished.

No implication as to dominant tenement where real burden created in grant in feu

48.—Where a real burden is created (or has at any time been created) in a grant in feu, the superior having the dominium utile, or allodial ownership, of land (the "superior's land") in the vicinity of the land feued, no implication shall thereby arise that the superior's land is a dominant tenement.

GENERAL NOTE

The mere fact that a former superior actually owns the *dominium utile* or holds allodial ownership of adjoining or neighbouring land will not create any implication that that adjoining or neighbouring land is to be regarded as a dominant tenement for the purpose of enforcing existing feudal real burdens enforceable by the superior *qua* superior. The superior will require to serve the appropriate reallotment notice or attempt to enter into an agreement whereby the neighbouring or adjoining land is specifically nominated.

Interpretation

Interpretation of Part 4

[1] **49.**—In this Part of this Act, unless the context otherwise requires—
"conservation body" means a body prescribed by order under section 38(4) of the Title Conditions (Scotland) Act 2003 (asp 9);
"conservation burden" shall be construed in accordance with sections 27(1) and 27A(1) of this Act;
"development value burden" and "development value" shall be construed in accordance with section 33 of this Act;
"economic development burden" shall be construed in accordance with section 18B(3) of this Act;
"health care burden" shall be construed in accordance with section 18C(3) of this Act;
"local authority" means a council constituted under section 2 of the Local Government etc. (Scotland) Act 1994 (c.39);
"notary public" includes any person duly authorised by the law of the country (other than Scotland) in which the swearing or affirmation takes place to administer oaths or receive affirmations in that other country;
"personal pre-emption burden" and "personal redemption burden" shall be construed in accordance with section 18A(5) of this Act;
"real burden"—
  (a) includes—
    (i) a right of pre-emption;
    (ii) a right of redemption; or
    (iii) [*Repealed by the Title Conditions (Scotland) Act 2003 (asp 9), Sch.15, (effective April 4, 2003).*]
  (b) does not include a pecuniary real burden or sporting rights (as defined by section 65A(9) of this Act);
"registering" means registering an interest in land (or information relating to such an interest) in the Land Register of Scotland or, as the case may be, recording a document in the Register of Sasines; and cognate expressions shall be construed accordingly; and "superior" means a person who has right to the immediate superiority or to any over-superiority, whether or not he has completed title (and if more than one person comes within either of those descriptions then, in relation to that description, the person who has most recently acquired such right) and "former superior" shall be construed accordingly.

AMENDMENT

1. As amended by the Title Conditions (Scotland) Act 2003 (asp 9), Sch.13, para.10, (effective April 4, 2003).

GENERAL NOTE
This is an interpretation section restricted to Part 4. The term "superior" includes an immediate superior and an over-superior and it does not matter whether such a person has a completed title.

PART 5

ENTAILS

Disentailment on appointed day

50.—(1) Land which, immediately before the appointed day, is held under an entail is disentailed on that day.

(2) Section 32 of the Entail Amendment Act 1848 (c.36) (which makes provision as respects an instrument of disentail executed and recorded under that Act) shall apply to the effect of disentailment by subsection (1) above as that section applies to the effect of such an instrument so executed and recorded.

GENERAL NOTE
All land held under entail on the appointed day is disentailed on that day to the same effect as if an instrument of disentail were executed and recorded.

Compensation for expectancy or interest of apparent or other nearest heir in an entailed estate

51.—(1) Where, immediately before the appointed day—
(a) land is held under an entail; and
(b) the consent of a person who is an apparent or other nearest heir is required to any petition for authority of the court for the purpose of presenting an instrument of disentail,
the valuation of any expectancy or interest of the person, which on his refusal to give such consent would fall, before the appointed day, to be ascertained under section 13 of the Entail (Scotland) Act 1882 (c.53) may, within two years after the appointed day, be referred by him to, and determined by, the Lands Tribunal.

(2) The Tribunal shall direct that any sum ascertained by them in a valuation by virtue of subsection (1) above shall be secured on the land, for the benefit of the person, in such manner as they think fit.

GENERAL NOTE
If the consent of an apparent or nearest heir of entail would have been required to any petition for authority to execute an instrument of disentail, the valuation of that person's expectancy or interest will be ascertained by the Lands Tribunal if the matter is referred within 2 years of the appointed day. Under the entail legislation where a consent is dispensed with the interest is valued and paid over or properly secured (see Gordon, *Scottish Land Law* (2nd ed.) 18–54).

Closure of Register of Entails

52.—The Keeper of the Registers of Scotland shall, immediately before the appointed day, close the Register of Entails; and as soon as is practicable thereafter, he shall transmit that register to the Keeper of the Records of Scotland for preservation.

GENERAL NOTE
There were existing entails but after the appointed day all these entails will be disentailed and there will be no need for a separate register. The Register of Entails will be transferred to the Keeper of the Records of Scotland purely for preservation purposes.

PART 6

MISCELLANEOUS

Discharge of certain rights and extinction of certain obligations and payments

Discharge of rights of irritancy

53.—(1) All rights of irritancy held by a superior are, on the day on which this section comes into force, discharged; and on that day any proceedings already commenced to enforce any such right shall be deemed abandoned and may, without further process and without any requirement that full judicial expenses shall have been paid by the pursuer, be dismissed accordingly.

(2) Subsection (1) above shall not affect any cause in which final decree (that is to say, any decree or interlocutor which disposes of the cause and is not subject to appeal or review) is granted before the coming into force of this section.

GENERAL NOTE

This section is one of the few sections which came into force on Royal Assent. This was necessary because of the fear that superiors might rush to enforce real burdens by irritancy in the run up to abolition on the appointed day. The abolition of the superior's right to irritancy applies to any proceedings already commenced prior to Royal Assent unless final decree has already been obtained prior to that date. Final decree, however, is defined as a decree or interlocutor not subject to appeal or review. Presumably, therefore, a vassal, if facing a decree by a sheriff granted in May 2000 will have taken the opportunity to lodge an appeal and will have taken steps to ensure that any appeal or further appeal has taken the matter beyond the date of Royal Assent.

Extinction of superior's rights and obligations qua superior

54.—[1] (1) Subject to section 13, to Part 4, and to sections 60(1) and 65A, of this Act, a right or obligation which, immediately before the appointed day, is enforceable by, or as the case may be against, a superior qua superior (including, without prejudice to that generality, sporting rights as defined by subsection (9) of that section 65A) shall, on that day, be extinguished.

(2) Subject to subsection (3) below—

(a) on or after the appointed day, no proceedings for such enforcement shall be commenced;

(b) any proceedings already commenced for such enforcement shall be deemed to have been abandoned on that day and may, without further process and without any requirement that full judicial expenses shall have been paid by the pursuer, be dismissed accordingly; and

(c) any decree, or interlocutor, already pronounced in proceedings for such enforcement shall be deemed to have been reduced, or as the case may be recalled, on that day.

(3) Subsection (2) above shall not affect any proceedings, decree or interlocutor in relation to—

(a) a right of irritancy held by a superior; or

[2] (aa) a right of enforcement held by virtue of section 13, 33, 60(1) or 65A of this Act;

(b) a right to recover damages or to the payment of money.

AMENDMENTS

   1. As amended by the Title Conditions (Scotland) Act 2003 (asp 9), Sch.13, para.11, (effective April 4, 2003).

   2. Inserted by the Title Conditions (Scotland) Act 2003 (asp 9), Sch.13, para.11, (effective April 4, 2003).

GENERAL NOTE
Ancillary rights enforceable by or against the superior are extinguished on the appointed day and any proceedings already commenced deemed to be abandoned. Decrees or interlocutors already pronounced are deemed to have been reduced or recalled, with the exception of the right of irritancy which is dealt with separately and the right to recover damages or payment of money.

Abolition of thirlage

55.—Any obligation of thirlage which has not been extinguished before the appointed day is extinguished on that day.

GENERAL NOTE
Thirlage is an odd form of burden. It has been described as a servitude or pseudo servitude requiring the servient proprietor to have corn ground at a particular mill (see Cusine and Paisley, *Servitudes and Rights of Way*, para.3.75; Gordon, *Scottish Land Law* (2nd ed.) 10–79 to 10–90). Whatever the right or obligation may be, it is abolished on the appointed day.

Extinction etc. of certain payments analogous to feuduty

56.—[1] (1) The provisions of Part 3 of this Act shall apply as regards ground annual, skat, teind, stipend, standard charge, dry multures (including compensation payable in respect of commutation pursuant to the Thirlage Act 1799 (c.55)) and, subject to the exceptions mentioned in subsection (2) below, as regards any other perpetual periodical payment in respect of the tenure, occupancy or use of land or under a title condition, as those provisions apply as regards feuduty; but for the purposes of that application—
   (a) references in the provisions to "vassal" and "superior" shall be construed as references to, respectively, the payer and the recipient of the ground annual, skat, teind, stipend, standard charge, dry multures or other payment in question ("former vassal" and "former superior" being construed accordingly); and
   (b) a form (and its explanatory note) contained in a schedule to this Act shall be modified so as to accord with the kind of payment to which it relates.
   (2) The exceptions are any payments—
   (a) in defrayal of, or as a contribution towards, some continuing cost related to land; or
   (b) made under a heritable security.
   [2] (3) The definition of "title condition" in section 122(1) of the Title Conditions (Scotland) Act 2003 (asp 9) shall apply for the purposes of this section as that definition applies for the purposes of that Act.
   (4) Nothing in subsections (1) to (3) above shall be taken to prejudice the tenure, occupancy or use of land.

AMENDMENTS
   1. As amended by the Title Conditions (Scotland) Act 2003 (asp 9), Sch.13, para.12, (effective April 4, 2003).
   2. Inserted by the Title Conditions (Scotland) Act 2003 (asp 9), Sch.13, para.12, (effective April 4, 2003).

GENERAL NOTE
There are various odd forms of periodical payment which derive from tenure. Ground annuals are payable generally in old burgh properties where subinfeudation was not possible. Skat was payable in udal property. All of these payments analogous to feuduty will be treated in the same way as feuduty (see Part 3, ss.7–16).

Extinction by prescription of obligation to pay redemption money for feuduty, ground annual etc.

57.—Notwithstanding the terms of Schedule 1 to the Prescription and Limitation (Scotland) Act 1973 (c.52) (which defines obligations affected by prescriptive periods of five years), any obligation under section 5 (redemption of feuduty, ground annual etc. on transfer for valuable consideration) or 6 (redemption of feuduty, ground annual etc. on compulsory acquisition) of the Land Tenure Reform (Scotland) Act 1974 (c.38) to pay redemption money is an obligation to which section 6 of that Act of 1973 (extinction of obligation by prescriptive period of five years) applies; and for the purposes of that application, the reference in subsection (1) of section 6 of that Act of 1973 to the "appropriate date" is a reference to the date of redemption within the meaning of—

(a) except in the case mentioned in paragraph (b) below, section 5 (read, as the case may be, with section 6(2)(a)); or

(b) in the case of an obligation arising out of the acquisition of land by means of a general vesting declaration, section 6(4),

of that Act of 1974.

GENERAL NOTE

This section makes it clear that where an obligation to redeem feuduty has arisen under sections 5 or 6 of the Land Tenure Reform (Scotland) Act 1974, the obligation to make payment of the redemption sum will prescribe after five years.

The Crown, the Lord Lyon and Barony

Crown application

58.—(1) This Act binds the Crown and accordingly such provision as is made by section 2 of this Act as respects feudal estates of dominium shall apply to the superiority of the Prince and Steward of Scotland and to the ultimate superiority of the Crown; but nothing in this Act shall be taken to supersede or impair any power exercisable by Her Majesty by virtue of Her prerogative.

(2) Without prejudice to the generality of subsection (1) above, in that subsection—

(a) Her Majesty's prerogative includes the prerogative of honour; and

(b) "any power exercisable by Her Majesty by virtue of Her prerogative" includes—

(i) prerogative rights as respects ownerless or unclaimed property; and

(ii) the regalia majora.

GENERAL NOTE

The Act binds the Crown and accordingly the paramount superiorities of the Crown and the Prince and Steward of Scotland are extinguished on the appointed day without prejudice to any other rights of prerogative.

Crown may sell or otherwise dispose of land by disposition

59.—It shall be competent for the Crown, in selling or otherwise disposing of any land, to do so by granting a disposition of that land.

GENERAL NOTE

This section merely makes it clear that after the appointed day, when the feudal system has ceased to exist, the Crown will be able to dispose of any Crown lands by disposition, thus divesting the Crown entirely of any right, title or interest in that land.

Preserved right of Crown to maritime burdens

60.—(1) Where, immediately before the appointed day, the Crown has the right as superior to enforce a real burden against part of the sea bed or part of the foreshore, then, on and after that day, the Crown shall—

(a) subject to any counter-obligation, have title to enforce; and

(b) be presumed to have an interest to enforce,

the burden; and any burden as respects which the Crown has such title and interest shall, on and after the appointed day, be known as a "maritime burden".

(2) [*Repealed by the Title Conditions (Scotland) Act 2003 (asp 9), Sch.15, (effective April 4, 2003).*]

(3) For the purposes of this section—

"sea bed" means the bed of the territorial sea adjacent to Scotland; and

"territorial sea" includes any tidal waters.

(4) In this section, "real burden" has the same meaning as in Part 4 of this Act.

GENERAL NOTE

There are certain burdens which the Crown enforces against the seabed or parts of the foreshore where the Crown is superior. These burdens are preserved subject to any counter-obligation and the Crown is presumed to have an interest to enforce despite the fact that after the appointed day the right to enforce will not be attached to a title. After the appointed day such burdens will be known as "maritime burdens". Maritime burdens are not capable of assignation by the Crown. (See s.44(2) of the Title Conditions (Scotland) Act 2003).

Mines of gold and silver

61.—The periodical payment to the Crown, in respect of the produce of a mine which by the Royal Mines Act 1424 (c.12) belongs to the Crown, of an amount which is not fixed but is calculated as a proportion of that produce is not—

(a) a payment to the Crown qua superior for the purposes of section 54 of this Act;

(b) a perpetual periodical payment for the purposes of section 56 of this Act; or

(c) a feuduty for the purposes of Part 3 of this Act.

GENERAL NOTE

Certain royalties are payable to the Crown in terms of the Royal Mines Act 1424 and the Mines and Metals Act 1592. This section makes it clear that payment of royalties of this type will remain unaffected and will not be subject to the abolition and compensatory payments provisions in the same way as feuduty and other analogous tenure payments (see ss.7–16).

Jurisdiction and prerogative of Lord Lyon

62.—Nothing in this Act shall be taken to supersede or impair the jurisdiction or prerogative of the Lord Lyon King of Arms.

GENERAL NOTE

The Lord Lyon deals with matters heraldic. The abolition of the superior's status has nothing to do with peerages or other heraldic matters even although a peerage may appear to be attached to particular lands.

Baronies and other dignities and offices

63.—(1) Any jurisdiction of, and any conveyancing privilege incidental to, barony shall on the appointed day cease to exist; but nothing in this Act affects the dignity of baron or any other dignity or office (whether or not of feudal origin).

(2) When, by this Act, an estate held in barony ceases to exist as a feudal

estate, the dignity of baron, though retained, shall not attach to the land; and on and after the appointed day any such dignity shall be, and shall be transferable only as, incorporeal heritable property (and shall not be an interest in land for the purposes of the Land Registration (Scotland) Act 1979 (c.33) or a right as respects which a deed can be recorded in the Register of Sasines).

(3) Where there is registered, before the appointed day, a heritable security over an estate to which is attached the dignity of baron, the security shall on and after that day (until discharge) affect—

    (a) in the case of an estate of dominium utile, both the dignity of baron and the land; and

    (b) in any other case, the dignity of baron.

(4) In this section—

"conveyancing privilege" includes any privilege in relation to prescription;

"dignity" includes any quality or precedence associated with, and any heraldic privilege incidental to, a dignity; and

"registered" has the same meaning as in Part 4 of this Act.

GENERAL NOTE

Barony titles are different from peerages. Baronies were estates brought together and erected by the Crown. The owner of the lands was entitled to the dignity of baron. These estates were, over time, sub-divided. Feus and dispositions were granted to various parties. The dignity of baron remains with the *caput* or hearthstone of the barony (see *Spencer-Thomas of Buquhollie v Newell,* 1992 S.L.T. 973). Where the title to the barony remains in the Sasine Register, it has been relatively easy to sell barony titles with the dignity. The disposition merely conveyed all of the original barony lands under a host of exceptions. The dignity or lordship was also conveyed. In many cases, of course, it would have been almost impossible to decide where the original *caput* or hearthstone was and indeed whether it remained as part of a rump of the barony lands still able to be conveyed. Difficulties have arisen when the land in which the barony is situated falls within an operational or area for land registration purposes. The Keeper has so far refused to issue any title sheets in respect of a barony with full indemnity in respect of the dignity or title. An inordinate amount of time would have to be spent analysing various exceptions and feus and other historical documents before one could say with any certainty that the barony title remained with the rump of the estate. Section 63 abolishes any jurisdiction and conveyancing privilege incidental to barony after the appointed day but preserves the dignity of baron. The dignity, however, no longer attaches to any land but is treated as an incorporeal heritable right which presumably is capable of assignation. There will, however, be no official register of baronies and no official facility for recording or registering any assignation. This removes a considerable difficulty for the Keeper but may impose difficult obligations on members of the profession who are advising parties who wish to acquire a barony title. Prior to the appointed day, where the title was in the Sasine Register, there would at least have been a disposition bearing to transfer the barony and if one were purchasing a barony a search could be brought down to ensure at least that the rump of the estate had not already been conveyed away with the barony to another party. After the appointed day, no such search will be of any value and the possibility exists that an unscrupulous "baron" may attempt to sell the barony to more than one person granting more than one assignation. For this reason an unofficial register with no legal standing has been set up. Where a heritable security exists on a barony title, the security will remain on any *dominium utile* title left and on the dignity. Where there is no *dominium utile* title left, the standard security will remain as an encumbrance over the dignity, although how it would be enforced is not clear. The Lord Lyon may have difficulty in relation to verification of a barony title which is unregistered where the holder seeks arms.

Kindly Tenants of Lochmaben

Abolition of Kindly Tenancies

64.—(1) The system of land tenure whereby the persons known as the Kindly Tenants of Lochmaben hold land on perpetual tenure without requiring to procure infeftment is, on the appointed day, abolished.

(2) On the appointed day the interest of a Kindly Tenant shall forthwith become the ownership of the land (which shall be taken to include any right

of salmon fishing inseverable from the kindly tenancy); and, in so far as is consistent with the provisions of this Act, the land shall be subject to the same subordinate real rights and other encumbrances as was the kindly tenancy.

(3) A right of salmon fishing inseverable from a kindly tenancy shall on and after the appointed day be inseverable from the ownership of the land in question.

GENERAL NOTE

This is an odd form of tenure which is akin to feudal tenure but expressed in the form of a perpetual lease. As a matter of theory the tenancy is only evidenced, however, in the rental book of the Crown Steward, the Earl of Mansefield. It is equivalent to ownership (see Gordon, *Scottish Land Law* (2nd ed.) 19-15). On the appointed day this unusual form of tenure will be abolished and converted into ownership along with any rights to salmon fishing which cannot be severed from the tenancy. Oddly enough, where a salmon fishing right is inseverable it remains inseverable after the appointed day.

Miscellaneous

Creation of proper liferent

65.—(1) A proper liferent over land is created—
(a) in a case where the right is registrable under section 2 of the Land Registration (Scotland) Act 1979 (c.33)—
   (i) (unless the deed granting or reserving the right makes provision for some later date) on registration; or
   (ii) (where provision is made for such a date and the right has been registered) on that date; or
(b) in any other case—
   (i) (unless the deed granting or reserving the right makes provision for some later date) on recording of the deed in the Register of Sasines; or
   (ii) (where provision is made for such a date and such deed has been so recorded) on that date.

(2) This section is without prejudice to any other enactment, or rule of law, by or under which a proper liferent over land may be created.

(3) In subsection (1)(a) above, "registrable" and "registration" have the meanings respectively assigned to those expressions by section 1(3) of the Land Registration (Scotland) Act 1979 (c.33).

(4) The references, in subsection (1)(b) above, to a deed being recorded include references to a notice of title deducing title through a deed being recorded.

GENERAL NOTE

This makes it clear that, in general terms, a proper liferent is created on registration or on a later date specified in the deed.

Sporting rights

[1]**65A.**—(1) Where a feudal estate of *dominium utile* of land is subject to sporting rights which are enforceable by a superior of the feu or which would be so enforceable were the person in question to complete title to the *dominium directum* the superior may, before the appointed day, by duly executing and registering against the *dominium utile* a notice in, or as nearly as may be in, the form contained in schedule 11A to this Act, prospectively convert those rights into a tenement in land.

(2) The notice shall—
(a) set out the title of the superior;
(b) describe, sufficiently to enable identification by reference to the Ordnance Map, the land the *dominium utile* of which is subject to the sporting rights (or any part of that land);

(c) describe those rights; and

(d) set out the terms of any counter-obligation to those rights if it is a counter-obligation enforceable against the superior.

(3) Before submitting any notice for registration under this section, the superior shall swear or affirm as is mentioned in subsection (4) of section 18 of this Act.

(4) Subsection (5) of that section applies for the purposes of subsection (3) above as it applies for the purposes of subsection (4) of that section.

(5) If subsections (1) to (3) above are, with subsection (4) of that section, complied with and immediately before the appointed day the sporting rights are still enforceable by the superior (or his successor) or would be so enforceable, or still so enforceable, were the person in question to complete title to the *dominium directum* then, on that day, the sporting rights shall be converted into a tenement in land.

(6) No greater, or more exclusive, sporting rights shall be enforceable by virtue of such conversion than were (or would have been) enforceable as mentioned in subsection (5) above.

(7) Where the *dominium utile* comprises parts each held by a separate vassal, each part shall be taken to be a separate feudal estate of *dominium utile*.

(8) Where sporting rights become, under subsection (5) above, a tenement in land, the right to enforce those rights shall be subject to any counter-obligation enforceable against the superior immediately before the appointed day; and section 47 of this Act shall apply in relation to any counter-obligation to sporting rights as it applies in relation to any counter-obligation to a real burden.

(9) In this section, "sporting rights" means a right of fishing or game.

(10) This section is subject to section 41 of this Act.

(11) Subsections (1) and (2)(a) of section 43 of this Act apply in relation to a notice submitted for registration under this section as they apply in relation to a notice so submitted under any of the provisions mentioned in those subsections; and paragraph (a) of subsection (3) of that section applies in relation to a determination for the purposes of subsection (5) of this section as it applies in relation to a determination for the purposes of any of the provisions mentioned in that paragraph.

(12) Subsections (1), (3) and (4) of section 46 of this Act apply in relation to sporting rights extinguished by virtue of section 54 of this Act as they apply in relation to a real burden extinguished by section 17(1)(a) of this Act.

AMENDMENT

1. Inserted by the Title Conditions (Scotland) Act 2003 (asp 9), s.114 (effective April 4, 2003).

GENERAL NOTES

Subs.(5)

Sporting rights

This is in many ways an unusual provision. The generally accepted position is that only salmon fishings are capable of ownership. Other fishings and indeed sporting rights of shooting cannot be owned as separate tenements of land (see *Gordon Scottish Land Laws* (2nd ed.) 8–45). These other so-called sporting rights are apparently inseparable from ownership of the land, although they can be leased. Prior to the introduction of the 2000 Act the Scottish Law Commission considered sporting rights and the reservation of these rights in feudal grants. The view of the Commission was that non-exclusive reservations could be treated as real burdens, and accordingly could be re-allotted in terms of s.18 of the 2000 Act. There was, however, considerable doubt as to the classification of the right. It is clear that fishings and shootings cannot be a servitude as such (see Cusine and Paisley, *Servitudes and Rights of Way*, 3.08; *Earl of Galloway v Duke of Bedford* (1902) 4 F 851). Presumably Scottish Ministers took the view that if the effect of abolition of the feudal system was to extinguish rights of fishing and shooting which had been reserved to superiority titles, then there might be a claim under Art.1 of Protocol 1 to the European Convention on Human Rights, especially since no compensation is payable to superiors for the loss of the superiority title. The new section allows a superior to preserve sporting rights if these were enforceable by a superior prior to the appointed day for abolition. The superior must execute and register against the dominium utile title a notice in the form contained in Sch.11A. The superior must swear an oath in terms of s.18(4) of the 2000 Act and must give the appropriate intimation. Apparently, if a notice is registered this converts the sporting rights into a tenement in land, something which they would not have been before. The question which arises is whether or not this section elevates so-called sporting rights to ownership rights in other non-feudal situations. Presumably it does not. One could be left therefore with the anomalous situation. Where sporting rights have been reserved to a superiority title and the superior has executed and registered the appropriate notice then the Keeper of the Land Register will have to create a separate title sheet for the sporting rights, even although these were not salmon fishing rights. Presumably, the former superior could then dispone these sporting rights to other parties. However, sporting rights which have been reserved in a disposition will presumably not be capable of separate conveyance but will be merely a personal licence. Presumably, therefore, the Keeper will require some sort of evidence that sporting rights derive from a feudal title and have been appropriately preserved in terms of the new section. It is unfortunate that the new system of land tenure will allow ownership of sporting rights in one sort of case. This section goes against the notion of a unitary concept of ownership. Presumably, however, as a result of this section someone may attempt to argue, given the rather confused nature of the old case law on the subject, that the law has now recognised that sporting rights in general (whether they derive from a feudal title or not) can be regarded as separate tenements of land. The definition of "incorporeal heritable rights" in section 28(1) of the Land Registration (Scotland) Act 1979 is expanded to include sporting rights as defined by s.65A(9). The definition there is simply "a right of fishing or game".

Subs.(1)

The reserved sporting rights must have been enforceable by a superior before the appointed day. If so, the superior can execute and register against the dominium utile title a notice in the form of Sch.11A which will convert these rights into a tenement in land.

Subs.(2)

This subsection prescribes what the notice must contain.

Subs.(3)

The superior must swear or affirm in terms of s.18(4) of the 2000 Act before executing and registering a notice.

Subs.(4)

Where the superior by reason of legal disability or incapacity cannot swear or affirm, then a legal representative may swear or affirm and where the superior is not an individual but a corporate or other entity, then any person authorised to sign documents may swear or affirm.

Subs.(5)

This reiterates that on registration of the notice and compliance with the other provisions the sporting rights in so far as they are enforceable are converted into a tenement in land. There is no definition of "tenement in land" in s.110, but the definition of "land" includes heritable property held as a separate tenement. The term "tenement" usually denotes a building divided into flats, but it has been used simply to describe a piece of land especially in relation to servitudes where there is a dominant and servient tenement of land. Perhaps it is because reserved sporting rights appear to have something of the character of a servitude that this rather vague term has been used. It is almost as if the legislators were frightened to use the word "ownership". (For a discussion of separate tenements of land in general see Gordon, *Scottish Land Law* (2nd ed.) Ch.10).

Subs.(6)

Only the sporting rights which have been reserved can be converted. There may of course be general arguments in relation to the terminology used in the reservation. Rights to general fishings which have been reserved to a superior have been upheld, presumably as a pertinent of the superiority (*MacDonald v Farquharson* (1836) 15 S 259). So far as game is concerned, Professor Gordon expresses a doubt that a right to shoot game can actually be reserved to a superior (Gordon, *Scottish Land Law* (2nd ed.) pp.9–12). In the second edition of his text he indicates that the right will go in any event with abolition of the feudal system. This may not now be the case. If, however, there was no enforceable right to take game prior to the coming into effect of this new section, a question must remain. Reservations have been expressed as to the possibility of reserving a right to shoot game to a superiority (*Hemming v Duke of Athole* (1883) 11 R 93 at 97). In that case a reservation of a right to all deer that might be found was restricted to deer which had already been killed and was not interpreted as a right to hunt or stalk.

Subs.(7)
The right to convert will apply even although a dominium utile is held by different parties.

Subs.(8)
Where sporting rights become a tenement of land the rights are subject to counter-obligations enforceable against the superior.

Subs.(9)
Sporting rights mean a right of fishing or game.

Subs.(10)
The superior will require to serve notice under s.41 of the 2000 Act to the owner of the servient tenement of the attempt to re-allot.

Subs.(11)
This applies subs.(1) and (2)(a) of s.43 of the 2000 Act to any notices under s.65A. This means that the Keeper of the Registers will not require to determine whether the superior has notified the owner of the dominium utile. Nor will the Keeper be required to determine whether, prior to conversion, the superior actually had the ability to enforce the right. No doubt this will mean that the Keeper will not require to make the difficult decisions on interpretation which are almost bound to arise.

Subs.(12)
The Keeper will not require to remove sporting rights which are extinguished by s.54 from the Register unless there is an application for registration or rectification or the Keeper is ordered to remove it. The Keeper also cannot remove sporting rights subject to proceedings before the court or the Lands Tribunal. This will apply when no notice is served to preserve the sporting rights.

Obligation to make title deeds and searches available

66.—A possessor of title deeds or searches which relate to any land shall make them available to a person who has (or is entitled to acquire) a real right in the land, on all necessary occasions when the person so requests, at the person's expense.

GENERAL NOTE
The custodians of deeds and searches relating to large areas of land must make them available to persons who have, or are entitled to acquire, a real right in the land or any part.

Prohibition on leases for periods of more than 175 years

67.—(1) Notwithstanding any provision to the contrary in any lease, no lease of land executed on or after the coming into force of this section (in this section referred to as the "commencement date") may continue for a period of more than 175 years; and any such lease which is still subsisting at the end of that period shall, by virtue of this subsection, be terminated forthwith.

(2) If a lease of land so executed includes provision (however expressed) requiring the landlord or the tenant to renew the lease then the duration of any such renewed lease shall be added to the duration of the original lease for the purposes of reckoning the period mentioned in subsection (1) above.

(3) Nothing in subsection (1) above shall prevent—
(a) any lease being continued by tacit relocation; or
(b) the duration of any lease being extended by, under or by virtue of any enactment.

(4) Subsections (1) and (2) above do not apply—

(a) to a lease executed on or after the commencement date in implement of an obligation entered into before that date;

(b) to a lease executed after the commencement date in implement of an obligation contained in a lease such as is mentioned in paragraph (a) above; or

(c) where—

    (i) a lease for a period of more than 175 years has been executed before the commencement date; or

    (ii) a lease such as is mentioned in paragraph (a) or (b) above is executed on or after that date,

to a sub-lease executed on or after that date of the whole, or part, of the land subject to the lease in question.

(5) For the purposes of this section "lease" includes sub-lease.

GENERAL NOTE

    This is an anti avoidance provision which came into effect on the Act receiving Royal Assent. It is designed to prevent the recreation of the feudal system by means of long leasehold tenure. There is, of course, already a prohibition of leases of domestic property in excess of 20 years (Land Tenure Reform (Scotland) Act 1974, s.8). The prohibition applies not only to a lease for more than 175 years but also to a lease for a lesser term which requires the landlord to renew for a period which would make the total length of the lease in excess of 175 years. Tacit relocation is, however, not affected and the provisions do not apply to leases executed after Royal Assent in implement of obligations entered into before that date. Sub-leases are included within the prohibition. There is no such prohibition in England and there has been some concern that this limit may restrict commercial development in Scotland.

Certain applications to Sheriff of Chancery

    68.—After section 26 of the Titles to Land Consolidation (Scotland) Act 1868 (c.101) there shall be inserted—

"Application for declarator of succession as heir in general or to specified lands

    26A.—On an application being made by any person having an interest, the Sheriff of Chancery may, if satisfied that—

(a) such deceased person as may be specified in the application died before 10th September 1964 and that person either—

    (i) was domiciled in Scotland at the date of his death; or

    (ii) was the owner of lands situated in Scotland to which the application relates; and

(b) the applicant, or as the case may be such person as may be specified in the application, has succeeded as heir to that deceased, and is either—

    (i) heir in general; or

    (ii) heir to such lands as may be specified in the application,

grant declarator that the applicant, or as the case may be such person as may be specified in the declarator, is the heir in general or heir to the lands so specified.

Application for declarator of succession as heir to last surviving trustee under a trust

    26B.—On an application being made under this section, the Sheriff of Chancery may, if satisfied that—

(a) such deceased person as may be specified in the application was the last surviving trustee named in, or assumed under, a trust;

(b) the trust provides for the heir of such last surviving trustee to be a trustee;

(c) either—

(i) the trust is governed by the law of Scotland; or

(ii) lands subject to the trust and to which the application relates are situated in Scotland; and

(d) the applicant has succeeded as heir to the deceased,

Construction of reference to service of heir

26C.—A reference in any enactment or deed to a decree of service of heir (however expressed) shall include a reference to a declarator granted under section 26A or 26B of this Act.".

Petitions of special or general service are becoming rare but they are still required in certain cases where a death occurs prior to September 10, 1964. This is a useful provision which will clarify procedure.

Application of 1970 Act to earlier forms of heritable security

69.—(1) Sections 14 to 30 of the Conveyancing and Feudal Reform (Scotland) Act 1970 (c.35) (which provisions relate to the assignation, variation, discharge and calling-up etc. of standard securities) shall apply (with the substitution of the word "heritable" for "standard" and subject to such other modifications as may be necessary) as respects any heritable security granted before 29th November 1970 as those provisions apply as respects a standard security.

(2) For the purposes of the said sections 14 to 30 (as modified by, or by virtue of, subsection (1) above), "heritable security" shall, with the modification mentioned in subsection (3) below, include a pecuniary real burden but shall not include a security constituted by ex facie absolute disposition.

(3) The modification is that the reference to the date in subsection (1) above shall be disregarded.

GENERAL NOTE

This section applies various sections of the Conveyancing and Feudal Reform (Scotland) Act 1970 to earlier forms of heritable security apart from those constituted by *ex facie* absolute disposition.

Ownership of land by a firm

70.—A firm may, if it has a legal personality distinct from the persons who compose it, itself own land.

GENERAL NOTE

Partnerships are regarded as a separate legal personae in the law of Scotland, separate from the personae of the partners. However, a partnership was not regarded as having sufficient legal personality to hold a feudal estate. The superior was normally entitled to have an individual vassal. This rather brief section simply states that if a firm has legal personality then it may own land. Presumably title would be taken in the firm's name and the rights of the partners would be regulated by a partnership agreement or alternatively by the Partnership Act 1890. Presumably if there was to be a complete dissolution of a firm, the heritable property would simply be treated as a firm asset. However, on one view at least as a technical matter a firm is dissolved and reconstituted each time a partner dies, retires or is assumed and there have been many difficulties surrounding leases where the tenant is a partnership (see *Lujo Properties Ltd v Green*, 1997 S.L.T. 225; *Moray Estates Development Co. v Butler*, 1999 S.C.L.R. 447). Presumably the framers of this section take the view that in any well ordered partnership, the partnership agreement will cater for all these eventualities. Presumably no one would suggest that on a technical dissolution caused by an assumption, death or resignation the previous legal entity would cease to exist and the title would go into some sort of vacuum. There is likely to be legislation in relation to partnerships in which this problem will be addressed (*Partnership Law: A Joint Consultative Paper*, Scot. Law. Com. No.111).

PART 7

GENERAL

The appointed day

71.—The Scottish Ministers may, for the purposes of this Act, by order appoint a day (in this Act referred to as the "appointed day"), being a day which—

(a) falls not less than six months after the order is made; and

(b) is one or other of the terms of Whitsunday and Martinmas.

GENERAL NOTE

The appointed day was November 28, 2004, the same day as the Title Conditions (Scotland) Act 2003 and Tenements (Scotland) Act 2004 came into force.

Interpretation

72.—In this Act, unless the context otherwise requires—

"land" includes all subjects of heritable property which, before the appointed day, are, or of their nature might be, held of a superior according to feudal tenure;

"Lands Tribunal" means Lands Tribunal for Scotland; and

"the specified day" and "the transitional period" shall be construed in accordance with section 20(6) of this Act.

GENERAL NOTE

This is a general interpretation section.

Feudal terms in enactments and documents: construction after abolition of feudal system

73.—[1](1) Where a term or expression, which before the appointed day would ordinarily, or in the context in which it is used, depend for its meaning on there being a feudal system of land tenure, requires to be construed, in relation to any period from that day onwards—

(a) in an enactment (other than this Act) passed before that day;

(b) in an enactment contained in subordinate legislation made before that day;

(c) in a document executed before that day; or

[2] (d) in the Land Register of Scotland or in—

    (i) a land certificate;

    (ii) a charge certificate; or

    (iii) an office copy,

issued, whether or not before that day, under the Land Registration (Scotland) Act 1979 (c.33), before the appointed day,

then in so far as the context admits, where the term or expression is, or contains, a reference to—

    (i) the dominium utile of the land, that reference shall be construed either as a reference to the land or as a reference to the ownership of that land;

    (ii) an estate in land, that reference shall be construed as a reference to a right in land and as including ownership of land;

    (iii) a vassal in relation to land, that reference shall be construed as a reference to the owner of the land;

    (iv) feuing, that reference shall be construed as a reference to disponing;

    (v) a feu disposition, that reference shall be construed as a reference to a disposition;

(vi) taking infeftment, that reference shall be construed as a reference to completing title,

analogous terms and expressions being construed accordingly.

[1] (2) On and after the appointed day, any reference—

(a) in any document executed before that day; or

[2] (b) in the Land Register of Scotland or in any certificate or copy such as is mentioned in subsection (1)(d) above (whenever issued),

to a superior shall, where that reference requires to be construed in relation to a real burden which a person is entitled, by virtue of section 18, 18A, 18B, 18C, 19, 20, 28, 28A or 60 of this Act or section 56 of the Title Conditions (Scotland) Act 2003 (asp 9) (facility burdens and service burdens), to enforce on and after that day, be construed as a reference to that person.

[2] (2A) In construing, after the appointed day and in relation to a right enforceable on or after that day, a document, or entry in the Land Register, which—

(a) sets out the terms of a real burden; and

(b) is not a document or entry references in which require to be construed as mentioned in subsection (2) above,

any provision of the document or entry to the effect that a person other than the person entitled to enforce the burden may waive compliance with, or mitigate or otherwise vary a condition of, the burden shall be disregarded.

(3) Subsection (1) above is without prejudice to section 76 of, and schedules 12 and 13 to, this Act or to any order made under subsection (3) of that section.

(4) In subsection (1) above—

(a) in paragraph (a), "enactment" includes a local and personal or private Act; and

(b) in paragraph (b), "subordinate legislation" has the same meaning as in the Interpretation Act 1978 (c.30) (but includes subordinate legislation made under an Act of the Scottish Parliament).

AMENDMENTS

1. As amended by the Title Conditions (Scotland) Act 2003 (asp 9), Sch.13, para.13, (effective April 4, 2003).
2. Inserted by the Title Conditions (Scotland) Act 2003 (asp 9), Sch.13, para.13, (effective April 4, 2003).

GENERAL NOTE

This is a general section which attempts to deal with well known feudal terms in earlier statutes and documents. *Dominium utile* and estates in land will simply be construed as ownership and a vassal will simply be an owner. Any references to feuing shall be construed as references to simple disponing and a reference to a feudal writ will be construed as a reference to a disposition. The taking of infeftment shall be construed simply as a reference to completion of title presumably by registration. Only those with title to enforce a real burden shall be capable of granting consents or waivers.

Orders, regulations and rules

74.—(1) Any power of the Scottish Ministers under this Act to make orders, regulations or rules shall be exercisable by statutory instrument; and a statutory instrument containing any such orders, regulations or rules, other than an order under section 71, 76(3) or 77(4), shall be subject to annulment in pursuance of a resolution of the Scottish Parliament.

(2) A statutory instrument containing an order under section 76(3) of this Act shall not be made unless a draft of the instrument has been—

(a) laid before; and

(b) approved by a resolution of,

the Scottish Parliament.

GENERAL NOTE
Any orders, regulations or rules shall be promulgated by statutory instrument. Apart from a few obvious exceptions, the statutory instrument shall be subject to a negative resolution annulment procedure in the Scottish Parliament. The Scottish Ministers are given delegated power in terms of s.76(3) to make further amendments or repeals in other enactments as appear necessary in consequence of any provision of the Act. In such a case, however, the statutory instrument must be laid before and approved by resolution of the Scottish Parliament.

Saving for contractual rights

[1] **75.**—(1) As respects any land granted in feu before the appointed day, nothing in this Act shall affect any right (other than a right to feuduty) included in the grant in so far as that right is contractual as between the parties to the grant (or, as the case may be, as between one of them and a person to whom any such right is assigned).

(2) In construing the expression "parties to the grant" in subsection (1) above, any enactment or rule of law whereby investiture is deemed renewed when the parties change shall be disregarded.

AMENDMENT
1. As amended by the Title Conditions (Scotland) Act 2003 (asp 9), Sch.13, para.14, (effective April 4, 2003).

GENERAL NOTE
Any contractual rights (as opposed to tenure rights) are not affected even if they are contained in a feudal writ, and such rights are capable of assignation. On one, perhaps unlikely, view, this does not mean that a former superior will be able to enforce real burdens and conditions as against the original vassal where the *dominium utile* has not changed hands before the appointed day. Real burdens would not be regarded as personal contractual rights. On another view, a burden is not real until successors are involved and the original superior and original vassal are merely contracting policies after abolition with normal contractual personal rights. The latter view is thought to be preferable although it may come as a shock to first time vassals who think they will be free of feudal fetters on November 28, 2004. Contractual liability will, however, cease when the first vassal ceases to be owned even as against that first vassal.

Minor and consequential amendments, repeals and power to amend or repeal enactments

76.—(1) Schedule 12 to this Act, which contains minor amendments and amendments consequential upon the provisions of this Act, shall have effect.

(2) The enactments mentioned in schedule 13 to this Act are hereby repealed to the extent specified in the second column of that schedule.

(3) The Scottish Ministers may by order make such further amendments or repeals, in such enactments as may be specified in the order, as appear to them to be necessary or expedient in consequence of any provision of this Act.

(4) In this section "enactment" has the same meaning as in section 73(1)(a) of this Act.

GENERAL NOTE
Schedule 12 contains a formidable list of minor and consequential amendments to earlier statutes. Previous conveyancing statutes have, of course, contained feudal terminology. One of the more significant amendments is to the Conveyancing and Feudal Reform (Scotland) Act 1970. Note 1 to Sch.2 to that Act is now amended to the effect that the security subjects in a standard security must only be described sufficiently to identify them without prejudice to any other additional requirement imposed as respects any register. This places descriptions in standard securities on the same footing as descriptions in ordinary dispositions. The description must not be too vague otherwise it may not be acceptable to the Keeper (see *MacDonald v The Keeper of the General Register of Sasines,* 1914 S.C. 854). Where the property to be secured is already registered in the Land Register, the title number must of course be used in any description. Schedule 13 contains a list of total or partial repeals. In terms of subs.(3) Scottish Ministers may make further amendments or repeals by statutory instrument approved by the Scottish Parliament. This is a necessary provision. It seems likely that there will be sections, sub-

sections or paragraphs in earlier legislation which require alteration in the light of the abolition of the feudal system.

Short title and commencement

77.—(1) This Act—

(a) may be cited as the Abolition of Feudal Tenure etc. (Scotland) Act 2000; and

(b) subject to subsections (2) and (4) below, comes into force on Royal Assent.

[1] (2) There shall come into force on the appointed day—

[2,3] (a) sections 1 and 2, 4 to 13, 35 to 37, 46, 50 and 51, 54 to 57, 59 to 61, 64, 65, 66, 68 to 70, 73, 75 and 76(1) (except in so far as relating to paragraph 30(23)(a) of schedule 12) and (2);

(b) schedules 1 to 3;

(c) subject to paragraph 46(3) of schedule 12, that schedule, except paragraph 30(23)(a); and

(d) schedule 13.

(3) Note 1 to Schedule 2 to the Conveyancing and Feudal Reform (Scotland) Act 1970 (c.35) shall be deemed to have been originally enacted as amended by the said paragraph 30(23)(a).

[1] (4) There shall come into force on such day as the Scottish Ministers may by order appoint—

[2] (a) sections 17 to 31, 33, 34, 38 to 45, 47 to 49, 63 and 65A;

(b) schedules 5 to 11;

and different days may be so appointed for different provisions.

(c)–(d) [*Repealed by the Title Conditions (Scotland) Act 2003 (asp 9), Sch.15 (effective April 4, 2003).*]

AMENDMENTS

1. Repealed in part by the Title Conditions (Scotland) Act 2003 (asp 9), Sch.15, (effective April 4, 2003).

2. Amended in part by the Title Conditions (Scotland) Act 2003 (asp 9), Sch 13, para. 15, (effective April 4, 2003).

3. As amended by the Title Conditions (Scotland) Act 2003 (Consequential Provisions) Order (SSI 2003/503), art.2, Sch.1, para.5 (effective October 22, 2003).

GENERAL NOTE

This section sets out when the various provisions will come into effect. So far as the change to the law relating to descriptions in standard securities is concerned, this is retrospective. There are two appointed days. After the first appointed day it will be possible to serve the various notices in respect of reallotment and reserved development values. These notices will all require to be served prior to the second appointed day (November 28, 2004) on which the abolition of the feudal system will take effect.

SCHEDULE 1

(introduced by section 8(2))

FORM OF NOTICE REQUIRING COMPENSATORY PAYMENT ETC.: CUMULO FEUDUTY

"NOTICE UNDER SECTION 8(1) OF THE ABOLITION OF FEUDAL TENURE ETC. (SCOTLAND) ACT 2000 (CUMULO FEUDUTY)

To: [*name and address of former vassal*].

This notice is sent by [*name and address of former superior*]. You are required to pay the sum of £ [*amount*] as a compensatory payment for the extinction of the cumulo feuduty of £ [*amount*] per annum due in respect of [*give sufficient identification of the land in respect of which the cumulo feuduty was due*].

The attached appendix shows the total sum due as compensation for the extinction of the feuduty and the compensatory payment due by each owner.

(*If arrears of the feuduty are also sought, then add*:

You are also required to pay the sum of £ [*amount*] as arrears of the feuduty.)

Signed: [*signature either of the former superior or of his agent; and if an agent signs he should put the word "Agent" after his signature*]

Date:

(*If payment is to be made to an agent of the former superior then add*:

Payment should be made to: [*name and address of agent*].)".

Appendix referred to in the Notice:

Total compensation payable is £ [*amount*], allocated as follows:

Owner (see note for completion 1) Property (see note for completion 2) Compensatory payment (see note for completion 3)

Explanatory Note

(This explanation, and the "Notes for completion of the Appendix" which immediately follows it, have no legal effect)

The feudal system was abolished on [*insert date of abolition*]. By this notice your former feudal superior is claiming compensation from you for the extinction of the cumulo feuduty which affected your property. A cumulo feuduty is one which affects two or more properties in separate ownership. This notice must have been sent within two years after the date of abolition.

The appendix sets out the total sum due as compensation for the extinction of the cumulo feuduty and divides that sum among the owners of the affected properties.

The total compensation payable is that sum which would, if invested in 2½% Consolidated Stock at the middle market price at the close of business last preceding the date of abolition, produce an annual sum equal to the cumulo feuduty. In practice the sum is arrived at by multiplying the feuduty by a factor known as the "compensation factor". This factor is [*insert factor*].

If the amount of the compensatory payment allocated to you is £50 or more you can choose to pay the sum due by instalments. You may do this by signing, dating and returning, within eight weeks, the enclosed instalment document.

If, having received the instalment document, you sell, or transfer for valuable consideration, the property or any part of it you will lose the option of paying by instalments.

Unless you are paying by instalments you must pay the compensatory payment allocated to you within eight weeks.

Your former feudal superior may also be claiming arrears of feuduty for the period before the date of abolition.

If at one time you had right to the property in question but, immediately before the feudal system was abolished, you no longer had that right (because, for example, you had sold that property to someone else) then this notice has been served on you in error and no payment will be due; but you nevertheless have to provide the person who sent you the notice, if you can, with such information as you have which might enable him to identify the person who should have received notice instead of you.

If you think that the amount required from you is not due for that or any other reason, you are advised to consult your solicitor or other adviser.

Notes for completion of the Appendix

1 Insert the name of each owner.
2 Give sufficient identification of each part of the land held in separate ownership (including, where appropriate, the postal address) which was subject to the cumulo feuduty.
3 Insert the amount of the compensation allocated to each owner.

SCHEDULE 2
(introduced by section 8(3))

FORM OF NOTICE REQUIRING COMPENSATORY PAYMENT ETC.: ORDINARY CASE
NOTICE UNDER SECTION 8(1) OF THE ABOLITION OF FEUDAL TENURE ETC. (SCOTLAND) ACT 2000 (ORDINARY CASE)

To: [*name and address of former vassal*].

This notice is sent by [*name and address of former superior*]. You are required to pay the sum of £ [*amount*] as a compensatory payment for the extinction of the feuduty of £ [*amount*] per annum due in respect of [give sufficient identification of the land in respect of which the feuduty was due].

(*If arrears of the feuduty are also sought, then add*:

You are also required to pay the sum of £ [*amount*] as arrears of the feuduty.)

Signed: [*signature either of the former superior or of his agent; and if an agent signs he should put the word "Agent" after his signature*]

Date:

(*If payment is to be made to an agent of the former superior then add*:

Payment should be made to: [*name and address of agent*].)".

Explanatory Note

(This explanation has no legal effect)

The feudal system was abolished on [*insert date of abolition*]. By this notice your former feudal superior is claiming compensation from you for the extinction of the feuduty which affected your property. This notice must have been sent within two years after the date of abolition.

The compensatory payment is that sum which would, if invested in 2½% Consolidated Stock at the middle market price at the close of business last preceding the date of abolition, produce an annual sum equal to the feuduty. In practice the sum is arrived at by multiplying the feuduty by a factor known as the "compensation factor". This factor is [insert factor].

If the compensatory payment is £50 or more you can choose to pay the sum by instalments. You may do this by signing, dating and returning, within eight weeks, the enclosed instalment document.

If, having received the instalment document, you sell, or transfer for valuable consideration, the property or any part of it you will lose the option of paying by instalments.

Unless you are paying by instalments you must pay the compensatory payment within eight weeks.

Your former feudal superior may also be claiming arrears of feuduty for the period before the date of abolition.

If at one time you had right to the property in question but, immediately before the feudal system was abolished, you no longer had that right (because, for example, you had transferred that property to someone else) then this notice has been served on you in error and no payment will be due in terms of the notice; but you nevertheless have to provide the person who sent you the notice, if you can, with such information as you have which might enable him to identify the person who ostensibly (that is to say, disregarding questions such as whether the feuduty has already been redeemed in the case of a transfer by conveyance for valuable consideration) should have received notice instead of you.

If you think that the amount required from you is not due for whatever reason, you are advised to consult your solicitor or other adviser.

SCHEDULE 3
(introduced by section 10(1))

FORM OF INSTALMENT DOCUMENT

"INSTALMENT DOCUMENT

To: [*name and address of former superior or of his agent*].

I [*name and address of former vassal*] opt to make the compensatory payment of £ [*amount*] due under the notice dated [*date*] by [number of instalments: see note for completion] equal half-yearly instalments of £ [*amount*] on 28 May and 28 November each year, commencing on [*28 May or 28 November*] [*year*].

I enclose payment of £ [amount] as an amount payable in addition to the compensatory payment.

Signed:

Date: .".

Explanatory Note

(This explanation has no legal effect)

You can choose to pay by instalments by signing, dating and returning this form within eight weeks, but if you do so you must enclose the additional amount (10% over and above the compensatory payment) mentioned in this notice.

The compensatory payment will be payable in 5, 10, 15, or 20 equal instalments (depending on the total amount). The first payment will be made at the first term day of Whitsunday (28 May) and Martinmas (28 November) which follows the return of the instalment document. Payments will be due half-yearly thereafter on 28 May and 28 November until payment in full has been made.

If you fail to pay an instalment within 42 days after the day on which it is due, the whole balance of the compensatory payment will be due at once.

If, having chosen to pay by instalments, you sell, or transfer for valuable consideration, the property or any part of it the whole balance of the compensatory payment will be due seven days after the sale or transfer.

If, after you receive this document, you sell, or so transfer, the property or any part of it without having signed, dated and returned this form, you will lose the right to obtain the option to pay by instalments and the entire compensatory payment will be payable in accordance with the notice which accompanied this document.

If you have difficulty in making the compensatory payment you may be able to make arrangements with your former superior different from those you would obtain by signing, dating and completing this form; but that is a matter on which you are advised to consult your solicitor or other adviser without delay.

Note for completion of the form by the former superior

(This note has no legal effect)
Insert the number of instalments in accordance with the following table:

Compensatory Payment	Number of Instalments
£50 but not exceeding £500	5
exceeding £500 but not exceeding £1,000	10
exceeding £1,000 but not exceeding £1,500	15
exceeding £1,500	20

SCHEDULE 4
(introduced by section 11(2))

PROCEDURES AS TO SERVICE UNDER SECTION 8(1)

FORM A

I, [*name of former vassal*], acknowledge receipt of a notice under section 8(1) of the Abolition of Feudal Tenure etc. (Scotland) Act 2000 requiring a compensatory payment [*add if applicable, of an instalment document*] and of an explanatory note relating to the notice.

Signed: [*signature of former vassal*]
Date: .".

FORM B

"Notice under section 8(1) of the Abolition of Feudal Tenure etc. (Scotland) Act 2000 requiring a compensatory payment was posted to [*name of former vassal*], together with [*add if applicable an instalment document and*] the requisite explanatory note relating to the notice, on [*date*].

Signature: [*signature either of the former superior or of his agent; and if an agent signs he should put the word "Agent" after his signature*]
Date: .".

SCHEDULE 5
(introduced by section 18(1))

FORM OF NOTICE PROSPECTIVELY NOMINATING DOMINANT TENEMENT

"NOTICE PROSPECTIVELY NOMINATING DOMINANT TENEMENT

Superior:
(see note for completion 1)

Description of land which is to be the servient tenement:
(see note for completion 2)

Description of land nominated as dominant tenement:
(see note for completion 2)

Specification of condition met:
(see note for completion 3)

Terms of real burden:
(see note for completion 4)

Any counter-obligation:
(see note for completion 4)

Title to the superiority:
(see note for completion 5)

Title to land nominated as dominant tenement:
(see note for completion 5)

Service:
(see note for completion 6)

I swear [or affirm] that the information contained in the notice is, to the best of my knowledge and belief, true.

Signature of superior:
(see note for completion 7)

Signature of notary public:

Date: .".

Explanatory Note

(This explanation has no legal effect)

This notice is sent by your feudal superior, who is also a neighbour. In this notice your property (or some part of it) is referred to (prospectively) as the "servient tenement" and neighbouring property belonging to the superior is referred to (again prospectively) as the "dominant tenement".

By this notice the feudal superior asserts that at present the use of your property is subject to certain burdens and conditions enforceable by him and claims the right to continue to enforce the burdens and conditions, not as superior but in his capacity of owner of neighbouring property. The notice, if it is registered in the Land Register or Register of Sasines under section 18 of the Abolition of Feudal Tenure etc. (Scotland) Act 2000, will allow him and his successors, as such owners, to enforce the burdens and conditions after the feudal system is abolished (which will be shortly).

Normally, for the notice to be valid, there must, on the dominant tenement, be a permanent building which is within 100 metres of the servient tenement. That building must be in use as a place of human habitation or of human resort. However, the presence of a building is not required if the burden gives a right to enter or otherwise make use of the servient tenement, or if it gives a right of pre-emption or redemption, or if the dominant tenement comprises, and the real burden was created for the benefit of, minerals, salmon fishings or some other incorporeal property.

If you think that there is a mistake in this notice or if you wish to challenge it, you are advised to contact your solicitor or other adviser.

Notes for completion of the notice

(These notes have no legal effect)

1 Insert name and address of superior.
2 Describe the land in a way that is sufficient to enable the Keeper to identify it by reference to the Ordnance Map. Where the title to the land has been registered in the Land Register the description should refer to the title number of the land or of the larger subjects of which the land forms part. Otherwise it should normally refer to and identify a deed recorded in a specified division of the Register of Sasines.
3 Insert one or more of the following:
"The dominant tenement has on it a [*specify type of building*] at [*specify address of building*] which is within 100 metres of the servient tenement.";

"The real burden comprises a right to enter, or otherwise make use of, the servient tenement.";
"The real burden comprises a right of [*specify pre-emption or redemption (or both)*].".
"The dominant tenement comprises, and (as is apparent from the terms of the real burden) that burden was created for the benefit of, [*specify minerals or salmon fishings or some other incorporeal property*].".

4 Specify by reference to the appropriate Register the deed or deeds in which the real burden or counter-obligation was imposed. Set out the real burden or counter-obligation in full or refer to the deed in such a way as to identify the real burden or counter-obligation.

5 Where the title has been registered in the Land Register of Scotland and the superior is—
  (a) registered as proprietor, specify the title number;
  (b) not registered as proprietor, specify the title number and set out the midcouples or links between the person last registered and the superior so as sufficiently to identify them.

Where the title has not been registered in the Land Register and the superior—
  (a) has a recorded title, specify by reference to the Register of Sasines the deed constituting the immediate title;
  (b) does not have a recorded title, either—
    (i) specify by reference to the Register of Sasines the deed constituting the immediate title of the person with the last recorded title and set out the midcouples or links between that person and the superior so as sufficiently to identify them; or
    (ii) if there is no such deed, specify the nature of the superior's title

6 Do not complete until a copy of the notice has been sent to the owner of the prospective servient tenement (except in a case where this is not reasonably practicable). Then insert whichever is applicable of the following:

"The superior has sent a copy of this notice by [*specify whether by recorded delivery or registered post or by ordinary post*] on [*date of posting*] to the owner of the prospective servient tenement at [*state address*]."; or

"It has not been reasonably practicable to send a copy of this notice to the owner of the prospective servient tenement for the following reason: [*specify the reason*].".

7 The superior should not swear or affirm, or sign, until a copy of the notice has been sent (or otherwise) as mentioned in note 6. Before signing the superior should swear or affirm before a notary public (or, if the notice is being completed outwith Scotland, before a person duly authorised under the local law to administer oaths or receive affirmations) that, to the best of the superior's knowledge and belief, all the information contained in the notice is true. The notary public should also sign. Swearing or affirming a statement which is known to be false or which is believed not to be true is a criminal offence under the False Oaths (Scotland) Act 1933. Normally the superior should swear or affirm, and sign, personally. If, however, the superior is legally disabled or incapable (for example, because of mental disorder) his legal representative should swear or affirm and sign. If the superior is not an individual (for example, if it is a company) a person entitled by law to sign formal documents on its behalf should swear or affirm and sign.

[1] SCHEDULE 5A
(introduced by section 18A(1))

FORM OF NOTICE PROSPECTIVELY CONVERTING REAL BURDEN INTO PERSONAL PRE-EMPTION BURDEN OR PERSONAL REDEMPTION BURDEN

"NOTICE PROSPECTIVELY CONVERTING REAL BURDEN INTO PERSONAL PRE-EMPTION BURDEN OR PERSONAL REDEMPTION BURDEN

Superior:
(see note for completion 1)

Description of land which is to be servient tenement:
(see note for completion 2)

Terms of real burden:
(see note for completion 3)

Any counter obligation:
(see note for completion 3)

Title to the superiority:
(see note for completion 4)

Service:
(see note for completion 5)

I swear [*or* affirm] that the information contained in the notice is, to the best of my knowledge and belief, true.

Signature of superior:
(see note for completion 6)

Signature of notary public:

Date: .”

Explanatory Note
(This explanation has no legal effect)

This notice is sent by your feudal superior. In this notice your property (or some part of it) is referred to (prospectively) as the "servient tenement". By this notice the feudal superior asserts that at present your property is subject to a right of pre-emption [*or* of redemption] enforceable by him and claims the right to continue to enforce it not as superior but in a personal capacity. The notice, if it is registered in the Land Register or Register of Sasines under section 18A of the Abolition of Feudal Tenure etc. (Scotland) Act 2000, will allow him to enforce the right after the feudal system is abolished (which will be shortly). If you think that there is a mistake in this notice or if you wish to challenge it, you are advised to contact your solicitor or other adviser.

Notes for completion of the notice
(These notes have no legal effect)

1 Insert name and address of superior.
2 Describe the land in a way that is sufficient to enable the Keeper to identify it by reference to the Ordnance Map. Where the title to the land has been registered in the Land Register the description should refer to the title number of the land or of the larger subjects of which the land forms part. Otherwise it should normally refer to and identify a deed recorded in a specified division of the Register of Sasines.
3 Specify by reference to the appropriate Register the deed or deeds in which the real burden or counter-obligation was imposed. Set out the real burden or counter-obligation in full or refer to the deed in such a way as to identify the real burden or counter-obligation.
4 Where the title has been registered in the Land Register of Scotland and the superior is—
  (a) registered as proprietor, specify the title number;
  (b) not so registered, specify the title number and set out the midcouples or links between the person last registered and the superior so as sufficiently to identify them.
Where the title has not been registered in the Land Register and the superior—
  (a) has a recorded title, specify by reference to the Register of Sasines the deed constituting the immediate title;
  (b) does not have a recorded title, either—
    (i) specify by reference to the Register of Sasines the deed constituting the immediate title of the person with the last recorded title and set out the midcouples or links between that person and the superior so as sufficiently to identify them; or
    (ii) if there is no such deed, specify the nature of the superior's title.
5 Do not complete until a copy of the notice has been sent to the owner of the prospective servient tenement (except in a case where this is not reasonably practicable). Then insert whichever is applicable of the following:
"The superior has sent a copy of this notice by [*specify whether by recorded delivery or registered post or by ordinary post*] on [*date of posting*] to the owner of the prospective servient tenement at [*state address*]."; or
"It has not been reasonably practicable to send a copy of this notice to the owner of the prospective servient tenement for the following reason: [*specify the reason*]".
6 The superior should not swear or affirm, or sign, until a copy of the notice has been sent (or otherwise) as mentioned in note 5. Before signing, the superior should swear or affirm before a notary public (or, if the notice is being completed outwith Scotland, before a person duly

authorised under the local law to administer oaths or receive affirmations) that, to the best of the superior's knowledge and belief, all the information contained in the notice is true. The notary public should also sign. Swearing or affirming a statement which is known to be false or which is believed not to be true is a criminal offence under the False Oaths (Scotland) Act 1933. Normally the superior should swear or affirm, and sign, personally. If, however, the superior is legally disabled or incapable (for example, because of mental disorder) his legal representative should swear or affirm and sign. If the superior is not an individual (for example, if it is a company) a person entitled by law to sign formal documents on its behalf should swear or affirm and sign.

AMENDMENT
1. Inserted by the Title Conditions (Scotland) Act 2003 (asp 9), Sch.13, para.16, (effective April 4, 2003).

[1] SCHEDULE 5B
(introduced by section 18B(1))

FORM OF NOTICE PROSPECTIVELY CONVERTING REAL BURDEN INTO ECONOMIC DEVELOPMENT BURDEN

"NOTICE PROSPECTIVELY CONVERTING REAL BURDEN INTO ECONOMIC DEVELOPMENT BURDEN

Superior:
(see note for completion 1)

Description of land which is to be servient tenement:
(see note for completion 2)

Terms of real burden:
(see note for completion 3)

Statement that purpose was to promote economic development:
(with supporting evidence: see note for completion 3)

Any counter obligation:
(see note for completion 3)

Title to the superiority:
(see note for completion 4)

Service:
(see note for completion 5)

Signature on behalf of superior:

Date: ."

Explanatory Note
(This explanation has no legal effect)

This notice is sent by your feudal superior; that is to say by [the Scottish Ministers] *or* [*specify local authority*]. By this notice the feudal superior asserts that at present your property is subject to a real burden enforceable by the superior and claims both the right to continue to enforce it, not as superior but in a personal capacity, and that the real burden is for the purpose of promoting economic development. The notice, if it is registered in the Land Register or Register of Sasines under section 18B of the Abolition of Feudal Tenure etc. (Scotland) Act 2000, will allow the superior to enforce that right after the feudal system is abolished (which will be shortly). If you think that there is a mistake in this notice or if you wish to challenge it, you are advised to contact your solicitor or other adviser.

Notes for completion of the notice
(These notes have no legal effect)

1 Insert "the Scottish Ministers" or as the case may be the name and address of the local authority.

2 Describe the land in a way that is sufficient to enable the Keeper to identify it by reference to the Ordnance Map. Where the title to the land has been registered in the Land Register the description should refer to the title number of the land or of the larger subjects of which the land forms part. Otherwise it should normally refer to and identify a deed recorded in a specified division of the Register of Sasines.

3 Specify by reference to the appropriate Register the deed or deeds in which the real burden or counter-obligation was imposed. Set out the terms of the real burden, or as the case may be the terms of the counter-obligation, in full or refer to the deed in such a way as to identify the real burden or counter-obligation. Provide the statement specified and set out any information which supports it.

4 Where the title has been registered in the Land Register of Scotland and the superior is—

    (a) registered as proprietor, specify the title number;

    (b) not so registered, specify the title number and set out the midcouples or links between the person last registered and the superior so as sufficiently to identify them.

Where the title has not been registered in the Land Register and the superior—

    (a) has a recorded title, specify by reference to the Register of Sasines the deed constituting the immediate title;

    (b) does not have a recorded title, either—

        (i) specify by reference to the Register of Sasines the deed constituting the immediate title of the person with the last recorded title and set out the midcouples or links between that person and the superior so as sufficiently to identify them; or

        (ii) if there is no such deed, specify the nature of the superior's title.

5 Do not complete until a copy of the notice has been sent to the owner of the prospective servient tenement (except in a case where such sending is not reasonably practicable). Then insert whichever is applicable of the following:

"The superior has sent a copy of this notice by [*specify whether by recorded delivery or registered post or by ordinary post*] on [*date of posting*] to the owner of the prospective servient tenement at [*state address*]."; or

"It has not been reasonably practicable to send a copy of this notice to the owner of the prospective servient tenement and the reason is that: [*specify the reason*]."

AMENDMENT

    1. Inserted by the Title Conditions (Scotland) Act 2003 (asp 9), Sch.13, para.16, (effective April 4, 2003).

[1] SCHEDULE 5C
(introduced by section 18C(1))

FORM OF NOTICE PROSPECTIVELY CONVERTING REAL BURDEN INTO HEALTH CARE BURDEN

"NOTICE PROSPECTIVELY CONVERTING REAL BURDEN INTO HEALTH CARE BURDEN

Superior:
(see note for completion 1)

Description of land which is to be servient tenement:
(see note for completion 2)

Terms of real burden:
(see note for completion 3)

Statement that purpose was to promote the provision of facilities for health care:
(with supporting evidence: see note for completion 3)

Any counter obligation:
(see note for completion 3)

Title to the superiority:
(see note for completion 4)

Service:
(see note for completion 5)

Signature on behalf of superior:

Date: .''

Explanatory Note
(This explanation has no legal effect)

This notice is sent by your feudal superior; that is to say by [the Scottish Ministers] *or* [*specify National Health Service trust*]. By this notice the feudal superior asserts that at present your property is subject to a real burden enforceable by the superior and claims both the right to continue to enforce it, not as superior but in a personal capacity, and that the real burden is for the purpose of promoting the provision of facilites for health care. The notice, if it is registered in the Land Register or Register of Sasines under section 18C of the Abolition of Feudal Tenure etc. (Scotland) Act 2000, will allow the superior to enforce that right after the feudal system is abolished (which will be shortly). If you think that there is a mistake in this notice or if you wish to challenge it, you are advised to contact your solicitor or other adviser.

Notes for completion of the notice
(These notes have no legal effect)

1 Insert "the Scottish Ministers" or as the case may be the name and address of the National Health Service trust.
2 Describe the land in a way that is sufficient to enable the Keeper to identify it by reference to the Ordnance Map. Where the title to the land has been registered in the Land Register the description should refer to the title number of the land or of the larger subjects of which the land forms part. Otherwise it should normally refer to and identify a deed recorded in a specified division of the Register of Sasines.
3 Specify by reference to the appropriate Register the deed or deeds in which the real burden or counter-obligation was imposed. Set out the terms of the real burden, or or as the case may be the terms of the counter-obligation, in full or refer to the deed in such a way as to identify the real burden or counter-obligation. Provide the statement specified and set out any information which supports it.
4 Where the title has been registered in the Land Register of Scotland and the superior is—
    (a) registered as proprietor, specify the title number;
    (b) not so registered, specify the title number and set out the midcouples or links between the person last registered and the superior so as sufficiently to identify them.
Where the title has not been registered in the Land Register and the superior—
    (a) has a recorded title, specify by reference to the Register of Sasines the deed constituting the immediate title;
    (b) does not have a recorded title, either—
        (i) specify by reference to the Register of Sasines the deed constituting the immediate title of the person with the last recorded title and set out the midcouples or links between that person and the superior so as sufficiently to identify them; or
        (ii) if there is no such deed, specify the nature of the superior's title.
5 Do not complete until a copy of the notice has been sent to the owner of the prospective servient tenement (except in a case where such sending is not reasonably practicable). Then insert whichever is applicable of the following:
"The superior has sent a copy of this notice by [*specify whether by recorded delivery or registered post or by ordinary post*] on [*date of posting*] to the owner of the prospective servient tenement at [*state address*]."; or
"It has not been reasonably practicable to send a copy of this notice to the owner of the prospective servient tenement and the reason is that: [*specify the reason*].

AMENDMENT
    1. Inserted by the Title Conditions (Scotland) Act 2003 (asp 9), Sch.13, para.16, (effective April 4, 2003).

SCHEDULE 6
(introduced by section 19(1)(a))

FORM OF NOTICE SEEKING AGREEMENT TO THE PROSPECTIVE NOMINATION
OF A DOMINANT TENEMENT

"NOTICE SEEKING AGREEMENT TO PROSPECTIVE NOMINATION OF
DOMINANT TENEMENT

Superior:
(see note for completion 1)

Person who has the feudal estate of dominium utile:
(see note for completion 2)

**Description of land which, if agreement is reached and the agreement is registered, shall be the
prospective servient tenement:**

**Description of land which, if agreement is reached and the agreement is registered, shall be the
prospective dominant tenement:**

Terms of real burden:
(see note for completion 3)

Any counter-obligation:
(see note for completion 3)

Title to the superiority:
(see note for completion 4)

Title to land which would be the prospective dominant tenement:
(see note for completion 4)

Service:
(see note for completion 5)

Signature of superior:

Date: .".

Explanatory Note
(This explanation has no legal effect)

This notice is sent by your feudal superior. In this notice your property (or some part of it) is
referred to (prospectively) as the "servient tenement" and property belonging to the superior is
referred to (again prospectively) as the "dominant tenement".

By this notice the feudal superior asserts that at present the use of your property is subject to
certain burdens and conditions enforceable by him. He wishes to be able to continue to enforce
the burdens and conditions, not as superior but in his capacity of owner of the prospective
dominant tenement. If you agree and if the agreement is registered in the Land Register or
Register of Sasines under section 19 of the Abolition of Feudal Tenure etc. (Scotland) Act 2000,
he and his successors, as such owners, will be able to enforce the burdens and conditions after
the feudal system is abolished (which will be shortly).

In the absence of agreement the superior may yet be able to enforce the burdens and conditions
provided that he can meet certain statutory conditions or if he applies to the Lands Tribunal for
Scotland and the Tribunal grants an appropriate order on being satisfied by him that there
would be substantial loss or disadvantage to him as owner of the prospective dominant
tenement were the real burden to be extinguished or to cease to be enforceable by him.

If the superior does apply to the Tribunal you may oppose the application and in doing so may
be eligible for Legal Aid. You would not ordinarily have to meet the superior's expenses. You

are advised to consult your solicitor or other adviser if you wish to consider opposing the application or if you are uncertain about what is said in this notice.

Notes for completion of the notice
(These notes have no legal effect)

1 Insert name and address of superior.
2 Insert name and address of person who has the feudal estate of dominium utile
3 Specify by reference to the appropriate Register the deed or deeds in which the real burden or counter-obligation was imposed. Set out the real burden or counter-obligation in full or refer to the deed in such a way as to identify the real burden or counter-obligation. You may if you wish propose and set out a modification to either the real burden or to the counter-obligation (or modifications to both).
4 Where the title has been registered in the Land Register of Scotland and the superior is—
  (a) registered as proprietor, specify the title number;
  (b) not registered as proprietor, specify the title number and set out the midcouples or links between the person last registered and the superior so as sufficiently to identify them.
Where the title has not been registered in the Land Register and the superior–
  (a) has a recorded title, specify by reference to the Register of Sasines the deed constituting the immediate title;
  (b) does not have a recorded title, either—
      (i) specify by reference to the Register of Sasines the deed constituting the immediate title of the person with the last recorded title and set out the midcouples or links between that person and the superior so as sufficiently to identify them; or
      (ii) if there is no such deed, specify the nature of the superior's title.
5 Do not complete until a copy of the notice has been delivered or sent to the person with right to the feu. Then insert the following:
"The superior has served this notice by [*specify whether by delivery, by recorded delivery, by registered post or by ordinary post*] on [*date of posting*] to the person with right to the feu at [*state address*].".
6 The notice should not be signed until a copy of it has been so delivered or sent.

SCHEDULE 7
(introduced by section 20(3))

FORM OF NOTICE INTIMATING APPLICATION TO LANDS TRIBUNAL UNDER SECTION 20(1)

"NOTICE INTIMATING APPLICATION TO LANDS TRIBUNAL UNDER SECTION 20(1) OF THE ABOLITION OF FEUDAL TENURE ETC. (SCOTLAND) ACT 2000

Superior:
(see note for completion 1)

Description of land which is the prospective servient tenement:
(see note for completion 2)

Description of land which is the prospective dominant tenement:
(see note for completion 2)

Terms of real burden:
(see note for completion 3)

Any counter-obligation:
(see note for completion 3)

Title to the superiority:
(see note for completion 4)

Title to the dominium utile of the prospective dominant tenement:
(see note for completion 4)

Terms of description given, in application to Lands Tribunal, of attempt to reach agreement:
(see note for completion 5)

Service:
(see note for completion 6)

I swear [*or affirm*] that the information contained in the notice is, to the best of my knowledge and belief, true.

Signature of superior:
(see note for completion 7)

Signature of notary public:

Date: .".

Explanatory Note
(This explanation has no legal effect)

This notice is sent by your feudal superior. In this notice your property (or some part of it) is referred to as the "prospective servient tenement" and the superior's property is referred to as the "prospective dominant tenement".

At present the use of your property is subject to certain burdens and conditions enforceable by the feudal superior. The feudal system is shortly to be abolished. The feudal superior cannot satisfy any of the conditions in section 18(7) of the Abolition of Feudal Tenure etc. (Scotland) Act 2000 but is applying to the Lands Tribunal for Scotland to be allowed the right to continue to enforce the burdens and conditions, not as superior but in his capacity of owner of the prospective dominant tenement. The Lands Tribunal's order, if it is registered in the Land Register or Register of Sasines under section 20 of the 2000 Act, would allow him and his successors, as such owners, to enforce the burdens and conditions after the feudal system is abolished. He claims that there would be substantial loss or disadvantage to him as owner of the prospective dominant tenement were the real burden to be extinguished or no longer to be enforceable by him.

You may oppose his application to the Tribunal and in doing so may be eligible for Legal Aid. You would not ordinarily have to meet the superior's expenses. You are advised to consult your solicitor or other adviser if you wish to consider opposing the application or if you think that there is a mistake in this notice.

The effect of the superior registering this notice will be that the burdens and conditions to which the notice relates will continue to be burdens and conditions (though, after the feudal system is abolished, non-feudal burdens and conditions) until the order made by the Lands Tribunal in respect of the application is registered as mentioned above unless the order is registered before the feudal system is abolished in which case until the feudal system is abolished (or, if there is no such registration at all, until a date specified by the Scottish Ministers) at which time the burdens and conditions would either be saved as non-feudal burdens and conditions or would be extinguished because the superior had been unsuccessful in his application.

Notes for completion of the notice
(These notes have no legal effect)

1 Insert name and address of superior.
2 Describe the land in a way that is sufficient to enable the Keeper to identify it by reference to the Ordnance Map. Where the title to the land has been registered in the Land Register the description should refer to the relevant title number of the land or of the larger subjects of which the land forms part. Otherwise it should normally refer to and identify a deed recorded in a specified division of the Register of Sasines.
3 Specify by reference to the Register the deed or deeds in which the real burden or counter-obligation was imposed. Set out the real burden or counter-obligation in full or so as sufficiently to identify it.
4 The superiority referred to in the box "Title to the superiority" is the superiority of land which comprises the prospective servient tenement.

Where the title—
  (a) has been registered in the Land Register and the applicant is infeft, specify the title number or if he is uninfeft specify the title number and set out the midcouples or links between the person last infeft and the applicant in such terms as are sufficient to identify them;
  (b) has not been registered in the Land Register and the applicant is infeft, specify by reference to the Register the deed constituting the title or if he is uninfeft specify the deed constituting the title of the person last infeft and the date of recording and set out the midcouples or links as in paragraph (a).

5 Set out in full the description which was, in pursuance of section 20(2) of the Abolition of Feudal Tenure etc. (Scotland) Act 2000, included in the application.

6 Insert either: "The applicant has sent a copy of this notice by [*specify recorded delivery mail or registered post*] to the owner of the prospective servient tenement at [*specify the address of the prospective servient tenement, or the place of residence or place of business, or the most recently known place of residence or place of business, of the owner of the servient tenement*]." or "It has not been reasonably practicable to serve a copy of this notice on the owner of the prospective servient tenement for the following reasons: [*specify the reasons*].".

7 The superior should not swear or affirm, or sign, until a copy of the notice has been sent (or otherwise) as mentioned in note 6. Before signing the superior should swear or affirm before a notary public (or, if the notice is being completed outwith Scotland, before a person duly authorised under the local law to administer oaths or receive affirmations) that, to the best of the superior's knowledge and belief, all the information contained in the notice is true. The notary public should also sign. Swearing or affirming a statement which is known to be false or which is believed not to be true is a criminal offence under the False Oaths (Scotland) Act 1933. Normally the superior should swear or affirm, and sign, personally. If, however, the superior is legally disabled or incapable (for example, because of mental disorder) his legal representative should swear or affirm and sign. If the superior is not an individual (for example, if it is a company) a person entitled by law to sign formal documents on its behalf should swear or affirm and sign.

SCHEDULE 8
(introduced by section 27(1))

FORM OF NOTICE PRESERVING CONSERVATION BODY'S OR SCOTTISH MINISTERS' RIGHT TO REAL BURDEN

"NOTICE PRESERVING CONSERVATION BODY'S OR SCOTTISH MINISTERS' RIGHT TO REAL BURDEN

Superior (being a conservation body or the Scottish Ministers):
(see note for completion 1)

Description of land subject to the real burden:
(see note for completion 2)

Terms of real burden:
(see note for completion 3)

Any counter-obligation:
(see note for completion 3)

Title to the superiority:
(see note for completion 4)

Service:
(see note for completion 5)

Signature of superior:
(see note for completion 6)

Signature of witness:

Name and address of witness:

Date: .".

[1] Explanatory Note
(This explanation has no legal effect)

This notice is sent by your feudal superior.

At present the use of your property is subject to certain burdens and conditions enforceable by the feudal superior. The feudal system is shortly to be abolished. [By the regulations mentioned in the notice, the Scottish Ministers have prescribed that your superior should be a conservation body. Such a body is entitled to enforce certain real burdens (referred to prospectively as "conservation burdens").] or [The feudal superior is the Scottish Ministers and it is intended that they shall enforce certain real burdens (referred to prospectively as "conservation burdens").] These are burdens which have been imposed in the public interest for the preservation or protection either of architectural or historic characteristics of land or of some other special characteristic of land derived from the flora, fauna, or general appearance of the land. By this notice [the conservation body is] [the Scottish Ministers are] claiming the right to continue to enforce a conservation burden, not as superior but [in its capacity as a conservation body] [in their capacity as the Scottish Ministers]. The notice, if it is registered in the Land Register of Scotland or recorded in the Register of Sasines under section 27 of the Abolition of Feudal Tenure etc. (Scotland) Act 2000, will allow the burden and conditions to be so enforced after the feudal system has been abolished.

If you think that there is a mistake in this notice or if you wish to challenge it, you are advised to consult your solicitor or other adviser.

Notes for completion of the notice
(These notes have no legal effect)
[2] 1 In the case of a conservation body, insert the year and number of the relevant statutory instrument and the name and address of body.
2 Describe the land in a way that is sufficient to enable the Keeper to identify it by reference to the Ordnance Map. Where the title to the land has been registered in the Land Register the description should refer to the title number of the land or of the larger subjects of which the land forms part. Otherwise it should normally refer to and identify a deed recorded in a specified division of the Register of Sasines.
3 Specify by reference to the appropriate Register the deed or deeds in which the real burden or counter-obligation was imposed. Set out the real burden or counter-obligation in full or refer to the deed in such a way as to identify the real burden or counter-obligation.
4 Where the title has been registered in the Land Register of Scotland and the superior is-
    (a) infeft, specify the title number;
    (b) uninfeft, specify the title number and set out the midcouples or links between the person last infeft and the superior so as sufficiently to identify them.
Where the title has not been registered in the Land Register and the superior—
    (a) has a recorded title, specify by reference to the Register of Sasines the deed constituting the immediate title;
    (b) does not have a recorded title, either—
        (i) specify by reference to the Register of Sasines the deed constituting the immediate title of the person last infeft and set out the midcouples or links between the person last infeft and the superior so as sufficiently to identify them; or
        (ii) if there is no such deed, specify the nature of the superior's title.
5 Do not complete until a copy of the notice has been sent to the owner of the land subject to the burden (except in a case where this is not reasonably practicable). Then insert whichever is applicable of the following:
"The superior has sent a copy of this notice by [*specify whether by recorded delivery or registered post or by ordinary post*] on [*date of posting*] to the owner of the land subject to the real burden at [*state address*]."; or
"It has not been reasonably practicable to send a copy of this notice to the owner of the land subject to the real burden for the following reason: [*specify the reason*].".
6 The notice should not be signed until a copy of it has been sent (or otherwise) as mentioned in note 5. The conservation body or the Scottish Ministers should sign.

AMENDMENTS
1. As amended by the Title Conditions (Scotland) Act 2003 (asp 9), Sch.15, (effective April 4, 2003).
2. As amended by the Title Conditions (Scotland) Act 2003 (asp 9), Sch.13, para.17, (effective April 4, 2003).

[1] SCHEDULE 8A
(introduced by section 27A(1))

FORM OF NOTICE NOMINATING CONSERVATION BODY OR SCOTTISH MINISTERS TO HAVE TITLE TO ENFORCE REAL BURDEN

"NOTICE NOMINATING CONSERVATION BODY OR SCOTTISH MINISTERS TO HAVE TITLE TO ENFORCE REAL BURDEN

Superior:

Nominee (being a conservation body or the Scottish Ministers):
(see note for completion 1)

Description of land subject to the real burden:
(see note for completion 2)

Terms of real burden:
(see note for completion 3)

Any counter-obligation:
(see note for completion 3)

Title to the superiority:
(see notes for completion 4 and 5)

Service:
(see note for completion 6)

Signature of superior:
(see note for completion 7)

Signature of consenting nominee:
(see note for completion 8)

Signature of superior's witness:

Name and address of witness:

Signature of nominee's witness:

Name and address of witness:

Date: ."

Explanatory note
(This explanation has no legal effect)

This notice is sent by your feudal superior. At present the use of your property is subject to certain burdens and conditions enforceable by the feudal superior. The feudal system is shortly to be abolished. The feudal superior intends to nominate a conservation body or the Scottish Ministers to have title to enforce certain of those burdens (referred to prospectively as "conservation burdens") when he ceases to have such title. These are burdens which have been imposed in the public interest for the preservation or protection either of architectural or historic characteristics of land or of some other special characteristic of land derived from the flora, fauna or general appearance of the land. By virtue of this notice the nominee would have the right to enforce a conservation burden in the capacity of conservation body or of the Scottish Ministers, as the case may be. The notice, if it is registered in the Land Register of Scotland or recorded in the Register of Sasines under section 27A of the Abolition of Feudal Tenure etc. (Scotland) Act 2000, will allow the burden to be so enforced after the feudal system has been abolished. If you think there is a mistake in this notice or if you wish to challenge it, you are advised to consult your solicitor or other adviser.

Notes for completion of the notice
(These notes have no legal effect)

1 In the case of a conservation body, insert the year and number of the relevant statutory instrument and the name and address of that body.
2 Describe the land in a way that is sufficient to enable the Keeper to identify it by reference to the Ordnance Map. Where the title to the land has been registered in the Land Register the description should refer to the title number of the land or of the larger subjects of which the land forms part. Otherwise it should normally refer to and identify a deed recorded in a specified division of the Register of Sasines.
3 Specify by reference to the appropriate Register the deed or deeds in which the real burden or counter-obligation was imposed. Set out the real burden or counter-obligation in full or refer to the deed in such a way as to identify the real burden or counter-obligation.
4 Where the title has been registered in the Land Register of Scotland and the superior is—
   (a) infeft, specify the title number;
   (b) uninfeft, specify the title number and set out the midcouples or links between the person last infeft and the superior so as sufficiently to identify them.
5 Where the title has not been registered in the Land Register and the superior—
   (a) has a recorded title, specify by reference to the Register of Sasines the deed constituting the immediate title;
   (b) does not have a recorded title, either—
      (i) specify by reference to the Register of Sasines the deed constituting the immediate title of the person last infeft and set out the midcouples or links between the person last infeft and the superior so as sufficiently to identify them; or
      (ii) if there is no such deed, specify the nature of the superior's title.
6 Do not complete until a copy of the notice has been sent to the owner of the land subject to the burden (except in a case where this is not reasonably practicable). Then insert whichever is applicable of the following:
"The superior has sent a copy of this notice by [*specify whether by recorded delivery or registered post or by ordinary post*] on [*date of posting*] to the owner of the land subject to the real burden at [*state address*]."; or
"It has not been reasonably practicable to send a copy of this notice to the owner of the land subject to the real burden for the following reason: [*specify the reason*]."
7 The notice should not be signed by the superior until a copy of it has been sent (or otherwise) as mentioned in note 6.
8 The nominee should sign, so as to indicate consent, before that copy is sent (or otherwise) as so mentioned.

AMENDMENT
   1. Inserted by the Title Conditions (Scotland) Act 2003 (asp 9), Sch.13, para.18, (effective April 4, 2003).

SCHEDULE 9
(introduced by section 33(1))

FORM OF NOTICE RESERVING RIGHT TO COMPENSATION IN RESPECT OF EXTINCTION OF DEVELOPMENT VALUE BURDEN

A. NOTICE RESERVING RIGHT TO COMPENSATION IN RESPECT OF EXTINCTION OF DEVELOPMENT VALUE BURDEN

Superior:
(see note for completion 1)

Description of land (or part) subject to the real burden:
(see note for completion 2)

Terms of real burden:
(see note for completion 3)

Statement that burden reserves development value:
(see note for completion 4)

Title to the superiority:
(see note for completion 5)

Details of feu grant:
(see note for completion 6)

Amount by which consideration reduced:
(see note for completion 7)

Service:
(see note for completion 8)

By this notice I [A.B.] (superior) reserve the right to claim compensation in respect of the extinction of the development value burden(s) set out in this form.

I swear [or affirm] that the information contained in the notice is, to the best of my knowledge and belief, true.

Signature of superior:
(see note for completion 9)

Signature of notary public:

Date: .".

Explanatory Note
(This explanation has no legal effect)

This notice is sent by your feudal superior.
The feudal system is shortly to be abolished. By this notice the feudal superior is claiming that your property is subject to a development value burden. He is reserving the right to claim compensation for the loss of the burden. Compensation so claimed is payable if either during the five year period ending on [*insert date of appointed day*] or during the twenty year period starting on that date something happens which, had the feudal system not been abolished, would have been a breach of the burden.

A development value burden is a special type of real burden designed to reserve for the superior the benefit of any increase in the value of the land arising from the land being freed to be used or dealt with in a way prohibited by the burden. Burdens of this type were typically inserted in feudal grants where the superior gave away land, or sold it very cheaply, on condition that it was used only for some charitable or community purposes (for example, for use only as a community hall or sports field).
For the superior to be entitled to reserve the right to claim compensation, the burden must have led to the price paid for your property when it was first sold by the superior being significantly lower than it would otherwise have been.
This notice will be registered in the Land Register of Scotland, or recorded in the Register of Sasines, under section 33 of the Abolition of Feudal Tenure etc. (Scotland) Act 2000.

If you think that there is a mistake in this notice or if you wish to challenge it, you are advised to consult your solicitor or other adviser.

Notes for completion of notice
(These notes have no legal effect)

1 Insert name and address of superior.

2 Describe the land in a way that is sufficient to enable the Keeper to identify it by reference to the Ordnance Map. Where the title to the land has been registered in the Land Register the description should refer to the title number of the land or of the larger subjects of which the land forms part. Otherwise it should normally refer to and identify a deed recorded in a specified division of the Register of Sasines.

3 Specify by reference to the appropriate Register the deed or deeds in which the development value burden was imposed. Set out the burden in full or refer to the deed in such a way as to identify the burden. If the notice is used to reserve rights in relation to more than one development value burden, details of each burden should be set out separately, in numbered paragraphs.

4 State that the burden reserves the development value. Section 33(5) of the Abolition of Feudal Tenure etc. (Scotland) Act 2000 defines "development value" as "any significant increase in the value of the land arising as a result of the land becoming free to be used, or dealt with, in some way not permitted under the grant in feu". Set out any information (additional to that provided in the other boxes) which supports that statement.

5 Where the title has been registered in the Land Register of Scotland and the superior is—
    (a) infeft, specify the title number;
    (b) uninfeft, specify the title number and set out the midcouples or links between the person last infeft and the superior so as sufficiently to identify them.

Where the title has not been registered in the Land Register and the superior—
    (a) has a recorded title, specify by reference to the Register of Sasines the deed constituting the immediate title;
    (b) does not have a recorded title, either—
        (i) specify by reference to the Register of Sasines the deed constituting the immediate title of the person last infeft and set out the midcouples or links between the person last infeft and the superior so as sufficiently to identify them; or
        (ii) if there is no such deed, specify the nature of the superior's title.

6 Specify by reference to the appropriate Register the writ granting the relevant land in feu.

7 State the amount by which the consideration was reduced because of the imposition of the burden. (If the notice relates to more than one burden, the amounts should be shown separately for each burden.) The statement should be made to the best of the superior's knowledge and belief.

8 Do not complete until a copy of the notice has been sent to the owner of the land subject to the burden (except in a case where this is not reasonably practicable). Then insert whichever is applicable of the following:

"The superior has sent a copy of this notice by [*specify whether by recorded delivery or registered post or by ordinary post*] on [*date of posting*] to the owner of the land subject to the burden at [*state address*]."; or

"It has not been reasonably practicable to send a copy of this notice to the owner of the land subject to the burden for the following reason: [*specify the reason*].".

9 The superior should not swear or affirm, or sign, until a copy of the notice has been sent (or otherwise) as mentioned in note 8. Before signing the superior should swear or affirm before a notary public (or, if the notice is being completed outwith Scotland, before a person duly authorised under the local law to administer oaths or receive affirmations) that, to the best of the superior's knowledge and belief, all the information contained in the notice is true. The notary public should also sign. Swearing or affirming a statement which is known to be false or which is believed not to be true is a criminal offence under the False Oaths (Scotland) Act 1933. Normally the superior should swear or affirm, and sign, personally. If, however, the superior is legally disabled or incapable (for example, because of mental disorder) his legal representative should swear or affirm and sign. If the superior is not an individual (for example, if it is a company) a person entitled by law to sign formal documents on its behalf should swear or affirm and sign.

SCHEDULE 10

(introduced by section 36(2))

PROCEDURES AS TO SERVICE UNDER SECTION 35(3)

FORM A

"I [*name of owner*] acknowledge receipt of a notice under section 35(3) of the Abolition of Feudal Tenure etc. (Scotland) Act 2000 claiming compensation of [*amount*].
Signed: [*signature of owner*]
Date: .".

FORM B

"Notice under section 35(3) of the Abolition of Feudal Tenure etc. (Scotland) Act 2000 claiming compensation was posted to [*name of owner*] on [*date*].

Signature: [*signature either of the owner or his agent; and if an agent signs he should put the word "Agent" after his signature*]
Date: .".

SCHEDULE 11
(introduced by section 40)

FORM OF ASSIGNATION, DISCHARGE OR RESTRICTION OF RESERVED RIGHT TO CLAIM COMPENSATION

"ASSIGNATION [OR DISCHARGE OR RESTRICTION] OF RESERVED RIGHT TO CLAIM COMPENSATION

I, [*A. B.*] (designation), hereby [assign to C. D. (designation)] or [discharge] the right to claim compensation reserved by a notice dated (specify date) and [recorded in the Register of Sasines for (*specify county*) on (*specify date*) under (*specify fiche and frame*) or registered in the Land Register of Scotland on (*specify date*) against the subjects in title number (*specify number*)] [*add if applicable but only to the extent of* (specify percentage) of each claim which may come to be made] or [add if applicable but only to the extent of (specify restriction) or but only in relation to (specify restriction)]. [Where the person assigning or as the case may be discharging or restricting the right to claim compensation is not registered as having that right, add a note setting out the midcouples or links between that person and the person last so registered so as sufficiently to identify them.]".

(Execute in accordance with section 3 of the Requirements of Writing (Scotland) Act 1995.)

[1] SCHEDULE 11A
(introduced by section 65A(1))

FORM OF NOTICE PROSPECTIVELY CONVERTING SPORTING RIGHTS INTO TENEMENT IN LAND

"NOTICE PROSPECTIVELY CONVERTING SPORTING RIGHTS INTO TENEMENT IN LAND

Superior:
(see note for completion 1)

Description of land subject to sporting rights:
(see note for completion 2)

Description of sporting rights:
(see note for completion 3)

Any counter-obligation:
(see note for completion 3)

Title to the superiority:
(see note for completion 4)

Service:
(see note for completion 5)

I swear [*or* affirm] that the information contained in this notice is, to the best of my knowledge and belief, true.

Signature of superior:
(see note for completion 6)

Signature of notary public:

Date: .''

Explanatory note
(This explanation has no legal effect)

This notice is sent by your feudal superior. By it the feudal superior asserts that at present your property is subject to certain sporting rights (that is to say, to rights of fishing or game) enforceable by him as superior and he seeks to continue to enjoy those rights on a different basis: that is to say, as a tenement in land. The notice, if it is registered in the Land Register of Scotland or recorded in the Register of Sasines under section 65A of the Abolition of Feudal Tenure etc. (Scotland) Act 2000, will have that effect when (shortly) the feudal system is abolished. If you think there is a mistake in this notice or if you wish to challenge it, you are advised to consult your solicitor or other adviser.

Notes for completion of the notice
(These notes have no legal effect)

1 Insert name and address of superior.
2 Describe the land in a way that is sufficient to enable the Keeper to identify it by reference to the Ordnance Map. Where the title to the land has been registered in the Land Register the description should refer to the title number of the land or of the larger subjects of which the land forms part. Otherwise it should normally refer to and identify a deed recorded in a specified division of the Register of Sasines.
3 Specify by reference to the appropriate Register the deed or deeds in which the sporting rights were reserved or the counter-obligation was imposed. Describe the sporting rights or set out the counter-obligation in full or refer to the deed in such a way as to identify those rights or that counter-obligation.
4 Where the title has been registered in the Land Register of Scotland and the superior is—
    (a) infeft, specify the title number;
    (b) uninfeft, specify the title number and set out the midcouples or links between the person last infeft and the superior so as sufficiently to identify them.
Where the title has not been registered in the Land Register and the superior—
    (a) has a recorded title, specify by reference to the Register of Sasines the deed constituting the immediate title;
    (b) does not have a recorded title, either—
        (i) specify by reference to the Register of Sasines the deed constituting the immediate title of the person last infeft and set out the midcouples or links between the person last infeft and the superior so as sufficiently to identify them;
        (ii) if there is no such deed, specify the nature of the superior's title.
5 Do not complete until a copy of the notice has been sent to the owner of the land subject to the sporting rights (except in a case where this is not reasonably practicable). Then insert whichever is applicable of the following:
"The superior has sent a copy of this notice by [*specify whether by recorded delivery or registered post or by ordinary post*] on [*date of posting*] to the owner of the land subject to the sporting rights at [*state address*]".; or
"It has not been reasonably practicable to send a copy of this notice to the owner of the land subject to the sporting rights for the following reason: [*specify the reason*]".
6 The notice should not be signed by the superior until a copy of it has been sent (or otherwise) as mentioned in note 5. Before signing, the superior should swear or affirm before a notary public (or, if the notice is being completed outwith Scotland, before a person duly authorised under the local law to administer oaths or receive affirmations) that, to the best of the superior's knowledge and belief, all the information contained in the notice is true. The notary public should also sign. Swearing or affirming a statement which is known to be false or which is believed not to be true is a criminal offence under the False Oaths (Scotland) Act 1933. Normally the superior should swear or affirm, and sign, personally. If, however, the superior is legally disabled or incapable (for example, because of mental disorder) his legal representative should swear or affirm and sign. If the superior is not an individual (for example, if it is a company) a person entitled by law to sign formal documents on its behalf should swear or affirm and sign.

1. Inserted by the Title Conditions (Scotland) Act 2003 (asp 9), Sch.13, para.19, (effective April 4, 2003).

SCHEDULE 12
(introduced by section 76(1))

MINOR AND CONSEQUENTIAL AMENDMENTS

PART 1

MINOR AND CONSEQUENTIAL AMENDMENTS: GENERAL

Mines and Metals Act 1592 (c.31) (Act of the Parliaments of Scotland)
1. In the Mines and Metals Act 1592—
    (a) for the words "sett in few ferme" substitute "dispone";
    (b) for the word "frehalder" substitute "owner";
    (c) the words "or few" shall cease to have effect;
    (d) for the words "saidis fewis" substitute "disposition of the saidis mynis";
    (e) for the words "four witnesses" substitute "ane witness"; and
    (f) for the words "set the same in few" substitute "dispone the same or set the same".

Redemptions Act 1661 (c.247) (Act of the Parliaments of Scotland)
2. [*Repealed by the Title Conditions (Scotland) Act 2003 (asp 9), Sch.15, (effective April 4, 2003).*]

Real Rights Act 1693 (c.22) (Act of the Parliaments of Scotland)
3. In the Real Rights Act 1693 (determination of preferences according to date and priority of registration), for the words from "All Infeftments" to the end substitute "reall rights in land shall in all competitions be preferable and preferred according to the date and priority of registration in the General Register of Sasines".

Lands Clauses Consolidation (Scotland) Act 1845 (c.19)
4. (1) The Lands Clauses Consolidation (Scotland) Act 1845 shall be amended in accordance with this paragraph.
(2) In section 7 (parties under disability enabled to sell and convey), the words "heirs of entail,", "estate or", "married women seised in their own right or entitled to terce or dower, or any other right or interest, husbands,", "or feoffees", "and as to such married women as if they were sole," and, in the last two places where they occur, "married women," shall cease to have effect.
(3) In section 8 (parties under disability may exercise other powers), the words from "power herein" to "therewith, and the" and, in both places where they occur, "feu duties, ground annuals,", shall cease to have effect.
(4) Sections 10 (where vendor absolutely entitled, lands may be sold on feu duties, &c.) and 11 (provisions incidental to section 10) shall cease to have effect.
(5) In section 12 (power to purchase lands required for additional accommodation), the word ", feu,", in both places where it occurs, shall cease to have effect.
(6) In section 67 (purchase money payable to parties under disability to be deposited in bank), the words "heir of entail,", "married woman seised in her own right or entitled to terce or dower or any other right or interest, husband,", "on the same heirs, or", ", or affecting succeeding heirs of entail in any such lands, whether imposed and constituted by the entailer, or in virtue of powers given by the entail, or in virtue of powers conferred by any Act of Parliament" and "same heirs, and the" shall cease to have effect.
(7) In each of sections 69 (sums to be deposited, or paid to trustees) and 70 (sums to be paid to parties), the word "coverture," and the word "husbands," shall cease to have effect.
(8) Section 73 (special provision for lands to be held under entail etc.) shall cease to have effect.
(9) In each of sections 74 (completion of title on deposit of purchase money or compensation) and 76 (further provision in that regard), for the word "estate" substitute "right".
(10) In section 77 (application of money deposited), for the word "estates" substitute "rights".
(11) In section 79 (expenses in cases of money deposited), the words "feu or" and ", and of re-entailing any of such lands," shall cease to have effect.
(12) In section 80 (form of conveyances)—
    (a) the words "feus and", in both places where they occur, shall cease to have effect;

(b) for the words "the Schedules (A.) and (B.) respectively" substitute "Schedule (A.)"; and

(c) the words "the particular register of sasines kept for the county, burgh, or district in which the lands are locally situated, or in", "for Scotland kept at Edinburgh, within sixty days from the last date thereof, which the respective keepers of the said registers are hereby authorized and required to do,", "feudal" and from ": Provided always" to the end shall cease to have effect.

(13) In section 93 (proceedings in regard to lands in commonty etc.), the words "; and if such lands be part of a barony a like notice shall be given to the superior or baron" shall cease to have effect.

(14) In section 100 (deposit of money on refusal to accept redemption), for the word "estate" substitute "right".

(15) In the preamble to sections 107 to 111, the words "any feu duty, ground annual, casualty of superiority, or" shall cease to have effect.

(16) In section 109 (discharge of part of lands from charge), the words "such feu duty, ground annual, casualty of superiority, or any" shall cease to have effect.

(17) In section 110 (deposit in case of refusal to discharge), the words "feu duty, ground annual, casualty of superiority," shall cease to have effect.

(18) In section 117 (power to purchase interests in lands the purchase of which may have been omitted by mistake), the word "estate,", in each place where it occurs, shall cease to have effect.

(19) In section 118 (valuation of lands), for the words—

(a) "estate or interests" substitute "right or interest"; and

(b) "estate, or interest" substitute "right, or interest".

(20) In section 119 (payment of expenses of litigation), for the word "estate", in both places where it occurs, substitute "right".

(21) In section 124 (lands to be conveyed to the purchasers), the words from ", by deed" to the end shall cease to have effect.

(22) In section 125 (effect of word "dispone" in conveyances), for the word "estate" substitute "right".

(23) Sections 126 (superiorities not to be affected by lands being taken for the purposes of the Act) and 127 (antiquated provisions relating to the prison assessment) shall cease to have effect.

(24) Schedule (B.) (form of conveyance in consideration of feu duty or rent-charge) shall cease to have effect.

Entail Amendment Act 1848 (c.36)

5. (1) The Entail Amendment Act 1848 shall be amended in accordance with this paragraph.

(2) Sections 1 to 31 (heir born after date of entail may disentail; and heir born before such date may do so with consent of heir apparent under entail, etc.) shall cease to have effect.

(3) In section 32 (form and effect of instrument of disentail etc.), the words from "may be in the form" to "in terms of this Act;" shall cease to have effect.

(4) Sections 33 to 45 (application to court by heir of entail in possession of entailed estate, etc.) shall cease to have effect.

(5) In section 47 (Act not to be defeated by trusts)—

(a) for the words "land or estate", wherever they occur, substitute "land";

(b) the words "dated on or after the first day of August one thousand eight hundred and forty-eight" shall cease to have effect;

(c) the words "fee simple", in each of the three places where they occur, shall cease to have effect;

(d) for the words "lands or estate, with infeftment thereon in favour of such party" substitute "land";

(e) the words "the superior of such lands or estate, and of" shall cease to have effect; and

(f) for the words "securities thereon" substitute "securities over such land".

(6) In section 48 (Act not to be defeated by life-rents—

(a) for the words "It shall be competent to grant an estate in Scotland limited to a liferent interest in favour only of a party in life at the date of such grant; and where any land or estate" substitute "Where any land";

(b) the words "dated on or after the first day of August one thousand eight hundred and forty eight", "fee simple" and "the superior of such lands or estate, and of" shall cease to have effect;

(c) for the words "such estate" substitute "such land"; and

(d) for the word "thereon" substitute "over such land".

(7) In section 49 (Act not to be defeated by leases), the words "or estate", in both places where they occur, and the words "dated on or after the said first day of August one thousand eight hundred and forty eight" shall cease to have effect.

(8) Sections 50 (consents to be in writing and to be irrevocable) and 51 (court may make acts of sederunt) shall cease to have effect.

(9) For section 52, substitute—

"**Interpretation**

52.–In this Act, the word "land" shall include all heritages.".

(10) The Schedule (form of instrument of disentail) shall cease to have effect.

Registration of Leases (Scotland) Act 1857 (c.26)

6. (1) The Registration of Leases (Scotland) Act 1857 shall be amended in accordance with this paragraph.

(2) In section 2 (effectuality of recorded leases), for the words "infeftment is posterior in date to" substitute "title is completed after".

(3) Sections 4 (assignations in security), 5 (presentation for registration by person who is not original lessee or assignee), 8 (executor's completion of title by recording notarial instrument), 9 (assignee dying without recording assignation) and 11 (entering trustee on sequestrated estate on register) shall cease to have effect.

(4) In section 16(1) (equivalence of registration to possession), for the words ", writs of acknowledgment, and notarial instruments" substitute "and writs of acknowledgment".

(5) Schedules (C) (form of notarial instrument in favour of party who is not original grantee) and (F) (form of notarial instrument in favour of executor in recorded lease or assignation in security or of trustee on sequestrated estate) shall cease to have effect.

Land Registers (Scotland) Act 1868 (c.64)

7. (1) The Land Registers (Scotland) Act 1868 shall be amended in accordance with this paragraph.

(2) In section 3 (writs of each county to be kept separate in general register of sasines), for the words—

   (a) "warrant of registration herein-after provided for," substitute "application for registration"; and

   (b) "said warrant," substitute "that application".

(3) In section 5 (registration of writ in other county to which it refers etc.)—

   (a) for the words from the beginning to "thereon applicable" substitute "Where any writ contains land or heritages in more than one county and application has not been made for registration in relation";

   (b) for the word "warrant", where it occurs for the second time, substitute "application";

   (c) for the words "by a new warrant of registration thereon" substitute "for registration";

   (d) the words "in terms of such new warrant" shall cease to have effect; and

   (e) for the words "such writ applies, and to which such new warrant is applicable" substitute "it applies".

(4) In section 6 (provision for writs transmitted by post to general register of sasines), the words "in terms of the warrant of registration thereon" shall cease to have effect.

(5) In section 12 (registration in general register of sasines equivalent in certain cases to registration in the books of council and session)–

   (a) for the words from the beginning to "being so registered in the said register of sasines," substitute—

"A writ competent to be registered in the general register of sasines need not be presented to be registered in the books of council and session for the purpose of—

   (a) preservation; or

   (b) preservation and execution.

If an application for registration of such a writ in the general register of sasines specifies that registration is for either of those purposes, then on registration in that register the writ shall be held to be registered also in the books of council and session for the purpose in question; and the writ registered"; and

   (b) the words "and shall be in the form, as nearly as may be, of the Schedule (B.) to this Act annexed," shall cease to have effect.

(6) [*Repealed by the Title Conditions (Scotland) Act 2003 (asp 9), Sch.15, (effective April 4, 2003).*]

Titles to Land Consolidation (Scotland) Act 1868 (c.101)

8. (1) The Titles to Land Consolidation (Scotland) Act 1868 shall be amended in accordance with this paragraph.

(2) In section 3 (interpretation)—

   (a) for the words "The words "superior," "vassal," "grantor,"" substitute "The words "grantor",";

   (b) for the words "such superior, vassal, grantor" substitute "such grantor";

   (c) the words "The words "Crown writ" shall extend to and include all charters, precepts, and writs from Her Majesty, and from the Prince; and" shall cease to have effect;

   (d) the definition of "charter" and of "writ" shall cease to have effect;

(e) in the definition of "deed" and of "conveyance", the words "charters,", "whether containing a warrant or precept of sasine or not, and", "feu contracts, contracts of ground annual,", ", whether such decrees contain warrant to infeft or precept of sasine or not," and ", procuratories of resignation ad remanentiam," shall cease to have effect;

(f) the definition of "deed of entail" shall cease to have effect;

(g) in the definition of "instrument", the words "authorized by this Act, or by any of the Acts hereby repealed," shall cease to have effect; and

(h) the definition of "infeft" and "infeftment" shall cease to have effect.

(3) Sections 4 (Acts repealed), 5 (in conveyances of land etc. not held burgage, certain clauses may be inserted in short forms), 6 (import of clause expressing manner of holding) and 7 (in conveyances of burgage property certain clauses may be inserted in given forms) shall cease to have effect.

(4) In section 8 (import of certain clauses)—

(a) for the words "forms Nos. 1 and 2" substitute "form No. 1";

(b) the words ", and to all open procuratories, clauses, and precepts, if any, and as the case may be," shall cease to have effect;

(c) for the words "rents in these forms" substitute "rents";

(d) for the words "warrandice in these forms" substitute "warrandice";

(e) for the words "feu duties, casualties, and public burdens, in form No. 1 of schedule (B.) hereto annexed," substitute "public burdens";

(f) for the words "feu duties or other duties and services or casualties payable or prestable to the superior, and of all public, parochial," substitute "public";

(g) the words from "; and the clause of obligation" to "other public, parochial, and local burdens, due from or on account of the lands conveyed prior to the date of entry" shall cease to have effect; and

(h) for the words from "in these two forms" to "to them" substitute "shall, unless specially qualified, have the meaning and effect assigned".

(5) Sections 9 (conditions of entail may, in conveyances of entailed lands, be inserted by reference merely) and 10 (real burdens may be referred to as already in the register of sasines) shall cease to have effect.

(6) In section 12 (clause directing part of conveyance to be recorded)—

(a) the words from "with a warrant of registration" to "hereto annexed)," shall cease to have effect;

(b) for the words "such keeper shall" substitute "the keeper may"; and

(c) the words from—

(i) and warrant of registration;" to "on whose behalf the conveyance is presented"; and

(ii) or to expede and record" to the end,

shall cease to have effect.

(7) Sections 14 (certain clauses in entails no longer necessary), 15 (instrument of sasine no longer necessary), 17 (not necessary to record the whole conveyance or discharge), 18 (instrument of resignation ad remanentiam unnecessary), 19 (notarial instruments in favour of general disponees) and 23 (notarial instruments in favour of parties acquiring rights to unrecorded conveyances) shall cease to have effect.

(8) In section 24 (mode of completing title by judicial factor on trust estate etc.), the words ", with warrant of registration thereon," shall cease to have effect.

(9) For section 25 (mode of completing title by trustee in sequestration etc.) substitute—

"Deduction of title by liquidator

25.—The liquidator in the winding up of a company shall, for the purposes of sections 3 (disposition etc. by person with unrecorded title) and 4 (completion of title) of the Conveyancing (Scotland) Act 1924 (c.27) (including those sections as applied to registered leases by section 24 of that Act), be taken to be a person having right to any land belonging to the company.".

(10) In section 26 (heritable property conveyed for religious or educational purposes to vest in disponees or their successors), the words "with warrant of registration thereon in terms of this Act, or when followed by notarial instrument expede, and with warrant of registration thereon recorded" and "feued," shall cease to have effect.

(11) Sections 27 to 50 (service of heirs: as saved by section 37(1)(d) of the Succession (Scotland) Act 1964 (c.41)) shall cease to have effect.

(12) In section 51 (power of Court of Session to pass acts of sederunt)—

(a) the word "said", where it first occurs; and

(b) the words from "or Sheriffs of counties" to the end,

shall cease to have effect.

(13) In section 62 (effect of decree of adjudication or sale), for the words from "feudal titles to said lands" to the end, substitute "title by recording the decree as a conveyance or by using the decree as a midcouple or link of title.".

(14) Sections 63 to 93 (Crown writs), 96 (provision for temporary absence or disability of Sheriff of Chancery), 100 (all writs and charters from subject superiors may refer to tenendas and reddendo) 104 to 109 (ways of completing title where superior did not or could not grant entry), 110 (mode of relinquishing superiority), 111 (investiture by over superior), 112 (forfeiture or relinquishment of rights of superiority does not operate as contravention of entail, etc.), 113 (payment in lieu of casualties of superiority in case of lands conveyed for religious purposes), 114 and 116 (provisions as respects writs of clare constat, etc.) shall cease to have effect.

(15) For section 117 (heritable securities to form moveable estate; except where conceived in favour of heirs, excluding executors, and quoad fiscum) there shall be substituted—
"Heritable security in succession of creditor in the security
117.–In the succession of the creditor in a heritable security, the security shall be moveable estate; except that in relation to the legal rights of the spouse, or of the descendants, of the deceased it shall be heritable estate.".

(16) Sections 118 (form of bond and disposition in security) and 119 (import of standard clauses in bond and disposition in security) shall cease to have effect.

(17) In section 120 (securities may be registered during lifetime of grantee etc.)—
  (a) ", whether dated before or after the commencement of this Act,"; and
  (b) the proviso,
shall cease to have effect.

(18) Sections 121 to 123 (sale under pre-1970 heritable securities), 124 (form for transfer of pre-1970 heritable security) 126, 127 and 130 (completion of title by notarial instrument), 131 (saving), 132 and 133 (provision for forms as respects pre-1970 heritable securities), 134 (application of the Act to all heritable securities), 135 (applicability of pre-1845 forms for heritable securities), 137 (applicability to lands held by any description of tenure) and 141 (requirement for warrant of registration) shall cease to have effect.

(19) In section 140 (additional sheets added to writs), the words ", and subsequent sheets (if any) shall be chargeable with the appropriate progressive duty" shall cease to have effect.

(20) In section 142 (recording of conveyances in register of sasines)—
  (a) the words ", and all instruments hereby" and ", with warrants of registration written thereon respectively," shall cease to have effect; and
  (b) for the words ", in the same manner as instruments of sasine, or notarial instruments, are at present recorded, and the same" substitute "and".

(21) For section 143 substitute—
"Recording anew
143.–Where there is an error or defect in recording a deed or conveyance in the Register of Sasines it shall be competent to record it anew.".

(22) Sections 144 (erasures), 145 (challenge to pre-1868 warrant of registration), 146 (insertion of real burdens etc. in a conveyance or deed applicable to lands), 147 (nothing in Act to affect prohibition against sub-infeudation or to take away or impair certain rights or remedies competent to a superior), 150 (debts affecting lands exchanged for other lands), 152 (lands held by the tenure of booking), 154 (personal interest of keeper of register), 156 (short form of letters of inhibition), 161 (review of certain judgments etc.), 162 (acts of sederunt for purposes of Act etc.) and 163 (old forms of conveyances may still be used) shall cease to have effect.

(23) The Schedules, except Schedules (B.) No.1, (F.) No.1, (G.), (PP.) and (RR.), shall cease to have effect; and in Schedule (B.) No. 1 the words—
  (a) from "to be holden" to "as the case may be];"; and
  (b) feu duties, casualties, and",
shall cease to have effect.

Conveyancing (Scotland) Act 1874 (c.94)
9. (1) The Conveyancing (Scotland) Act 1874 shall be amended in accordance with this paragraph.
(2) In section 3 (interpretation)—
  (a) in the definition of "Land" or "lands", for the words "are or may be" substitute "prior to the day appointed by order made under section 71 of the Abolition of Feudal Tenure etc. (Scotland) Act 2000 (asp 5) were, or might be,";
  (b) the definitions of "Estate in land" and of "Superior" and "superiority" shall cease to have effect;
  (c) in the definition of "heritable securities" and "securities", the words ", and shall also,

when used in this Act, include real burdens and securities by way of ground annual" shall cease to have effect; and

(d) the definitions of "Infeftment", "Feu" and "feu-duty" and "Casualties" shall cease to have effect.

(3) Sections 4 (abolition of renewal of investiture), 5 (compositions payable by corporations or trustees or persons having separate interests), 6 (consolidation of superiority with property), 7 (consolidation not to affect or extend superior's rights) and 8 (memorandum of allocation of feu-duty) shall cease to have effect.

(4) In section 10 (completion of title when deceased heir not served etc.) (as saved by section 37(1)(d) of the Succession (Scotland) Act 1964 (c.41))—

(a) the words "neither infeft nor served, but" and "by virtue of this Act," shall cease to have effect;

(b) for the words "last infeft in" substitute "who held the last recorded title to";

(c) the words "and assignation" shall cease to have effect;

(d) for the words—

(i) be infeft in" substitute "complete title to"; and

¹ (ii) be held to be duly infeft in" substitute "have a completed title to"; and

(e) the words from "Such petition" to the end shall cease to have effect.

(5) Sections 14 (legal remedies to prevent redemption preserved), 18 (entails not to bar redemption), 19 (redemption of casualties by a mid-superior), 20 (commutation of carriages and services by agreement etc.), 21 (commuted value to be feu-duty: not barred by entails), 22 (monopolies of superior's agents annulled), 24 (where feu rights stipulating or inferring casualties are contracted to be granted), 25 (distinction between burgage and feu abolished etc.) and 26 (form of conveyances) shall cease to have effect.

(6) In section 29 (general dispositions forming links of series of titles not objectionable on certain grounds)—

(a) the words "under this Act, and no other decree, instrument, or conveyance" shall cease to have effect; and

(b) for the words "last infeft, shall contain" substitute "who last held a recorded title contains".

(7) Section 30 (conveyances and discharges of real burdens) shall cease to have effect.

(8) [*Repealed by the Title Conditions (Scotland) Act 2003 (asp 9), Sch.15, (effective April 4, 2003).*]

(9) In section 35 (registration of a decree of division)—

(a) the word "joint" shall cease to have effect;

(b) for the words "infeftment in, or of acquiring a personal right" substitute "deducing title"; and

(c) the words from ", as an assignation" to the end shall cease to have effect.

(10) In section 36 (effect of decree of sale of glebe), the words from ", with a holding" to the end shall cease to have effect.

(11) Section 37 (distinction between heritage and conquest abolished) shall cease to have effect.

(12) In section 44 (provisions for the case of a person appointed by the court to administer a trust)—

(a) after the words "When a trust title" insert "to land or to a real right in or over land";

(b) for the words "a title by infeftment in the estate" substitute "to complete,"; and

(c) after the words "thereby appointed," insert "title to the land or real right".

(13) In section 45 (how title is completed when the holder of an office or proprietor is ex officio a trustee and his successor in office takes the trust), for the words—

(a) "estate in land" substitute "land, or any real right in or over land,"; and

(b) "by infeftment in the estate" substitute "to the land or real right".

(14) In section 47 (securities upon land, and relative personal obligations, to transmit against heirs and disponees), for the words—

(a) "upon an estate in land" substitute "over land, or over a real right in land,";

(b) "such estate" substitute "such land or real right"; and

(c) "the estate" substitute "the land or real right".

(15) Sections 48 (provisions for disencumbering lands sold under heritable securities when no surplus emerges) and 49 (provision for disencumbering lands of heritable security) shall cease to have effect.

(16) In section 51 (probate equivalent to will or extract for completing title)—

(a) the words "production to any notary public of the" shall cease to have effect;

(b) for the words "of an exemplification of such probate, shall for the purpose of expediing a notarial instrument, or otherwise completing a title to any estate in land" substitute "an exemplification of such probate, shall for the purpose of completing a title to any land, or real right in land,"; and

(c) the words "the production to such notary of" and from ", and it shall not" to the end shall cease to have effect.

[2] (17) Sections 52 (decrees of service unchallengeable on certain grounds), 53 (form of completing title to heritable securities under a general disposition), 57 (certain offices abolished, and the duties of the Sheriff of Chancery, &c. enlarged) and 58 (provisions as to Chancery office) shall cease to have effect.

(18) In section 59 (application to lands held of the Crown and Prince) the words "shall apply to lands held of the Crown and of the Prince, in the same way as to lands held of a subject superior, but" shall cease to have effect.

(19) Section 60 (title to private estates of Her Majesty in Scotland) shall cease to have effect.

(20) Schedules A (form of notice to be given to a superior of change of ownership), B (form of summons of declarator and for payment of a casualty), C (form of minute for effecting consolidation of lands), D (being the form of memorandum of allocation of feu-duty; and not that Schedule D substituted for Schedule O by section 8(1) of the Conveyancing (Scotland) Act 1924), F (form of discharge of casualties) and G (form of memorandum constituting a feu-duty or additional feu-duty) shall cease to have effect.

(21) [*Repealed by the Title Conditions (Scotland) Act 2003 (asp 9), Sch.15, (effective April 4, 2003).*]

(22) Schedule L (form of certificate where lands are sold under a heritable security and no surplus emerges and form of certificate where lands have been redeemed of a heritable security but discharge cannot be obtained) shall cease to have effect.

(23) In Schedule M (form of assignation of right of relief etc.), the words from ", e.g.]," to "or as the case may be" shall cease to have effect.

(24) Schedule N (form of instrument in favour of a general disponee or his assignee in right of a heritable security) shall cease to have effect.

Writs Execution (Scotland) Act 1877 (c.40)

10. In section 6 of the Writs Execution (Scotland) Act 1877 (provision that writs registered in the Register of Sasines for preservation only may afterwards be registered for preservation and execution)—

(a) the words "upon a warrant of registration" shall cease to have effect; and

(b) for the words "having a warrant of registration written thereon, bearing" substitute "with, written on the extract, a statement to the effect".

Conveyancing (Scotland) Acts (1874 and 1879) Amendment Act 1887 (c.69)

11. (1) The Conveyancing (Scotland) Acts (1874 and 1879) Amendment Act 1887 shall be amended in accordance with this paragraph.

(2) Sections 1 (limitation of liability of trustees for casualties), 3 (novodamus not challengeable because lands not resigned into superior's hands) and 4 (decree of irritancy not final till extract recorded) shall cease to have effect.

(3) In section 5 (letters of administration of will, &c. equivalent to will for authorisation of notary to expede instrument)—

(a) the words "The production to any notary public of" shall cease to have effect;

(b) for the words "or of an exemplification" substitute "or an exemplification";

(c) the words "expeding a notarial instrument, or otherwise" shall cease to have effect;

(d) for the word "estate" substitute "land or real right"; and

(e) the words from "; and it shall not" to the end shall cease to have effect.

Military Lands Act 1892 (c.43)

12. In section 25 of the Military Lands Act 1892 (application to Scotland), after subsection (1) there shall be added—

"(1A) Any reference to an "estate" in land shall be construed as a reference to a right in land and as including a reference to ownership of land.".

Heritable Securities (Scotland) Act 1894 (c.44)

13. (1) The Heritable Securities (Scotland) Act 1894 shall be amended in accordance with this paragraph.

(2) In section 6 (power to lease security subjects for seven years or under), for the words "disponed in security" substitute "by virtue of an adjudication".

(3) In section 7 (sheriff may grant power to lease security subjects for longer periods, not more than 21 years for heritable property in general and 31 years for minerals)—

(a) for the words "disponed in security", where they first occur, substitute "by virtue of an adjudication"; and

(b) where they occur for the second time they shall cease to have effect.

(4) Sections 8 (provisions for security holders becoming proprietors of security subjects), 9 (completion of title of security holders etc.) and 10 (purchaser's title indefeasible) shall cease to have effect.

(5) In section 12 (provisions anent procedure), the word ", eight," shall cease to have effect.

(6) In section 13 (provisions of Act to have effect notwithstanding incapacity of debtor etc.), for the words—

(a) "conferred by this Act" substitute "under a heritable security";

(b) "under this Act" substitute "by a creditor in exercise of those rights and powers"; and

(c) "such debtor, proprietor," substitute "the debtor, proprietor, other".

(7) Sections 14 (provision as respects security holders under Registration of Leases (Scotland) Act 1857), 15 (jurisdiction of sheriff in all cases instituted under or in connection with Act), 16 (provision as to notice where debtor has died and heir cannot be traced) and 17 (saving) shall cease to have effect.

(8) Schedule (D.) (form of decree whereby security holder becomes proprietor of security subjects) shall cease to have effect.

Entail (Scotland) Act 1914 (c.43)

14. (1) The Entail (Scotland) Act 1914 shall be amended in accordance with this paragraph.

(2) In section 2 (Entail Act 1685 not to apply to future deeds)—

(a) for the words "The Entail Act, 1685, shall not apply to any" substitute "No";

(b) for the words ", the effect of which would be" substitute "shall be effective"; and

(c) the words "and any clause of consent to registration in the register of entails", and the provisos, shall cease to have effect.

(3) Sections 3 to 8 (further facilities for disentail, etc.) shall cease to have effect.

(4) In section 10 (interpretation), the words ", unless the contrary intention appears," and ", and the words "heir of entail" shall include the institute" shall cease to have effect.

Conveyancing (Scotland) Act 1924 (c.27)

15. (1) The Conveyancing (Scotland) Act 1924 shall be amended in accordance with this paragraph.

(2) In section 2(1)(b) (definition of "heritable securities" and "securities"), the words from "real burdens" to "them, and" shall cease to have effect.

(3) In section 3 (disposition etc. by person uninfeft)—

(a) the words "last infeft or" shall cease to have effect; and

(b) for the words from "in all respects" to the end substitute "completed".

(4) In section 4 (completion of title)—

(a) in subsection (1), for the words "last infeft" substitute "having the last recorded title";

(b) in subsection (2)—

(i) for the words "last infeft" substitute "having the last recorded title"; and

(ii) the words "by infeftment" shall cease to have effect;

(c) in subsection (3)—

(i) the words from ", or in the case" to "that Schedule" shall cease to have effect; and

(ii) for the words from "last infeft" to the end substitute "having the last recorded title to the heritable security"; and

(d) in subsection (4)—

(i) for the words "infeft him therein and in" substitute "completed his title thereto and to";

(ii) the words ", or in the case of a ground annual in or as nearly as may be in the terms of Form No. 6 of that Schedule" and from "And on such notice" to the end, shall cease to have effect.

(5) In section 5 (deduction of title)—

(a) in subsection (1)—

(i) for the words "any estate or interest in or security over" substitute "any real right in";

(ii) after the words "instrument could" insert "(before the day appointed by order made under section 71 of the Abolition of Feudal Tenure etc. (Scotland) Act 2000 (asp 5))"; and

(iii) for the words "an estate or interest in or security over" substitute "a real right in";
(b) in subsection (2)(a)—
(i) the words "infeft or uninfeft, or" shall cease to have effect; and
(ii) for the words "and seventh sections" substitute "section"; and
(c) in subsection (3)(a), the words "last infeft or" shall cease to have effect.
(6) Section 6 (notice of title equivalent to notarial instrument) shall cease to have effect.
(7) In section 8 (description by reference), subsection (2) shall cease to have effect.
(8) [*Repealed by the Title Conditions (Scotland) Act 2003 (asp 9), Sch.15, (effective April 4, 2003).*]
(9) Sections 10 (warrants of registration), 11 (consolidation of superiority and property), 12 (abolition and commutation of grain, etc., feu-duties) and 13 (allocation of feu-duty) shall cease to have effect.
(10) In section 19 (applicability of forms prescribed by Act), the words "or fee" shall cease to have effect.
(11) Sections 20 (ratification by married woman) and 23 (assignation of ground-annuals) shall cease to have effect.
(12) In section 24 (registered leases: assimilation of forms)–
(a) the words ", including power of sale and other rights under a bond and disposition in security," and ", and such forms shall have the same force and effect as the corresponding forms prescribed by the Registration of Leases (Scotland) Act 1857," shall cease to have effect;
(b) in paragraph (1) of the proviso—
(i) after the word "'lessee'" there shall be inserted "and"; and
(ii) the words from ", for 'infeft'" to the end shall cease to have effect; and
(c) in paragraph (5) of the proviso, the words from "by notarial instrument" to "law and practice" shall cease to have effect.
(13) Sections 25 (form of bond and disposition in security) and 26 (heritable creditors' remedies for recovery of feu-duties and ground-annuals) shall cease to have effect.
(14) Sections 28 to 39 (provisions as respects heritable securities) shall cease to have effect.
(15) In section 40(1) (exposure in lots and apportionment of feu-duty)—
(a) for the words "The land, or any part thereof," substitute "Land, or any part thereof, sold in exercise of a power of sale under a bond and disposition in security"; and
(b) the words "feu-duty, ground-annual, stipend," and "feu-duty and casualties, ground annual, stipend or" shall cease to have effect.
(16) In section 41(1) (purchasers protected), for the words "under sections thirty-two to forty, inclusive, of this Act" substitute "relating to the redemption or calling up of, or a sale under, a bond and disposition in security".
(17) Sections 42 (mode of disburdening land sold under power of sale in heritable security) and 43 (application of Act to all heritable securities) shall cease to have effect.
(18) In section 49 (saving), subsection (1) shall cease to have effect.
(19) In Schedule A—
(a) the heading to Form No.1 shall be–

"CLAUSE OF DEDUCTION OF TITLE IN A DISPOSITION OF LAND WHERE THE GRANTER DOES NOT HAVE A RECORDED TITLE"

and
(b) in Form No.1, for the words—
(i) "ast infeft" substitute "having last recorded title"; and
(ii) "infeftment" substitute "recorded title".
(20) In Schedule B (notice of title)—
(a) in Form No.1, for the words-
(i) "last infeft" substitute "having last recorded title"; and
(ii) "infeftment" substitute "recorded title";
(b) in Form No. 3, the words "last infeft therein, or" shall cease to have effect; and
(c) Forms Nos. 4 and 6 shall cease to have effect.
(21) In the Notes to Schedule B—
(a) in Note 1, for the word "infeftment" substitute "recorded title"; and
(b) in Note 3—
(i) for the words "infeftment upon" substitute "title to"; and

(ii) for the words "including a ground annual has been taken" substitute "has been completed".

(22) Schedules F (warrants of registration), G (minute of consolidation) and H (memorandum of allocation of feu duty not endorsed on a deed), and the Notes to Schedule F, shall cease to have effect.

(23) Schedules K, L, M and N (forms relating to bonds and dispositions in security), and the Notes to Schedule K, shall cease to have effect.

Church of Scotland (Property and Endowments) Act 1925 (c.33)

16. (1) The Church of Scotland (Property and Endowments) Act 1925 shall be amended in accordance with this paragraph.

(2) In section 22 (burgh churches)—

(a) [*Repealed by the Title Conditions (Scotland) Act 2003 (asp 9), Sch.15, (effective April 4, 2003).*]

(b) in subsection (3), the word "feu,",

shall cease to have effect.

(3) Section 27 (proceedings relating to certain matters) shall cease to have effect.

(4) In section 28 (transfer of rights in parish churches and manses)—

(a) in subsection (3)(b)—

(i) for the words "all rights of property in" substitute "the ownership of"; and

(ii) the words from ", to the same effect" to the end shall cease to have effect; and

(b) subsections (6) to (8) shall cease to have effect.

(5) In section 30(3) (orders relating to glebes)—

(a) in paragraph (c), the words from ", whether as" to "in place of the minister";

(b) in paragraph (e), the words "feu-duties and Government or other" and from "under or in pursuance" to "made by a minister"; and

(c) paragraph (f),

shall cease to have effect.

(6) Section 31 (redemption of feu-duty affecting glebe) shall cease to have effect.

(7) In section 34 (provisions relating to quoad sacra parishes)—

(a) in subsection (1)—

(i) in paragraph (b), the words "and certified by the Clerk of Teinds"; and

(ii) paragraph (e);

(b) subsection (3); and

(c) in subsection (4)(iii), the words "feu-duties, ground annuals, bonds of annual rent, or other", "with the sanction of the Court of Teinds" and "or payment of the feu-duty thereon",

shall cease to have effect.

(8) In section 35(7) (interpretation), the words "uninfeft or infeft" shall cease to have effect.

(9) In section 36 (requirements of parish to be first charge on endowments), the proviso shall cease to have effect.

(10) In section 37 (powers of General Trustees), the words "heritor or other" shall cease to have effect.

(11) Sections 39 (allocation of certain money by General Trustees), 40 (redemption of manse maill, etc.) and 41 (provisions relating to Court of Teinds) shall cease to have effect.

(12) In section 42 (application to Crown lands), the words from ", and to the teinds" to the end shall cease to have effect.

(13) Sections 45 (saving for obligations of relief) and 46 (saving for superiors) shall cease to have effect.

(14) In section 47 (interpretation)—

(a) in subsection (1), in the definition of "Stipend", the words ", including any allowance for communion elements payable by heritors out of teinds"; and

(b) subsections (2) and (3),

shall cease to have effect.

(15) The First to the Seventh Schedules shall cease to have effect.

Church of Scotland (Property and Endowments) Amendment Act 1933 (c.44)

17. (1) The Church of Scotland (Property and Endowments) Amendment Act 1933 shall be amended in accordance with this paragraph.

(2) In section 7 (suppression or union of parishes)—

(a) paragraph (ii) of the proviso; and

(b) the word "and" immediately preceding that paragraph,
shall cease to have effect.

(3) In section 8(1) (obligation of third party as respects endowments of parish quoad sacra etc.), the words ", or any obligation at common law for payment of the stipend or part of the stipend of the parish being a parish quoad omnia" shall cease to have effect.

(4) In section 9 (rights of superiors and others)—
   (a) subsections (1) and (2) shall cease to have effect; and
   (b) in subsection (3)—
      (i) for the word "heritor", in both places where it occurs, substitute "person"; and
      (ii) the words "or take in feu" and "or feu-duty" shall cease to have effect.

(5) Sections 10 (vesting of stipends of ministers of burgh churches, etc.) and 11 (vesting of glebe feu-duties etc.) shall cease to have effect.

Conveyancing Amendment (Scotland) Act 1938 (c.24)
18. (1) The Conveyancing Amendment (Scotland) Act 1938 shall be amended in accordance with this paragraph.

(2) Sections 6 (actions of declarator of irritancy) and 8 (prohibition of subinfeudation annulled) shall cease to have effect.

(3) [*Repealed by the Title Conditions (Scotland) Act 2003 (asp 9), Sch.15, (effective April 4, 2003).*]

National Parks and Access to the Countryside Act 1949 (c.97)
19. (1) The National Parks and Access to the Countryside Act 1949 shall be amended in accordance with this paragraph.

(2) For section 26 substitute—
"Application of Part III to Scotland
26.—In the application of this Part of this Act to Scotland the expression "limited owner", in relation to land, means a liferenter in possession of that land.".

(3) In section 114(1) (interpretation), in the definition of "owner"—
   (a) after the words "except in Part III of this Act" insert "or in relation to Scotland,"; and
   (b) the words "and as respects Scotland has the meaning assigned to it by section twenty-six of this Act" shall cease to have effect.

Town and Country Planning (Scotland) Act 1954 (c.73)
20. (1) The Town and Country Planning (Scotland) Act 1954 shall be amended in accordance with this paragraph.

(2) In section 55 (compensation for damage to requisitioned land), for subsection (2) substitute—
"(2) The said values are—
   (a) the value, at the time when the compensation accrues due, of the land in question (it being presumed that the land is subject to any servitude or other restriction then affecting it but otherwise is free from burdens); and
   (b) the value which such land would have at that time (on the same presumption as is mentioned in paragraph (a) above) if the land were then in the state in which it was when possession was taken in the exercise of emergency powers.".

(3) Section 69 (interpretation) shall cease to have effect.

Land Powers (Defence) Act 1958 (c.30)
21. In section 25(2) of the Land Powers (Defence) Act 1958 (interpretation), after paragraph (b) there shall be inserted—
"(bb) any reference to an "interest" in land, however expressed, shall be construed as a reference to a right in, or interest in, land and as including a reference to ownership of land;".

Opencast Coal Act 1958 (c.69)
22. In section 52 of the Opencast Coal Act 1958 (general application to Scotland)—
   (a) in subsection (2) in the definitions of "freehold interest" and "owner", the words "of the dominium utile" shall cease to have effect; and
   (b) subsections (6) to (8) shall cease to have effect.

Caravan Sites and Control of Development Act 1960 (c.62)
23. In section 32(1) of the Caravan Sites and Control of Development Act 1960 (application of Part I of Act to Scotland), for paragraph (d) substitute—
"(d) the reference in subsection (3) of section one of this Act to an estate or interest in land shall

be construed as a reference to a right in, or to, land and the references in that subsection and in section twelve of this Act to a licence in respect of land shall be construed as not including a tenancy of land;".

Flood Prevention (Scotland) Act 1961 (c.41)
24. In section 15(1) of the Flood Prevention (Scotland) Act 1961 (interpretation), in the definition of "interest", for the words "estate in or right" substitute "right in or".

Land Compensation (Scotland) Act 1963 (c.51)
25. (1) The Land Compensation (Scotland) Act 1963 shall be amended in accordance with this paragraph.

(2) In section 10 (consolidation of proceedings on claims in respect of several interests in the same land), for the words "acquisition of the several interests" substitute "acquisition of several interests".

(3) In section 20 (consideration in respect of discharge of feu-duty etc.)—

(a) in subsection (1), the words "the dominium utile in", in both places where they occur, shall cease to have effect;

(b) in subsection (2), the words "feu-duty, or ground annual or other" and "(not being stipend or standard charge in lieu of stipend)" shall cease to have effect;

(c) in subsection (3), for the words "dominium utile" substitute "land";

(d) in subsection (7), the words "dominium utile in any" shall cease to have effect; and

(e) in subsection (8), the words "the dominium utile in" shall cease to have effect.

(4) In section 27(3) (application for certificate of alternative development), the words "and that interest is the dominium utile of the land,", "feu-duty or ground annual or other" and "(not being stipend or standard charge in lieu of stipend)" shall cease to have effect.

(5) In section 28 (provisions as respect certain regulations under section 275(1)(c) of the Town and Country Planning (Scotland) Act 1997)—

(a) in paragraph (e), the words "the dominium utile of" and, in both places where they occur, "feu-duty or"; and

(b) in paragraph (f), the words "the dominium utile of",

shall cease to have effect.

(6) In section 32(6)(b) (provision for notification to planning authority in certain circumstances), for the words "dominium utile" substitute "ownership".

(7) In section 45 (interpretation)—

(a) after subsection (1) insert—

"(1A) Any reference in this Act to an "interest" in land shall be construed as a reference to a right in land and as including a reference to ownership of land."; and

(b) subsections (8) and (9) shall cease to have effect.

(8) In Schedule 2 (acquisition of houses which do not meet the tolerable standard), in paragraph 2(2), the words "the superior of, and" shall cease to have effect.

Local Government (Development and Finance)(Scotland) Act 1964 (c.67)
26. In section 7 of the Local Government (Development and Finance)(Scotland) Act 1964 (power to make advances for erection of buildings), for subsection (6) substitute—

"(6) The security for an advance made under this section shall be taken at the time of making or, in the case of an agreement to sell or let the land, at the time of the conveyance or of the lease.".

Forestry Act 1967 (c.10)
27. (1) The Forestry Act 1967 shall be amended in accordance with this paragraph.

(2) In section 5(3) (recording of forestry dedication agreement affecting land in Scotland), in the proviso, for the words "completed by infeftment" substitute "title has been completed".

(3) In section 34(3) (Scottish interpretation of expression "owner"), the words "the proprietor of the dominium utile or, in the case of land other than feudal land, is" shall cease to have effect.

(4) In section 49 (interpretation), subsection (3) shall cease to have effect.

(5) In Schedule 2 (conveyancing and other provisions connected with forestry dedication), in paragraph 4, for sub-paragraph (1) substitute—

"(1) In the case of land in Scotland, a liferenter in possession of the land shall have power to enter into forestry dedication agreements relating to, or to any part of, the land.".

Countryside (Scotland) Act 1967 (c.86)
28. (1) The Countryside (Scotland) Act 1967 shall be amended in accordance with this paragraph.

(2) In section 13(4) (certain persons who have power to enter access agreements), for the words "person, being the liferenter or the heir of entail," substitute "liferenter".

(3) In section 16 (effect of access agreement or order on rights and liabilities of persons interested in land)—

    (a) in each of subsections (6)(a) and (7)(a), for the words "an interest" substitute "a right"; and

    (b) in subsection (9), for the words "completed by infeftment" substitute "title has been completed".

(4) In each of sections 24(1) (acquisition, by planning authority, of land for public access) and 25(1) (acquisition, by Secretary of State, of land for public access), the word "feu," shall cease to have effect

(5) In section 38(5) (recording of public path creation agreement), in the proviso, for the words "completed by infeftment" substitute "title has been completed".

(6) In section 49A (management agreements)—

    (a) in subsection (5), for the words "person, being the liferenter or the heir of entail," substitute "liferenter"; and

    (b) in subsection (9), for the words "completed by infeftment" substitute "title has been completed".

(7) In section 78(1) (interpretation), in the definition of "interest", for the words "the ownership of an interest in land" substitute "ownership".

Countryside Act 1968 (c.41)
29. (1) The Countryside Act 1968 shall be amended in accordance with this paragraph.

(2) In section 15(6) (modification of section in its application to Scotland), in the proviso to the inserted subsection (4), for the words "completed by infeftment" substitute "title has been completed".

(3) In section 24(2) (acquisition of land for planting trees in interests of amenity), the word "feu," shall cease to have effect.

Conveyancing and Feudal Reform (Scotland) Act 1970 (c.35)
30. (1) The Conveyancing and Feudal Reform (Scotland) Act 1970 shall be amended in accordance with this paragraph.

(2)–(3) [*Repealed by the Title Conditions (Scotland) Act 2003 (asp 9), Sch.15, (effective April 4, 2003).*]

(4) Sections 3 to 6 (allocation of feuduties and ground annuals) shall cease to have effect.

(5) [*Repealed by the Title Conditions (Scotland) Act 2003 (asp 9), Sch.15, (effective April 4, 2003).*]

(6) In section 9 (which introduces the form of heritable security known as a standard security)—

    (a) in subsection (2), for the words "interest in land" substitute "land or real right in land,";

    (b) in subsection (3), for the words "an interest" substitute "land or a real right";

    (c) in subsection (4), for the words "of an interest" substitute "of land or of a real right"; and

    (d) in subsection (8)—

        (i) in paragraph (a), for the word "interest", in both places where it occurs, substitute "land or real right";

        (ii) [*Repealed by the Title Conditions (Scotland) Act 2003 (asp 9), Sch.15, (effective April 4, 2003).*]

        (iii) in paragraph (c), the words "feuduty, ground annual," shall cease to have effect.

(7) In section 10(2) (clause of warrandice to import absolute warrandice), for the word "interest" substitute "land or real right".

(8) In section 11(1) (effect of recorded standard security), for the words from "the interest" to "a security" substitute "in the grantee a real right in security".

(9) In section 12 (standard security may be granted by person uninfeft)—

    (a) in subsection (1)—

        (i) for the words "an interest" substitute "land or a real right";

        (ii) the words "having right to that interest, but" shall cease to have effect; and

        (iii) for the word "interest", where it last occurs, substitute "land or real right";

    (b) in subsection (2)—

        (i) for the word "interest" substitute "land or real right in land"; and

        (ii) for the words "last infeft" substitute "having the last recorded title".

(10) In section 13(1) (ranking of standard securities), for the words "interest in land or any part thereof, or of the subsequent assignation or conveyance of that interest" substitute "land

or real right in land or over any part thereof, or of the subsequent assignation or conveyance of that land or real right,".

(11) In section 15(1) (restriction of standard security)—

    (a) for the word "interest", where it first occurs, substitute "land or real right"; and

    (b) for the words from "to the interest" to "and the interest in land" substitute "to the land or real right contained in the standard security other than the part of that land or real right disburdened by the deed; and the land or real right".

(12) In section 16 (variation of standard security)—

    (a) in each of subsections (1) and (2), for the word "interest" substitute "land or real right"; and

    (b) in subsection (4), for the words "interest in land, or" substitute "land or real right in land, or over".

(13) In section 17 (discharge of standard security), for the word "interest" substitute "land or real right".

(14) In section 18(3) (redemption of standard security), for the word "interest" substitute "land or real right".

(15) In section 19 (calling-up of standard security)—

    (a) in subsection (2), for the words "last infeft in" substitute "having the last recorded title to"; and

    (b) in subsection (3), for the words—

        (i) "last infeft in" substitute "having the last recorded title to"; and

        (ii) "last infeft have" substitute "having the last recorded title have".

(16) In section 30 (interpretation)—

    (a) in subsection (1), for the definition of "interest in land" substitute—

    " 'real right in land' has the meaning assigned to it by the said section 9(8);"; and

    (b) in subsection (2), the definition of "infeft" shall cease to have effect.

(17) Sections 33 (form of notice calling-up heritable security), 34 (amendment of section 34 of Conveyancing (Scotland) Act 1924), 35 (power of creditor in bond and disposition in security to sell to include power to sell by private bargain) and 39 (amendment of section 8 of Heritable Securities (Scotland) Act 1894) shall cease to have effect.

(18) In section 41(1) (restriction on effect of reduction of certain discharges of securities)—

    (a) for the words "to any subsequent interest in the land, acquired" substitute "who subsequently acquires the land or a real right in or over it"; and

    (b) the words "of the interest" shall cease to have effect.

(19) In section 43(1) (interpretation), the definition of "the Act of 1894" shall cease to have effect.

(20) Section 49 (abolition of heritor's right of pre-emption of glebe) shall cease to have effect.

(21) In section 51 (application to the Crown), for the words "held of the Crown and of" substitute "owned by the Crown or by".

(22) [*Repealed by the Title Conditions (Scotland) Act 2003 (asp 9), Sch.15, (effective April 4, 2003).*]

(23) In the Notes to Schedule 2 (which relates to forms of standard security)—

    (a) for note 1 substitute—

    "Note 1.-The security subjects shall be described sufficiently to identify them; but this note is without prejudice to any additional requirement imposed as respects any register.".

    (b) in note 2—

        (i) the words "ground annual or" shall cease to have effect; and

        (ii) for the word "infeftment" substitute "recorded title"; and

    (c) in note 3—

        (i) for the words "has been infeft in" substitute "has a recorded title to";

        (ii) for the words "has not previously been infeft in" substitute "does not have a recorded title to";

        (iii) the words "ground annual or" shall cease to have effect;

        (iv) for the words "last infeft in" substitute "who last had a recorded title to"; and

        (v) for the word "infeftment" substitute "recorded title".

(24) In Schedule 3 (the standard conditions), in condition 10(3), the words "feuduties, ground annuals or, as the case may be," shall cease to have effect.

(25) In the Notes to Schedule 4 (which relates to forms of deeds of assignation and of restriction etc.), in note 3, for the words "infeftment upon a standard security has been taken" substitute "title to a standard security has been completed".

(26) In schedule 8 (excluded enactments), paragraphs 2, 3, 7 to 14, 16 and 17, 18 to 22, 24 and 26 to 30 shall cease to have effect.

Agriculture Act 1970 (c.40)

31. (1) Section 33 of the Agriculture Act 1970 (miscellaneous amendments relating to amalgamations) shall be amended in accordance with this paragraph.

(2) In subsection (2)—

    (a) in paragraph (b), for the words "in which an estate or interest is held by a liferenter or an heir of entail" substitute "which is held by a liferenter";

    (b) for the words "the liferenter or the heir of entail" substitute "or the liferenter"; and

    (c) for the words "that estate or interest" substitute "the land".

(3) Subsection (5) shall cease to have effect.

Housing (Financial Provisions) (Scotland) Act 1972 (c.46)

32. In section 78(1) of the Housing (Financial Provisions) (Scotland) Act 1972 (interpretation), in the definition of "land", for the word "estate" substitute "right".

Prescription and Limitation (Scotland) Act 1973 (c.52)

33. (1) The Prescription and Limitation (Scotland) Act 1973 shall be amended in accordance with this paragraph.

(2) For sections 1 and 2 there shall be substituted—

> **"Validity of right**
>
> **1.**—(1) If land has been possessed by any person, or by any person and his successors, for a continuous period of ten years openly, peaceably and without any judicial interruption and the possession was founded on, and followed—
>
> (a) the recording of a deed which is sufficient in respect of its terms to constitute in favour of that person a real right in—
>
>   (i) that land; or
>
>   (ii) land of a description habile to include that land; or
>
> (b) registration of a real right in that land, in favour of that person, in the Land Register of Scotland, subject to an exclusion of indemnity under section 12(2) of the Land Registration (Scotland) Act 1979 (c.33),
>
> then, as from the expiry of that period, the real right so far as relating to that land shall be exempt from challenge.
>
> (2) Subsection (1) above shall not apply where—
>
> (a) possession was founded on the recording of a deed which is invalid ex facie or was forged; or
>
> (b) possession was founded on registration in the Land Register of Scotland proceeding on a forged deed and the person appearing from the Register to have the real right in question was aware of the forgery at the time of registration in his favour.
>
> (3) In subsection (1) above, the reference to a real right is to a real right which is registrable in the Land Register of Scotland or a deed relating to which can competently be recorded; but this section does not apply to servitudes or public rights of way.
>
> (4) In the computation of a prescriptive period for the purposes of this section in a case where the deed in question is a decree of adjudication for debt, any period before the expiry of the legal shall be disregarded.
>
> (5) Where, in any question involving any foreshore or any salmon fishings, this section is pled against the Crown as owner of the regalia, subsection (1) above shall have effect as if for the words "ten years" there were substituted "twenty years".
>
> (6) This section is without prejudice to section 2 of this Act.
>
> **Special cases**
>
> **2.**—(1) If—
>
> (a) land has been possessed by any person, or by any person and his successors, for a continuous period of twenty years openly, peaceably and without any judicial interruption; and
>
> (b) the possession was founded on, and followed the execution of, a deed (whether recorded or not) which is sufficient in respect of its terms to constitute in favour of that person a real right in that land, or in land of a description habile to include that land,
>
> then, as from the expiry of that period, the real right so far as relating to that land shall be exempt from challenge except on the ground that the deed is invalid ex facie or was forged.
>
> (2) This section applies—
>
> (a) to the real right of the lessee under a lease; and
>
> (b) to any other real right in land, being a real right of a kind which, under the law in force immediately before the commencement of this Part of this Act, was sufficient to form a foundation for positive prescription without the deed constituting the title to the real right having been recorded,
>
> but does not apply to servitudes or public rights of way.

(3) This section is without prejudice to section 1 of this Act or to section 3(3) of the Land Registration (Scotland) Act 1979 (c.33).".

(3) In section 5(1) (provision as to what is to be treated as a deed for the purposes of sections 1, 2 and 3 of the Act), for the words "title to an interest in land shall be treated as a deed sufficient to constitute that title" substitute "right in land shall be treated as a deed sufficient to constitute that right".

(4) In section 15(1) (interpretation), the definition of "interest in land" shall cease to have effect.

(5) In Schedule 1 (obligations affected by certain prescriptive periods)—

    (a) in paragraph 1, heads (iii) and (iv) of sub-paragraph (a); and

    (b) in paragraph 2(f), the words "terce, courtesy,"

shall cease to have effect.

34. Paragraph 33(1) and (5)(a) of this schedule, and the provisions of schedule 13 to this Act in so far as relating to Schedule 1.1(a)(iii) and (iv) to the Prescription and Limitation (Scotland) Act 1973, shall not affect the application of section 6 of that Act to any obligation falling due on or before the appointed day.

Land Compensation (Scotland) Act 1973 (c.56)

35. In section 80 of the Land Compensation (Scotland) Act 1973 (interpretation), after subsection (1) insert—

"(1A) Any reference in this Act to an "interest" in land shall be construed as a reference to a right in land and as including a reference to ownership of land.".

Offshore Petroleum Development (Scotland) Act 1975 (c.8)

36. (1) The Offshore Petroleum Development (Scotland) Act 1975 shall be amended in accordance with this paragraph.

(2) In section 14(1) (power to require information as to interests in land), the word "superior," shall cease to have effect.

(3) In section 20 (short title, interpretation and extent)—

    (a) in subsection (2)—

        (i) in the definition of "Crown interest", the words "estate or" shall cease to have effect; and

        (ii) for the definition of "land" substitute—

"land" includes the foreshore and other land covered with water and, except where the context otherwise requires—

    (a) any interest in, or right over, land; and

    (b) any other heritable property;"; and

    (c) in subsection (3), the words "estate or" shall cease to have effect.

Scottish Development Agency Act 1975 (c.69)

37. (1) The Scottish Development Agency Act 1975 shall be amended in accordance with this paragraph.

(2) In section 9 (acquisition and disposal of land), in subsection (1)(a), the word "feu," shall cease to have effect.

(3) In section 11(1) (power to obtain information), the word "superior," shall cease to have effect.

(4) In section 25(1) (interpretation), for the definition of "land" substitute—

"land" includes—

    (a) the foreshore and other land covered with water;

    (b) any interest in, or right over, land; and

    (c) any other heritable property;".

Aircraft and Shipbuilding Industries Act 1977 (c.3)

38. In section 56(3) (interpretation of expressions relating to land in Scotland), for paragraph (b) substitute—

"(b) "rights of ownership" means the rights—

    (i) of an owner; or

    (ii) of a tenant under a lease;".

Land Registration (Scotland) Act 1979 (c.33)

39. (1) The Land Registration (Scotland) Act 1979 shall be amended in accordance with this paragraph.

(2) In section 2(1)(a) (provision for registration in the land register)—

(a) in sub-paragraph (i)—

(i) for the words "feu, long lease or security by way of contract of ground annual" substitute "long lease"; and

(ii) for the words "feuar, lessee or debtor in the ground annual" substitute "lessee"; and

(b) in sub-paragraph (v), for the words ", udal tenure or a kindly tenancy" substitute "or udal tenure".

[1] (3) In section 3 (effect of registration)—

(a) in subsection (3), paragraph (c) shall cease to have effect;

(b) in subsection (4), paragraph (b) shall cease to have effect.

(c) [*Repealed by the Title Conditions (Scotland) Act 2003 (asp 9), Sch.15 (effective April 4, 2003).*]

(4) In section 6 (title sheets)—

(a) in subsection (1)(a), for the words "dominium utile" substitute "land"; and

(b) in subsection (3), the words "over-feuduty or", in both places where they occur, shall cease to have effect.

(5) In section 12 (indemnity in respect of loss)—

(a) in subsection (3)(m), the words "a superior, a creditor in a ground annual or", "the feu writ, the contract of ground annual or", ", as the case may be,", "superior, creditor or" and, in both places where they occur, "feuduty, ground annual or"; and

(b) in subsection (4)(a) the words "over-feuduty or",

shall cease to have effect.

(6) [*Repealed by the Title Conditions (Scotland) Act 2003 (asp 9), Sch.15, (effective April 4, 2003).*]

(7) In section 16 (omission of certain clauses in deeds)—

(a) subsection (2); and

(b) in subsection (3)(b), the words "feuduties, ground annuals," and "and, in the case of a grant of land in feu, of all feuduties payable by the grantor to his superiors from and after the date of entry",

shall cease to have effect.

(8) In section 20 (tenants-at-will)—

(a) in subsection (3), paragraph (ii), and the word "; and" immediately preceding that paragraph, shall cease to have effect;

(b) in subsection (5), for the words ", restriction or redemption" substitute "or restriction";

(c) in subsection (6), the words ", and all such feuduties, ground annuals or other periodical payments as are mentioned in subsection (3)(ii) above" shall cease to have effect; and

(d) in subsection (8)(a), sub-paragraph (ii) shall cease to have effect.

(9) In section 21 (provisions supplementary to section 20)–

(a) in subsection (8), for the words "infeft in" substitute "owner of";

(b) for subsection (9) substitute—

"(9) Any condition or provision to the effect that a person with an interest in land shall be entitled to a right of pre-emption in the event of a sale of the land, or of any part of the land, by the proprietor for the time being, shall not be capable of being enforced where the sale is by a landlord to his tenant-at-will under section 20 of this Act."; and

(c) in subsection (10) for the words "grant by him of a feu" substitute "disposition by him".

(10) In section 26 (application to Crown), for the words "held of the Crown and of" substitute "owned by the Crown or by".

(11) In section 28(1) (interpretation)—

(a) the definition of "feu" shall cease to have effect;

(b) in the definition of "incorporeal heritable right", after the word "include" insert "a right of ownership of land, the right of a lessee under a long lease of land, a right to mines or minerals or";

(c) for the definition of "interest in land" substitute—

"interest in land"—

(a) means any right in or over land, including any heritable security or servitude but excluding any lease which is not a long lease; and

(b) where the context admits, includes the land;".

Ancient Monuments and Archaeological Areas Act 1979 (c.46)

40. (1) The Ancient Monuments and Archaeological Areas Act 1979 shall be amended in accordance with this paragraph.

(2) In section 12(9) (certain persons acquiring rights to monuments in Scotland not bound by guardianship deeds), in paragraph (b), for the words "completed by infeftment" substitute "title has been completed".

(3) In section 18(4) (capacities relevant to limited ownership), in paragraph (c), the words "or heir of entail" shall cease to have effect.

(4) In section 57(1) (power to require information), the words "of the dominium utile," shall cease to have effect.

Education (Scotland) Act 1980 (c.44)

41. (1) The Education (Scotland) Act 1980 shall be amended in accordance with this paragraph.

(2) In section 16(2)(b) (method of effecting transference of school), in sub-paragraph (i), for the words "interest in the land to be transferred" substitute "transferee's right in the land".

(3) In each of sections 20(1)(a) (power of education authority to acquire land) and 22(1)(a) (power of education authority to sell land), the word "feu," shall cease to have effect.

Water (Scotland) Act 1980 (c.45)

42. (1) The Water (Scotland) Act 1980 shall be amended in accordance with this paragraph.

(2) In section 65 (power of council to make charging order for expenses of executing works), as saved by section 179 of the Local Government etc. (Scotland) Act 1994 (c.39)—

(a) in subsection (5)—

(i) the word "estates,"; and

(ii) paragraph (a),

shall cease to have effect;

(b) in subsection (7), for the words "absolute order made under and in terms of the Improvement of Land Act 1864" substitute "a standard security"; and

(c) in subsection (8), the words "or rentcharge" shall cease to have effect.

(3) In Schedule 4 (provisions to be incorporated in orders relating to water undertakings), in paragraph 8, the words "feuduties, ground annuals," shall cease to have effect.

British Telecommunications Act 1981 (c.38)

43. In Schedule 2 to the British Telecommunications Act 1981 (provisions as to transfers of property, rights and liabilities), in paragraph 1(3), for the words from "Sub-paragraph (2)" to "that sub-paragraph" substitute "In the application of sub-paragraph (2)".

Mobile Homes Act 1983 (c.34)

44. In section 5 of the Mobile Homes Act 1983 (interpretation), at the end add—

"(4) In relation to land in Scotland, any reference in this Act to an "estate or interest" shall be construed as a reference to a right in, or to, the land.".

Roads (Scotland) Act 1984 (c.54)

45. In each of sections 53(4) (enforceability against third parties of agreements as to use of land near roads) and 72(3) (enforceability against third parties of agreements as to stopping up of private access to land) of the Roads (Scotland) Act 1984, for the words "completed by infeftment" substitute "title has been completed".

Companies Act 1985 (c.6)

46. (1) The Companies Act 1985 shall be amended in accordance with this paragraph.

(2) In—

(a) section 396(1)(a)(ii) (charges requiring registration) unless the circumstance mentioned in sub-paragraph (4) below arises; or

(b) section 410(4)(a) (charges void unless registered) if that circumstance does arise, the words ", ground annual" shall cease to have effect.

(3) If the amendment in head (b) above falls to be made, the amendment in head (a) above shall, on section 92 of the Companies Act 1989 coming into force, have effect.

(4) The circumstance is that section 92 of the Companies Act 1989 has not come into force by the date on which this schedule comes into force.

(5) In Schedule 4, in paragraph 93 (interpretation of Schedule), the words "is the proprietor of the dominium utile or, in the case of land not held on feudal tenure," and "; and the reference to ground-rents, rates and other outgoings includes feu-duty and ground annual" shall cease to have effect.

(6) In Schedule 9, in paragraph 86 (interpretation of Schedule), the words "is the proprietor of the dominium utile or, in the case of land not held on feudal tenure," and "; and the reference to ground-rents, rates and other outgoings includes a reference to feu-duty and ground annual" shall cease to have effect.

Housing Associations Act 1985 (c.69)
47. In section 106(2) of the Housing Associations Act 1985 (application of Act in Scotland), in the definition of "heritable security", for the words "interest in land by disposition or assignation of that interest" substitute " land, or real right in land, by disposition of the land, or assignation of the real right,".

Housing (Scotland) Act 1987 (c.26)
48. (1) The Housing (Scotland) Act 1987 shall be amended in accordance with this paragraph.

(2) In section 16 (disposal of land for erection of churches etc.), for the word "feu" substitute "disposition".

(3) In section 84A (application of right to buy to cases where landlord is lessee), for the word "interest", wherever it occurs, substitute "real right".

(4) In section 125(2) (notice to certain persons of time and place at which question of demolishing building will be considered), the words "of the superior of whom such owner holds, and" shall cease to have effect

(5) In section 132, subsection (1) (notice to superiors of certain proceedings in relation to lands and heritages) shall cease to have effect.

(6) In section 155(1) (power to require information), for the words "an estate" substitute "a right".

(7) In section 175(1) (protection of superiors and owners)–
   (a) the words "superior or" shall cease to have effect; and
   (b) for the word "estate" substitute "right".

(8) In section 177(b) (interpretation), for the words "an estate" substitute "a right".

(9) In section 179 (general effect of control order)—
   (a) in subsection (1)(b), for the words "an estate" substitute "a right"; and
   (b) in subsection (2), for the words "under this section have an interest amounting to an estate in" substitute "own".

(10) In section 180 (effect of control order on occupier)—
   (a) in subsection (2)—
      (i) in paragraph (a), for the words "an estate" substitute "a right"; and
      (ii) in paragraph (b), for the words "an estate in" substitute "ownership of"; and
   (b) in subsection (6), for the words "an estate" substitute "a right".

(11) In section 186 (appeal against control order), in each of subsections (1) and (2), for the words "an estate" substitute "a right".

(12) In section 190(1) (interpretation), in the definition of "licence", for the words "an estate or interest therein" substitute "ownership, tenancy or a real right".

(13) Section 334 (power of heir of entail to sell land for housing purposes) shall cease to have effect.

(14) In section 338(1) (interpretation)—
   (a) in the definition of "land", for the word "estate" substitute "right"; and
   (b) the definitions of—
      (i) "sell" and "sale"; and
      (ii) "superior",
shall cease to have effect.

(15) In Schedule 9 (recovery of expenses by charging order), in paragraph 7, for the words "bond and disposition in" substitute "standard".

(16) In Schedule 11 (houses in multiple occupation: control orders)—
   (a) in paragraph 4(1), for the words "an estate" substitute "a right"; and
   (b) in paragraph 5(3), for the words—

    (i) "an estate" substitute "a right"; and

    (ii) "that estate" substitute "that right".

Consumer Protection Act 1987 (c.43)
49. In section 23(3) of the Consumer Protection Act 1987 (interpretation), in paragraph (b) of the definition of "relevant interest", for the words "dominium utile" substitute "ownership".

Income and Corporation Taxes Act 1988 (c.1)
50. (1) The Income and Corporation Taxes Act 1988 shall be amended in accordance with this paragraph.

    (2) In section 15(1) (in which is set out Schedule A), in Schedule A, in paragraph 1(4)(b), the words ", ground annuals and feu duties" shall cease to have effect.

    (3) In section 119 (rent etc. payable in connection with mines, quarries and similar concerns), in subsection (3), in the definition of "rent", the word ", feuduty" shall cease to have effect.

    (4) In section 776 (transactions in land: taxation of capital gains), in subsection (6), in the definition for Scotland of "freehold", for the words "estate or interest of the proprietor of the dominium utile or, in the case of property other than feudal property," substitute "interest".

    (5) In section 832(1) (interpretation of the Tax Acts), after the definition of "distribution" insert—
"'estate in land', in relation to any land in Scotland, includes the land;".

Capital Allowances Act 1990 (c.1)
51. In each of sections 51(3) and 125(1) of the Capital Allowances Act 1990 (interpretation), for paragraph (b) substitute—
"(b) in Scotland, the interest of the owner or an agreement to acquire such an interest,".

Enterprise and New Towns (Scotland) Act 1990 (c.35)
52. In section 32(2) of the Enterprise and New Towns (Scotland) Act 1990 (enforceability of registered agreements), for the words "completed by infeftment" substitute "title has been completed".

Natural Heritage (Scotland) Act 1991 (c.28)
53. (1) The Natural Heritage (Scotland) Act 1991 shall be amended in accordance with this paragraph.

    (2) In section 22(1) (interpretation), in the definition of "land", the word "estate," shall cease to have effect.

    (3) In Schedule 1 (constitution and proceedings of Scottish Natural Heritage), in paragraph 19—

    (a) in sub-paragraph (1), after the words "to land" insert "which or"; and

    (b) for sub-paragraph (2) substitute—
"(2) In sub-paragraph (1) above—
"interest" includes any right over the land, whether exercisable by virtue of ownership or by virtue of a licence or agreement and, without prejudice to that generality, includes sporting rights; and
"land" includes—
    (i) land covered by water; and
    (ii) salmon fishings.".

"Coal Mining Subsidence Act 1991 (c.45)
54.(1) The Coal Mining Subsidence Act 1991 shall be amended in accordance with this paragraph.

    (2) In section 52(1) (interpretation), in the definition of "owner", paragraph (b) shall cease to have effect.

    (3) In Schedule 1 (determination of amount of depreciation payments), in paragraph 2(6)—

    (a) in the definition of "fee simple", for the words ", in the case of feudal property, the estate or interest of the proprietor of the dominium utile or, in the case of property other than feudal property, the estate or" substitute "the"; and

    (b) the definition of "incumbrance" shall cease to have effect.

    (4) In Schedule 2 (recipients of depreciation payments: special cases)—

    (a) in paragraph 3(2), head (b); and

    (b) in paragraph 4(2)(b), the words "an entail or",
shall cease to have effect.

    (5) In Schedule 6 (farm loss payments), in paragraph 1(5)–

    (a) in head (a), for the words "an interest as infeft proprietor of" substitute "a right as proprietor with completed title to"; and

    (b) the words ", but do not include references to an interest as a superior only" shall cease to have effect.

Crofters (Scotland) Act 1993 (c.44)

55. (1) The Crofters (Scotland) Act 1993 shall be amended in accordance with this paragraph.

(2) In section 16 (provisions relating to conveyance)—

(a) in subsection (3), the words "estates or" shall cease to have effect;

(b) in subsection (5), for the words "is infeft in" substitute "has a completed title to"; and

(c) subsection (7) shall cease to have effect.

(3) In section 17(3) (certain conditions or provisions to be unenforceable), paragraph (a), the words "or (b)" and in paragraph (b) the word "other", shall cease to have effect.

(4) In section 19(4) (heritable securities)—

(a) paragraph (a); and

(b) in each of paragraphs (b) and (c), the words "otherwise than in feu",

shall cease to have effect.

(5) In section 20(3) (interpretation), in paragraph (a), for the word "feuing" substitute "disposing".

Coal Industry Act 1994 (c.21)

56. (1) The Coal Industry Act 1994 shall be amended in accordance with this paragraph.

(2) In section 8 (exploitation rights: territorial waters and continental shelf), in subsection (6), for the words "a proprietor of the dominium utile" substitute "an owner".

(3) In section 9 (exploitation rights: oil and gas), in subsection (4)(b), for the words "proprietor of the dominium utile as respects" substitute "an owner in".

(4) In section 10 (protection for certain interests in coal and coal mines), in subsection (7), paragraph (b) and the word "and" immediately preceding that paragraph shall cease to have effect.

Value Added Tax Act 1994 (c.23)

57. In section 96(1) of the Value Added Tax Act 1994 (interpretation) in the definition of—

(a) "fee simple", in paragraph (a), the words "estate or interest of the proprietor of the dominium utile or, in the case of land not held on feudal tenure, the estate or" shall cease to have effect; and

(b) "major interest", for the words from "-(a) the estate" to "tenure, the estate or" substitute "the".

Requirements of Writing (Scotland) Act 1995 (c.7)

58. In section 1 of the Requirements of Writing (Scotland) Act 1995 (writing required for certain contracts, obligations, trusts, conveyances and wills)—

(a) in subsection (2), in each of paragraphs (a)(i) and (b), for the words "an interest" substitute "a real right"; and

(b) in subsection (7), for the words "'interest in land' means any estate, interest or" substitute "'real right in land' means any real".

Atomic Energy Authority Act 1995 (c.37)

59. In section 1 of the Atomic Energy Authority Act 1995 (schemes for transfer of property, rights and liabilities), for subsection (6) substitute—

"(6) In the application of subsection (3)(b) above to Scotland, the reference to the fee simple estate shall be construed as a reference to the interest of the owner.".

Town and Country Planning (Scotland) Act 1997 (c.8)

60. (1) The Town and Country Planning (Scotland) Act 1997 shall be amended in accordance with this paragraph.

(2) In section 75(4) (restriction on enforceability of agreement regulating development or use of land), for the words "completed by infeftment" substitute "title has been completed".

(3) In section 191 (disposal of land held for planning purposes), subsection (9) shall cease to have effect.

(4) In section 272(2) (matters as to which information may be required), in paragraph (b), the word "superior," shall cease to have effect.

(5) In section 277 (interpretation)—

(a) in subsection (1), in the definition of—

(i) "disposal", the words ", except in section 191(9),"; and

(ii) "heritable security", in paragraph (a), the words "a security by way of ground annual and",

shall cease to have effect; and

(b) subsection (8) shall cease to have effect.

(6) In Schedule 15 (general vesting declarations)—

(a) in paragraph 7, the words "feuduty, ground annual or"; and

(b) in paragraph 34, the words "a feuduty, ground annual,",

shall cease to have effect.

Finance Act 1999 (c.16)

61. (1) In Part III of Schedule 13 to the Finance Act 1999 (other instruments), in paragraph 18(1), head (c) shall cease to have effect.

(2) Sub-paragraph (1) above and, in so far as relating to the Finance Act 1999, section 76 of, and schedule 13 to, this Act shall not affect any instrument executed before the appointed day.

PART 2

MINOR AND CONSEQUENTIAL AMENDMENTS RELATING TO THE NATIONAL TRUST FOR SCOTLAND

National Trust for Scotland Order Confirmation Act 1935 (c.ii)

62. (1) The Order contained in the Schedule to the National Trust for Scotland Order Confirmation Act 1935 (incorporation, conferring of powers etc.) shall be amended in accordance with this paragraph.

(2) In section 4(2) (powers of National Trust), the word "feu" shall cease to have effect.

(3) In section 6(2) (completion of title by National Trust), the words "notarial instrument or" shall cease to have effect.

National Trust for Scotland Order Confirmation Act 1947 (c.xxxviii)

63. (1) 63 (1) The Order contained in the Schedule to the National Trust for Scotland Order Confirmation Act 1947 (extension of powers of National Trust etc.) shall be amended in accordance with this paragraph.

(2) In section 3(a) (extension of powers of National Trust: feuing of land for feu duties etc.)—

(a) for the word "feus" substitute "dispositions"; and

(b) the words from "feu duties" to "any" shall cease to have effect.

(3) In section 4 (exercise of extended powers)—

(a) in subsection (2)—

(i) for the word "feu", where it first occurs, substitute "dispone"; and

(ii) for the words "feu charter feu contract" substitute "disposition"; and

(b) in subsection (4), for the word "feued" substitute "disponed".

AMENDMENTS

1. As amended by the Title Conditions (Scotland) Act 2003 (asp 9), Sch.15, (effective April 4, 2003).

2. As amended by the Title Conditions (Scotland) Act 2003 (asp 9), Sch.13, para.20, (effective April 4, 2003).

¹ SCHEDULE 13

(introduced by section 76(2))

REPEALS

PART 1

REPEALS: GENERAL

Enactment	Extent of Repeal
Registration Act 1661 (c.243) (Act of the Parliaments of Scotland)	The whole Act.
Ann Act 1672 (c.24) (Act of the Parliaments of Scotland)	
Entail Act 1685 (c.26) (Act of the Parliaments of Scotland)	The whole Act.
Udal Tenure Act 1690 (c.61) (Act of the Parliaments of Scotland)	The whole Act.
Teinds Act 1690 (c.63) (Act of the Parliaments of Scotland)	The whole Act.

Enactment	Extent of Repeal
Tenures Abolition Act 1746 (c.50)	The whole Act except sections 21 and 22.
Entail Improvement Act 1770 (c.51)	The whole Act.
Burghs of Barony (Scotland) Act 1795 (c.122)	The whole Act.
Thirlage Act 1799 (c.55)	The whole Act.
Teinds Act 1808 (c.138)	The whole Act.
Entail Provisions Act 1824 (c.87)	The whole Act.
Register of Sasines Act 1829 (c.19)	The whole Act.
Public Revenue (Scotland) Act 1833 (c.13)	In section 1, the words from "or in relation to the issuing or paying any stipend" to "behalf, or others entitled thereto;"; and the words "granting tacks of teinds, or to the".
New Churches (Scotland) Act 1834 (c.41)	The whole Act.
Erasures in Deeds (Scotland) Act 1836 (c.33)	The whole Act.
Entail Powers Act 1836 (c.42)	The whole Act.
Entail Act 1838 (c.70)	The whole Act.
Court of Session (No.2) Act 1838 (c.118)	The whole Act.
Court of Session Act 1839 (c.36)	The whole Act.
Entail Sites Act 1840 (c.48)	The whole Act.
New Parishes (Scotland) Act 1844 (c.44)	The whole Act.
Lands Clauses Consolidation (Scotland) Act 1845 (c.19)	In section 7, the words "heirs of entail,", "estate or", "married women seised in their own right or entitled to terce or dower, or any other right or interest, husbands,", "or feoffees", "and as to such married women as if they were sole," and, in the last two places where they occur, "married women,".
	In section 8, the words from "power herein" to "therewith, and the" and, in both places where they occur, the words "feu duties, ground annuals,".
	Sections 10 and 11.
	In section 12, the word ", feu,", in both places where it occurs.
	In section 67, the words "heir of entail,", "married woman seised in her own right or entitled to terce or dower or any other right or interest, husband,", "on the same heirs, or", ", or affecting succeeding heirs of entail in any such lands, whether imposed and constituted by the entailer, or in virtue of powers given by the entail, or in virtue of powers conferred by any Act of Parliament" and "same heirs, and the".
	In each of sections 69 and 70, the word "coverture," and the word "husbands,".
	Section 73.
	In section 79, the words "feu or" and ", and of re-entailing any of such lands,".
	In section 80, the words "feus and", in both places where they occur; and the words "the particular register of sasines kept for the

Enactment	Extent of Repeal
	county, burgh, or district in which the lands are locally situated, or in", "for Scotland kept at Edinburgh, within sixty days from the last date thereof, which the respective keepers of the said registers are hereby authorized and required to do,", "feudal" and from ": Provided always" to the end.
	In section 93, the words " and if such lands be part of a barony a like notice shall be given to the superior or baron".
	In the preamble to sections 107 to 111, the words "any feu duty, ground annual, casualty of superiority, or".
	In section 109, the words "such feu duty, ground annual, casualty of superiority, or any".
	In section 110, the words "feu duty, ground annual, casualty of superiority,".
	In section 117, the word "estate,", in each place where it occurs.
	In section 124, the words from ", by deed" to the end.
	Sections 126 and 127.
	Schedule (B.).
Infeftment Act 1845 (c.35)	The whole Act.
Entail Amendment Act 1848 (c.36)	Sections 1 to 31.
	In section 32, the words from "may be in the form" to "in terms of this Act;".
	Sections 33 to 45.
	In section 47, the words "dated on or after the first day of August one thousand eight hundred and forty-eight", "fee simple" in each of the three places where they occur and "the superior of such lands or estate, and of".
	In section 48, the words "dated on or after the said first day of August one thousand eight hundred and forty eight", "fee simple" and "the superior of such lands or estate, and of".
	In section 49, the words "or estate" in both places where they occur and "dated on or after the said first day of August one thousand eight hundred and forty eight".
	Sections 50 and 51.
	The Schedule.
Judicial Factors Act 1849 (c.51)	In section 7, the words from "and if the estate be held under entail," to "could have charged the estate under the said Acts, or either of them;".
Entail Amendment Act 1853 (c.94)	The whole Act.
Registration of Leases (Scotland) Act 1857 (c.26)	Sections 4, 5, 8, 9 and 11. Schedules (C) and (F).

Enactment	Extent of Repeal
Defence Act 1859 (c.12)	In section 3, the words "feus and", in both places where they occur; the word "feudal"; and the words from "; provided always" to the end.
Entail Cottages Act 1860 (c.95)	The whole Act.
Lands Clauses Consolidation Acts Amendment Act 1860 (c.106)	Section 3.
	In each of sections 4 and 5, the words ", annual feu duty or ground annual", in each place where they occur.
	In section 8, the words ", or of the Lands Clauses Consolidation (Scotland) Act, 1845, in all matters in which it relates to the said Act respectively.".
Parochial Buildings (Scotland) Act 1862 (c.58)	The whole Act.
Church of Scotland Courts Act 1863 (c.47)	In section 2, the words from ", and at the same time" to "shall subsist".
	In section 3, the words from ", and to apportion" to the end.
Fish Teinds (Scotland) Act 1864 (c.33)	The whole Act.
Improvement of Land Act 1864 (c.114)	The whole Act.
Glebe Lands (Scotland) Act 1866 (c.71)	The whole Act.
Parochial Buildings (Scotland) Act 1866 (c.75)	The whole Act.
United Parishes (Scotland) Act 1868 (c.30)	The whole Act.
Land Registers (Scotland) Act 1868 (c.64)	In section 5, the words "in terms of such new warrant".
	In section 6, the words "in terms of the warrant of registration thereon".
	In section 12, the words "and shall be in the form, as nearly as may be, of the Schedule (B.) to this Act annexed,"
Entail Amendment (Scotland) Act 1868 (c.84)	The whole Act
Ecclesiastical Buildings and Glebes (Scotland) Act 1868 (c.96)	The whole Act
Titles to Land Consolidation (Scotland) Act 1868 (c.101)	In section 3, the words "The words "Crown writ" shall extend to and include all charters, precepts, and writs from Her Majesty, and from the Prince; and" the definition of "charter" and of "writ" in the definition of "deed" and of "conveyance", the words "charters,", "whether containing a warrant or precept of sasine or not, and", "feu contracts, contracts of ground annual,", ", whether such decrees contain warrant to infeft or precept of sasine or not," and ", procuratories of resignation ad remanentiam," the definition of "deed of entail" in the definition of "instrument", the words "authorized by this Act, or by any of the Acts hereby repealed," and the definition of "infeft" and "infeftment".
	Sections 4 to 7.

Enactment	Extent of Repeal
	In section 8, the words ", and to all open procuratories, clauses, and precepts, if any, and as the case may be," and the words from " and the clause of obligation" to "other public, parochial, and local burdens, due from or on account of the lands conveyed prior to the date of entry".
	Sections 9 and 10.
	In section 12, the words from "with a warrant of registration" to "hereto annexed)," the words from "and warrant of registration;" to "on whose behalf the conveyance is presented" and the words from "or to expede and record" to the end.
	Sections 14 to 19.
	Section 23.
	In section 24, the words ", with warrant of registration thereon,".
	In section 26, the words "with warrant of registration thereon in terms of this Act, or when followed by notarial instrument expede, and with warrant of registration thereon recorded" and "feued,".
	Sections 27 to 50.
	In section 51, the word "said", where it first occurs; and the words from "or Sheriffs of counties" to the end.
	Sections 63 to 116.
	Sections 118 and 119.
	In section 120, the words ", whether dated before or after the commencement of this Act," and the proviso.
	Sections 121 to 127.
	Sections 130 to 137.
	In section 140, the words ", and subsequent sheets (if any) shall be chargeable with the appropriate progressive duty".
	Section 141.
	In section 142, the words ", and all instruments hereby" and ", with warrants of registration written thereon respectively,".
	Sections 144 to 147.
	Sections 150 to 154.
	Section 156.
	Sections 161 to 163.
	The Schedules, except Schedules (B.) No.1, (F.) No.1, (G.), (PP.) and (RR.).
	In Schedule (B.) No. 1, the words from "to be holden" to "as the case may be];" and the words "feu duties, casualties, and".
Titles to Land Consolidation (Scotland) Amendment Act 1869 (c.116)	The whole Act.

Enactment	Extent of Repeal
Limited Owners Residences Act 1870 (c.56)	The whole Act.
Limited Owners Residences Act (1870) Amendment Act 1871 (c.84)	The whole Act.
Church Patronage (Scotland) Act 1874 (c.82)	In section 8, the words from ", or the right to teind" to the end.
Conveyancing (Scotland) Act 1874 (c.94)	In section 3, the definitions of "Estate in land" and of "Superior" and "superiority" in the definition of "heritable securities" and "securities", the words ", and shall also, when used in this Act, include real burdens and securities by way of ground annual" and the definitions of "Infeftment", "Feu" and "feu-duty" and "Casualties".
	Sections 4 to 8.
	In section 10 (as saved by section 37(1)(d) of the Succession (Scotland) Act 1964), the words "neither infeft nor served, but", "by virtue of this Act,", "and assignation" and from "Such petition" to the end.
	Sections 14 to 26.
	In section 29, the words "under this Act, and no other decree, instrument, or conveyance".
	Section 30.
	In section 35, the word "joint" and the words from ", as an assignation" to the end.
	In section 36, the words from ", with a holding" to the end.
	Section 37.
	Sections 48 and 49.
	In section 51, the words "production to any notary public of the" the words "the production to such notary of" and the words from ", and it shall not" to the end.
	Sections 52, 53, 57 and 58.
	In section 59, the words "shall apply to lands held of the Crown and of the Prince, in the same way as to lands held of a subject superior, but".
	Section 60.
	Schedules A to C.
	Schedule D (being the form of memorandum of allocation of feu-duty; and not that Schedule D substituted for Schedule O by section 8(1) of the Conveyancing (Scotland) Act 1924).
	Schedules F and G.
	Schedule L.
	In Schedule M, the words from ", e.g.]," to "or as the case may be".
	Schedule N.
Entail Amendment (Scotland) Act 1875 (c.61)	The whole Act.

Enactment	Extent of Repeal
United Parishes (Scotland) Act 1876 (c.11)	The whole Act.
Writs Execution (Scotland) Act 1877 (c.40)	In section 6, the words "upon a warrant of registration".
Entail Amendment (Scotland) Act 1878 (c.28)	The whole Act.
Settled Land Act 1882 (c.38)	The whole Act.
Entail (Scotland) Act 1882 (c.53)	The whole Act.
Conveyancing (Scotland) Acts (1874 and 1879) Amendment Act 1887 (c.69)	Sections 1, 3 and 4.
	In section 5, the words "The production to any notary public of" "expeding a notarial instrument, or otherwise" and from " and it shall not" to the end.
Judicial Factors (Scotland) Act 1889 (c.39)	In section 6, the words "the Entail (Scotland) Act, 1882,".
Universities (Scotland) Act 1889 (c.55)	In section 24, the words ", without prejudice to the rights of Her Majesty as superior of the said garden and buildings, and to the rights of any subject superior in and to the said garden and buildings,".
Settled Land Act 1890 (c.69)	The whole Act.
Registration of Certain Writs (Scotland) Act 1891 (c.9)	The whole Act.
Heritable Securities (Scotland) Act 1894 (c.44)	In section 7, the words "disponed in security", where they occur for the second time.
	Sections 8 to 10.
	In section 12, the word ", eight,".
	Sections 14 to 17.
	Schedule (D.).
Improvement of Land Act 1899 (c.46)	The whole Act.
Ecclesiastical Assessments (Scotland) Act 1900 (c.20)	The whole Act.
Entail (Scotland) Act 1914 (c.43)	In section 2, the words "and any clause of consent to registration in the register of entails" and the provisos.
	Sections 3 to 8.
	In section 10, the words ", unless the contrary intention appears," and ", and the words "heir of entail" shall include the institute".
Feudal Casualties (Scotland) Act 1914 (c.48)	The whole Act.
Land Settlement (Scotland) Act 1919 (c.97)	Section 4.
Duplicands of Feu-duties (Scotland) Act 1920 (c.34)	The whole Act.
Trusts (Scotland) Act 1921 (c.58)	In section 4(1), paragraph (b).
	In section 6, the words from "sell subject to" to "be lawful to".
	In section 12(1), the words from "on any charge or" to "1899, or".
	Section 13.
Agricultural Credits Act 1923 (c.34)	Section 3(4) and (5).

Enactment	Extent of Repeal
	In section 5, in paragraph (a), the definitions of "freehold or copyhold land", "mortgage", "devisee" and "incumbrance" and paragraph (b).
Conveyancing (Scotland) Act 1924 (c.27)	In section 2(1)(b), the words from "real burdens" to "them, and".
	In section 3, the words "last infeft or".
	In section 4, in subsection (2), the words "by infeftment" in subsection (3), the words from ", or in the case" to "that Schedule" and in subsection (4), the words ", or in the case of a ground annual in or as nearly as may be in the terms of Form No. 6 of that Schedule" and from "And on such notice" to the end.
	In section 5, in subsection (2)(a), the words "infeft or uninfeft, or" and in subsection (3)(a), the words "last infeft or".
	Section 6.
	In section 8, subsection (2).
	Sections 10 to 13.
	In section 19, the words "or fee".
	Sections 20 and 23.
	In section 24, the words ", including power of sale and other rights under a bond and disposition in security," and ", and such forms shall have the same force and effect as the corresponding forms prescribed by the Registration of Leases (Scotland) Act 1857," in paragraph (1) of the proviso, the words from ", for "infeft"" to the end; and in paragraph (5) of the proviso, the words from "by notarial instrument" to "law and practice".
	Sections 25, 26 and 28 to 39.
	In section 40(1), the words "feu-duty, ground-annual, stipend," and "feu-duty and casualties, ground-annual, stipend or".
	Sections 42 and 43.
	In section 49, subsection (1).
	In Schedule B, in Form No. 3, the words "last infeft therein, or" and Forms Nos. 4 and 6.
	Schedules F to H and the Notes to Schedule F.
	Schedules K to N and the Notes to Schedule K.
Church of Scotland (Property and Endowments) Act 1925 (c.33)	Part I.
	In section 22, the word "feuing," and in subsection (3), the word "feu,".
	Section 27.
	In section 28, in subsection (3)(b), the words from ", to the same effect" to the end; and subsections (6) to (8).

Enactment	Extent of Repeal
	In section 30(3), in paragraph (c), the words from ", whether as" to "in place of the minister" in paragraph (e), the words "feuduties and Government or other" and from "under or in pursuance" to "made by a minister" and paragraph (f).
	Section 31.
	In section 34, in subsection (1), in paragraph (b), the words "and certified by the Clerk of Teinds", and paragraph (e); subsection (3); and in subsection (4)(iii) the words "feuduties, ground annuals, bonds of annual rent, or other", "with the sanction of the Court of Teinds" and "or payment of the feu-duty thereon".
	In section 35(7), the words "uninfeft or infeft".
	In section 36, the proviso.
	In section 37, the words "heritor or other".
	Sections 39 to 41.
	In section 42, the words from ", and to the teinds" to the end.
	Sections 45 and 46.
	In section 47, in subsection (1), in the definition of "Stipend", the words ", including any allowance for communion elements payable by heritors out of teinds" and subsections (2) and (3).
	Schedules 1 to 7.
Agricultural Credits (Scotland) Act 1929 (c.13)	In section 6(2), the words "or to the superior of the lands occupied by the society", "or superior" and "or feuduty".
Church of Scotland (Property and Endowments) Amendment Act 1933 (c.44)	In section 7, paragraph (ii) of the proviso; and the word "and" immediately preceding that paragraph.
	In section 8(1), the words ", or any obligation at common law for payment of the stipend or part of the stipend of the parish being a parish quoad omnia".
	In section 9, subsections (1) and (2); and in subsection (3), the words "or take in feu" and "or feu-duty".
	Sections 10 and 11.
Harbours, Piers and Ferries (Scotland) Act 1937 (c.28)	In section 31(1), in the definition of "owner", the words "deed of entail or other".
Conveyancing Amendment (Scotland) Act 1938 (c.24)	Sections 6 and 8.
Requisitioned Land and War Works Act 1945 (c.43)	In section 60(4), the words "the dominium utile or, in the case of land other than feudal land,".

Enactment	Extent of Repeal
Coal Industry Nationalisation Act 1946 (c.59)	In section 64, in subsection (2), the words ", and does not include any stipend"; and subsection (3).
Requisitioned Land and War Works Act 1948 (c.17)	In section 18(4), the words "the dominium utile or, in the case of land other than feudal land,".
Public Registers and Records (Scotland) Act 1948 (c.57)	In section 1(2), the words ", the Register of Entails".
National Parks and Access to the Countryside Act 1949 (c.97)	In section 114(1), the words "and as respects Scotland has the meaning assigned to it by section twenty-six of this Act".
Long Leases (Scotland) Act 1954 (c.49)	Part I. Section 30. The Schedules.
Town and Country Planning (Scotland) Act 1954 (c.73)	Section 69.
Church of Scotland (Property and Endowments) (Amendment) Act 1957 (c.30)	The whole Act.
Land Drainage (Scotland) Act 1958 (c.24)	In section 18(1), in the definition of "owner", paragraph (a).
Opencast Coal Act 1958 (c.69)	In section 52, in subsection (2), in the definitions of "freehold interest" and "owner", the words "of the dominium utile" and subsections (6) to (8).
Town and Country Planning (Scotland) Act 1959 (c.70)	In section 27(5)(d), the words ", feu duty". In section 44, the words "such an interest in", "dominium utile in the" and "feu duty, any ground annual and any". In section 54, subsection (7).
Trustee Investments Act 1961 (c.62)	In Schedule 1, Part II, in paragraph 14, the words ", and in feu-duties or ground annuals in Scotland".
Land Compensation (Scotland) Act 1963 (c.51)	In section 20, in subsection (1), the words "the dominium utile in", in both places where they occur; in subsection (2), the words "feu-duty, or ground annual or other" and "(not being stipend or standard charge in lieu of stipend)" in subsection (7), the words "dominium utile in any" and in subsection (8), the words "the dominium utile in". In section 27(3), the words "and that interest is the dominium utile of the land,", "feu-duty or ground annual or other" and "(not being stipend or standard charge in lieu of stipend)". In section 28, in paragraph (e), the words "the dominium utile of" and, in both places where they occur, "feu-duty or" and in paragraph (f), the words "the dominium utile of". Section 45(8) and (9). In Schedule 2, in paragraph 2(2), the words "the superior of, and".

Enactment	Extent of Repeal
Harbours Act 1964 (c.40)	In section 57(1), in the definition of "owner", in paragraph (a), the words ", if the land is feudal property, the proprietor of the dominium utile or, if the land is not feudal property,".
Succession (Scotland) Act 1964 (c.41)	In section 18, subsection (1).
Gas Act 1965 (c.36)	In section 28(1), in the definition of "owner", in paragraph (a), the words ", if the land is feudal property, the proprietor of the dominium utile or, if the land is not feudal property,".
Forestry Act 1967 (c.10)	In section 34(3), the words "the proprietor of the dominium utile or, in the case of land other than feudal land, is".
	In section 49, subsection (3).
Countryside (Scotland) Act 1967 (c.86)	In section 6, in each of subsections (1)(a) and (2), the word "feu,"..
	In each of sections 24(1) and 25(1), the word "feu,".
Law Reform (Miscellaneous Provisions) (Scotland) Act 1968 (c.70)	In section 18(2), paragraph (c).
Mines and Quarries (Tips) Act 1969 (c.10)	In section 36(3)(b)(i), the words "the dominium utile or, in the case of land not held on feudal tenure, the proprietor, of".
Conveyancing and Feudal Reform (Scotland) Act 1970 (c.35)	Sections 3 to 6.
	In section 9(8)(c), the words "feuduty, ground annual,".
	In section 12(1), the words "having right to that interest, but".
	In section 30(2), the definition of "infeft".
	Sections 33 to 35.
	Section 39.
	In section 41(1), the words "of the interest".
	In section 43(1), the definition of "the Act of 1894".
	Section 49.
	In the Notes to Schedule 2, in each of notes 2 and 3, the words "ground annual or".
	In Schedule 3, in condition 10(3), the words "feuduties, ground annuals or, as the case may be,".
	In Schedule 8, paragraphs 2, 3, 7 to 14, 16 and 17, 18 to 22, 24 and 26 to 30.
Agriculture Act 1970 (c.40)	In section 33, subsection (5).
Prescription and Limitation (Scotland) Act 1973 (c.52)	In section 15(1), the definition of "interest in land".
	In Schedule 1, in paragraph 1(a), heads (iii) and (iv); and in paragraph 2(f), the words "terce, courtesy,".
Land Tenure Reform (Scotland) Act 1974 (c.38)	Part I, except section 2.
	In section 2, the words "(other than feuduty)"

Enactment	Extent of Repeal
	and "a payment of teind, stipend or standard charge,".
	Sections 14 and 15.
	In section 22, the words "held of the Crown and of the Prince and Steward of Scotland, and to land in which there is any other interest".
	In section 23(1), the words "ground annual or other".
	Schedules 1 to 4.
Offshore Petroleum Development (Scotland) Act 1975 (c.8)	In section 14(1), the word "superior,".
	In section 20, in subsection (2), in the definition of "Crown interest", the words "estate or" and in subsection (3), the words "estate or".
Scottish Development Agency Act 1975 (c.69)	In section 9(1)(a), the word "feu,".
	In section 11(1), the word "superior,".
Land Registration (Scotland) Act 1979 (c.33)	In section 3, in subsection (3), paragraph (c); in subsection (4), paragraph (b).
	In section 6(3), the words "over-feuduty or" in both places where they occur.
	In section 12, in subsection (3)(m), the words "a superior, a creditor in a ground annual or", "the feu writ, the contract of ground annual or", ", as the case may be,", "superior, creditor or" and, in both places where they occur, "feuduty, ground annual or" and in subsection (4)(a), the words "over-feuduty or".
	In section 16, subsection (2); and in subsection (3)(b) the words "feuduties, ground annuals," and "and, in the case of a grant of land in feu, of all feuduties payable by the grantor to his superiors from and after the date of entry".
	In section 20, in subsection (3), paragraph (ii), and the word " and" immediately preceding that paragraph; in subsection (6), the words ", and all such feuduties, ground annuals or other periodical payments as are mentioned in subsection (3)(ii) above" and subsection (8)(a)(ii).
	In section 28(1), the definition of "feu".
Ancient Monuments and Archaeological Areas Act 1979 (c.46)	In section 18(4), the words "or heir of entail".
	In section 57(1), the words "of the dominium utile,".
Slaughter of Animals (Scotland) Act 1980 (c.13)	In section 1, the word "feu,".
Education (Scotland) Act 1980 (c.44)	In each of sections 20(1)(a) and 22(1)(a), the word "feu,".
Water (Scotland) Act 1980 (c.45)	In section 20, the word "feu,".

Enactment	Extent of Repeal
	In section 65, in subsection (5), the word "estates," and paragraph (a); and in subsection (8), the words "or rentcharge".
	In Schedule 4, in paragraph 8, the words "feuduties, ground annuals,".
Companies Act 1985 (c.6)	In section 396(1)(a)(ii) or (if section 92 of the Companies Act 1989 has not come into force by the date on which, subject to paragraph 46(3) of schedule 12 to this Act, that schedule and this schedule come into force) in section 410(4)(a), the words ", ground annual".
	In Schedule 4, in paragraph 93, the words "is the proprietor of the dominium utile or, in the case of land not held on feudal tenure," and " and the reference to ground-rents, rates and other outgoings includes feu-duty and ground annual".
	In Schedule 9, in paragraph 86, the words "is the proprietor of the dominium utile or, in the case of land not held on feudal tenure," and " and the reference to ground-rents, rates and other outgoings includes a reference to feu-duty and ground annual".
Insolvency Act 1986 (c.45)	In Schedule 1, in paragraph 2, the word "feu,".
	In Schedule 2, in paragraph 2, the word "feu,".
Debtors (Scotland) Act 1987 (c.18)	In section 15(1), in the definition of "adjudication for debt", paragraph (b) and the word "or" immediately preceding that paragraph.
	In section 99(1), the words "or superior's" and "or feuduty".
	In section 101, the words "(other than an action under section 23(5) of the Conveyancing (Scotland) Act 1924)".
Housing (Scotland) Act 1987 (c.26)	In section 125(2), the words "of the superior of whom such owner holds, and".
	Section 132(1). In section 175(1), the words "superior or".
	Section 334.
	In section 338(1), the definitions of "sell" and "sale" and of "superior".
Income and Corporation Taxes Act 1988 (c.1)	In section 15(1), in Schedule A, in paragraph 1(4)(b), the words ", ground annuals and feu duties".
	In section 119(3), in the definition of "rent", the word ", feuduty".
Self-Governing Schools etc. (Scotland) Act 1989 (c.39)	In section 39(4)(a), the words "an interest in".
	In section 80(1), the definition of "interest in land".
Enterprise and New Towns (Scotland) Act 1990 (c.35)	In section 10(1), the word "superior,".
	In section 36(2), the words "estate or".

Enactment	Extent of Repeal
Natural Heritage (Scotland) Act 1991 (c.28)	In section 22(1), in the definition of "land", the word "estate,".
Coal Mining Subsidence Act 1991 (c.45)	In section 52(1), in the definition of "owner", paragraph (b).
	In Schedule 1, in paragraph 2(6), the definition of "incumbrance".
	In Schedule 2, in paragraph 3(2), head (b); and in paragraph 4(2)(b), the words "an entail or".
	In Schedule 6, in paragraph 1(5), the words ", but do not include references to an interest as a superior only".
Agricultural Holdings (Scotland) Act 1991 (c.55)	In section 74, the words "estate or" and "dominium utile of the".
	In section 75, in subsection (1), the words "dominium utile of the" and in subsection (3), the words "dominium utile of the" and "absolute".
Crofters (Scotland) Act 1993 (c.44)	In section 16, in subsection (3), the words "estates or" and subsection (7).
	In section 17(3), paragraph (a); the words ", or (b)" and in paragraph (b) the word "other".
	In section 19(4), paragraph (a); and, in each of paragraphs (b) and (c), the words "otherwise than in feu".
Coal Industry Act 1994 (c.21)	In section 10(7), paragraph (b) and the word "and" immediately preceding that paragraph.
Value Added Tax Act 1994 (c.23)	In section 96(1), in the definition of "fee simple", in paragraph (a), the words "estate or interest of the proprietor of the dominium utile or, in the case of land not held on feudal tenure, the estate or".
Town and Country Planning (Scotland) Act 1997 (c.8)	In section 191, subsection (9).
	In section 272(2), in paragraph (b), the word "superior,".
	In section 277, in subsection (1), in the definition of "disposal", the words ", except in section 191(9)," and in paragraph (a) of the definition of "heritable security", the words "a security by way of ground annual and" and subsection (8).
	In Schedule 15, in paragraph 7, the words "feuduty, ground annual or" and in paragraph 34, the words "a feuduty, ground annual,".
Planning (Listed Buildings and Conservation Areas) (Scotland) Act 1997 (c.9)	In section 81, subsection (7).

<small>AMENDMENT</small>
1. As amended by the Title Conditions (Scotland) Act 2003 (asp 9), Sch.15 (effective April 4, 2003).

PART 2

REPEALS RELATING TO THE NATIONAL TRUST FOR SCOTLAND

National Trust for Scotland Order Confirmation Act 1935 (c.ii)	In the Order contained in the Schedule, in section 4(2), the word "feu" and, in section 6(2), the words "notarial instrument or".
National Trust for Scotland Order Confirmation Act 1947 (c.xxxviii)	In the Order contained in the Schedule, in section 3(a), the words from "feu duties" to "any".

LEASEHOLD CASUALTIES (SCOTLAND) ACT 2001

(asp 5)

[April 12, 2001]

An Act of the Scottish Parliament to provide for the extinction of leasehold casualties; for the payment of compensation on their extinction; for irritancy provisions in certain leases of land to be void; for the disapplication, in relation to certain leases, of the rule of law entitling a landlord in certain circumstances to terminate a lease; and for connected purposes.

INTRODUCTION AND GENERAL NOTE
On February 26, 1967 the then Secretary of State for Scotland asked the Scottish Law Commission to consider the law on leasehold casualties and to advise on possible abolition. Although leasehold tenure is a significant feature of land law in England and Wales, it only features in a few areas in Scotland. In these areas titles are commonly held on long leases, the period varying, but generally being between terms of 700–999 years. Some of these leases contained casualties which could be of a fixed figure of one year's ground rent or tackduty or of an unascertained figure such as one full year's market rent at the time the casualty was incurred. Casualties in feudal writs were effectively abolished by the Feudal Casualties (Scotland) Act 1914. Casualties unlike a periodic payment such as feu duty or ground rent are payable on the occurrence of a particular event such as the entry of an heir or a singular successor. The Feudal Casualties (Scotland) Act 1914 did provide that the Court of Session could by Act of Sederunt apply the redemption scheme for feudal casualties to leasehold casualties but this power has never been exercised. It has been incompetent to create leasehold casualties since the coming into effect of the Land Tenure Reform (Scotland) Act 1974 (s.16). Indeed it has been incompetent to grant leases over domestic property for periods in excess of 20 years by virtue of the same Act (ss 8–10). Many practitioners took the view that casualties in long leases could be ignored probably on the mistaken assumption that they had been abolished in 1914. In many cases, the landlords could not be traced and where the landlords were still in existence, very often they did not bother to collect small amounts of ground rent or tackduty nor enforce any of the conditions of the lease. Matters were to change when certain landlords sold their interests to firms of property speculators who enforced the conditions of the leases including the casualties. This caused some publicity and there was pressure for urgent reform. The Scottish Law Commission issued a final report on April 30, 1998 (Scot Law Com no.165). Because of the advent of devolution, however, it was left to the Scottish Parliament to pass the necessary legislation. A private member's bill (the first to be introduced) was the vehicle chosen and since the measure was regarded as non-partisan it received full support. After some amendment the bill received Royal Assent on April 12, 2001. It contains 11 sections and 2 schedules. Section 1 deals with the abolition of leasehold casualties, sections 2 and 3 with a limited compensation for landlords, Section 4 with prescription, section 5 and 6 with irritancies, section 7 with arrears of

casualty and sections 9–11 with transitional matters and interpretations. The schedules provide a table of multipliers and a method for calculating the compensation.

Extinction of leasehold casualties

1.—(1) In a relevant lease (that is to say, in a lease of land granted before 1st September 1974 for a period of not less than one hundred and seventy-five years), any provision which stipulates for payment of a casualty is void; and, accordingly, any such payment which would, but for this subsection, have fallen due on or after the relevant day shall not be exigible.

(2) In subsection (1) above, any reference to a payment falling due shall be construed, in a case where the provision in the relevant lease stipulates for payment to be deferred until the death of the last person to pay a casualty, as a reference to its falling due on the date of death of that person.

(3) This section shall be deemed to have come into force on the relevant day.

GENERAL NOTE

Section 1 provides that in a lease of land granted before September 1, 1974 for a period of not less than 175 years, any provision which stipulates for a payment of a casualty is void and accordingly any such casualty payment falling due after the relevant day is not exigible. Where the casualty stipulates for payment to be deferred until the death of the last person to pay such a casualty, then the date of falling due shall be the date of the death of that person. Although the act received Royal Assent on April 12, 2001, the abolition provisions are retrospective since the relevant day is defined in section 10 as May 10, 2000 which was the date of introduction of the bill. The fear of course was that landlords might, having been alerted to the likely abolition of leasehold casualties, take steps to collect the casualties or otherwise enforce provisions of the lease by irritancy while the bill was in progress.

Landlord's right to require compensation in respect of extinction of casualty

2.—(1) Where a casualty is extinguished by virtue of section 1 of this Act, a landlord may, not later than one year after the day on which this Act received Royal Assent, give written notice to the tenant—

(a) requiring the tenant to pay to him compensation calculated in accordance with section 3 of this Act; and

(b) specifying the amount of compensation required as calculated by him; and the tenant shall be liable to pay such compensation.

(2) Any error in a calculation under paragraph (b) of subsection (1) above shall not affect the validity of the notice under that subsection.

(3) For the purposes of this section, "tenant" means the person who, on the relevant day, has the interest of tenant in the relevant lease.

GENERAL NOTE

The approach to compensation which is adopted in the act is the same as that adopted in the Abolition of Feudal Tenure, etc (Scotland) Act 2000. Nominal compensation for landlords is the order of the day. Section 2 provides that where a casualty is extinguished the landlord may, not later than one year after Royal Assent, give written notice to the tenant requiring payment of compensation calculated in accordance with section 3. The notice must specify the amount of compensation due and when the notice is served the tenant is liable to pay. A mistake in the calculation of the compensation will not affect the validity of the notice. The tenant is the person who on May 10, 2000 held the interest of tenant under the lease in question. What should be noted here is that the abolition of leasehold casualties in terms of section 1 on May 10, 2000 does not of itself trigger an obligation on the part of the tenant to pay compensation. If the landlord has not served the appropriate notice by April 12, 2002 the right to compensation will be lost.

Calculation of compensation

3.—(1) Subject to subsection (2) below, where by virtue of section 2(1) of this Act a tenant is liable to pay compensation, the amount payable shall be—

(a) in a case where—
    (i) a period of eighty or more years of the relevant lease is unexpired on the relevant day; and
    (ii) the lease stipulated for payment of a casualty of an unvarying amount at fixed and regularly recurring intervals of nineteen, twenty, twenty-one, twenty-five or, as the case may be, thirty years,
the product of the amount of the casualty and the multiplier obtained from the Table of Multipliers in schedule 1 to this Act (the reference in the first column of that table to the relevant period being a reference to the period (if any) between the relevant day and the date on which the casualty would, but for this Act, next be payable);

(b) in a case where—
    (i) sub-paragraph (ii), but not sub-paragraph (i), of paragraph (a) above is satisfied; or
    (ii) the relevant lease stipulated for payment of a casualty of an unvarying amount at fixed and regularly recurring intervals other than any interval mentioned in sub-paragraph (ii) of that paragraph,
the product of the amount of the casualty and the multiplier obtained in accordance with schedule 2 to this Act;

(c) in a case where the relevant lease stipulated for–
    (i) payment of a casualty on, or by reference to, the entry of an assignee; and
    (ii) the payment to be made at any time other than on the death of the person who last paid a casualty,
the product of the amount of the casualty and 0.75;

(d) in a case where the relevant lease stipulated for payment of a casualty on, or by reference to—
    (i) the entry of an heir; or
    (ii) the death of any person,
the product of the amount of the casualty and 0.03; and

(e) in any other case, the sum of the discounted values as at the relevant day of the amounts which would, but for this Act, have been payable in respect of the casualty; and any dispute as to the amount payable under this paragraph shall be referred to and determined by the Lands Tribunal for Scotland.

(2) Where compensation is payable in respect of the extinction of a casualty based on the rent (other than ground rent or tack duty), or rental value, of the land held under the relevant lease, subsection (1) above shall apply subject to the following modifications–

(a) in each of paragraphs (a) to (d) of that subsection, for the words "amount of the casualty" there shall be substituted the words "amount of the ground rent or, as the case may be, tack duty payable under the relevant lease"; and

(b) in paragraph (e) of that subsection, the amounts which would have been payable shall be taken to be amounts each of which is equal to the ground rent or, as the case may be, tack duty payable under the relevant lease; but no other modification of the terms of the casualty (including any provision as to when the casualty is payable) shall be made for the purposes of this paragraph.

GENERAL NOTE

The calculation of compensation is regulated by section 3 and the schedules. The schedules are set out as tables for ease of calculation. Given the fact that the amount of compensation to be paid is very small it may be that few, if any, landlords will actually serve the appropriate notice. Where the period of 80 or more years of the lease is unexpired on May 10, 2000 and the lease stipulated for payment of a casualty of a fixed amount at fixed and regularly recurring intervals of 19, 20, 21, 25 or as the case may be 30 years, then the compensation payable is the product of the amount of the fixed casualty and the multiplier set out in schedule 1. The first column in the schedule shows a relevant period in years and that is the period (if any) between the relevant date (May 10, 2000) and the date at which the casualty would but for the abolition have been next payable. Multipliers are then set out for the various time intervals. Where the casualty is for a fixed amount at the intervals already mentioned but the period unexpired is not 80 or more years or where the fixed casualty is due at other intervals then the multiplier to be used is that to be found in schedule 2. Where the lease stipulates for a payment of a fixed casualty by reference to the entry of an assignee and the payment is to be made at any other time than the death of a person who last paid the casualty the compensation is fixed at the casualty times 0.75. Where the casualty is due on the entry of an heir or the death of a person then the compensation is the amount of the casualty time 0.03. In any other case, compensation is the sum of the discounted values at the relevant day of the amounts which would but for the act have been payable in respect of the casualty. Any dispute as to what is meant by discounted values goes to the Lands Tribunal. The Scottish Law Commission referred to this last category as being a residual category for all non-rental value casualties other then those already dealt with. This catch-all provision does not apply to full rental value casualties because sub-section (1) of section 3 is made subject to sub-section (2). It is of course the rental value casualties which cause the difficulty because they can amount to many thousands of pounds depending on the nature of the property concerned. In relation to these casualties sub-section (2) provides that the sum to be payable shall be as calculated in sub-section (1) with the modification that the words "amount of the casualty" shall be removed and the words "amount of the ground rent or as the case may be tackduty payable under the relevant lease" substituted. Accordingly, the multipliers in schedules 1 and 2 will be applied in the case of a rental value casualty not to the amount of the casualty itself but to the amount of the ground rent or tackduty. Given the fact that most ground rents or tackduties are £5 or less the amount of compensation payable in respect of rental value casualties will be small.

Prescriptive period for payment of compensation on extinction of casualty

4. In Schedule 1 to the Prescription and Limitation (Scotland) Act 1973 (c.52) (obligations affected by prescriptive periods of five years to which section 6 of that Act applies)—
   (a) after paragraph 1(a) there shall be inserted—
      "(aa) to any obligation to pay compensation by virtue of section 2 of the Leasehold Casualties (Scotland) Act 2001 (asp 5);"; and
   (b) in paragraph 2(e), after the words "paragraph 1(a)" there shall be inserted "or (aa)".

GENERAL NOTE
   Section 4 inserts a provision into schedule 1 of the Prescription and Limitation (Scotland) Act 1973 by adding an obligation to pay compensation under section 2 of the Leasehold Casualties (Scotland) Act 2001 to the list of obligations which are affected by the five year negative prescription. Accordingly, if a notice has been served by a landlord within the one year period requiring payment in terms of sections 2 and 3 but the tenant makes no payment and the landlord does not enforce payment for a period of five years, then the right to demand the compensation will go. This makes it clear that the right to demand compensation is not imprescribable as the right to casualty itself might have been; the right to compensation is not *res merae faculatis*. The starting point for the five year prescription will be the date of service of the notice.

Irritancy provisions in certain leases to be void

5.—(1) This section applies to any relevant lease—
   (a) granted before 10th August 1914; and
   (b) stipulating for payment of a ground rent, or tack duty, of not more than £150 in respect of each year.
   (2) In so far as any provision in a relevant lease to which this section applies—
   (a) purports to terminate the lease, or to entitle the landlord to terminate it, in the event of a failure of the tenant to comply with any provision in the lease; or
   (b) deems such a failure to be a material breach of contract,
that provision is void.

(3) This section shall be deemed to have come into force on the relevant day.

GENERAL NOTE

Many long leases contain irritancy provisions in respect of non-payment of tackduty and contravention of the conditions of the lease. Given the fact that many landlords were difficult to trace or did not bother to collect tackduties these irritancy provisions could cause difficulty when leasehold properties were changing hands. In some cases ridiculously small amounts of money equal to five years the tackduty were consigned in case the landlord should ever reappear. Section 5 of the Act provides, in relation to any ground lease granted before August 10, 1914 which stipulated for payment of a ground rent or tackduty of not more than £150 per annum, that any irritancy provision which purports to terminate the lease or entitles the landlord to terminate in the event of failure to comply with a provision of the lease or indeed which deems such a failure to be material breach of the lease in void. The abolition of irritancies came into force on the relevant day, May 10, 2000.

Irritancy: limited disapplication of common law

6.—(1) The rule of law entitling a landlord to terminate a lease in the event of a failure of the tenant to pay the rent due under the lease for a continuous period of two years shall not apply in relation to a relevant lease to which section 5 of this Act applies.

(2) This section shall be deemed to have come into force on 12th February 2001.

GENERAL NOTE

Any existing rule of law entitling a landlord to terminate a lease in the event of failure to pay rent for a continuous period of two years does not apply to any lease to which section 5 applies. This provision came into force on February 12, 2001. The provisions in sections 5 and 6 only apply to relevant leases as defined in Section 1(1). The lease has to be for a period of not less than 175 years and the lease must have been granted before August 10, 1914.

Liability for casualty due by former tenant not to transmit on assignation, or other transfer, of lease

7.—(1) Where—
(a) before, on or after the relevant day a relevant lease is assigned, or otherwise transferred, to a new tenant; and
(b) any casualty payable under the lease by a former tenant is, on such assignation or other transfer, due but unpaid,
the new tenant shall not be liable to pay it.

(2) Nothing in subsection (1) above shall–
(a) entitle a new tenant to recover any amount which he has paid to the landlord;
(b) affect any agreement concluded before the relevant day between a new tenant and the landlord; or
(c) prevent a landlord enforcing any decree obtained before the relevant day against a new tenant.

(3) Any reference in this section to a relevant lease being assigned, or otherwise transferred, includes a reference to the lease being partially assigned or, as the case may be, partially transferred.

(4) This section shall be deemed to have come into force on the relevant day.

GENERAL NOTE

When landlords began to pursue tenants for casualty payments one of the difficulties which arose related to casualties which would have been incurred in the past by previous tenants. Section 7 provides that if a lease has been assigned or transferred prior to May 10, 2000 and casualty was not paid, the new tenant shall have no liability. No new tenant can however recover an amount already paid nor will the section affect any agreement concluded prior to May 10, 2000 between a new tenant and the landlord. If a decree has already been obtained against a new tenant before May 10, 2000, it will still be enforceable. The provisions cover not only an assignation of the whole lease but also a partial assignation or partial transfer. This section came into force on May 10, 2000.

Transitional application of sections 5 to 7

8.—(1) Without prejudice to the generality of section 5 of this Act, that section shall apply for the purposes of any action commenced before the relevant day which concerns a provision such as is mentioned in subsection (2) of that section and in which final decree is not granted before that day.

(2) Without prejudice to the generality of section 6(1) of this Act, that section shall apply for the purposes of any action for irritancy founded on the rule of law mentioned in that section which is commenced before 12th February 2001 and in which final decree is not granted before that day.

(3) Without prejudice to the generality of section 7 of this Act, that section shall apply for the purposes of any action against a new tenant commenced before the relevant day for payment of a casualty such as is mentioned in subsection (1)(b) of that section and in which final decree is not granted before that day.

(4) For the purposes of this section "final decree" means any decree or interlocutor which—

(a) disposes of an action; and

(b) is not subject to appeal or review.

GENERAL NOTE

There was some concern that landlords might raise irritancy proceedings before the act came into force, especially given the fact that the Scottish Law Commission report had been publicised and was clearly in favour of abolition. Accordingly section 8 provides that the abolition of irritancy provisions in section 5 will apply to any action commenced before May 10, 2000 in which final decree has not been granted. So far as the provisions of section 6(1) are concerned, that section will apply to any action of irritancy founded on any existing rule of law which was commenced before February 12, 2001 and in which final decree has not been granted before that day. The provisions in relation to arrears of casualty set out in section 7 will apply for the purposes of any action against a new tenant which has commenced before May 10, 2000 in respect of which final decree has not been granted before that day. Final decree means any decree or interlocutor which disposes of the action and is not subject to appeal or review.

Saving: proceedings in respect of section 12 of Land Registration (Scotland) Act 1979

9. Nothing in this Act shall affect any proceedings in respect of a claim to indemnity under section 12 of the Land Registration (Scotland) Act 1979 (c.33) (circumstances in which person entitled to indemnification by Keeper) which have commenced, but have not been finally disposed of, before the relevant day.

GENERAL NOTE

Nothing in the Act will affect any proceedings in respect of an indemnity claim against the Keeper which has not been finally disposed of before May 10, 2000.

Interpretation

10.—(1) In this Act, unless the context otherwise requires—

"casualty" means any duplicand or other periodical or casual payment stipulated in a relevant lease to be payable by the tenant to the landlord in addition to the rent;

"lease" includes sublease;

"relevant day" means 10th May 2000; and

"relevant lease" shall be construed in accordance with section 1(1) of this Act.

(2) For the purposes of reckoning the periods mentioned in sections 1(1) and 3(1)(a)(i) of this Act—

(a) any provision in a lease (however expressed) enabling the lease to be terminated earlier than the date on which the lease would otherwise terminate shall be disregarded; and

(b) where a lease includes provision (however expressed) requiring the landlord to renew the lease, the duration of any such renewed lease shall be added to the duration of the original lease.

GENERAL NOTE

The definition of lease includes sub-lease but a relevant lease for the purposes of the act is a lease granted before September 1, 1974 for a period of not less than 175 years. For the purposes of reckoning these periods any provision in a lease enabling the lease to be terminated earlier than the natural expiry date is disregarded and where the lease includes a renewal provision which is binding on the landlord the duration of the renewed lease is added to the duration of the original lease.

Short title and Crown application

11.—(1) This Act may be cited as the Leasehold Casualties (Scotland) Act 2001.

(2) This Act binds the Crown.

SCHEDULE 1

(introduced by section 3(1)(a))

TABLE OF MULTIPLIERS

Relevant period	Multipliers for casualties payable at intervals of:				
(in years)	*19 years*	*20 years*	*21 years*	*25 years*	*30 years*
Nil or less than ½	1.196	1.174	1.155	1.102	1.060
½ but less than 1	1.140	1.119	1.102	1.050	1.011
1 but less than 2	1.087	1.067	1.051	1.002	0.964
2 but less than 3	0.988	0.970	0.955	0.910	0.876
3 but less than 4	0.898	0.882	0.869	0.827	0.796
4 but less than 5	0.816	0.802	0.789	0.753	0.724
5 but less than 6	0.743	0.729	0.718	0.683	0.659
6 but less than 7	0.673	0.662	0.651	0.621	0.598
7 but less than 8	0.613	0.602	0.592	0.564	0.544
8 but less than 9	0.557	0.548	0.540	0.514	0.496
9 but less than 10	0.506	0.497	0.490	0.467	0.449
10 but less than 11	0.461	0.453	0.446	0.425	0.409
11 but less than 12	0.418	0.411	0.404	0.385	0.371
12 but less than 13	0.381	0.374	0.369	0.351	0.338
13 but less than 14	0.346	0.340	0.335	0.319	0.308
14 but less than 15	0.314	0.309	0.305	0.289	0.279
15 but less than 16	0.285	0.281	0.276	0.263	0.254
16 but less than 17	0.261	0.256	0.252	0.240	0.231
17 but less than 18	0.236	0.233	0.229	0.218	0.210
18 but less than 19	0.215	0.212	0.207	0.199	0.191
19 but less than 20	-	0.193	0.189	0.180	0.174
20 but less than 21	-	-	0.172	0.164	0.158
21 but less than 22	-	-	-	0.148	0.143
22 but less than 23	-	-	-	0.135	0.130
23 but less than 24	-	-	-	0.123	0.118
24 but less than 25	-	-	-	0.112	0.108
25 but less than 26	-	-	-	-	0.097
26 but less than 27	-	-	-	-	0.089
27 but less than 28	-	-	-	-	0.080
28 but less than 29	-	-	-	-	0.073
29 but less than 30	-	-	-	-	0.067

SCHEDULE 2

(introduced by section 3(1)(b))

METHOD FOR CALCULATING MULTIPLIER

(1) As respects each date on which, but for this Act, a payment of the casualty would have fallen due, a value shall, subject to paragraphs 2 and 3 below, be calculated, rounded to three decimal places, in accordance with the formula—

$$\frac{1}{1.1n}$$

where n is the period, in years, between the relevant date and the date of the payment; and the sum of all the values so calculated shall be the multiplier for the purposes of section 3(1)(b) of this Act.

(2) For the purposes of paragraph 1 above, for any case where the period is—

(a) less than ½ year (or is nil), the value shall be 1;

(b) ½ but less than 1 year, the value shall be 0.953.

(3) For the purposes of reckoning n in paragraph 1 above, where the period is more than one year, n shall be the whole number of years in question (with any time in excess of that number being ignored).

GENERAL NOTE

This section contains the citation and also a statement that it binds the Crown.

¹TITLE CONDITIONS (SCOTLAND) ACT 2003

(asp 9)

[April 3, 2003]

NOTE

1. Only those sections specified in s.129 of this Act, as coming into force on Royal Assent (April 4, 2003) and brought into force by the Title Conditions (Scotland) Act 2003 (Commencement No.1) Order 2003 (SSI 2003/454) (effective November 1, 2003 and November 28, 2004) and Abolition of Feudal Tenure etc. (Scotland) Act 2000 (Commencement No.2) (Appointed Day) Order 2003 (SSI 2003/456) (effective November 28, 2004) are in force. Sections 71–74 of this Act are not in force to date (March 2005).

PART 2

COMMUNITY BURDENS

Meaning, creation etc.

Management of community

Variation, discharge etc.

PART 3

CONSERVATION AND OTHER PERSONAL REAL BURDENS

Conservation burdens

Rural housing burdens

Maritime burdens

Economic development burdens

Health care burdens

General

PART 4

TRANSITIONAL: IMPLIED RIGHTS OF ENFORCEMENT

Extinction of implied rights of enforcement

New implied rights of enforcement

PART 5

REAL BURDENS: MISCELLANEOUS

PART 6

DEVELOPMENT MANAGEMENT SCHEME

PART 7

SERVITUDES

Positive servitudes

Negative servitudes

The Bill for this Act of the Scottish Parliament was passed by the Parliament on 26th February 2003 and received Royal Assent on 3rd April 2003

An Act of the Scottish Parliament to make further provision as respects real burdens, servitudes and certain other obligations affecting land; to amend the law relating to the ranking of standard securities; and for connected purposes.

INTRODUCTION AND GENERAL NOTE

The Abolition of Feudal Tenure etc. (Scotland) Act 2000 ("the 2000 Act") received Royal Assent on June 9, 2000. The main provisions of that Act relating to the abolition of the feudal system came into effect on the second appointed day, November 28, 2004. That Act was the first step in a fundamental reform of the Scottish Law of land tenure. Effectively, it abolishes the entire system whereby land in Scotland is held by a vassal on perpetual tenure from a superior introducing a system of simple or, to use a more contentious term, absolute ownership. One of the questions which arose during the discussions which led up to the enactment of the Abolition Act was what to do with real burdens and conditions. On one view real burdens and conditions were essentially a feature of the feudal system whereby land was granted in return for certain services. The superior was the focal point of the feudal system and the party with the primary title to enforce these conditions. Accordingly, it would have made some sense to abolish real burdens and conditions with the feudal system. The view which was taken, however, was that real burdens and conditions did have a valuable role to play in any system of land tenure. Indeed, they do feature in land tenure systems in other jurisdictions although they tend to be known as land covenants. Once the policy decision was taken to retain real burdens, a new legislative framework had to be put in place to cater for them in a non-feudal system. The Title Conditions (Scotland) Act 2003 is that legislative framework and it is the second part of the Scottish Executive's programme of property law reform. In terms of s.117, the Act, apart from certain sections, came into effect on the appointed day. The appointed day was November 28, 2004 so there was a seamless progression from a feudal system of land tenure to a non-feudal system. Sections 63, 66, 67, 86 and 88 except in so far as it inserts sub-para.(ab)(ii) into para.1 of Sch.1 to the Prescription and Limitation (Scotland) Act 1973, Pt 9 for the purposes of any application under ss.107(5), 111, 113, 114, 117, 118, 122–124, 126, 127, 128(3), Schs 12, 13 and in Sch.14: paras 7(1), (3) and (6) came into force on the day after Royal Assent (April 3, 2003). Parts 3 and 6 and ss.95–98 are now in force. Other provisions which came into force on the day after Royal Assent are s.129 in so far as it relates to paras 7(1), (3) and (5) of Sch.14, s.129 in so far as it relates to the 2000 Act, Sch.15 in so far as it relates to the 2000 Act and Pt 1 in so far as is necessary for the purposes of Pt 3 and s.63. Part 6, sections 71–74 (Development Management Scheme) are not in force as at March 2005.

The genesis of the Act is the report of the Scottish Law Commission on real burdens (*Real Burdens*, Scot. Law Comm. no.181 October 2000). A draft Bill was annexed to the report. Despite the fact that there had been an extensive consultation process prior to the publication of the report the Scottish Executive embarked on a worthwhile but more restrictive consultation process before introducing their own bill. The Act contains 129 sections and 15 Schedules. Part 1 of the Act re-enacts and redefines real burdens and the law relating to enforceability and interpretation. It should be noted that in terms of s.119(10) most of the Act is retrospective in that, unless a contrary intention appears, or unless otherwise specifically provided in the Act, the provisions apply to all real burdens whenever created. Thus, for example, the provisions relating to how real burdens are to be interpreted (ss.2(5) and (14)) may alter the way in which courts interpret real burdens created prior to November 28, 2004. Part 2 of the Act introduces the notion of community burdens. Part 3 of the Act provides for conservation burdens, (introduced by the 2000 Act in relation to existing feudal burdens), and other personal real burdens such as rural housing burdens, economic development burdens and healthcare burdens. In many ways this is a legislative compromise because a personal real burden is of course a contradiction in terms. Part 4 is an attempt to deal with the vexed question of implied third party rights of enforcement (*ius quaesitum tertio*). One of the difficulties of reform in this area was that the law was so confused that no-one could really understand it. There was also a policy question over whether or not the Act should extend rights to enforce burdens to neighbouring proprietors who might not have had a third party right to enforce in the past. Part 5 contains certain miscellaneous provisions including provisions dealing with manager burdens and the power to dismiss and appoint a manager. Non-feudal irritancies are also abolished in terms of s.67 and this provision comes into effect the day after Royal Assent as did the corresponding provision in relation to feudal irritancies in s.53 of the 2000 Act. Part 6 is a late addition to the Bill. This introduces the concept of development management schemes. Part 7 reforms the law of servitudes. Section 76 abolishes the rule that servitudes have to be known to the law but provides that any new servitude must not be repugnant with ownership. The creation of negative servitudes is prohibited in terms of s.70 but negative servitudes can become real burdens in terms of the transitional provision in s.71. Part 8 deals with pre-emptions and reversions. The existing provisions in s.8 of the Conveyancing Amendment (Scotland) Act 1938 as amended by the Conveyancing and Feudal Reform (Scotland) Act 1970 and the Land Tenure Reform (Scotland) Act 1974, provided that an offer had to be made to the party entitled to the pre-emption. This provision, however, was honoured more in the breach than in the observance and the practice had grown up of the seller simply writing to the party entitled to the pre-emption asking whether they wished to exercise the right. As a policy matter, the Keeper of the Registers is prepared to accept a letter of declinature as evidence that the pre-emption is not being exercised. The new provisions effectively give that practice legal status by providing that the party entitled to the pre-emption can give an undertaking not to exercise it within a period set out in the undertaking. Reversions under the Schools Site Act 1841 are dealt with in terms of s.86 and that section comes into effect on Royal Assent. Part 9 recasts the jurisdiction of the Lands Tribunal in respect of the variation and discharge of title conditions repealing the original ss.1, 2 and 7 of the Conveyancing and Feudal Reform (Scotland) Act 1970. Part 10 contains certain miscellaneous provisions in relation to the Land Register and compulsory acquisition of land. Sections 106 and 107 make clear what many people have believed, namely that an acquisition of land by compulsory purchase or schedule conveyance will extinguish the burdens. Sections 96A–106 deal with various statutory amendments and miscellaneous matters. Section 117 makes clear that it shall not be competent to create a pecuniary real burden by way of a reservation in a conveyance, and s.118 provides that it shall not be competent to create a light of common interest by agreement. These two sections come into force on the day after Royal Assent. Part 11 contains the usual savings and transitional and general provisions. The schedules contain the various statutory forms brought into being by the Act and the usual statutory amendments and repeals.

The Abolition of Feudal Tenure etc. (Scotland) Act 2000 was fundamentally anti-superior. The Title Conditions (Scotland) Act 2003 is a more general piece of legislation and accordingly less controversial. It will be followed by the Tenements (Scotland) Act and a new Act dealing with land registration. It is clear that automated registration of title to land ("ARTL") will also be introduced in the near future. All in all, the new century will be an exciting one for conveyancers.

PART 1

REAL BURDENS: GENERAL

Meaning and creation

The expression "real burden"

1.—(1) A real burden is an encumbrance on land constituted in favour of the owner of other land in that person's capacity as owner of that other land.

(2) In relation to a real burden—

(a) the encumbered land is known as the "burdened property"; and

(b) the other land is known as the "benefited property".

(3) Notwithstanding subsections (1) and (2) above, the expression "real burden" includes a personal real burden; that is to say a conservation burden, a rural housing burden, a maritime burden, an economic development burden, a health care burden, a manager burden, a personal pre-emption burden and a personal redemption burden (being burdens constituted in favour of a person other than by reference to the person's capacity as owner of any land).

General Note

This section emphasises the praedial nature of a real burden. The basic definition does not alter the law as set out in the leading case of *Tailors of Aberdeen v Coutts* (1840) 1 Rob. App. 296. Section 1(3) however, does introduce an anomaly by providing that the expression "real burden" includes a personal real burden within the meaning of the Act. The Act uses the terminology of "burdened" and "benefited" property whereas the 2000 Act used the term "dominant tenement" for the purposes of reallotment of feudal burdens. In terms of s.122 (the interpretation Section) "land" is defined as including all heritable property both corporeal and incorporeal capable of being held as a separate tenement including land covered with water. Accordingly, heritable incorporeal properties such as salmon fishings and tenemental properties are included within the definition. The expression "owner" is defined in s.123 as a person who has right to the property whether or not that person has a completed title and this could include a person who has most recently acquired a right if more than one person could fall within the definition.

Affirmative, negative and ancillary burdens

2.—(1) Subject to subsection (3) below, a real burden may be created only as—

(a) an obligation to do something (including an obligation to defray, or contribute towards, some cost); or

(b) an obligation to refrain from doing something.

(2) An obligation created as is described in—

(a) paragraph (a) of subsection (1) above is known as an "affirmative burden"; and

(b) paragraph (b) of that subsection is known as a "negative burden".

(3) A real burden may be created which—

(a) consists of a right to enter, or otherwise make use of, property; or

(b) makes provision for management or administration,

but only for a purpose ancillary to those of an affirmative burden or a negative burden.

(4) A real burden created as is described in subsection (3) above is known as an "ancillary burden".

(5) In determining whether a real burden is created as is described in subsection (1) or (3) above, regard shall be had to the effect of a provision rather than to the way in which the provision is expressed.

Burdens are categorised into distinct types. Affirmative burdens impose a positive obligation on the owner of the burdened property to do something. This would include an obligation to contribute towards some cost. A negative burden is a burden which prohibits the burdened proprietor from carrying out certain activities. An ancillary burden is a burden which consists of a right to enter or make use of property or makes provision for management where these purposes are tied to an affirmative or negative burden. An obvious example of this would be a provision in a deed of conditions relating to the appointment of a factor. This is neither positive nor negative; it is ancillary to the positive obligation to maintain the common property of the tenement or the development. Under the existing law a real burden was always construed strictly in accordance with the presumption of freedom. This led to what has been described as a malign or malignant construction. Section 2(5) provides for some relaxation and this should be read together with s.14 which provides in relation to construction of real burdens that they are to be construed in the same manner as other provisions of deeds which relate to land and are intended for registration. Although the provisions of the Act apply for the most part to all real burdens, a real burden which was void from uncertainty prior to the Act will not revive by value of this provision.

Other characteristics

3.—(1) A real burden must relate in some way to the burdened property.

(2) The relationship may be direct or indirect but shall not merely be that the obligated person is the owner of the burdened property.

(3) In a case in which there is a benefited property, a real burden must, unless it is a community burden, be for the benefit of that property.

(4) A community burden may be for the benefit of the community to which it relates or of some part of that community.

(5) A real burden may consist of a right of pre-emption; but a real burden created on or after the appointed day must not consist of—

(a) a right of redemption or reversion; or

(b) any other type of option to acquire the burdened property.

(6) A real burden must not be contrary to public policy as for example an unreasonable restraint of trade and must not be repugnant with ownership (nor must it be illegal).

(7) Except in so far as expressly permitted by this Act, a real burden must not have the effect of creating a monopoly (as for example, by providing for a particular person to be or to appoint—

(a) the manager of property; or

(b) the supplier of any services in relation to property).

(8) It shall not be competent—

(a) to make in the constitutive deed provision; or

(b) to import under section 6(1) of this Act terms which include provision,

to the effect that a person other than a holder of the burden may waive compliance with, or mitigate or otherwise vary, a condition of the burden.

(9) Subsection (8) above is without prejudice to section 33(1)(a) of this Act.

AMENDMENT
1. As amended by the Tenements (Scotland) Act 2004 (asp 11), s.25, Sch.4, para.2 (effective October 23, 2004).

GENERAL NOTE

This section restates the existing law in relation to what is permissible in a real burden. It deals with the content of the burden. The principles relating to the constitution of real burdens were set out in the leading case of *Tailors of Aberdeen v Coutts*, 1840 1 Rob. App. 296 and subsequent cases. The praedial rule is effectively reaffirmed although the relationship between the burden and the property may be direct or indirect provided the burden is not imposed because a particular person is the owner of the burdened property. The burden must be praedial both in relation to the burdened property and the benefited property. It must not simply benefit a person because they happen to be owner of another property.

Subs.(4)

A community burden will be a real burden if it benefits the community to which it relates or some part of that community. Community burdens are defined in s.24. Pre-emptions will still be capable of being created real burdens but rights of redemption or reversion or other options to acquire created after the appointed day will not be capable of creation as real burdens. Personal pre-emption burdens and personal redemption burdens are possible, but not as burdens under this Act. These burdens can only arise as a result of the newly introduced conversion provisions in s.18A of the 2000 Act which is introduced by s.114 of the 2003 Act.

Subs.(6)

This is a restatement of the existing law although it does not make it much clearer. Obviously examples of an illegal condition would be one which prevented someone from selling their own property (other than a pre-emption) or one which contravened a statutory code, such as might be contained in the race or sex discrimination laws. Difficulty has always surrounded burdens which confer commercial benefit. These are burdens which are likely to be caught by the prohibition of a burden in unreasonable restraint of trade (see *Aberdeen Varieties Ltd v Jas. F. Donald (Aberdeen Cinemas) Ltd*, 1939 S.C. 788; 1940 S.C. (HL) 45; *Phillips v Lavery*, 1962 S.L.T. (Sh. Ct) 57; *Giblin v Murdoch*, 1979 S.L.T (Sh. Ct.) 5). In a small development of shop units it has been held that a prohibition of competing businesses could be a real burden because it protected, in the context of a very small development, a praedial as well as a commercial interest (*Co-operative Wholesale Society Ltd v Ushers Brewery*, 1975 S.L.T. (Lands Tr.) 9).

Subs.(7)

Except as expressly permitted by the Act a real burden must not have the effect of creating a monopoly. Under the provisions relating to manager burdens a temporary monopoly for a maximum of five years is permitted in certain circumstances (see ss.28 and 63). In the case of manager burdens created in deed by a local authority in a right to buy sale the period is 30 years, and in the case of manager burdens imposed under common schemes involving sheltered or retirement housing the period is three years. These periods do not run from the coming into force of the Act but from the day on which the burden is or has been created by registration.

Subs.(8)

It is the holder of the burden who must waive compliance or vary the burden apart from the rights of a majority to vary or discharge a community burden in terms of s.33(1)(a).

Creation

4.—(1) A real burden is created by duly registering the constitutive deed except that, notwithstanding section 3(4) of the 1979 Act (creation of real right or obligation on date of registration etc.), the constitutive deed may provide for the postponement of the effectiveness of the real burden to—

    (a) a date specified in that deed (the specification being of a fixed date and not, for example, of a date determinable by reference to the occurrence of an event); or

    (b) the date of registration of some other deed so specified.

(2) The reference in subsection (1) above to the constitutive deed is to a deed which—

(a) sets out (employing, unless subsection (3) below is invoked, the expression "real burden") the terms of the prospective real burden;

(b) is granted by or on behalf of the owner of the land which is to be the burdened property; and

(c) except in the case mentioned in subsection (4) below, nominates and identifies—

(i) that land;

(ii) the land (if any) which is to be the benefited property; and

(iii) any person in whose favour the real burden is to be constituted (if it is to be constituted other than by reference to the person's capacity as owner of any land).

(3) Where the constitutive deed relates, or purports to relate, to the creation of a nameable type of real burden (such as, for example, a community burden), that deed may, instead of employing the expression "real burden", employ the expression appropriate to that type.

(4) Where the constitutive deed relates to the creation of a community burden, that deed shall nominate and identify the community.

(5) For the purposes of this section, a constitutive deed is duly registered in relation to a real burden only when registered against the land which is to be the burdened property and (except where there will be no benefited property or the land in question is outwith Scotland) the land which is to be the benefited property.

(6) A right of ownership held pro indiviso shall not in itself constitute a property against which a constitutive deed can be duly registered.

[1](7) This section is subject to sections 53(3A), 73(2) and 90(8) and (8A) of this Act and is without prejudice to section 6 of this Act.

AMENDMENT

1. As amended by the Title Conditions (Scotland) Act 2003 (Consequential Provisions) Order (SSI 2003/503), Sch.1, para.7 (effective October 22, 2003) and the Tenements (Scotland) Act 2004 (asp 11), s.25, Sch.4, para.3 (effective October 23, 2004).

GENERAL NOTE

The previous law was to the effect that a real burden had to appear in the infeftment of the property and in the appropriate register at length. Normally, it would also require to appear in the dispositive clause of a deed or in a deed of conditions. All that s.4 requires is that the real burden is created in a constitutive deed which is registered. The deed, however, must be registered against the titles to both the burdened and benefited properties.

Subs.(1)

Registration is essential for the creation of a real burden and the time of creation will normally be the date of registration. However, the constitutive deed may provide that the burden will come into effect at a date specified in the deed or the date of registration of some other deed. Section 17 of the Land Registration (Scotland) Act 1979 is repealed by Sch.15 which means that the granter of a deed of conditions who wishes to postpone the creation of real burdens until an estate is developed will require to specify that the burdens are not to come into effect until a certain date.

Subs.(2)

A constitutive deed is a deed which sets out the terms of the burden using the expression "real burden" and is granted by the owner of the burdened land. It must identify the land both burdened and benefited. The term "owner" includes a party who has not completed title. So far as conservation burdens, maritime burdens and some manager burdens are concerned there may be no benefited property in which case the person in whose favour the burden is created must be identified.

Subs.(3)

In the case of a named type of burden such as a community burden the constitutive deed may instead of using the expression "real burden" employ the expression appropriate to the type. A community burden therefore may be referred to as "community burden" rather than a real burden.

Subs.(5)
This emphasises the need for registration against the titles of both burdened and benefited properties.

Subs.(6)
A burden cannot be registered against a *pro indiviso* share. This is probably the law at the moment.

Subs.(7)
This proviso is to cater for real burdens which are created by the Lands Tribunal in terms of s.90(6) and also for the special provisions for third party rights where these are related properties under s.53.

Further provision as respects constitutive deed

5.—(1) It shall not be an objection to the validity of a real burden (whenever created) that—

(a) an amount payable in respect of an obligation to defray some cost is not specified in the constitutive deed; or

(b) a proportion or share payable in respect of an obligation to contribute towards some cost is not so specified provided that the way in which that proportion or share can be arrived at is so specified.

(2) Without prejudice to the generality of subsection (1) above, such specification may be by making reference to another document the terms of which are not reproduced in the deed; but for reference to be so made the other document must be a public document (that is to say, an enactment or a public register or some record or roll to which the public readily has access).

GENERAL NOTE
This section deals with various anomalies in the existing law. The law is restated with certain changes. There has been some doubt as to whether a burden which provides that a party will be liable for a share of the cost of maintenance could be a real burden because it was effectively a burden to pay an uncertain sum of money (see *David Watson Property Management v Woolwich Equitable Building Society*, 1992 S.L.T. 430). This situation is to be contrasted with the situation where there is a burden to the effect that a proprietor or proprietors must actually maintain property and then pay a share for the cost of that maintenance. Section 5 provides that it will not be an objection to a real burden whenever created that the amount payable to defray some cost is not specified in the deed or that a proportion of share is not so specified provided the way in which that proportion or share can be arrived at is specified. The section also provides that specification may be by reference to an outside document provided that outside document is a public document such as an enactment or public register or some record or roll to which the public readily has access. Accordingly, a real burden which provides that a proprietor will pay a proportionate share of the cost of maintenance of common subjects by reference to the last rateable value in a valuation roll will be valid. This provision is retrospective and will apply to existing burdens of this type.

Further provision as respects creation

6.—(1) A real burden is created by registering against the land which is to be the burdened property a deed which—

(a) is granted by or on behalf of the owner of that land; and

(b) imports the terms of the prospective burden.

(2) "Imports" in subsection (1)(b) above means imports into itself from a deed of conditions; and importation in, or as near as may be in, the form set out in schedule 1 to this Act shall suffice in that regard.

(3) A right of ownership held pro indiviso shall not in itself constitute a property against which a deed such as is mentioned in subsection (1) above

can be duly registered. (4) This section is without prejudice to section 4 of this Act.

GENERAL NOTE

This is a transitional provision in relation to burdens created in deeds of condition registered before the appointed day. Section 32 and Sch.H of the Conveyancing (Scotland) Act 1874 are repealed in Sch.14. Burdens will of course be able to be created in terms of s.4(1) in the future. Effectively, s.6 allows a deed of conditions which excludes s.17 of the Land Registration (Scotland) Act 1979 to impose real burdens after the appointed day by importation to subsequent conveyances. This provision cannot be used to create a burden over a *pro indiviso* share.

Duration, enforceability and liability

Duration

7. Subject to any enactment (including this Act) or to any rule of law, the duration of a real burden is perpetual unless the constitutive deed provides for a duration of a specific period.

GENERAL NOTE

This section merely confirms the existing law that the duration of a real burden is perpetual unless the constitutive deed provides for a specific period. This section is subject to the termination provisions contained in ss.15–24.

Right to enforce

8.—(1) A real burden is enforceable by any person who has both title and interest to enforce it.

(2) A person has such title if an owner of the benefited property; but the following persons also have such title—

(a) a person who has a real right of lease or proper liferent in the benefited property (or has a pro indiviso share in such right);

(b) a person who—

(i) is the non-entitled spouse of an owner of the benefited property or of a person mentioned in paragraph (a) above; and

(ii) has occupancy rights in that property; and

(c) if the real burden was created as mentioned in subsection (3)(b) below, a person who was, at the time the cost in question was incurred—

(i) an owner of the benefited property; or

(ii) a person having such title by virtue of paragraph (a) or (b) above.

(3) A person has such interest if—

(a) in the circumstances of any case, failure to comply with the real burden is resulting in, or will result in, material detriment to the value or enjoyment of the person's ownership of, or right in, the benefited property; or

(b) the real burden being an affirmative burden created as an obligation to defray, or contribute towards, some cost, that person seeks (and has grounds to seek) payment of, or as respects, that cost.

(4) A person has title to enforce a real burden consisting of—

(a) a right of pre emption, redemption or reversion; or

(b) any other type of option to acquire the burdened property, only if the owner of the benefited property.

(5) In subsection (2)(b) above, "non-entitled spouse" and "occupancy rights" shall be construed in accordance with section 1 of the Matrimonial Homes (Family Protection) (Scotland) Act 1981 (c.59) (right of spouse without title to occupy matrimonial home).

(6) Subsections (2) to (5) above do not apply in relation to a personal real burden.

GENERAL NOTE

One of the great difficulties in relation to the enforcement of real burdens has been the identification the party or parties who may have both title and interest to enforce. The abolition of the feudal system may make this an even more difficult task because the focal point of the superior is removed. The purpose of this section is to identify the party who will have the right to enforce a real burden for the future.

Subs.(1)

This simply restates the existing law that a party who wishes to enforce a real burden or condition must have both title and interest to enforce. Until the abolition of the feudal system a superior's title to enforce a burden was obvious; it was the superiority title itself. The interest of a superior was presumed at least in the first instance (*Earl of Zetland v Hislop* (1882) 9 R (HL) 40).

Subs.(2)

This controversial provision allows parties other than the owner of the benefited property to enforce real burdens. The right to enforce is extended to tenants under real leases, proper liferenters in the benefited property and non-entitled spouses of the owner of the benefited property or of tenants and liferenters provided that party has occupancy rights. It should be remembered that owner is defined in s.123 as including a heritable creditor in lawful possession. Paragraph (c) contains an enabling provision in respect of former owners who will have the right to recover costs incurred when they were owners. One of the problems here is whether or not a burdened proprietor seeking some sort of consent from a benefited proprietor will also have to make enquiry as to the existence of tenants, liferenters and spouses with occupancy rights. Section 15 provides that a real burden can be discharged by registration of a deed granted by the owner of the benefited property. This means that no discharge would be required from any of these other parties. That section relates to a discharge and not to a consent to plans within the terms of the burden. Section 16 does however provide that a consent by all benefited proprietors will be sufficient, so it should not be necessary to obtain a consent from those holding subsidiary enforcement rights.

Subs.(3)

A statutory definition of interest is welcome. The question of interest or the lack of interest will of course depend on the circumstances of each individual case but generally speaking a party will have an interest if failure to comply with the burden results in material detriment to the value or enjoyment of the benefited property. There will also be an interest where the burden relates to an obligation to defray or contribute towards some cost. It is anticipated that the interest of an owner of the benefited property is likely to be more significant than the interest of someone holding some sort of subordinate right such as occupancy rights. Section 17 tends to reinforce this view. For examples see Rennie, *Land Tenure in Scotland*, 8–24.

Subs.(4)

Only owners of benefited property will be entitled to enforce rights of pre-emption, redemption or reversion or other options to acquire burdened property. Obviously only one party should be in a position to exercise rights of this type. *Pro indiviso* owners will not have independent individual rights. In the future it will not be possible to create options as opposed to pre-emptions as real burdens in terms of s.3(5).

Subs.(5)

The terms "non-entitled spouse" and "occupancy rights" have the same meanings as are attached to them in terms of s.1 of the Matrimonial Homes (Family Protection) (Scotland) Act 1981.

Subs.(6)

There are special rules in connection with personal real burdens and accordingly the requirements for title and interest are modified in these cases.

Persons against whom burdens are enforceable

9.—(1) An affirmative burden is enforceable against the owner of the burdened property.

(2) A negative burden or an ancillary burden is enforceable against—

(a) the owner, or tenant, of the burdened property; or

(b) any other person having the use of that property.

GENERAL NOTE
Affirmative burdens are only enforceable against the owner of the burdened property whereas negative or ancillary burdens can be enforced against the owner or the tenant of the burdened property or any other person having the use of that property. Obviously, one would not expect a tenant to have an obligation to erect property in terms of a real burden but that tenant should comply with negative or ancillary burdens and accordingly use of a property by a tenant in contravention of a burden should be capable of prevention by direct enforcement action against the tenant.

Affirmative burdens: continuing liability of former owner

10.—(1) An owner of burdened property shall not, by virtue only of ceasing to be such an owner, cease to be liable for the performance of any relevant obligation.

[1] (2) Subject to subsection (2A) below, a person who becomes an owner of burdened property (any such person being referred to in this section as a "new owner") shall be severally liable with any former owner of the property for any relevant obligation for which the former owner is liable.

[2] (2A) A new owner shall be liable as mentioned in subsection (2) above for any relevant obligation consisting of an obligation to pay a share of costs relating to maintenance or work (other than local authority work) carried out before the acquisition date only if—

  (a) notice of the maintenance or work—

    (i) in, or as near as may be in, the form set out in schedule 1A to this Act; and

    (ii) containing the information required by the notes for completion set out in that schedule,

  (such a notice being referred to in this section and section 10A of this Act as a "notice of potential liability for costs") was registered in relation to the burdened property at least 14 days before the acquisition date; and

  (b) the notice had not expired before the acquisition date.

[2] (2B) In subsection (2A) above—

  "acquisition date" means the date on which the new owner acquired right to the burdened property; and

  "local authority work" means work carried out by a local authority by virtue of any enactment.

(3) A new owner who incurs expenditure in the performance of any relevant obligation for which a former owner of the property is liable may recover an amount equal to such expenditure from that former owner.

(4) For the purposes of subsections (1) to (3) above, "relevant obligation" means any obligation under an affirmative burden which is due for performance; and such an obligation becomes due—

  (a) in a case where—

    (i) the burden is a community burden; and

    (ii) a binding decision to incur expenditure is made,

  on the date on which that decision is made; or

  (b) in any other case, on—

    (i) such date; or

    (ii) the occurrence of such event,

  as may be stipulated for its performance (whether in the constitutive deed or otherwise).

[2] (5) This section does not apply in any case where section 12 of the Tenements (Scotland) Act 2004 (asp 11) applies.

AMENDMENT
1. As amended by the Tenements (Scotland) Act 2004 (asp 11), s.25, Sch.4, para.4 (effective October 23, 2004).
2. Inserted by the Tenements (Scotland) Act 2004 (asp 11), s.25, Sch.4, para.4 (effective October 23, 2004).

General Note

This section restates the existing law in relation to continuing liability of former owners and clarifies it but continuing liability of a former owner is now dependent on registration of a notice under subs. (2A) where the obligation is to pay a share of costs relating to maintenance.

Subs.(1)

As a general rule the owner of the burdened property does not cease to be liable for performance of certain obligations by virtue of ceasing to be owner. In terms of s.123 the expression "owner" includes those who have not completed title. Presumably one ceases to be an owner on delivery of a conveyance for the purposes of this section.

Subs.(2)

The new owner of property may also be liable for performance of the relevant obligation. Liability appears to be joint and several.

Subs.(2A)

As is the case with tenements, a new owner is not liable for arrears of common repairs costs unless a notice has been registered. This exclusion does not apply to work carried out by a local authority.

Subs.(3)

Despite the joint and several liability, the new owner is entitled to relief from the former owner in respect of expenditure incurred in the performance of the relevant obligation.

Subs.(4)

A "relevant obligation" is any obligation under an affirmative burden which is due for performance. In the case of community burdens the obligation is due for performance on the date when a binding decision to incur expenditure is made and in any other case on such date or the occurrence of such event as is stipulated in the burden for performance.

Notice of potential liability for costs: further provision

[1] **10A.**—(1) A notice of potential liability for costs—

(a) may be registered in relation to burdened property only on the application of—

   (i) an owner of the burdened property;

   (ii) an owner of the benefited property; or

   (iii) any manager; and

(b) shall not be registered unless it is signed by or on behalf of the applicant.

(2) A notice of potential liability for costs may be registered—

(a) in relation to more than one burdened property in respect of the same maintenance or work; and

(b) in relation to any one burdened property, in respect of different maintenance or work.

(3) A notice of potential liability for costs expires at the end of the period of 3 years beginning with the date of its registration, unless it is renewed by being registered again before the end of that period.

(4) This section applies to a renewed notice of potential liability for costs as it applies to any other such notice.

(5) The Keeper of the Registers of Scotland shall not be required to investigate or determine whether the information contained in any notice of potential liability for costs submitted for registration is accurate.

(6) The Scottish Ministers may by order amend schedule 1A to this Act.

AMENDMENT

1. Inserted by the Tenements (Scotland) Act 2004 (asp 11), s.25, Sch.4, para.5 (effective October 23, 2004).

GENERAL NOTE

This section sets out the procedure for registration of a notice of potential liability for costs.

Affirmative burdens: shared liability

11.—(1) If a burdened property as respects which an affirmative burden is created is divided (whether before or after the appointed day) into two or more parts then, subject to subsections (2) and (4) below, the owners of the parts—

(a) are severally liable in respect of the burden; and

(b) as between (or among) themselves, are liable in the proportions which the areas of their respective parts bear to the area of the burdened property.

(2) "Part" in subsection (1) above does not include a part to which the affirmative burden cannot relate.

(3) In the application of subsection (1) above to parts which are flats in a tenement, the reference in paragraph (b) of that subsection to the areas of the respective parts shall be construed as a reference to the floor areas of the respective flats.

[1] (3A) For the purposes of subsection (3) above, the floor area of a flat is calculated by measuring the total floor area (including the area occupied by any internal wall or other internal dividing structure) within its boundaries; but no account shall be taken of any pertinents or any of the following parts of a flat—

(a) a balcony; and

(b) except where it is used for any purpose other than storage, a loft or basement.

(4) Paragraph (a) of subsection (1) above shall not apply if, in the constitutive deed, it is provided that liability as between (or among) the owners of the parts shall be otherwise than is provided for in that paragraph; and paragraph (b) of that subsection shall not apply if, in the constitutive deed or in the conveyance effecting the division, it is provided that liability as between (or among) them shall be otherwise than is provided for in that paragraph.

(5) If two or more persons own in common a burdened property as respects which an affirmative burden is created then, unless the constitutive deed otherwise provides—

(a) they are severally liable in respect of the burden; and

(b) as between (or among) themselves, they are liable in the proportions in which they own the property.

AMENDMENT

1. Inserted by the Tenements (Scotland) Act 2004 (asp 11), s.25, Sch.4, para.6 (effective October 23, 2004).

GENERAL NOTE

This section deals with the vexed question of shared liability where the burdened property subject to an affirmative burden is divided. The section applies whether or not the division occurred before or after the appointed day.

Subs.(1)

Basically, the owner of each subdivided part is jointly and severally liable for the performance of any affirmative burden. If one owner is forced to comply at the instigation of the party entitled to enforce then a share of the expense of compliance can be recovered from the other burdened owner or owners. Here the proportion of expense would be determined in relation to the respective surface areas of the sub-divided parts.

Subs.(2)

There will be burdens which by their nature only apply to particular parts of the burdened property. There could, for example, be a burden to the effect that there is to be erected on a particular boundary a particular type of wall. That burden could only relate to that part of the burdened property on which the wall is to be erected. Accordingly the provisions in subs.(1) do not apply to a part of the burdened property to which the affirmative burden cannot relate.

Subs.(3)

Where the subdivided parts are flats in a tenement the calculation of liability will be by reference to the respective floor areas of the flats.

Subs.(3A)

In calculating floor area no account is taken of balconies or loft or basement storage areas.

Subs.(4)

It will be possible in the constitutive deed creating the affirmative burden to provide specifically that liability will attach to particular parts of the property.

Subs.(5)

So far as common owners are concerned they are each severally liable to the party entitled to enforce the burden. Between or among themselves they are liable in the proportions in which they actually own the burdened property.

Division of benefited or burdened property

Division of a benefited property

12.—(1) Where part of a benefited property is conveyed, then on registration of the conveyance the part conveyed shall cease to be a benefited property unless in the conveyance some other provision is made, as for example—

(a) that the part retained and the part conveyed are separately to constitute benefited properties; or

(b) that it is the part retained which is to cease to be a benefited property.

(2) Different provision may, under subsection (1) above, be made in respect of different real burdens.

(3) For the purposes of subsection (1) above, any such provision as is referred to in that subsection shall—

(a) identify the constitutive deed, say where it is registered and give the date of registration;

(b) identify the real burdens; and

(c) be of no effect in so far as it relates to—

(i) a right of pre-emption, redemption or reversion; or

(ii) any other type of option to acquire the burdened property,

if it is other than such provision as is mentioned in paragraph (b) of that subsection.

(4) Subsection (1) above does not apply where—

(a) the property, part of which is conveyed, is a benefited property only by virtue of any of sections 52 to 56 of this Act;

(b) the real burdens are community burdens; or

(c) the real burdens are set out in a common deed of conditions, that is to say in a deed which sets out the terms of the burdens imposed on the part conveyed, that part being one of two or more properties on which they are or will be imposed under a common scheme.

GENERAL NOTE

Sections 12 and 13 deal with division of the benefited or burdened property. Section 12 deals with the benefited property and s.13 with the burdened property. Section 11 has of course already provided in general terms what is to happen where the burdened property is divided. It is perhaps the division of the benefited property which causes the greatest difficulty in conveyancing transactions, especially where burdens have been created in dispositions and the land owned by the original granter of the disposition containing the burden has been subdivided. The first question is whether or not every proprietor of a subdivided part has a title to enforce. This is sometimes a difficult question to answer. As often as not a view is taken that very few proprietors of subdivided parts will have an interest to enforce even if they have a title. The clarity afforded by s.12 is welcome.

Subs.(1)

Where there is a subdivision of a benefited property after the appointed day and there is registration of the conveyance, the part conveyed will cease to be a benefited property unless, in that conveyance it is stated that both the part retained and the part conveyed are separately to constitute benefited properties, or the part retained is to cease to be a benefited property. This allows a certain degree of flexibility.

Subs.(2)

This caters for the situation where particular burdens will have greater significance for either the retained area or the conveyed area.

Subs.(3)

For a specific provision to have effect the constitutive deed and the burdens must be identified in the provision. This subsection also makes it clear that it will not be possible to pass over a right to a pre-emption, redemption or reversion or any other type of option. This will require to stay with the part retained. If no provision is made in the conveyance of the part of the benefited property then the fall back position will apply namely that the right of pre-emption, redemption, reversion or option will remain with retained property.

Subs.(4)

The subdivision provisions do not apply to real burdens imposed under a common scheme under ss.52–56 nor do they apply where the real burdens are community burdens or are set out in a common deed of conditions. Where property is subject to burdens in a deed of conditions then each conveyance of a part would amount to a division of the benefited property and the strict application of the provisions could mean that property conveyed away would cease to be a benefited property. Subsection (4) addresses this problem.

Division of a burdened property

13. Where part of a burdened property is conveyed (whether before or after the appointed day), then on registration of the conveyance the part retained and the part conveyed shall separately constitute burdened properties unless the real burden cannot relate to one of the parts, in which case that part shall, on that registration, cease to be a burdened property.

GENERAL NOTE

This section applies to burdens in general, whereas s.11 applies only to affirmative burdens. If there is, for example, a burden prohibiting a particular use of the burdened property then that burden will apply to each part of the subdivided burdened property unless the burden cannot relate to one of the parts.

Construction

Construction

14. Real burdens shall be construed in the same manner as other provisions of deeds which relate to land and are intended for registration.

GENERAL NOTE

This section should be read in conjunction with s.2(5) which provides that in determining whether a real burden is created regard is to be had to the effect of the provision rather than the manner in which the provision is expressed. Section 2(5) deals with the content of a real burden; s.14 deals with the construction or interpretation of a real burden. There is sometimes confusion between the sets of principles which apply to these distinct concepts. Section 14 effectively removes any suggestion that real burdens are to be subjected to a malign construction (see Reid, *The Law of Property in Scotland*, para.415). The attitude of judges varies. In *Lothian Regional Council v Rennie*, 1991 S.L.T. 465 two judges took the view that a real burden to the effect that a party would allow sufficient water through a lade to cleanse the lade to the reasonable satisfaction of another party, was too vague to be a real burden because the reasonable satisfaction of one person might be different from the reasonable satisfaction of another. A third judge however took the view that the burden was perfectly well phrased and capable of interpretation and enforcement. Presumably the effect of this section will be that real burdens will be subject to the same type of interpretation as is currently applied to servitudes (see *MacLean v Marwhirn Developments Ltd*, 1976 S.L.T. (Notes) 47).

Discharge

15.—(1) A real burden is discharged as respects a benefited property by registering against the burdened property a deed of discharge granted by or on behalf of the owner of the benefited property.

(2) In subsection (1) above, "discharged" means discharged—

(a) wholly; or

(b) to such extent as may be specified in the deed of discharge.

GENERAL NOTE

This section merely confirms the existing law whereby a real burden can be expressly discharged in a deed granted by the owner of the benefited property. The deed can relate to the burden in its entirety or to a limited extent. A discharge of a burden generally prohibiting the carrying on of any trade business or profession in a dwelling-house could, for example, be discharged in total or only to the extent of allowing the owner of the burdened property to give piano lessons. It should be noted that although in terms of s.8(2), parties other than the owner of the benefited property, such as tenants or holders of occupancy rights, can enforce burdens, the owner can discharge a burden apparently without reference to the rights of any of these other parties to enforce. These subordinate rights depend for their existence on the owner's right to enforce and when that has been discharged the subordinate rights are discharged also. The definition of "owner" as including a person who has right to property but no completed title should be borne in mind (s.123). If the benefited property is owned in common then the discharge will require to be granted by all *pro indiviso* proprietors. As regards to the form of the discharge, although a minute of waiver would normally be granted in favour of a person there is no such requirement to identify a grantee (s.69(1)). A deed of discharge can be registered by an owner of the burdened property or by any other person against whom the real burden is enforceable (s.69(2)). No particular form is specified in the Act, but the discharge must be registered.

Acquiescence

16.—(1) Where—

(a) a real burden is breached in such a way that material expenditure is incurred;

(b) any benefit arising from such expenditure would be substantially lost were the burden to be enforced; and

(c) in the case of—

(i) a burden other than a conservation burden, economic development burden or health care burden, the owner of the benefited property (if any) has an interest to enforce the burden in respect of the breach and consents to the carrying on of the activity which results in that breach, or every person by whom the burden is enforceable and who has such an interest, either so consents or, being aware of the carrying on of that activity (or, because of its nature, being in a position where that person ought to be aware of it), has not, by the expiry of such period as is in all the circumstances reasonable (being in any event a period which does not exceed that of twelve weeks beginning with the day by which that activity has been substantially completed), objected to its being carried on; or

(ii) a conservation burden, economic development burden or health care burden, the person by whom the burden is enforceable consents to the carrying on of that activity,

the burden shall, to the extent of the breach, be extinguished.

(2) Where the period of twelve weeks following the substantial completion of an activity has expired as mentioned in sub-paragraph (i) of subsection (1)(c) above, it shall be presumed, unless the contrary is shown, that the person by whom the real burden was, at the time in question, enforceable (or where a burden is enforceable by more than one person, each of those persons) was, or ought to have been, aware of the carrying on of the activity and did not object as mentioned in that sub-paragraph.

GENERAL NOTE

One of the unfortunate features of any land tenure system which includes real burdens or land covenants is the opportunity which it affords to warring neighbours to pursue unjustified vendettas against each other. The typical example is where someone has built a extension in contravention of a real burden which is enforceable by a neighbouring proprietor. The neighbouring proprietor or his or her predecessor in title may have taken no objection but the matter becomes an issue when the property with the extension comes to be sold. Acquiescence is of course a part of the existing law but it can be difficult to apply and the statutory statement contained in s.16 is very welcome as is the new negative prescription contained in s.17.

Subs.(1)

Acquiescence is of course a branch of the law of personal bar and this subsection sets out how that personal bar will operate in relation to a real burden. First of all there has to be a breach of the real burden which results in material expenditure being incurred by the party in breach which would be lost if the burden was to be enforced. Secondly, it has to be shown that the owner of the benefited property with an interest to enforce either has consented to the activity which results in the breach or every person by whom the burden is enforceable and who has an interest, has consented or has actual or constructive knowledge of the activity and took no action to oppose it. Parties having title and interest to enforce have a period not exceeding 12 weeks beginning with the day by which the activity resulting in the breach has been substantially completed to object. If they have not objected within that period then there will effectively be a deemed consent. There is no definition of the words "substantially completed". It is to be hoped that this does not prove to be an awkward provision. It does suggest that an adjoining proprietor with title and interest to enforce could take objection when an extension was three quarters complete having waited several months while his luckless neighbour incurred expense. Where the burden is a conservation burden, economic development burden or healthcare burden there is no presumed consent; actual consent is required. The section does not state that express consent requires to be in writing although it would obviously be preferable to have something in writing. It should be noted that where an express consent is obtained, this must come not just from the owner of the benefited property but all others entitled to enforce such as tenants, liferenters and spouses holding occupancy rights. The same applies to tacit consent by acquiescence. It would appear therefore that if, a spouse with occupancy rights objected, that would be sufficient to prevent extinguishment of the burden by acquiescence even if the owner of the benefited property consented or acquiesced. The provisions here are different from those relating to voluntary discharge in s.15 which only requires discharge by the owner of the benefited property. There is no statement that an objection by the party entitled to enforce must be in writing far less be judicial. Obviously evidence of the objection should be preserved.

Subs.(2)

Establishing acquiescence under the common law is difficult, mainly because knowledge has to be proved. Accordingly, after the expiry of the 12-week period, following substantial completion of the activity resulting in the breach, it will be presumed, unless the contrary is shown, that the person by whom the real burden was enforceable, or each of these persons was—or ought to have been—aware of the carrying on of the activity, and did not object. This will be a useful provision in many cases.

Further provision as regards extinction where no interest to enforce

17. Where at any time a real burden is breached but at that time no person has an interest to enforce it in respect of the breach, the burden shall, to the extent of the breach, be extinguished.

GENERAL NOTE

This is a statement of the existing law. If no party has an interest to enforce a breach the burden cannot be enforced to the extent of that breach. The burden itself is not extinguished.

Negative prescription

18.—(1) Subject to subsection (5) below, if—

(a) a real burden is breached to any extent; and

(b) during the period of five years beginning with the breach neither—

(i) a relevant claim; nor

(ii) a relevant acknowledgement,

is made,

then, subject to subsection (2) below, the burden shall, to the extent of the breach, be extinguished on the expiry of that period.

(2) Subject to subsections (5) and (6) below, where, in relation to a real burden which consists of—

(a) a right of pre-emption, redemption or reversion; or

(b) any other type of option to acquire the burdened property,

the owner of the burdened property fails to comply with an obligation to convey (or, as the case may be, to offer to convey) the property (or part of the property) and paragraph (b) of subsection (1) above is satisfied, the burden shall be extinguished in relation to the property (or part) on the expiry of the period mentioned in the said paragraph (b).

(3) Sections 9 and 10 of the Prescription and Limitation (Scotland) Act 1973 (c.52) (which define the expressions "relevant claim" and "relevant acknowledgement" for the purposes of sections 6, 7 and 8A of that Act) shall apply for the purposes of subsections (1) and (2) above as those sections apply for the purposes of sections 6, 7 and 8A of that Act but subject to the following modifications—

(a) in each of sections 9 and 10 of that Act—

(i) subsection (2) shall not apply;

(ii) for any reference to an obligation there shall be substituted a reference to a real burden; and

(iii) for any reference to a creditor there shall be substituted a reference to any person by whom a real burden is enforceable;

(b) in section 9 of that Act, for the reference to a creditor in an obligation there shall be substituted a reference to any person by whom a real burden is enforceable; and

(c) in section 10 of that Act, for any reference to a debtor there shall be substituted a reference to any person against whom the real burden is enforceable.

(4) Section 14 of the said Act of 1973 (which makes provision as respects the computation of prescriptive periods) shall apply for the purposes of subsections (1) and (2) above as that section applies for the purposes of Part I of that Act except that paragraph (a) of subsection (1) of that section shall for the purposes of those subsections be disregarded.

(5) In relation to a breach occurring before the appointed day, subsections (1) and (2) above apply with the substitution in paragraph (b) of subsection (1), for the words "period of five years beginning with the breach", of the words "appropriate period".

(6) In the case of a right of pre-emption constituted as a rural housing burden, subsection (2) above shall apply with the modification that for the words "the burden shall be extinguished in relation to the property (or part) on" there shall be substituted "it shall not be competent to commence any action in respect of that failure after".

(7) The reference, in subsection (5) above, to the "appropriate period" is to whichever first expires of—

(a) the period of five years beginning with the appointed day; and

(b) the period of twenty years beginning with the breach.

GENERAL NOTE

This is another very useful provision. Conveyancers will all have encountered situations where there has been a breach of a burden and successive benefited proprietors have done nothing about it. This can still cause problems when the burdened property comes to be sold. One can argue acquiescence under the present law and acquiescence may be easier to establish under s.16. However, it still does depend on knowledge, actual or constructive, on the part the party or parties entitled to enforce the burden. There may also be difficult questions if a benefited proprietor alleges that there was an objection. The new negative prescription of five years introduced by s.18 applies irrespective of knowledge or objection unless there has been judicial interpretation or acknowledgement.

Subs.(1)

If there is a breach of a real burden which is not acknowledged or made the subject of some form of action on the part of the benefited proprietor during a period of five years beginning with the breach then, in general terms, the burden is extinguished to the extent of the breach. Note that the burden is not totally abrogated. If there is a negative burden which prohibits the erection of additional buildings the new five-year prescription will apply only in relation to an additional building erected in breach of the burden. If further additional buildings are erected then they will still contravene the burden and a further five years would require to elapse. The expressions, "relevant claim" and "relevant acknowledgement" are expressions which are used in the context prescription generally.

Subs.(2)

Burdens of this type can cause difficulties, especially where there has been an apparent breach in the past. Situations can arise where evidence of the non-exercise of a pre-emption in the past has been lost or never obtained. Theoretically, this can lead to dispositions granted in the teeth of the pre-emption being subject to reduction at the instance of some former owner of the benefited property. If the party entitled to the pre-emption or other rights makes no claim within the five-year period from the granting of the deed in contravention of the pre-emption or other right, then the pre-emption will be extinguished. It is interesting to note that the words "to the extent of the breach" are not included in this sub-Section. This could mean therefore that if the breach occurs in relation to a pre-emption occurring in a non feudal deed executed prior to September 1, 1974, then the pre-exemption is extinguished forever, although that is not the implication in ss.82–85. Indeed, s.82 specifically preserves (presumably for human rights purposes) a distinction between pre-emptions in feudal deeds, pre-emptions in deeds executed before September 1, 1974 and pre-emptions created in deeds executed after September 1, 1974. Presumably, the reason for the distinction is that where a party does not exercise a right within a prescriptive period, then the right goes completely whereas if someone who declines to exercise a right which can in law be exercised on later occasions is not giving up the right for good.

Subs.(3)

This subsection applies various provisions of the Prescription and Limitation (Scotland) Act 1973 to the new prescription in relation to real burdens with the appropriate changes. A burdened proprietor will be regarded as having acknowledged that the burden is still in force if he or she has given an acknowledgement in writing that the burden is still in force or has acted in some way to actually implement the burden.

Subs.(4)

This subsection applies s.14 of the Prescription and Limitation (Scotland) Act 1973 to the new prescription in relation to real burdens. The prescriptive period will begin on the day after the breach if that occurs at a time other than the actual beginning of the day in question.

Subs.(5)

If the breach of the real burden has occurred before the appointed day then the period will be the "appropriate period" set out in subs.(6).

Subs.(5A)

This is a special provision relating to pre-emptions constituted as rural housing burdens.

Subs.(6)

In the case of breaches of real burdens which occur before the appointed day, the prescriptive period will either be 20 years from the date of the breach or five years from the appointed day whichever is earlier. So far as the period of 20 years from the date of breach is concerned, this reflects the period of long negative prescription which would have applied to breaches in any event. Note again that this only extinguishes the burden to the extent of the breach. It does not extinguish the burden for all purposes.

Confusio not to extinguish real burden

19.—A real burden is not extinguished by reason only that—

(a) the same person is the owner of the benefited property and the burdened property; or

(b) in a case in which there is no benefited property, the person in whose favour the real burden is constituted is the owner of the burdened property.

For a real burden to exist there must be a separate benefited and burdened property. This section makes it clear that the fact that both properties happen to be in the same ownership will not extinguish the burden. Under the Act this may have some significance in as much as burdens can now be enforced against tenants of burdened property. Effectively, therefore a landlord who owns the benefited property will be able to enforce the burden against his own tenant in the burdened property. The same will apply in connection with personal burdens such as conservation burdens, manager burdens and the like except that there will of course be no benefited property. The section will operate where the party in whose favour the conservation or other burden is constituted owns the burdened property.

Termination

Notice of termination

20.—(1) Subject to section 23 of this Act, if at least one hundred years have elapsed since the date of registration of the constitutive deed (whether or not the real burden has been varied or renewed since that date), an owner of the burdened property, or any other person against whom the burden is enforceable, may, after intimation under section 21(1) of this Act, execute and register, in (or as nearly as may be in) the form contained in schedule 2 to this Act, a notice of termination as respects the real burden.

(2) It shall be no objection to the validity of a notice of termination that it is executed or registered by a successor in title of the person who has given such intimation; and any reference in this Act to the "terminator" shall be construed as a reference to—

(a) except where paragraph (b) below applies, the person who has given such intimation; or

(b) where that person no longer has the right or obligation by virtue of which intimation was given, the person who has most recently acquired that right or obligation.

(3) Subsections (1) and (2) above do not apply in relation to—

(a) a conservation burden;

(b) a maritime burden;

(c) a facility burden;

(d) a service burden; or

(e) a real burden which is a title condition of a kind specified in schedule 11 to this Act.

(4) The notice of termination shall—

(a) identify the land which is the burdened property;

(b) describe the terminator's connection with the property (as for example by identifying the terminator as an owner or as a tenant);

(c) set out the terms of the real burden and (if it is not wholly to be terminated) specify the extent of the termination;

(d) specify a date on or before which any application under paragraph (b) of section 90(1) of this Act will require to be made if the real burden is to be renewed or varied under that paragraph (that date being referred to in this Act as the "renewal date");

(e) specify the date on which, and the means by which, intimation was given under subsection (1) of section 21 of this Act; and

(f) set out the name (in so far as known) and the address of each person to whom intimation is sent under subsection (2)(a) of that section.

(5) Any date may be specified under paragraph (d) of subsection (4) above provided that it is a date not less than eight weeks after intimation is last given under subsection (1) of the said section 21 (intimation by affixing being taken, for the purposes of this subsection, to be given when first the notice is affixed).

(6) Where a property is subject to two or more real burdens, it shall be competent to execute and register a single notice of termination in respect of both (or all) the real burdens.

GENERAL NOTE

When these legislative proposals were being considered by the Scottish Law Commission, there was a proposal that all burdens which had existed for more than 100 years should simply be extinguished. This would have had the benefit of clarity and in due course, the Keeper of the Registers would have been able, at a stroke, to remove from the title sheets of registered properties a large amount of irrelevant and obsolete burdens. However, this was thought to be too radical, and instead, the provisions in s.20 provide for burdens which are at least 100 years old to be subject to a notice of termination.

Subs.(1)

The burden must be at least 100 years old, the period beginning with the date of registration of the constitutive deed. In the case of deeds of condition the period will run from the date of registration irrespective of the fact that s.17 of the Land Registration (Scotland) Act 1979 has been disapplied. It will not matter that the real burden in question has been varied or indeed renewed within the 100-year period. The procedure is that a notice of termination is executed and registered after due intimation. The notice can be registered by an owner of the burdened property which presumably means that in the case of *pro indiviso* ownership, one common owner can execute the notice without the consent of the other. Notice can also be given by any other person against whom the burden is enforceable which would include a tenant. Intimation must first be given in terms of s.21 and on registration of the notice under s.24 the burden is extinguished provided that the benefited proprietor or some other party has not applied to renew the burden. Notice of termination cannot be registered unless the Lands Tribunal has endorsed a certificate on the notice in terms of s.23. A form of notice of termination is provided in Sch.2.

Subs.(2)

The party who registers the notice may be a successor of the party who gave the intimation. If the owner of the burdened property initiates the termination process and then sells the purchasers can continue with that process. The term "terminator" is used to describe the party who seeks to remove the burden.

Subs.(3)

The termination provisions do not apply to conservation burdens, maritime burdens, facility burdens, service burdens or other burdens specified in Sch.11. The burdens specified in Sch.11 are the burdens which are excluded from the jurisdiction of the Lands Tribunal, such as obligations relating to the right to work minerals and obligations created or imposed in a lease of an agricultural holding.

Subs.(4)

The statutory form of notice of termination is given in Sch.2. The notice must identify the burdened property and describe the terminator's connection with that property. The terms of the real burden and the extent to which it is to be terminated must be set out. It will be possible therefore to retain parts of a burden in terms of s.24(1). Strangely perhaps, there is no requirement to specify the benefited property or properties. In many cases of course such identification would involve extensive legal research which would be pointless in the case of benefited parties who have no idea that the burden even exists. The notice must list those to whom intimation has been sent and must also specify the date before which a renewal application in terms of s.90(1)(b) must be made.

Subs.(5)

The renewal date which is stipulated in terms of subs.(4)(d) must not be less than eight weeks after the date of the last intimation. An application for renewal can only be made after the renewal date with the consent of the terminator (s.90(4)(a)). Even where an application is made for renewal with the consent of the terminator, it must still be made before the Lands Tribunal have actually endorsed the certificate on the notice (s.90(4)(b)). Where intimation is given by affixing notice then the period will run from the date when the notice is first affixed.

Subs.(6)

Where two or more burdens are involved a single notice is all that is required provided it specifies both or all of the burdens.

Intimation

21.—(1) A proposal to execute and register a notice of termination shall be intimated—

(a) to the owner of each benefited property;

(b) in the case of a personal real burden, to the holder; and

(c) to the owner (or, if the terminator is an owner, to any other owner) of the burdened property.

(2) Subject to subsection (3) below, such intimation may be given—

(a) by sending a copy of the proposed notice of termination, completed as respects all the matters which must, in pursuance of paragraphs (a) to (d) and (f) of section 20(4) of this Act, be identified, described, set out or specified in the notice and with the explanatory note which immediately follows the form of notice of termination in schedule 2 to this Act;

(b) by affixing to the burdened property and to—

    (i) in a case (not being one mentioned in paragraph (c)(ii) below) where there exists one, and only one, lamp post which is situated within one hundred metres of that property, that lamp post; or

    (ii) in a case (not being one so mentioned) where there exists more than one lamp post so situated, each of at least two such lamp posts,

  a conspicuous notice in the form set out in schedule 3 to this Act; or

(c) in a case where—

    (i) it is not possible to comply with paragraph (b) above; or

    (ii) the burdened property is minerals or salmon fishings,

  by advertisement in a newspaper circulating in the area of the burdened property.

(3) Such intimation shall, except where it is impossible to do so, be given by the means described in subsection (2)(a) above if it is given—

(a) under subsection (1)(b) or (c) above; or

(b) under subsection (1)(a) above in relation to a benefited property which is at some point within four metres of the burdened property.

(4) An advertisement giving intimation under subsection (2)(c) above shall—

(a) identify the land which is the burdened property;

(b) set out the terms of the real burden either in full or by reference to the constitutive deed;

(c) specify the name and address of a person from whom a copy of the proposed notice of termination may be obtained; and

(d) state that any owner of a benefited property, or as the case may be any holder of a personal real burden, may apply to the Lands Tribunal for Scotland for the real burden to be renewed or varied but that if no such application is received by a specified date (being the renewal date) the consequence may be that the real burden is extinguished.

(5) The terminator shall provide a person with a copy of the proposed notice of termination (completed as is mentioned in subsection (2)(a) above and with the explanatory note referred to in that subsection) if so requested by that person.

(6) A person—

(a) is entitled to affix a notice to a lamp post in compliance with subsection (2)(b) above regardless of who owns the lamp post but must—

    (i) take all reasonable care not to damage the lamp post in doing so; and

    (ii) remove the notice no later than one week after the date specified in it as the renewal date; and

(b) must, until the day immediately following the date so specified, take all reasonable steps to ensure that the notice continues to be displayed and remains conspicuous and readily legible.

(7) Section 184 of the Town and Country Planning (Scotland) Act 1997 (c.8) (planning permission not needed for advertisements complying with regulations) applies in relation to a notice affixed in compliance with subsection (2)(b) above as that section applies in relation to an advertisement displayed in accordance with regulations made under section 182 of that Act (regulations controlling display of advertisements).

GENERAL NOTE

Before a notice of termination can be registered, intimation must be given of the intention to terminate the burden. Section 21 contains detailed provisions for intimation. The notices do not require to be signed. Although various methods of intimation are provided for there are restrictions where notice is to be given to certain parties in terms of subs.3.

Subs.(1)

Intimation must be given to the owner of each benefited property. If there are more than one benefited properties then intimation must be made to the owners of all benefited properties. In the case of a personal real burden there will be no owners so intimation must be made to the holder of that burden, for example, a conservation body. If the terminator is only one of the owners of the burdened property then intimation must also be given to any other such owner.

Subs.(2)

The great difficulty with the current law of real burdens is identifying all the benefited proprietors. The normal method of intimation will be by post. A copy of the proposed notice of termination with all the appropriate details as set out in Sch.2 with the explanatory note attached must be sent. So far as "sending" is concerned, s.124 provides that the notice is sent if it is sent to the person or an agent for the person. Where a notice requires to be sent to the owner but only the property is known it is sufficient that the notice is sent addressed to "the owner" or some other expression such as "the proprietor". Sending includes posting, physical delivery or transmission by electronic means. Where the notice is posted, it shall be taken to have been sent on the day of posting. Where a notice is transmitted by electronic means, it is deemed to be sent on the day of transmission. Section 124 makes no mention of sending by recorded delivery. The second method of intimation is by affixing a notice in the form of Sch.3 to the burdened property and one or two lampposts. Where it is not possible to actually affix a notice or where the burdened property is minerals or salmon fishings, intimation may be made by advertisement in a newspaper circulating in the area of the burdened property.

Subs.(3)

The first method of intimation (sending a copy) is compulsory, except where impossible, if the notice is given to the holder of a personal burden. Where the notice is given to any other owner or the owner of the burdened property, transmission of the notice must also be sent in the case of owners of benefited properties which are at some point within four metres of the burdened property. In terms of s.125, where a provision in the Act refers to distances, then the distance is measured along a horizontal plane, disregarding the width of any intervening road if of less than 20 metres, and any pertinent of either burdened or benefited property.

Subs.(4)

Any advertisement given in terms of subs.(2)(c), must identify the burdened land, set out the terms of the real burden either in full or by reference to the constitutive deed, specify the name and address of the person from whom a copy of the notice may be obtained and state that the owner of the benefited property or the holder of the personal real burden may apply to the Lands Tribunal for renewal or variation of the burden. The advertisement must also state that if no such application is received by the renewal date the consequence may be that the real burden is extinguished.

Subs.(5)

The terminator must provide a copy of the proposed notice of termination together with the explanatory note to any person. Oddly, this subsection does not appear to be restricted to owners of the benefited property. Presumably, only owners will be interested.

Subs.(6)

This subsection provides statutory authority for the affixation of the notice to a lamppost, regardless of who owns the lamppost, provided the person affixing takes reasonable care not to cause damage and removes the notice no later than one week after the date specified in it as the renewal date. There is also an obligation to take all reasonable steps to ensure that the notice continues to be displayed and remains conspicuous and readily legible. Presumably, a notice would require to be laminated or waterproofed in some manner.

Subs.(7)

This subsection applies s.184 of the Town and Country Planning (Scotland) Act 1987 in relation to affixed notices.

Oath or affirmation before notary public

22.—(1) Before submitting a notice of termination for registration, the terminator shall swear or affirm before a notary public that, to the best of the terminator's knowledge and belief, all the information contained in the notice is true and that section 21 of this Act has been complied with.

(2) For the purposes of subsection (1) above, if the terminator is—

(a) an individual unable by reason of legal disability, or incapacity, to swear or affirm as mentioned in that subsection, then a legal representative of the terminator may swear or affirm;

(b) not an individual, then any person authorised to sign documents on its behalf may swear or affirm;

and any reference in that subsection to a terminator shall be construed accordingly.

GENERAL NOTE

Before the terminator executes the notice, he must swear or affirm before a notary public that the information in the notice is true and that the notice has been duly intimated in terms of the statutory provisions. Where the terminator is an individual unable to swear of affirm by reason of legal disability or incapacity, then the legal representative of the terminator may swear or affirm. Where the person is not an individual but a juristic person then any person authorised to sign documents may swear or affirm.

Prerequisite certificate for registration of notice of termination

23.—(1) A notice of termination shall not be registrable unless, after the renewal date, there is endorsed on the notice (or on an annexation to it referred to in an endorsement on it and identified, on the face of the annexation, as being the annexation so referred to) a certificate executed by a member of the Lands Tribunal, or by their clerk, to the effect that no application in relation to the proposal to execute and register the notice has been received under section 90(1)(b) (and (4)) of this Act or that any such application which has been received—

(a) has been withdrawn; or

(b) relates (either or both)—

(i) to one or more but not to all of the real burdens the terms of which are set out in the notice (any real burden to which it relates being described in the certificate);

(ii) to one or more but not to all (or probably or possibly not to all) of the benefited properties (any benefited property to which it relates being described in the certificate),

and where more than one such application has been received the certificate shall relate to both (or as the case may be all) applications.

(2) At any time before endorsement under subsection (1) above, a notice of termination, whether or not it has been submitted for such endorsement, may be withdrawn, by intimation in writing to the Lands Tribunal, by the terminator; and it shall not be competent to endorse under that subsection a notice in respect of which such intimation is given.

GENERAL NOTE

A notice of termination is registered in the Land Register or Register of Sasines Since these registers are public, there has to be some protection against the registration of a notice where an application to preserve the burden has been lodged with the Lands Tribunal. Accordingly, in terms of this section the Lands Tribunal must certify that no application for renewal has been lodged. If an application for renewal, relating only to some of the benefited properties or some of the burdens, has been lodged, the Tribunal will certify the notice to the extent that it has not been opposed.

Subs.(1)

The content of certificate by the Tribunal is specified. It is to the effect either that no application for renewal has been received or that any such application has been withdrawn or that the application only applies to some of the real burdens or some of the benefited properties. If more than one renewal application has been received then the certificate by the Tribunal must relate to both or all applications. The certificate is endorsed on the notice before it is sent for registration or on an annexation referred to. The certificate given by the Lands Tribunal lists the burdens and the relevant properties that are subject to applications for renewal.

Subs.(2)

A notice of termination may be withdrawn at any time before the certificate is endorsed by the Lands Tribunal.

Effect of registration of notice of termination

24.—(1) Subject to subsection (2) below, a notice of termination, when registered against the burdened property, extinguishes the real burden in question wholly or as the case may be to such extent as may be described in that notice.

(2) A notice of termination registrable by virtue of a certificate under paragraph (b) of section 23(1) of this Act shall not, on being registered, extinguish a real burden which is the subject of an application disclosed by the certificate in so far as that burden—

    (a) is constituted in favour of the property of which the applicant is owner; or

    (b) is a personal real burden of which the applicant is holder,

but if under that section a further certificate is endorsed on the notice (or on an annexation to the notice) the notice may be registered again, the effect of the later registration being determined by reference to the further certificate rather than to the certificate by virtue of which the notice was previously registered.

GENERAL NOTE

The registration of the notice against the burdened property extinguishes the real burden wholly or to such an extent as may be described in the notice. Where there has been an application for renewal which relates only to some of the benefited properties or some of the burdens then registration of the notice of termination only extinguishes the real burden so far as not subject to application for renewal. A further certificate may be endorsed in the notice if the benefited proprietor later withdraws an application for renewal. If the application for renewal has not been withdrawn but the Lands Tribunal have refused the application and discharged the burden then it is the order of the Tribunal which should be registered in terms of s.104(2).

PART 2

COMMUNITY BURDENS

Meaning, creation etc.

The expression "community burdens"

25.—(1) Subject to subsection (2) below, where—

[1] (a) real burdens are imposed under a common scheme on two or more units; and

(b) each of those units is, in relation to some or all of those burdens, both a benefited property and a burdened property,

the burdens shall, in relation to the units, be known as "community burdens".

(2) Any real burdens such as are mentioned in section 54(1) of this Act are community burdens.

AMENDMENT

1. As amended by the Tenements (Scotland) Act 2004 (asp 11), s.25, Sch.4, para.7 (effective October 23, 2004).

GENERAL NOTE

Part 2 of the Act introduces a new concept into the law of real burdens. Conveyancers will be familiar with burdens which apply to all the flats in a tenement, or indeed to all the houses in a residential estate. This part of the Act defines that type of burden as a community burden and seeks to regulate how these burdens are to be enforced, varied or waived within the community which is subject to them. The basic principle is that the will of the majority will prevail. The concept of a community is legal rather than social. A community can be a block of flats, a housing estate or indeed an industrial estate or business park. This part of the Act applies to all burdens with the character of a community burden whether these burdens were created before or after the Act comes into force (s.119(10)). In legal terms a community is a group of two or more properties which are subject to the same or similar burdens which can be mutually enforced. The existing law of *ius quaesitum tertio* is of course extremely difficult to understand. Community burdens will fulfil a similar function and hopefully the statutory framework will make the law easier to understand and apply.

Subs.(1)

The definition is fairly clear. A community burden is a real burden imposed under a common scheme on two or more units where each of these units is, in relation to some or all of the burdens, both a benefited and burdened property.

Subs.(2)

For the avoidance of doubt, burdens imposed under a common scheme on units in a sheltered or retirement housing development in terms of s.54(1) are community burdens even in cases where a warden's flat is not subject to the burdens.

Creation of community burdens: supplementary provision

26.—(1) Without prejudice to section 2 of this Act, community burdens may make provision as respects any of the following—

(a) the appointment by the owners of a manager;
(b) the dismissal by the owners of a manager;
(c) the powers and duties of a manager;
(d) the nomination of a person to be the first manager;
(e) the procedures to be followed by the owners in making decisions about matters affecting the community;
(f) the matters on which such decisions may be made; and
(g) the resolution of disputes relating to community burdens.

(2) In this Act "community" means—

(a) the units subject to community burdens; and
(b) any unit in a sheltered or retirement housing development which is used in some special way as mentioned in section 54(1) of this Act.

GENERAL NOTE

This section is an enabling one indicating the type of burden which may be created as community burden and containing a further definition of "community".

Subs.(1)

The list is non-exclusive. A community burden may benefit a community rather than an individual property. "Manager" is defined in s.122(1). The subsection contains a list of enabling powers which indicates that community burdens need not just be positive obligations or prohibitions.

A community is made up of all the units that are subject to the community burdens. It is not necessary that all the units in the community be subject to all the community burdens. Some units may obtain a discharge and in a sheltered housing or retirement complex there will be units such as a warden's or caretaker's flat which will not be subject to the community burdens.

Effect on units of statement that burdens are community burdens
27.—Where, in relation to any real burdens, the constitutive deed states that the burdens are to be community burdens, each unit shall, in relation to those burdens, be both a benefited property and a burdened property.

GENERAL NOTE
This section is equivalent to a statement in a deed of conditions under the old law that each burdened proprietor will have a right to enforce the burden against other burdened proprietors. This is a very useful provision because it means that nobody has to actually interpret the burdens to see if they are truly community burdens. If the constitutive deed says that the burdens are to be community burdens then they will be and the proprietors of all units will be able to enforce them against each other.

Management of community

Power of majority to appoint manager etc.
28.—(1) Subject to sections 54(5)(a) and 63(8)(a) of this Act and to any provision made by community burdens, the owners of a majority of the units in a community may—
  (a) appoint a person to be the manager of the community on such terms as they may specify;
  (b) confer on any such manager the right to exercise such of their powers as they may specify;
  (c) revoke, or vary, the right to exercise such of the powers conferred under paragraph (b) above as they may specify; and
  (d) dismiss any such manager.
  (2) Without prejudice to the generality of subsection (1)(b) above, the powers mentioned there include—
  (a) power to carry out maintenance;
  (b) power to enforce community burdens; and
  (c) power to vary or discharge such burdens.
  (3) If a unit is owned by two or more persons in common, then, for the purposes of voting on any proposal to exercise a power conferred by subsection (1) above, the vote allocated as respects the unit shall only be counted for or against the proposal if it is the agreed vote of those of them who together own more than a half share of the unit.
  (4) The powers conferred by paragraphs (b) to (d) of subsection (1) above may be exercised whether or not the manager was appointed by virtue of paragraph (a) of that subsection.

GENERAL NOTE
The provisions contained in sections 28–31 might be said to be something of a conveyancing experiment. It would be fair to say that difficulty has been caused, as much through ambiguous provision as the lack of provision, particularly in flatted properties. The provisions in these sections relating to the management of the community are fallback provisions. They apply only where the titles to the property are silent. This section sets out the fallback powers of a manager. "Manager" is defined in s.122(1). Tenement property is governed by the Tenements (Scotland) Act 2004. Sections 28(1)(a) and (d) and (2)(a), 29 and 31 do not apply to a community consisting of one tenement. Sections 28(1)(a) and (d) and 31 do not apply where a development management scheme applies.

Subs.(1)
This sets out the power of the proprietors of a majority of units in a community to appoint a manager and confer powers on that manager. The majority may also revoke or vary the right to

exercise the powers and dismiss that manager. The right to dismiss is of course subject to ss.54(5)(a) and 63(8)(a) which provide for a two thirds majority in relation to a sheltered housing and time limited monopolies on the appointment of a manger in certain cases. There are no restrictions on who can be appointed a manager. It might be that an owner of a unit would be the manager or it could be a professional factor.

Subs.(2)

The list of powers is non-exclusive. Other powers may be conferred. It should be borne in mind however that a majority cannot confer on a manager, powers which the majority themselves do not have (see s.28(1)(b)). This provision is wide enough to permit qualified delegation. The powers include the power to carry out maintenance (but presumably not improvement), the power to actually enforce community burdens and the power to vary or discharge burdens. One can see situations where the majority might want to limit the exercise of these powers either by reference to a limit of expenditure or certain changes of use. In a sheltered or retirement housing complex the power to discharge or vary a community burden can only be delegated to a manager if the burden in question is not a core burden (see ss.54(4) and 54(5)(a) (ii)).

Subs.(3)

Where a unit is owned in common then there is only one vote per unit and more importantly the vote will not count unless it has been agreed by those common owners who together own more than a half share. In the normal case therefore of a couple owning a unit equally, both will require to agree.

Subs.(4)

Powers may be delegated even although the manager was not appointed in terms of s.28(1)(a). A manager may have been appointed in the constitutive deed under s.26(1)(d) or in terms of a manager burden under s.63.

Power of majority to instruct common maintenance

[1] **29.**—(1) This section applies where—

(a) community burdens impose an obligation on the owners of all or some of the units to maintain, or contribute towards the cost of maintaining, particular property; and

(b) the obligation so imposed accounts for the entire liability for the maintenance of such property.

(2) Subject to any provision made by community burdens, the owners of a majority of the units subject to the obligation may—

(a) decide that maintenance should be carried out;

(b) subject to subsection (3A) below, require each owner to deposit—

(i) by such date as they may specify (being a date not less than twenty-eight days after the requirement is made of that owner); and

(ii) with such person as they may nominate for the purpose, a sum of money (being a sum not exceeding that owner's apportioned share, in accordance with the terms of the community burdens, of a reasonable estimate of the cost of maintenance);

(c) [*Repealed by the Tenements (Scotland) Act 2004 (asp 11), s.25, Sch.4, para.8 (effective October 23, 2004).*]

(d) instruct or carry out such maintenance; and

(e) modify or revoke anything done by them by virtue of paragraphs (a) to (d) above.

(3) If a unit is owned by two or more persons in common, then, for the purposes of voting on any proposal to exercise a power conferred by subsection (2) above, the vote allocated as respects the unit shall only be counted for or against the proposal if it is the agreed vote of those of them who together own more than a half share of the unit.

(3A) A requirement under subsection (2)(b) above that each owner deposit a sum of money—

(a) exceeding £100; or

(b) of £100 or less where the aggregate of that sum taken together with any other sum or sums required (otherwise than by a previous notice

under this subsection) in the preceding 12 months to be deposited
under that subsection by each owner exceeds £200,

shall be made by written notice to each owner and shall require the sum to
be deposited into such account (the "maintenance account") as the owners
may nominate for the purpose.

(3B) The owners may authorise a manager or at least two other persons
(whether or not owners) to operate the maintenance account on their behalf.

(4) Any notice given under subsection (3A) above shall contain, or to it
shall be attached, a note comprising a summary of the nature and extent of
the maintenance to be carried out together with the following information—

   (a) the estimated cost of carrying out that maintenance;

   (b) why the estimate is considered a reasonable estimate;

   (c) how—

      (i) the sum required from the owner in question; and

      (ii) the apportionment among the owners,

   have been arrived at;

   (d) what the apportioned shares of the other owners are;

   (e) the date on which the decision to carry out the maintenance was
taken and the names of those by whom it was taken;

   (f) a timetable for the carrying out of the maintenance, including the
dates by which it is proposed the maintenance will be—

      (i) commenced; and

      (ii) completed;

   (g) the location and number of the maintenance account; and

   (h) the names and addresses of the persons who will be authorised to
operate that account on behalf of the community.

(5) The maintenance account shall be a bank or building society account
which is interest bearing; and the authority of at least two persons, or of a
manager on whom has been conferred the right to give authority, shall be
required for any payment from it.

(6) If modification or revocation under paragraph (e) of subsection (2)
above affects the information contained in a notice or note under subsection
(4) above, that information shall forthwith be sent again, modified
accordingly, to the owners.

(6A) The notice given under subsection (2)(b) above may specify a date as
a refund date for the purposes of subsection (7)(b)(i) below.

(7) An owner shall be entitled—

   (a) to inspect, at any reasonable time, any tender received in connection
with the maintenance to be carried out;

   (b) if—

      (i) that maintenance is not commenced by—

         (A) where the notice under subsection (2)(b) above specifies a
refund date, that date; or

         (B) where that notice does not specify such a date, the twenty-
eighth day after the date specified by virtue of subsection
(4)(f)(i) above; and

      (ii) the owner demands, by written notice, from the persons
authorised under subsection (3B) above repayment (with
accrued interest) of such sum as has been deposited by that
owner in compliance with the requirement under subsection
(2)(b) above,

   to be repaid accordingly; except that no requirement to make
repayment in compliance with a notice under paragraph (b)(ii) above
shall arise if the persons so authorised do not receive that notice
before the maintenance is commenced.

(7A) A former owner who, before ceasing to be an owner, deposited sums
in compliance with a requirement under subsection (2)(b) above, shall have
the same entitlement as an owner has under subsection (7)(b) above.

(8) Such sums as are held in the maintenance account by virtue of subsection (3A) above are held in trust for all the depositors, for the purpose of being used by the persons authorised to make payments from the account as payment for the maintenance.

(9) Any sums held in the maintenance account after all sums payable in respect of the maintenance carried out have been paid shall be shared among the owners—

    (a) by repaying each depositor, with any accrued interest and after deduction of that person's apportioned share of the actual cost of the maintenance, the sum which the person deposited; or

    (b) in such other way as the depositors agree in writing.

(10) The Scottish Ministers may by order substitute for the sums for the time being specified in subsection (3A) above such other sums as appear to them to be justified by a change in the value of money appearing to them to have occurred since the last occasion on which the sums were fixed.

AMENDMENT

    1. As amended by the Tenements (Scotland) Act 2004 (asp 11), s.25, Sch.4, para.8 (effective October 23, 2004).

GENERAL NOTE

This section applies where there are existing community burdens imposing an obligation of maintenance or an obligation to contribute towards the cost of maintenance and that obligation deals with the whole liability for maintenance of the property. In some cases there is a bare obligation of maintenance but no framework relating to the appointment of managers or indeed the instruction of repairs. This section provides a fall-back mechanism which allows the owners of a majority of units to instruct maintenance expenditure. The majority may require each owner to deposit a float based on an estimated share of the cost. Maintenance is defined in s.122 as including repair or replacement and such demolition, alteration or improvement as is reasonably incidental to maintenance. Accordingly, the section does not apply to what might be regarded as improvement or upgrading which is not allied to maintenance or repair as such. Presumably therefore a majority could decide in the context of reroofing that an improved type of slate be used rather than a replacement slate. A majority would not be able to commission an artist to decorate the outside of a block of flats with a mural on the basis that this improvement would increase the amenity value of the properties. Between these two extremes, of course, there are an infinite variety of situations. The dividing line between an improvement carried out in relation to maintenance and a pure improvement will be difficult to define. A unit is defined in s.122 as any land which is designed to be held on separate ownership whether it is so held or not.

Subs.(1)

This subsection makes it clear that the fall-back provisions only apply to matters of common maintenance. The sections do not apply, for example, to obligations on the owners of individual units to maintain their own units. The obligation would apply to obligations imposed on the proprietors of all the units to maintain or contribute towards the cost of maintaining a common close or stair. The power of the majority will not apply if due to some mistake in the conveyancing, the entire liability is not adequately dealt with in the title provisions.

Subs.(2)

Subsection 2 sets out the powers of the majority. The majority is the majority of units which are subject to the particular maintenance obligations. There will be cases where there are community burdens that apply generally to a whole development, which may comprise two or more blocks of flats. Some of these community burdens will apply to all the flats in each block, such as those relating to the maintenance of common landscaped areas, parking areas and the like. However, some of the burdens will relate only to particular blocks of flats such as obligations in relation to common closes, passages and stairs. The majority may decide that maintenance should be carried out and require each owner to lodge a deposit being a reasonable estimate of the cost. The majority may also instruct or carry out maintenance and they may change course if things do not appear to be working out.

Subs.(3)

This provision again applies to units owned in common. The vote will only count if those who together own more than a half share agree. In the normal case of property owned by a couple equally, both will have to agree.

Subs.(3A)

This subsection sets out provisions for a float to be deposited by a proprietor against the cost of a repair.

Subs.(3B)

A manager or at least two other persons may be authorised to operate the account.

Subs.(4)

Where notice is given in terms of subs.(2)(b) that a deposit is required the notice must contain a note comprising a summary of the nature and extent of the maintenance to be carried out together with other details relating to estimates, apportionment, timetable for work and the authority of those parties who can operate the bank account holding the deposits of behalf of the community.

Subs.(5)

Deposits must be held in a separate bank or building society account, which is interest bearing. The signature of two persons or the manager, if he has authority, will be required to operate the account.

Subs.(6)

If the maintenance programme is modified or revoked and this affects the information which was contained in the notice under s.29(4) then amended information must be sent to the owners.

Subs.(6A)

A refund date may be specified in the notice.

Subs.(7)

An owner of any unit is entitled to inspect tenders for maintenance work. Owners are also entitled to demand a refund of any deposit paid if the maintenance work has not been commenced by the refund date or within 28 days of the commencement date under subs.(4)(f)(i) within 14 days of the dates specified in the notice except where work commences prior to receipt of the repayment demand.

Subs.(7A)

Former owners are entitled to a refund of sums deposited by them.

Subs.(8)

Deposits held for maintenance are deemed to be held in trust.

Subs.(9)

In the unlikely event that there is a surplus in the maintenance account after the work has been carried out, the surplus is to be shared among the owners, in such manner as they agree in writing, or failing agreement, by paying each depositor with accrued interest the sum which each party deposited, less that party's share of the actual cost of maintenance.

Subs.(10)

Scottish Ministers may increase the deposit limits from time to time.

Owners' decision binding

30. Anything done (including any decision made) by—

(a) the owners in accordance with such provision as is made in community burdens; or

(b) a majority of them, in accordance with section 28 or 29 of this Act,

is binding on all the owners and their successors as owners.

GENERAL NOTE

This section makes it clear that the majority rule. Moreover the decision is binding on all the owners at the time it is taken and their successors as owners. It should be noted that this section applies not just to the fallback provisions in ss.28 and 29 but also to provisions and acts which are carried out in terms of community burdens contained in existing titles.

Remuneration of manager

31. Subject to any provision made by community burdens, liability for any remuneration due to a manager of the community (however appointed) shall be shared equally among the units in a community and each owner shall be liable accordingly; but if two or more persons have common ownership of a unit then—

    (a) they are severally liable for any share payable in respect of that unit; and

    (b) as between (or among) themselves, they are liable in the proportions in which they own the unit.

GENERAL NOTE

The manager is entitled to remuneration and unless the titles provide otherwise in a community burden liability for that remuneration is to be shared equally among the units in the community. This applies no matter how the manager is appointed. Where two or more people own a unit then the manager can demand payment from either or them but as between themselves they are liable in the proportions in which they own the unit.

Disapplication of provisions of sections 28, 29 and 31 in certain cases

[1]**31A.**—(1) Sections 28(1)(a) and (d) and (2)(a), 29 and 31 of this Act shall not apply in relation to a community consisting of one tenement.

(2) Sections 28(1)(a) and (d) and 31 of this Act shall not apply to a community in any period during which the development management scheme applies to the community.

GENERAL NOTE

Tenements are governed by the Tenements (Scotland) Act 2004.

AMENDMENT

    1. As inserted by the Tenements (Scotland) Act 2004 (asp 11), s.25, Sch.4, para.9 (effective October 23, 2004).

Variation, discharge etc.

The expressions "affected unit" and "adjacent unit"

32.—In this Part of this Act a unit in respect of which a community burden is to be varied ("varied" including imposed), or discharged, is referred to as an "affected unit"; and "adjacent unit" means, in relation to an affected unit, any unit which is at some point within four metres of the unit.

GENERAL NOTE

This is essentially a definition section but an important section in relation to variation and discharge of community burdens. There may be provision in the constitutive deed in relation to variation and discharge. If not, ss.33 and 35 provide methods which may be used to vary or discharge community burdens. Variation may be in relation to one property or a group of properties within the community. A majority may wish to vary burdens for the whole community. These are quite radical fallback provisions. The community is of course made up of units and it is for this reason that the terms "affected unit" and "adjacent unit" must be defined. An "affected unit" is a unit in respect of which a community burden is to be varied or discharged. An "adjacent unit" means in relation to an affected unit any unit which is at some point within four metres of the affected unit. It should be borne in mind that s.125 provides that where the Act refers to distances the width of any intervening road if of less than 20 metres and a pertinent of either property is to be disregarded. Many conveyancers will have come across problems in relation to alterations to burdens contained in deeds of conditions. Effectively, everyone affected by the burdens must agree. This can make practical alterations difficult. The provisions in ss.33 and 35 seek to address this.

Majority etc. variation and discharge of community burdens

[1] **33.**—(1) A community burden may be varied ("varied" including imposed), or discharged, by registering against each affected unit a deed of variation, or discharge, granted—

(a) where provision is made in the constitutive deed for it to be granted by the owners of such units in the community as may be specified, by or on behalf of the owners of those units; or

(b) in accordance with subsection (2) below.

(2) A deed is granted in accordance with this subsection if granted—

(a) where no such provision as is mentioned in subsection (1)(a) above is made, by or on behalf of the owners of a majority of the units in the community (except that, where one person owns a majority of those units, the deed must also be granted by at least one other owner); or

(b) where the manager of the community is authorised to do so (whether in the constitutive deed or otherwise), by that manager.

(3) An affected unit may, for the purposes of subsection (1)(a) or (2)(a) above, be included in any calculation of the number of units.

(4) For the purposes of this section, where a unit is owned by two or more persons in common a deed is granted by or on behalf of the owners of the unit if—

(a) granted in accordance with such provision as is made in that regard in the constitutive deed; or

(b) where no such provision is made, granted by or on behalf of those of them who together own more than a half share of the unit.

(5) This section is subject to section 54(5)(b) and (c) of this Act.

AMENDMENT

1. As amended by the Tenements (Scotland) Act 2004 (asp 11), s.25, Sch.4, para.10 (effective October 23, 2004).

GENERAL NOTE

This section allows a community burden to be varied or discharged by registration against each affected unit of a deed of variation or discharge. It should be noted that the term "varied" will include the imposition of another burden.

Subs.(1)

This subsection indicates who will have to grant the deed of discharge or variation and how it is to be granted. There may be provision in the constitutive deed but if not then variation and discharge is achieved in accordance with subs.(2).

Subs.(2)

A deed of variation or discharge may be granted by, or on behalf of the owners of a majority of the units in the community, unless one person owns a majority in which case the deed must be granted by at least one other owner. The deed can also be granted by a manager of the community if he is authorised to do so whether in the constitutive deed or otherwise. A majority of owners might give a manager appropriate authority in terms of s.28(1)(b) and s.28(2)(c).

Subs.(3)

The owners of affected units will be counted with a view to ascertaining the majority. Accordingly it is not just a majority of those who want change.

Subs.(4)

Where a unit is owned in common by two or more persons a deed is granted on their behalf if granted by both of them or by the party who owns more than one half share or in accordance with any provision in the constitutive deed. In the ordinary case of a couple owning one half share each both would require to grant the deed.

Subs.(5)

Section 50 deals with core burdens in sheltered housing complexes. A deed of variation or discharge granted under s.33(2) can only vary core burdens; it cannot discharge them. A two thirds majority would be required, rather than a simple majority. No real burden relating to a restriction as to any persons age may be varied or discharged by virtue of s.33(2).

Variation or discharge under section 33: intimation

34.—(1) Where a deed of variation or discharge is granted under section 33(2) of this Act, a proposal to register that deed shall be intimated to such other owners of the units in the community as have not granted the deed.

(2) Such intimation shall be given by sending a copy of the deed, together with—

(a) a notice in, or as near as may be in, the form set out in schedule 4 to this Act; and

(b) the explanatory note which immediately follows that form in that schedule.

(3) Where a deed has been granted as mentioned in subsection (1) above, any person to whom intimation is given under subsection (2) above may, during the period of eight weeks beginning with the latest date on which intimation of the proposal to register the deed is so given, apply to the Lands Tribunal for preservation, unvaried, of the community burden in so far as constituted in favour of, or against, any unit not all of whose owners have granted the deed.

(4) Subsections (2) to (4) of section 37 of this Act apply to a deed granted as mentioned in subsection (1) above as they apply in relation to a deed granted as mentioned in section 35 of this Act but with the modifications specified in subsection (5) below.

(5) The modifications are that—

(a) references in the said subsections (2) and (4) to subsection (1) of that section are to be construed as references to subsection (3) above;

(b) the reference in the former of those said subsections to no application having been received under section 37 is to be construed as a reference to none having been received under this section; and

(c) the reference in the latter of those said subsections to section 36 of this Act is to be construed as a reference to subsections (1) and (2) above.

(6) For the purposes of subsection (4) of section 37 of this Act as so applied, if the person proposing to submit for registration a deed granted as mentioned in subsection (1) above is—

(a) an individual unable by reason of legal disability, or incapacity, to swear or affirm as mentioned in the said subsection (4), then a legal representative of that person may swear or affirm;

(b) not an individual, then any person authorised to sign documents on its behalf may swear or affirm,

and any reference in the said subsection (4) to the person so proposing shall be construed accordingly.

GENERAL NOTE

A community burden cannot be varied or discharged in accordance with s.33 unless there has been appropriate intimation of the proposal in advance.

Subs.(1)

Intimation must be made by those who have signed the deed of variation or discharge, to owners of the units in the community who have not granted the deed. Note that this could include a *pro indiviso* proprietor who owned less than a one half share in a unit where the other *pro indiviso* proprietor has granted the deed.

Subs.(2)

Intimation is given by sending a copy of the deed of variation or discharge with a notice in the form set out in Sch.4 and an explanatory note. There are detailed provisions relating to the transmission of the notice set out in s.124. The notice contains an intimation to the owners of their right to make application to the Lands Tribunal to preserve the burden under subs.(3) and s.90(1)(c).

Subs.(3)

Any person to whom intimation has been given may during the period of eight weeks beginning with the last date or which intimation has been given apply to the Lands Tribunal for preservation of the community burden unvaried in so far as that burden is constituted in favour of or against any unit not all of whose owners have granted the deed. If the Lands Tribunal grants the application, then the burden will not be varied or discharged in respect of the minority who did not sign the deed. Intimation by the dissenting owners is given in terms of s.124. It is not necessary for the burden to be preserved that all proprietors of units who did not grant the deed of variation or discharge actually apply to the Lands Tribunal for renewal. If one of these owners is successful in the application then the burden is preserved for all those units whose proprietors did not sign.

Subs.(4)

This subsection applies subss.(2) to (4) of s.36 to a deed of variation or discharge subject to certain modifications. Effectively, a deed of variation or discharge will not be effective unless it has endorsed on it when registered a certificate from the Lands Tribunal. That certificate can only be endorsed after the expiry of the eight-week period in which applications to preserve the community burden can be made. If an application for renewal is made then the certificate cannot be endorsed until that application is refused or withdrawn. The application to preserve the burdens can relate to some of the community burdens to be varied or discharged in which case a certificate can be endorsed in relation to the others. The parties who wish to register the deed of variation or discharge must swear or affirm before a notary public that the intimation requirements have been carried out. They must also state in the oath or affirmation the date on which the eight-week period expired.

Subs.(5)

This indicates the technical changes required to the provisions in s.37(2)–(4).

Subs.(6)

This provides for execution by those subject to legal disability or by juristic persons.

Variation and discharge of community burdens by owners of adjacent units

35.—[1] (1) A community burden may be varied or discharged by registering against each affected unit a deed of variation, or discharge, granted, by or on behalf of the owners of the affected units and by or on behalf of the owners of all units (if any) which in relation to any of the affected units are adjacent units, except that this subsection—

(a) shall not apply where the burden is a facility burden or a service burden or where the units constitute a sheltered or retirement housing development;

(b) may expressly be disapplied by the constitutive deed; and

(c) is subject to sections 36 and 37 of this Act and to any determination of the Lands Tribunal.

(2) Subsection (4) of section 33 of this Act applies for the purposes of this section as it applies for the purposes of that section.

AMENDMENT

1. As amended by the Tenements (Scotland) Act 2004 (asp 11), s.25, Sch.4, para.11 (effective October 23, 2004).

GENERAL NOTE

This is an alternative fall-back provision for discharge and variation of community burdens. A community burden may be varied or discharged by the registration of a deed of variation or discharge granted by or on behalf of the owners of the affected units or by or on behalf of the owners of all units which are adjacent units. Adjacent units are those units within four metres of an affected unit. Effectively, the owners of affected units can therefore ask owners of adjacent units to join with them in a variation or discharge. This provision does not apply in relation to community burdens which are facility burdens or service burdens or where the units constitute a sheltered or retirement housing development. The constitutive deed may disapply this particular provision. Variation is subject to the intimation provisions contained in s.36 and the preservation provisions contained in s.37.

Variation and discharge under section 35: intimation

36.—(1) A proposal to register under section 35 of this Act a deed of variation or discharge shall be intimated to such owners of the units in the community as have not granted the deed.

(2) Such intimation may be given—

(a) by sending a copy of the deed together with—

    (i) a notice in, or as near as may be in, the form set out in schedule 5 to this Act; and

    (ii) the explanatory note which immediately follows that form in that schedule;

(b) by affixing to each affected unit and to—

    (i) in a case where there exists one, and only one, lamp post which is situated within one hundred metres of that unit, that lamp post; or

    (ii) in a case where there exists more than one lamp post so situated, each of at least two such lamp posts,

a conspicuous notice in the form set out in schedule 6 to this Act; or

(c) in a case where it is not possible to comply with paragraph (b) above, by advertisement in a newspaper circulating in the area of the affected unit.

(3) An advertisement giving intimation under subsection (2)(c) above shall—

(a) identify the land which is the affected unit;

(b) set out the terms of the community burden either in full or by reference to the constitutive deed;

(c) specify the name and address of the person who proposes to register the deed and state that from that person (or from some other person whose name and address are specified in the advertisement) a copy of that deed may be obtained;

(d) state that any owner of a unit who has not granted the deed may apply to the Lands Tribunal for Scotland for the community burden to be preserved but that if no such application is received by a specified date (being the date on which the period mentioned in section 37(1) of this Act expires) the consequence may be that the community burden is varied or discharged in relation to the affected unit.

(4) The person proposing to register the deed shall provide any other person with a copy of that deed if so requested by that other person.

(5) Subsections (6) and (7) of section 21 of this Act apply in relation to affixing, and to a notice affixed, under subsection (2)(b) above as they apply in relation to affixing, and to a notice affixed, under subsection (2)(b) of that section (the reference in paragraph (a)(ii) of the said subsection (6) to the date specified in the notice as the renewal date being construed as a reference to the date so specified by virtue of subsection (2)(b) above).

GENERAL NOTE

    Notification provisions apply to variations and discharges of burdens under s.35. The form of notice and explanatory notice are contained in Sch.5. Intimation may be made by sending a copy of the deed with the notice and explanatory note, or by affixing to each affected unit, and two lampposts or one lamppost where there is only one within 100 metres of that unit. The affixed notice is in the form of Sch.6. Where a notice cannot be affixed, there is the alternative of advertisement in a newspaper circulating in the area of the affected unit. An advertisement should identify the land which is the affected unit, set out the terms of the burden, specify the name and address of the person proposing to register the deed and identify the person from whom a copy of the deed may be obtained. The advertisement must also state that any owner of a unit who has not granted the deed may apply to the Lands Tribunal for the community burden to be preserved setting out the specified date by which application must be made. Effectively, the provisions of s.21(6) in relation to affixed notices are applied by subs.5, subject to modification.

Preservation of community burden in respect of which deed of variation or discharge has been granted as mentioned in section 35(1)

37.—(1) Where a deed of variation or, as the case may be, of discharge has been granted as mentioned in section 35(1) of this Act, any owner of a unit in the community who has not granted the deed may, during the period of eight weeks beginning with the latest date on which intimation of the proposal to register that deed is given under section 36(2) of this Act, apply to the Lands Tribunal for preservation, unvaried, of the community burden in so far as constituted in favour of, or against, any unit not all of whose owners have granted the deed.

(2) A deed of variation or discharge granted as so mentioned shall not, on registration, vary or discharge a community burden in so far as constituted in favour of, or against, any unit not all of whose owners have granted the deed unless, after the expiry of the period mentioned in subsection (1) above, there is endorsed on it (or on an annexation to it referred to in an endorsement on it and identified, on the face of the annexation, as being the annexation so referred to) a certificate executed by a member of the Lands Tribunal, or by their clerk, to the effect that no application in relation to the proposal to register the deed has been received under this section or that any such application which has been received—

(a) has been withdrawn; or

¹(b) relates to one or more but not to all of the community burdens the terms of which are set out or referred to in the deed (any community burden to which it relates being described in the certificate),

and where more than one such application has been received the certificate shall relate to both (or as the case may be all) applications.

(3) A deed of variation or discharge granted as so mentioned does not vary or discharge, in so far as constituted in favour of, or against, any unit not all of whose owners have granted the deed, a burden described by virtue of subsection (2)(b) above.

(4) A person who proposes to submit a deed of variation or discharge granted as so mentioned for registration shall, before doing so, swear or affirm before a notary public (the deed being endorsed accordingly)—

(a) that section 36 of this Act has been complied with; and

(b) as to the date on which the period mentioned in subsection (1) above expires,

but if more than one person so proposes only one of them need so swear or affirm.

(5) Subsection (2) of section 22 of this Act applies in relation to such a person and for the purposes of subsection (4) above as it applies in relation to a terminator and for the purposes of subsection (1) of that section.

(6) For the purposes of subsection (1) above, intimation by affixing shall be taken to be given when first the notice is affixed.

Amendment

1. As amended by the Title Conditions (Scotland) Act 2003 (Consequential Provisions) Order (SSI 2003/503), Sch.1, para.8 (effective October 22, 2003).

General Note

As a counterbalance to the right of the majority to vary or discharge community burdens the dissenting minority may apply to the Lands Tribunal to have the community burden preserved. If the existing application is granted the community burden is preserved in so far as it is constituted in favour of, or against any unit where not all of the owners have granted the deed of discharge or variation. The effect of the grant of an application is to isolate those who have not granted the deed of variation or discharge.

Subs.(1)

This details the right of the dissenting minority to apply within the eight-week period. It also allows a common owner who has not granted the deed to apply.

Subs.(2)

This details the requirement for a certificate to be endorsed on a deed of variation or discharge by the Lands Tribunal, indicating that no application for preservation has been made within the eight-week period, or if such an application has been made it has been withdrawn, or relates to one or more—but not all of—the community burdens, which are to be varied or discharged.

Subs.(3)

This inclusion makes it clear that if the deed of variation or discharge only relates to some burdens if granted it will not vary or discharge so far as owners who have not granted the deed are concerned any of the community burdens referred to in s.37(2)(b).

Subs.(4)

Any person submitting a deed of variation or discharge for registration must swear or affirm that s.36 of the Act has been complied with and the period has expired. Where more than one person wishes to register the deed then only one need swear or affirm.

Subs.(5)

The provisions of s.21(2) apply to the person swearing or affirming.

Subs.(6)

Intimation by affixing takes effect on the date when the notices are first affixed.

PART 3

CONSERVATION AND OTHER PERSONAL REAL BURDENS

Conservation burdens

38.—(1) On and after the day on which this section comes into force it shall, subject to subsection (2) below, be competent to create a real burden in favour of a conservation body, or of the Scottish Ministers, for the purpose of preserving, or protecting, for the benefit of the public—

   (a) the architectural or historical characteristics of any land; or

   (b) any other special characteristics of any land (including, without prejudice to the generality of this paragraph, a special characteristic derived from the flora, fauna or general appearance of the land);

and any such burden shall be known as a "conservation burden".

(2) If under subsection (1) above the conservation burden is to be created other than by the conservation body or the Scottish Ministers, the consent of—

   (a) that body to the creation of the burden in its favour; or

   (b) those Ministers to the creation of the burden in their favour,

must be obtained before the constitutive deed is registered.

(3) It shall not be competent to grant a standard security over a conservation burden.

(4) The Scottish Ministers may, subject to subsection (5) below, by order, prescribe such body as they think fit to be a conservation body.

(5) The power conferred by subsection (4) above may be exercised in relation to a body only if the object, or function, of the body (or, as the case may be, one of its objects or functions) is to preserve, or protect, for the benefit of the public such characteristics of any land as are mentioned in paragraph (a) or (b) of subsection (1) above.

(6) Where the power conferred by subsection (4) above is exercised in relation to a trust, the conservation body shall be the trustees of the trust.

(7) The Scottish Ministers may, by order, determine that such conservation body as may be specified in the order shall cease to be a conservation body.

GENERAL NOTE

Conservation burdens were first introduced by the 2000 Act. That Act was concerned with the preservation of existing feudal burdens where these burdens had been created in writs granted by conservation bodies. Conservation burdens are not realloted in terms of s.18 of the 2000 Act. They are simply preserved as conservation burdens by the execution and registration of a notice under Sch.8 to the 2000 Act. Scottish Ministers have prescribed certain bodies (including local authorities) to be conservation bodies, and they may also by order determine that any such a body may cease to be a conservation body. Sections 38–42 provide the legislative framework for conservation burdens in the post-feudal era. These will be burdens which are created in a constitutive deed, as opposed to a feudal writ.

Subs.(1)

The provision allows real burdens to be created in favour of conservation bodies or Scottish Ministers where these burdens are for the purpose of preserving or protecting for the benefit of the public the architectural or historical characteristics of any land or any other special characteristics of any land including a special characteristic derived from flora, fauna or general appearance of the land. These burdens are to be known as conservation burdens.

Subs.(2)

It will apparently be possible to create a conservation burden in favour of a conservation body or Scottish Ministers in a constitutive deed to which the conservation body or Scottish Ministers are not party, provided that the consent of the conservation body or Scottish Ministers has been obtained before the constitutive deed is registered.

Subs.(3)

Although the right to enforce a conservation burden must presumably be an incorporeal heritable right it will not be an interest in land for the purposes of the grant of a standard security.

Subs.(4)

Scottish Ministers will decide which bodies are conservation bodies.

Subs.(5)

Before a body can be declared a conservation body its object or function, or one of its objects or functions, must be to preserve or protect for the benefit of the public such characteristics as are mentioned in subs.(1).

Subs.(6)

Many conservation bodies are trusts of a public or quasi-public nature. In such a case trustees may be a conservation body.

Subs.(7)

Scottish Ministers may remove conservation bodies from the approved list.

Assignation

39.—The right to a conservation burden may be assigned or otherwise transferred to any conservation body or to the Scottish Ministers; and any such assignation or transfer takes effect on registration.

General Note

A conservation burden is as incorporeal heritable right and may be assigned or otherwise transferred to another conservation body or Scottish Ministers. Such an assignation will require to be registered and will take effect on registration. There does not appear to be any requirement to intimate the assignation to the owner for the time being of the burdened property although this would be sensible.

Enforcement where no completed title

40.—A conservation burden is enforceable by the holder of the burden irrespective of whether the holder has completed title to the burden.

General Note

This is a rather odd section. For a party to be able to enforce a real burden that party must have title and interest to enforce. Section 40 provides that the conservation body in whose favour the burden is conceived will have a title to enforce even if its right has not been registered. The first conservation body will presumably have an entitlement to enforce the burden as soon as the constitutive deed creating the burden is registered. This deed will, of course, be in favour of an owner of the burdened property, so there could be an argument that the conservation body or Scottish Ministers have no actual title to enforce. This section makes it clear that none is required. The position will be different where there is an assignation of the burden from one conservation body to another, or from one conservation body to Scottish Ministers. In such a situation, it could be argued that the assignee body does have a title to the conservation burden by virtue of the registered assignation.

Completion of title

41.—Where the holder of a conservation burden does not have a completed title—

  (a) title may be completed by the holder registering a notice of title; or

  (b) without completing title, the holder may grant—

  (i) under section 39 of this Act, a deed assigning the right to the burden; or

  (ii) under section 48 of this Act, a deed discharging, in whole or in part, the burden,

but unless the deed is one to which section 15(3) of the 1979 Act (circumstances where unnecessary to deduce title) applies, it shall be necessary, in the deed, to deduce title to the burden through the midcouples linking the holder to the person who had the last completed title.

GENERAL NOTE

  This section deals with a situation where a conservation body is reorganised and it is provided within the reorganisation scheme that any conservation burdens and the right to enforce them will pass to another successor body. The obvious example of this would be local government reorganisation or changes in the identity of trustees. In such a case, there is provision for a notice of title to be registered. A notice of title, of course, would only apply in a case where the conservation burden is somehow or other in the sasine register. It could apply in the case of a feudal burden which has been realloted in terms of s.26 of the 2000 Act. Section 30 of the 2000 Act contains a similar provision in relation to completion of title. In such a case a deduction of title would be required. Where, however, the conservation burden is registered in the Land Register no notice of title will be required. The Keeper will be able to update the title sheet. A successor body will be able to grant assignations and discharges.

Extinction of burden on body ceasing to be conservation body

42. Where—

  (a) the holder of a conservation burden is a conservation body or, as the case may be, two or more such bodies; and

  (b) that body ceases to be such a body, or those bodies cease to be such bodies (whether because an order under section 38(7) of this Act so provides or because the body in question has ceased to exist),

the conservation burden shall, on the body or bodies so ceasing, forthwith be extinguished.

GENERAL NOTE

  The right to enforce a conservation burden is not tied to the ownership of any interest in land. It is tied to the peculiar nature of the conservation body. Accordingly, if the body ceases to be a conservation body or if indeed it ceases to exist, the burden is extinguished. Presumably a conservation body which was in terminal decline might consider assigning a conservation burden to another conservation body or Scottish Ministers.

Rural housing burdens

Rural housing burdens

  [1]**43.**—(1) On and after the day on which this section comes into force it shall, subject to subsections (2) and (3) below, be competent to create a real burden over rural land which comprises a right of pre-emption in favour of

a rural housing body other than by reference to the body's capacity as owner of any land; and any such burden shall be known as a "rural housing burden".

(2) If under subsection (1) above the rural housing burden is to be created other than by the rural housing body, the consent of that body to the creation of the burden in its favour must be obtained before the constitutive deed is registered.

(3) It shall not be competent to create a rural housing burden on the sale of a property by virtue of section 61 of the Housing (Scotland) Act 1987 (c.26) (secure tenant's right to purchase).

(4) It shall not be competent to grant a standard security over a rural housing burden.

(5) The Scottish Ministers may, subject to subsection (6) below, by order, prescribe such body as they think fit to be a rural housing body.

(6) The power conferred by subsection (5) above may be exercised in relation to a body only if the object, or function, of the body (or, as the case may be one of its principal objects or functions) is to provide housing or land for housing.

(7) Where the power conferred by subsection (5) above is exercised in relation to a trust, the rural housing body shall be the trustees of the trust.

(8) The Scottish Ministers may, by order, determine that such rural housing body as may be specified in the order shall cease to be a rural housing body.

(9) In this section, "rural land" means land other than excluded land ("excluded land" having the same meaning as in Part 2 of the Land Reform (Scotland) Act 2003 (asp 2)).

(10) Sections 39 to 42 of this Act apply in relation to a rural housing burden and a rural housing body as they apply in relation to a conservation burden and a conservation body but with the modifications that in section 39 the words "or to the Scottish Ministers" shall be disregarded and in section 42(b) the reference to an order under section 38(7) of this Act shall be construed as a reference to an order under subsection (8) above.

AMENDMENT
1. As amended by the Tenements (Scotland) Act 2004 (asp 11), s.25, Sch.4, para.12 (effective October 23, 2004).

GENERAL NOTE
The provisions of s.43 create a special type of pre-emption right in favour of a rural housing body. A rural housing body is defined in s.122 as any body prescribed by order under subs.(5). Effectively, it will be up to Scottish Ministers to decide which bodies are to be rural housing bodies. It will be competent to create a right of pre-emption as a real burden on rural land in favour of a rural housing body whether or not that body actually owns any land which could be said to be benefited.

Subs.(1)
This subsection sets out the principle that a right of pre-emption can be a rural housing burden in favour of a rural housing body as a personal real burden.

Subs.(2)
The pre-emption may be created in a deed to which the rural housing body are not a party if that body consents to the creation of the burden before the constitutive deed is registered.

Subs.(3)
Where a secure tenant exercises his or her right to buy in terms of s.61 of the Housing (Scotland) Act 1987, it shall not be competent to create a personal right of pre-emption as a rural housing burden. There are of course other protections in respect of repayment of discount where there is a resale within the statutory period.

Subs.(4)

As with conservation burdens it is not competent to grant a standard security over a rural housing burden.

Subs.(5)

This gives Scottish Ministers the power to decide which bodies are to be rural housing bodies.

Subs.(6)

The only bodies which can become rural housing bodies shall be bodies whose object or function is to provide housing on rural land or to provide rural land for housing. The body may, however, have these objects or functions as principal objects or functions as opposed to sole objects or functions.

Subs.(7)

Where the rural housing body is a trust then the trustees are the body.

Subs.(8)

Scottish Ministers may determine when a rural housing body shall cease to have that status.

Subs.(9)

Rural land does not include excluded land in terms of Pt 2 of the Land Reform (Scotland) Act 2003.

Subs.(10)

The provisions in ss.39–42 apply with the necessary modifications.

Maritime burdens

Maritime burdens

44.—(1) On and after the day on which this section comes into force, it shall be competent to create a real burden over the sea bed or foreshore in favour of the Crown for the benefit of the public; and any such burden shall be known as a "maritime burden".

(2) The right of the Crown to a maritime burden may not be assigned or otherwise transferred.

(3) For the purposes of this section—

(a) "sea bed" means the bed of the territorial sea adjacent to Scotland; and

(b) "territorial sea" includes any tidal waters.

GENERAL NOTE

Maritime burdens were introduced as a concept by the 2000 Act (s.60). The right to enforce these burdens is restricted to the Crown.

Subs.(1)

It will be competent to create a real burden over the seabed or the foreshore in favour of the Crown for the benefit of the public and such a burden will be known as a maritime burden.

Subs.(2)

The right is restricted to the Crown to the extent that the maritime burden may not be assigned or otherwise transferred.

Subs.(3)

This contains definitions of the seabed and territorial sea.

Economic development burdens

Economic development burdens

45.—(1) On and after the day on which this section comes into force it shall, subject to subsection (2) below, be competent to create a real burden in favour of a local authority, or of the Scottish Ministers, for the purpose of promoting economic development; and any such burden shall be known as an "economic development burden".

(2) If under subsection (1) above the economic development burden is to be created other than by the local authority or the Scottish Ministers, the consent of that body or those Ministers to the creation of the burden in their favour must be obtained before the constitutive deed is registered.

(3) An economic development burden may comprise an obligation to pay a sum of money (the sum or the method of determining it being specified in the constitutive deed) to the local authority or the Scottish Ministers as the case may be.

(4) It shall not be competent—

(a) to grant a standard security over; or

(b) to assign the right to,

an economic development burden.

(5) Sections 40 and 41(a) and (b)(ii) of this Act apply in relation to an economic development burden as they apply in relation to a conservation burden.

(6) [*Repealed by the Tenements (Scotland) Act 2004 (asp 11), s.25, Sch.4, para.13 (effective October 23, 2004).*]

GENERAL NOTE

This new type of burden can only be created in favour of a local authority or Scottish Ministers for the purpose of promoting economic development. Normally, it would be created in a disposition by the local authority or Scottish Ministers of land sold with a view to development which would benefit the community. If the burden is created in a constitutive deed to which a local authority or Scottish Ministers are not parties then the consent of the local authority or Scottish Ministers must be obtained before the constitutive deed is registered. An economic development burden will normally be an obligation providing for a claw-back in the event, for example, that land is sold at a low price and then resold at a high price because of some development potential. Subsection 3 makes it clear that the sum of money to be recovered need not be exact provided that there is a method of calculating it in the constitutive deed. This is to get over the normal rule that any real burden in respect of a sum of money must be for an exact sum. Although an economic development burden must be regarded as an incorporeal heritable right, like other so-called personal real burdens it cannot be the subject of a standard security. It should be noted that this type of burden can only be granted in favour of local authorities or Scottish Ministers. Accordingly, it cannot be assigned. It has been the practice to insert claw-back burdens of this type in deeds granted by landowners or developers. Most of these real burdens are ineffective so far as singular successors of the original disponee are concerned because they involve complicated calculations by means of formulae relative to base values and development values. The law remains the same so far as this type of title provision is concerned. An economic development burden will be enforceable by the local authority or Scottish Ministers irrespective of whether they have a completed title to the burden and a successor local authority or a reconstituted body will be able to complete a title as with a conservation burden in terms of s.41. There does not appear to be a requirement that the economic development takes place at the burdened land.

Health care burdens

Health care burdens

46.—(1) On and after the day on which this section comes into force it shall, subject to subsection (2) below, be competent to create a real burden in favour of a National Health Service trust, or of the Scottish Ministers, for the purpose of promoting the provision of facilities for health care; and any such burden shall be known as a "health care burden".

(2) If under subsection (1) above the health care burden is to be created other than by the trust or the Scottish Ministers, the consent of the trust or those Ministers to the creation of the burden in its or their favour must be obtained before the constitutive deed is registered.

(3) A health care burden may comprise an obligation to pay a sum of

money (the sum or the method of determining it being specified in the constitutive deed) to the trust or the Scottish Ministers as the case may be.

(4) It shall not be competent—

(a) to grant a standard security over; or

(b) to assign the right to,

a health care burden.

(5) Sections 40 and 41(a) and (b)(ii) of this Act apply in relation to a health care burden as they apply in relation to a conservation burden.

(6) In subsection (1) above, "facilities for health care" includes facilities ancillary to health care; as for example (but without prejudice to that generality) accommodation for staff employed to provide health care.

GENERAL NOTE

A health care burden is a burden in favour of a National Health Service trust or Scottish Ministers for the purpose of promoting the provision of facilities for health care. As with economic development burdens these will normally be created in a deed granted by a Health Service trust or Scottish Ministers for health purposes but containing some sort of claw-back burden in relation to alternative development. If the burden is created in a constitutive deed to which the trust or Scottish Ministers are not parties then their consent must be obtained. It is not competent to grant a standard security over or assign a health care burden. The provisions in relation to completion of title also apply (see ss.40 and 41(a)(b)(ii)). The term "facilities for health care" includes facilities ancillary to health care as for example accommodation for staff employed to provide health care.

General

Interest to enforce

47.—The holder of a personal real burden is presumed to have an interest to enforce the burden.

GENERAL NOTE

Personal real burdens are something of an anomaly. They run contrary to the definition of real burdens contained in s.1. As a general rule, the holder of a real burden must have both title and interest to enforce. The interest, however, must be a praedial or patrimonial interest and not merely a personal one. Since the holder of a personal burden will not have such a praedial or patrimonial interest this section provides that the holder of a personal real burden is presumed to have an interest to enforce.

Discharge

48.—(1) A personal real burden is discharged by registering against the burdened property a deed of discharge granted by or on behalf of the holder of the burden.

(2) In subsection (1) above, "discharged" means discharged—

(a) wholly; or

(b) to such extent as may be specified in the deed of discharge.

GENERAL NOTE

A discharge of a personal real burden is registered against the burdened property. The discharge can be to the extent of the whole burden or only to a limited extent.

PART 4

TRANSITIONAL: IMPLIED RIGHTS OF ENFORCEMENT

Extinction of implied rights of enforcement

Extinction

49.—(1) Any rule of law whereby land may be the benefited property, in relation to a real burden, by implication (that is to say, without being nominated in the constitutive deed as the benefited property and without being so nominated in any deed into which the constitutive deed is incorporated) shall cease to have effect on the appointed day and a real burden shall not, on and after that day, be enforceable by virtue of such rule; but this subsection is subject to subsection (2) below.

(2) In relation to a benefited property as respects which, on the appointed day, it is competent (taking such rule of law as is mentioned in subsection (1) above still to be in effect) to register a notice of preservation or of converted servitude, subsection (1) above shall apply with the substitution, for the reference to the appointed day, of a reference to the day immediately following the expiry of the period of ten years beginning with the appointed day.

GENERAL NOTE

It is to be doubted whether anyone wholly understands the existing law, at least where a right is created by implication rather than expressly in a deed. The reason for this is mainly because the law is based on a number of conflicting decisions. This leads to the obvious difficulty of ascertaining just who might have the implied right. The thrust of the new legislation is to abolish rights which arise purely by implication, as opposed to those which are expressly created. This is a sensible and much needed reform. The new rules resolve the difficulties caused by the decisions in *J.A. Mactaggart & Co v Roemmele* (1906) 8 F 1101 and *Botanic Gardens Picture House Ltd v Adamson*, 1924 S.C. 549. The aim of the reform is to extinguish implied rights in a 10-year period other than those which may be preserved under s.50, and to prevent implied enforcement rights arising in the future. Sections 52–56, however, contain certain replacement enforcement rights under common schemes for related properties. There are special provisions in s.54 in relation to sheltered housing and in s.56 in relation to facility and service burdens. It should be noted, however, that these provisions, with the exception of s.53 apply only to real burdens which have been created prior to the appointed day.

Subs.(1)

On the appointed day implied enforcement rights will be abolished. After the appointed day it will be necessary to state expressly in the constitutive deed which properties are to be benefited properties.

Subs.(2)

Those who hold an implied enforcement right on the appointed day will be entitled to register a notice of preservation or a notice of converted servitude. If they do so then the implied enforcement right will be preserved.

Preservation

50.—(1) Subject to subsection (6) below, an owner of land which is a benefited property by virtue of such rule of law as is mentioned in section 49(1) of this Act may, during the period of ten years beginning with the appointed day, execute and duly register, in (or as nearly as may be in) the form contained in schedule 7 to this Act, a notice of preservation as respects the land; and if the owner does so then the land shall continue to be a benefited property after the expiry of that period (in so far as the burdened property, the benefited property and the real burden are the burdened property, the benefited property, and the real burden identified in the notice of preservation).

(2) The notice of preservation shall—

(a) identify the land which is the burdened property (or any part of that land);

(b) identify the land which is the benefited property (or any part of that land);

(c) where the person registering the notice does not have a completed title to the benefited property, set out the midcouples linking that person to the person who last had such completed title;

(d) set out the terms of the real burden; and

(e) set out the grounds, both factual and legal, for describing as a benefited property the land identified in pursuance of paragraph (b) above.

(3) For the purposes of subsection (1) above, a notice is, subject to section 116 of this Act, duly registered only when registered against both properties identified in pursuance of subsection (2)(a) and (b) above.

(4) A person submitting any notice for registration under this section shall, before doing so, swear or affirm before a notary public that to the best of the knowledge and belief of the person all the information contained in the notice is true.

(5) For the purposes of subsection (4) above, if the person is—

(a) an individual unable by reason of legal disability, or incapacity, to swear or affirm as mentioned in that subsection, then a legal representative of the person may swear or affirm;

(b) not an individual, then any person authorised to sign documents on its behalf may swear or affirm;

and any reference in that subsection to a person shall be construed accordingly.

(6) Subsection (1) above does not apply as respects a real burden which has been imposed under a common scheme affecting both the burdened and the benefited property.

(7) This section is subject to section 115 of this Act.

GENERAL NOTE

This makes it clear that the notice of preservation may be registered at any time during the 10-year period. The notice of preservation is in the form of Sch.7 to the Act. This section is intended to cover situations where there is clearly a benefited property and a burdened property and the burden is in the nature of a neighbour burden. It is not really intended to cover burdens which affect all properties in a common scheme. If the notice of preservation is registered within the 10-year period then the benefited property will remain a benefited property in so far as that burden is concerned after the 10-year period has expired.

Subs.(2)

This subsection lists the details which must appear in the notice of preservation. The burdened and benefited properties must be identified, as must any links in title. The terms of the burden must be specified and the grounds, both factual and legal, which justify the assertion that the land identified is indeed a benefited property.

Subs.(3)

This requires registration against the title of both benefited and burdened properties.

Subs.(4)

Anyone submitting a notice of preservation must swear or affirm before a notary public that, to the best of his or her knowledge and belief, all the information contained in the notice is true.

Subs.(5)

The usual provisions in relation to those with legal disability or incapacity apply as do the rules relating to corporate identities.

Subs.(6)

Separate provision is made in ss.52–54 for common schemes.

Subs.(7)

Section 105 contains further provisions relating to the intimation.

Duties of Keeper: amendments relating to unenforceable real burdens

51.—(1) Unless one of the circumstances mentioned in subsection (2) below arises, the Keeper of the Registers of Scotland shall not be required to remove from the Land Register of Scotland a real burden which section 49 of this Act makes unenforceable.

(2) The circumstances are that the Keeper—

(a) is requested, in an application for registration or rectification, to remove the real burden; or

(b) is, under section 9(1) of the 1979 Act (rectification of the register), ordered to do so by the court or the Lands Tribunal,
and no such request or order shall be competent during that period of ten years which commences with the appointed day.

(3) During the period mentioned in subsection (2) above a real burden, notwithstanding that it has been so made unenforceable, may at the discretion of the Keeper, for the purposes of section 6(1)(e) of the 1979 Act (entering subsisting real right in title sheet), be taken to subsist; but this subsection is without prejudice to subsection (4) below.

(4) The Keeper shall not, before the date mentioned in subsection (5) below, remove from the Land Register of Scotland a real burden which is the subject of a notice in respect of which application has been made for a determination by—

(a) a court; or

(b) the Lands Tribunal,

under section 115(6)(b) of this Act.

(5) The date is whichever is the earlier of—

(a) that two months after the final decision on the application; and

(b) that prescribed under section 115(6)(ii) of this Act.

GENERAL NOTE

In an ideal world, the Keeper would cleanse the registers of all unenforceable real burdens. After the abolition of feudal tenure superiors will, subject to the re-allotment provisions in the 2000 Act, lose the right to enforce. Those other parties who have a *ius quaesitum tertio* will retain that right. If it is an implied *ius quaesitum tertio*, then they may only retain it for 10 years unless a notice of preservation is registered. At the end of the 10-year period if no notice has been registered that right will also be lost. However, it would be impossible for the Keeper to immediately undertake the task of cleansing the registers. Section 51 therefore limits the duties of the Keeper in this regard in much the same way as s.46 of the 2000 Act does in relation to feudal burdens. Basically, the Keeper is not required to remove unenforceable burdens which rely on implied *ius quaesitum tertio* unless he is requested to do so in an application for registration or rectification or is ordered to do so by the court or the Lands Tribunal. However, no such request or order shall be competent during the period of 10 years, which commences with the appointed day.

New implied rights of enforcement

Common schemes: general

52.—(1) Where real burdens are imposed under a common scheme and the deed by which they are imposed on any unit, being a deed registered before the appointed day, expressly refers to the common scheme or is so worded that the existence of the common scheme is to be implied (or a constitutive deed incorporated into that deed so refers or is so worded) then, subject to subsection (2) below, any unit subject to the common scheme by virtue of—

(a) that deed; or

(b) any other deed so registered,

shall be a benefited property in relation to the real burdens.

(2) Subsection (1) above applies only in so far as no provision to the contrary is impliedly (as for example by reservation of a right to vary or waive the real burdens) or expressly made in the deed mentioned in paragraph (a) of that subsection (or in any such constitutive deed as is mentioned in that subsection).

(3) This section confers no right of pre-emption, redemption or reversion.

(4) This section is subject to sections 57(1) and 122(2)(ii) of this Act.

GENERAL NOTE

This section involves a restatement of the existing law of *ius quaesitum tertio* or, more accurately third party rights, where these arise by implication. Where burdens are imposed under a common scheme in a deed registered before the appointed day, and that deed expressly refers to a common scheme or is so worded that a common scheme can be implied, then any unit subject to the common scheme shall be a benefited property in relation to the burdens. A typical case would be a tenement property or block of flats subject to a deed of conditions applicable to all flats.

Subs.(1)

This sets out the general principle of reciprocity subject to the important exception in subsection (2).

Subs.(2)

This preserves the existing rule that a reservation to the party who has imposed the conditions to waive or alter these conditions is destructive of mutuality (see *Turner v Hamilton* (1890) 17 R 494).

Subs.(3)

Any burdens imposed will not be construed as rights of pre-emption, redemption or reversion but merely as rights to enforce the burdens.

Subs.(4)

If a right of enforcement has already been waived or has been lost, *e.g.* by acquiescence, as at the day immediately preceding the appointed day, then it will not be revived in terms of this section. Where a burden contains an obligation to maintain a public utility such as a road or a sewer and that obligation has been taken over by the local authority, s.52 will not result in a revival of that burden.

Common schemes: related properties

53.—(1) Where real burdens are imposed under a common scheme, the deed by which they are imposed on any unit comprised within a group of related properties being a deed registered before the appointed day, then all units comprised within that group and subject to the common scheme (whether or not by virtue of a deed registered before the appointed day) shall be benefited properties in relation to the real burdens.

(2) Whether properties are related properties for the purposes of subsection (1) above is to be inferred from all the circumstances; and without prejudice to the generality of this subsection, circumstances giving rise to such an inference might include—

(a) the convenience of managing the properties together because they share—
   (i) some common feature; or
   (ii) an obligation for common maintenance of some facility;
(b) there being shared ownership of common property;
(c) their being subject to the common scheme by virtue of the same deed of conditions; or
(d) the properties each being a flat in the same tenement.

(3) This section confers no right of pre-emption, redemption or reversion.

¹ (3A) Section 4 of this Act shall apply in relation to any real burden to which subsection (1) above applies as if—

(a) in subsection (2), paragraph (c)(ii);
(b) subsection (4); and
(c) in subsection (5), the words from "and" to the end,

were omitted.

(4) This section is subject to sections 57 and 122(2)(ii) of this Act.

AMENDMENT

1. Inserted by the Tenements (Scotland) Act 2004 (asp 11), s.25, Sch.4, para.14 (effective October 23, 2004).

GENERAL NOTE

It is possible that real burdens may be imposed under a common scheme by virtue of a conveyance or a succession of conveyances registered prior to the appointed day. It may be that some of the properties which are physically, if not legally, in the common scheme area are not made subject to the burdens until after the appointed day. These would be related properties. The typical example would be a local authority estate where there is no deed of conditions covering all the houses sold and unsold, the burdens being created in each conveyance. Whether a property is a related property or not is to be inferred from all the circumstances but taking into account various features such as the convenience of managing properties together because they share a common feature or common maintenance obligation. Other matters which would be taken into account would be the existence of common property and the fact that they are all subject to the same deed of conditions. Flats in a tenement are the obvious example. The idea behind this section is to allow for a rolling community. If conveyances (feudal or otherwise) have been granted prior to the appointed day with identical or very similar real burdens so that a common scheme has been created then each time a disposition is granted after the appointed day with the same or similar real burdens then that newly sold property will, on registration of the disposition, be added to the community. It will effectively become a burdened and a benefited property with enforcement rights against all the other properties subject to the burdens. There was an argument, however, that for this section to apply all the benefited properties previously sold would require to be listed. This was to comply with the provisions of section 4 which states that the burdened and benefited properties must be identified and there must be dual registration to preserve transparency in enforcement rights. This would have proved an extremely awkward provision. Accordingly, the section was amended by the Tenements (Scotland) Act 2004. For section 53 to apply it will not be necessary that all the benefited properties are identified nor will the burden be registered against the title of all the benefited properties. Where a deed of conditions has been granted and it applies to the whole of an estate (both sold and unsold properties) then the developer or local authority still owning the rump of the unsold estate will be able to continue to enforce the burdens. If, however, there is no deed of conditions and previous conveyances have been feudal then although the contractual right of the superior to enforce as against the first vassal will remain the superior will lose the right to enforce against singular successors because of feudal abolition. If previous conveyances have been by way of disposition the rights of real owner of the rump of the estate to enforce as against singular successors of the original disponees will depend on whether or not title to enforce in favour of the remaining portions of the estate has been expressly created. If not, then the provisions of sections 49–51 will apply. Burdens, however, which qualify as facility or service burdens in terms of section of section 56 will continue to be enforceable no matter what method of imposing burdens has been adopted. Accordingly, if for example, a local authority has granted feu dispositions and there is no deed of conditions then that local authority as owner of unsold units will be able to enforce facility and service burdens as owners of land to which the facility is, and is intended to be, of benefit. Alternatively, where a local authority or developer still holding the rump of an estate wishes more extensive enforcement rights then a deed of conditions may be granted by that local authority or developer over the rump of the estate. Provided that deed of conditions contains the same or very similar burdens to those contained in the original conveyances of sold properties (whether feudal or otherwise) then all the units (both sold and yet to be sold) will be part of a common scheme and will be related properties.

Sheltered housing

54.—(1) Where by a deed (or deeds) registered before the appointed day real burdens are imposed under a common scheme on all the units in a sheltered or retirement housing development or on all such units except a unit which is used in some special way, each unit shall be a benefited property in relation to the real burdens.

(2) Subsection (1) above is subject to section 122(2)(ii) of this Act.

(3) In this section, "sheltered or retirement housing development" means a group of dwelling-houses which, having regard to their design, size and other features, are particularly suitable for occupation by elderly people (or by people who are disabled or infirm or in some other way vulnerable) and which, for the purposes of such occupation, are provided with facilities substantially different from those of ordinary dwelling-houses.

(4) Any real burden which regulates the use, maintenance, reinstatement or management—

    (a) of—

        (i) a facility; or

        (ii) a service,

which is one of those which make a sheltered or retirement housing development particularly suitable for such occupation as is mentioned in subsection (3) above; or

(b) of any other facility if it is a facility such as is mentioned in that subsection,

is in this section referred to as a "core burden".

(5) In relation to a sheltered or retirement housing development—

(a) section 28 of this Act applies with the following modifications—

    (i) in subsection (1), the reference to the owners of a majority of the units in a community shall, for the purposes of paragraphs (b) and (c) of that subsection, be construed as a reference to the owners of at least two thirds of the units in the development; and

    (ii) in paragraph (c) of subsection (2), the reference to varying or discharging shall be construed as a reference only to varying and that to community burdens as a reference only to real burdens which are not core burdens (the words "Without prejudice to the generality of subsection (1)(b) above," which begin the subsection being, for the purposes of that modification, disregarded except in so far as they give meaning to the words "the powers mentioned there" which immediately follow them);

(b) section 33 of this Act, in relation to core burdens, applies with the following modifications—

    (i) in subsection (1), the reference to varying or discharging shall, in relation to a deed granted in accordance with subsection (2) of the section, be construed as a reference only to varying; and

    (ii) in subsection (2)(a) the reference to the owners of a majority of the units shall be construed as a reference to the owners of at least two thirds of the units of the development; and

(c) no real burden relating to a restriction as to any person's age may be varied or discharged by virtue of section 33(2) of this Act.

(6) This section confers no right of pre-emption, redemption or reversion and is subject to section 57 of this Act.

GENERAL NOTE

Section 54 contains special provision in relation to burdens imposed on sheltered housing complexes. A sheltered or retirement housing development is a group of dwelling houses which having regard to their design, size and other features are particularly suitable for occupation by elderly, disabled, infirm or vulnerable people and are provided with facilities for these purposes. Not all housing units within such developments will be so designed. There may be a warden's or caretaker's flat, or there may be a guest flat with accommodation for visiting relatives. Such special units will not necessarily be subject to the sheltered housing burdens but will be benefited units having enforcement rights being part of the sheltered housing community.

Subs.(1)

This provides that where burdens are imposed under a common scheme in a sheltered or retirement housing development in a deed registered prior to the appointed day, then each unit is to be a benefited property in relation to such real burdens. The burdens need not be imposed on units used in a special way such as a warden's flat.

Subs.(2)

Where a burden has been taken over by a local authority such as an obligation to maintain roads or sewers, then this obligation will not be a real burden for the purposes of a sheltered or retirement housing scheme.

Subs.(3)

This contains the definition of a sheltered or retirement housing development.

Subs.(4)

This defines "core burdens" for the purposes of subs.5. These are burdens which regulate the use, maintenance, re-instatement or management of a facility or a service which is designed to make the development suitable for the people defined in subs.(3).

Subs.(5)

This subsection makes it clear that burdens in common schemes relating to sheltered or retirement housing are community burdens and that the various powers vest in the majority of the owners. This subsection modifies s.28 of the Act which contains the power of a majority to appoint a manager and confer powers on that manager. The majority for sheltered and retirement housing purposes is two-thirds for the purposes of s.28(1)(b) and (c). It will not be competent under s.28 to confer on a manager the power to discharge burdens in a sheltered housing development where the burdens are core burdens. Similarly, it will not be possible to extinguish core burdens using the fall-back provisions in s.33 as a required majority for core burdens in a sheltered housing development will be two-thirds. There is a blanket prohibition of varying or discharging a real burden relating to an age restriction in a sheltered or retirement housing development. All provisions in this subsection will apply to burdens created both before and after the appointed day.

Subs.(6)

This simply confirms that no right of pre-emption, redemption or reversion is implied and also that even burdens in sheltered housing developments (core or otherwise) can be lost through waiver, acquiescence or other means in the usual way.

Grant of deed of variation or discharge of community burdens relating to sheltered or retirement housing: community consultation notice

55.—(1) Where in relation to a sheltered or retirement housing development it is proposed to grant, under section 33(1)(a) or (2) of this Act, a deed of variation or discharge, the proposal shall be intimated to all the owners of the units of the community.

(2) Such intimation shall be given by sending a notice (a "community consultation notice") in, or as near as may be in, the form set out in schedule 8 to this Act together with the explanatory note which immediately follows that form in that schedule.

(3) The deed of variation or discharge shall not be granted before the date specified in the community consultation notice as that by which any comments are to be made, being a date no earlier than that on which expires the period of three weeks beginning with the latest date on which such intimation is given.

(4) Subsection (4) of section 37 of this Act shall apply in relation to a deed of variation or discharge granted as mentioned in subsection (1) above and to the person giving intimation as it applies in relation to such a deed granted as mentioned in section 35(1) of this Act and to the person proposing to submit the deed but with the modifications that the reference—

(a) in paragraph (a) of the said subsection (4), to section 36 of this Act is to be construed as a reference to this section; and

(b) in paragraph (b) of that subsection, to subsection (1) of section 37 of this Act is to be construed as a reference to subsection (3) above.

(5) For the purposes of subsection (4) of section 37 as so applied, if the person giving intimation is—

(a) an individual unable by reason of legal disability, or incapacity, to swear or affirm as mentioned in the said subsection (4), then a legal representative of that person may swear or affirm;

(b) not an individual, then any person authorised to sign documents on its behalf may swear or affirm,

and any reference in the said subsection (4) (as so applied) to the person giving intimation shall be construed accordingly.

GENERAL NOTE

This section contains specific provision relating to variation and discharge of community burdens which relate to sheltered or retirement housing. Where it is proposed to grant a discharge under s.33, the deed of variation or discharge must be intimated to all owners of units of the community. The community consultation notice should be in the form set out in Sch.8 to the Act with an explanatory note. The deed of variation or discharge cannot be granted before the date specified in the community consultation notice by which comments must be made. This date must not be earlier than three weeks, beginning with the latest date on which intimation is given. A party who proposes to register a deed of discharge or variation must swear or affirm that appropriate intimation has been given.

Facility burdens and service burdens

56.—(1) Where by a deed registered before the appointed day—

(a) a facility burden is imposed on land, then—

    (i) any land to which the facility is (and is intended to be) of benefit; and

    (ii) the heritable property which constitutes the facility,

shall be benefited properties in relation to the facility burden;

(b) a service burden is imposed on land, then any land to which the services are provided shall be a benefited property in relation to the service burden.

(2) Subsection (1) above is subject to section 57 of this Act; and in paragraph (a) of that subsection "facility burden" does not include a manager burden.

GENERAL NOTE

This section replaces s.23 of the 2000 Act which is repealed by Sch.15. It provides that facility and service burdens are enforceable by the owners of those properties which benefit from the facility or the service. There is no requirement that the benefited properties are also subject to these burdens. There is no requirement to register every notice against any other property benefiting from this facility or service. A manager burden is not a facility burden. This section applies to deeds registered before the appointed day.

Further provisions as respects rights of enforcement

57.—(1) Nothing in sections 52 to 56 revives a right of enforcement waived or otherwise lost as at the day immediately preceding the appointed day.

(2) Where there is a common scheme, and a deed, had it nominated and identified a benefited property, would have imposed under that scheme the real burdens whose terms the deed sets out, the deed shall, for the purposes of sections 25 and 53 to 56 of this Act, be deemed so to have imposed them.

(3) Sections 53 to 56 do not confer a right of enforcement in respect of anything done, or omitted to be done, in contravention of the terms of a real burden before the appointed day.

GENERAL NOTE

The right to enforce burdens may have been specifically waived or may indeed have been lost through acquiescence, prescription or some other means. This section makes it clear that nothing in ss.52–56 in relation to common schemes will revive a burden in respect of which rights of enforcement have already been lost. Moreover, certain burdens created prior to the appointed day may not qualify as real burdens. Subsection (2) caters for the situation where there is obviously a common scheme but a deed does not actually nominate or identify a benefited property. If the deed nevertheless sets out the real burdens in the scheme then it shall be deemed to have imposed them for the purposes of ss.52–56 and s.25. No rights of enforcement are conferred in respect of anything done or omitted in contravention of a real burden before the appointed day.

Duty of Keeper to enter on title sheet statement concerning enforcement rights

58.—The Keeper of the Registers of Scotland—

(a) during that period of ten years which commences with the appointed day, may; and

(b) after the expiry of that period, shall,

where satisfied that a real burden subsists by virtue of any of sections 52 to 56 of this Act or section 60 of the 2000 Act (preserved right of Crown to maritime burdens), enter on the title sheet of the burdened property—

    (i) a statement that the real burden subsists by virtue of the section in question; and

    (ii) where there is sufficient information to enable the Keeper to
       describe the benefited property, a description of that property,

and where there is that sufficient information the Keeper shall enter
that statement on the title sheet of the benefited property also,
together with a description of the burdened property.

GENERAL NOTE

   The duty is imposed on the Keeper to show the new implied enforcement rights set out in
ss.52–56 on the title sheets of registered properties. The same applies to maritime burdens in
respect of feudal writs in terms of s.60 of the 2000 Act. Given the complicated provisions this
may be a difficult task.

PART 5

REAL BURDENS: MISCELLANEOUS

Effect of extinction etc. on court proceedings

59.—Where by virtue of this Act, a real burden is to any extent
discharged, extinguished or made unenforceable, then on and after the day
on which that happens (but only to the extent in question)—
    (a) no proceedings for enforcement shall be commenced;
    (b) any such proceedings already commenced shall, in so far as they do
       not relate to the payment of money, be deemed to have been
       abandoned on that day and may, without further process and without
       any requirement that full judicial expenses shall have been paid by the
       pursuer, be dismissed accordingly; and
    (c) any decree or interlocutor already pronounced in proceedings for
       such enforcement shall, in so far as it does not relate to the payment
       of money, be deemed to have been reduced, or as the case may be
       recalled, on that day.

GENERAL NOTE

   Where a real burden is discharged, extinguished or made unenforceable by virtue of the Act,
then after the day on which that happens, no proceedings for enforcement can be commenced,
and any such proceedings as have already been commenced in so far as they do not relate to
payment of money, shall be deemed to be abandoned without any requirement for full judicial
expenses to be paid. Any decree or interlocutor already pronounced in so far as it does not
relate to the payment of money is deemed to have been reduced or recalled. Decrees in respect
of the payment of money could relate to the cost of common repairs.

Grant of deed where title not completed: requirements

60.—(1) Subject to subsection (2) below, where an owner who does not
have a completed title to land is to grant, as respects a real burden—
    (a) a constitutive deed;
    (b) a deed of discharge; or
    (c) a deed of variation,

then unless the deed is one to which section 15(3) of the 1979 Act
(circumstances where unnecessary to deduce title) applies, it shall be
necessary in the deed to deduce title to the land through the midcouples
linking the owner to the person who had the last completed title to the land.

   (2) Where, under section 33 of this Act, a manager is to grant a deed of
variation or discharge, it shall not be necessary to comply with subsection
(1) above or with section 15(3) of the 1979 Act.

GENERAL NOTE

   Where a party grants any sort of deed in respect of a real burden and does not have a
completed title then a deduction of title will be required unless the title is already registered in
the Land Register. Where, however, the deed is a variation or discharge granted by a manager
under powers in terms of s.33 then there is no need to comply with the requirement for a
deduction of title.

Contractual liability incidental to creation of real burden

61.—Incidental contractual liability which a constitutive deed (or a deed into which a constitutive deed is incorporated) gives rise to as respects a prospective real burden, ends when the deed has been duly registered and the real burden has become effective.

GENERAL NOTE

As the law stood prior to feudal abolition a burden (whether created in a feudal or non-feudal writ) operated as a personal contract between the original granter and grantee of the deed (*Scottish Co-operative Wholesale Society v Finnie*, 1937 S.C. 835). This provision makes it clear that once the constitutive deed is registered contractual liability ends and liability depends on the obligation being a real burden. This is to avoid dual liability. If, however, a burden cannot be a real burden because it does not comply with the rules relating to the constitution of a real burden as set out in s.3, then the contractual liability will remain as between the original parties. The provisions of this section are to be contrasted with s.75 of the 2000 Act which simply preserves contractual rights as between the parties to the grant. s.75 is amended in Sch.12 of the 2003 Act simply to make it clear that the words "parties to the grant" in s.75 will not be construed as including successors. There is a question over whether s.75 means that burdens in a feudal grant which would be real burdens and accordingly be abolished when feudal abolition takes effect could remain as personal obligations between the original contracting parties, even although they were of the nature of real burdens. The provisions in s.61 of the 2003 Act make it clear that contractual liability ends, even as between the original parties, when the burden becomes real.

Real burdens of combined type

62.—(1) Where an obligation is constituted both as a nameable type of real burden (such as, for example, a community burden) and as a real burden which is not of that nameable type, then in so far as a provision of this Act relates specifically to real burdens of the nameable type the obligation shall be taken, for the purpose of determining the effect of that provision, to be constituted as two distinct real burdens.

(2) The owner of a benefited property which is a unit of a community shall not be entitled to enforce that obligation against the community constituted other than as a community burden or as a burden mentioned in section 1(3) of this Act.

GENERAL NOTE

There may be some burdens that are both community burdens and also burdens enforceable by parties outside the community. Where this is the case then the obligation will be treated as two distinct real burdens subject to the proviso that the owner of a benefited property in a community cannot enforce the obligation against the community other than as a community burden.

Manager burdens

63.—(1) A real burden (whenever created) may make provision conferring on such person as may be specified in the burden power to—

(a) act as the manager of related properties;

(b) appoint some other person to be such manager; and

(c) dismiss any person appointed by virtue of paragraph (b) above,

a real burden making any such provision being referred to in this Act as a "manager burden".

(2) A power conferred by a manager burden is exercisable only if the person on whom the power is conferred is the owner of one of the related properties.

(3) The right to a manager burden may be assigned or otherwise transferred; and any such assignation or transfer shall take effect on the sending of written intimation to the owners of the related properties.

(4) A manager burden shall be extinguished on the earliest of the following dates—

(a) the date on which such period as may be specified in the burden expires;

(b) the relevant date;

(c) the ninetieth day of any continuous period throughout which, by virtue of subsection (2) above, the burden is not exerciseable; and

(d) if a manager is dismissed under section 64 of this Act (in the case mentioned in subsection (6) below), the date of dismissal.

(5) In this section, the "relevant date"—

(a) in the case so mentioned means the date thirty years after the day specified in subsection (7) below;

(b) in a case where the manager burden is imposed under a common scheme on any unit of a sheltered or retirement housing development, means the date three years after the day so specified; and

(c) in any other case, means the date five years after the day so specified.

(6) The case is where the manager burden is imposed on the sale, by virtue of section 61 of the Housing (Scotland) Act 1987 (c.26) (secure tenant's right to purchase), of a property by—

(a) a person such as is mentioned in any of the sub-paragraphs of subsection (2)(a) of that section; or

(b) a predecessor of any such person,

to a tenant of such a person.

(7) The day is that on which the constitutive deed setting out the terms of the burden is registered (and if there is more than one day on which such a constitutive deed is registered in respect of the related properties, then the first such day).

(8) Where a power conferred by a manager burden is exercisable, any person who is, by virtue of that burden, a manager may not be dismissed—

(a) under section 28(1)(d) of this Act; or

(b) in a case other than that mentioned in subsection (6) above, under section 64 of this Act.

(9) Section 17(1) of the 2000 Act (extinction on appointed day of certain rights of superior) shall not apply to manager burdens.

GENERAL NOTE

This section applies to existing real burdens and to real burdens created after the section comes into force which is the day after Royal Assent. A manager burden is a burden which allows a party to appoint a manager in a development. There has always been doubt as to whether or not administrative or management burdens of this type were praedial in nature. Section 61 gives them this status. For examples of how these provisions may operate see Rennie, *Land Tenure in Scotland*, 6–32.

Subs.(1)

A manager burden is defined as one which confers on a person the power to act as manager of related properties, appoint a person to be such a manager and dismiss any such person. "related properties" are defined in s.66 and "manager" is defined in s.122(1). This power is to a certain extent a relaxation of the prohibition of monopolies contained in s.3(7). If however, a manager burden in an existing deed provides a right to nominate a manager for all time then that will become subject to the time limitations contained in subs.(2)(4) and (5).

Subs.(2)

The power conferred by a manager burden will only be exercised if the person on whom the power is conferred is the owner of one of the related properties. Accordingly, a manager burden is not a personal burden which does not need to attach to a benefited property. However, no one specific property need be specified. Typically, such a power of appointment may rest with a developer, but the developer would have required to exercise the power of appointment before selling the last property.

Subs.(3)

The holder of the manager burden may assign the right, and apparently, this assignation need not be registered provided it is intimated to the owners of the other related properties. Presumably, the assignee would normally own one of the related properties. If he or she did not then the burden would be extinguished in terms of the 90-day provision.

Subs.(4) and (5)

A manager burden is extinguished either on the expiry of a period specified in the burden or on a relevant date. Alternatively it may be terminated on the 90th day of any continuous period throughout which the burden is not exercisable in terms of subs.(2). It is also extinguished on dismissal of the manager under s.64. In normal circumstances, if there is no expiry date in the manager burden the burden comes to an end five years after the date of registration of the deed containing the manager burden. Where, however, the manager burden has been constituted by virtue of a sale to a secure tenant under the right-to-buy legislation, then the period is 30 years from that date. The relevant date, however, is not the date of the coming into effect of the section, but the date on which the constitutive deed setting out the terms of the manager burden is registered. The period is three years in the case of a manager burden in a sheltered or retirement housing scheme.

Subs.(6)

This provision allows the 30-year period where the burden was imposed in a right to buy sale, or otherwise in a sale by a local authority to its tenant. This definition does not include property sold by local authorities in other circumstances.

Subs.(7)

This defines the relevant date.

Subs.(8)

This prevents dismissal of the manager in terms of s.28 as long as the manager burden is in operation. The overriding power of dismissal contained in s.64 will not apply except in the case of manager burdens imposed on a sale by virtue of the right to buy legislation (see subs.(6)).

Subs.(9)

If the manager burden is imposed in a feudal grant which is extinguished by the 2000 Act s.17(1) of the 2000 Act will not apply and the superior will be able to continue until a manager burden is extinguished in terms of subs.(4).

Overriding power to dismiss and appoint manager

64.—(1) Where a person is the manager of related properties, the owners of two thirds of those properties may—

(a) dismiss that person; and

(b) where they do so, appoint some other person to be such manager, and such actings shall be effective notwithstanding the terms of any real burden affecting those properties; but this section is subject to section 63(8)(b) of this Act.

(2) If a property is owned by two or more persons in common, then, for the purposes of voting on any proposal to exercise a power conferred by subsection (1) above, the vote allocated as respects the property shall only be counted for or against the proposal if it is the agreed vote of those of them who together own more than a half share of the property.

General Note

There is an overriding power to dismiss a manager and appoint another notwithstanding anything in the deeds where a two-thirds majority of related properties subject to community burdens so decide. Where a property is owned in common then the vote will only count if the common owners owning more than half of the property are in agreement. In the majority of cases where property is held in common by husband and wife or a couple there will have to be unanimity. This overriding power to dismiss does not apply to a manager appointed under a manager burden until the time-limits have elapsed, except in cases where the manager burden is imposed in a right to buy sale. In terms of s.63(8)(b) and s.64(1) a two-thirds majority could dismiss such a manager within the 30-year period. For examples of how these provisions may operate see Rennie, *Land Tenure in Scotland*, 6–32.

Manager: transitory provisions

65.—Where, immediately before the appointed day, any person is, by virtue of any real burden or purported real burden, ostensibly the manager of related properties that person shall be deemed to have been validly appointed as such.

GENERAL NOTE
There are many burdens relating to factoring and management which are not valid because they fail to comply with the existing rules relating to the constitution of real burden. This section, however, makes it clear that such appointments will continue until they are terminated either in terms of s.28(1)(d) or 64.

The expression "related properties"

66.—(1) Whether properties are related properties for the purposes of sections 63 to 65 of this Act is, subject to subsection (2) below, to be inferred from all the circumstances; and without prejudice to the generality of this section circumstances giving rise to such an inference might include—
  (a) the convenience of managing the properties together because they share—
      (i) some common feature; or
      (ii) an obligation for common maintenance of some facility;
  (b) it being evident that the properties constitute a group of properties on which real burdens are imposed under a common scheme; or
  (c) there being shared ownership of common property.
  (2) For the purposes of section 63(2) of this Act, the following are not related properties—
  (a) any property which, being a unit in a sheltered or retirement housing development, is used in some special way (that is to say, is the unit mentioned as an exception in section 54(1) of this Act);
  (b) any property to which a development management scheme applies; or
  (c) any facility which benefits two or more properties (examples of such a facility being, without prejudice to the generality of this paragraph, a private road and a common area for recreation).

GENERAL NOTE
This section contains the definition of related properties. Essentially, whether a property is a related property or not will be a question of fact taking into account all the circumstances, including the circumstances mentioned in subs.(1)(a). Subsection 2 makes it clear that a warden's flat which is not subject to the community burdens in a sheltered or retirement housing development will not be a related property. Similarly, any property to which a development managing scheme in terms of Pt 6 applies cannot be a related property, nor can any common facility.

Discharge of rights of irritancy

67.—(1) All rights of irritancy in respect of a breach of a real burden are, on the day on which this section comes into force, discharged; and on and after that day—
  (a) it shall not be competent to create any such right; and
  (b) any proceedings already commenced to enforce any such right shall be deemed abandoned and may, without further process and without any requirement that full judicial expenses shall have been paid by the pursuer, be dismissed accordingly.
  (2) Subsection (1)(b) above shall not affect any cause in which final decree (that is to say, any decree or interlocutor which disposes of the cause and is not subject to appeal or review) is granted before the coming into force of this section.

GENERAL NOTE
Irritancies in non-feudal deeds have always been something of an oddity, but they do exist. They are abolished with effect from the day after Royal Assent, albeit subject to the usual transitory provisions.

Requirement for repetition etc. of terms of real burden in future deed

68.—In any deed (whenever executed) a requirement to the effect that the terms of a real burden shall be repeated or referred to in any subsequent deed shall be of no effect.

Conveyancers will be familiar with the provision in dispositive clauses of deeds which impose real burdens to the effect that the burdens must be repeated or referred to in subsequent deeds. This section removes that requirement. Section 9(3) and (4) of the Conveyancing (Scotland) Act 1924 is repealed by virtue of Sch.15. These changes do not mean that burden writs should not be referred to in sasine transactions. As land registration takes over, however, there will be no need to refer to burden writs at all in dispositions.

Further provision as respects deeds of variation and of discharge

69.—(1) Where a deed of variation or deed of discharge is granted under this Act, it is not requisite that there be a grantee.

(2) Any such deed so granted may be registered by an owner of the burdened property or by any other person against whom the real burden is enforceable.

(3) Without prejudice to subsection (2) above, a deed of variation or deed of discharge granted under section 33 or 35 of this Act may be registered by a granter.

GENERAL NOTE
It will not be necessary to specify a grantee in any deed of variation or discharge and any such deed may be registered by an owner of the burdened property or any other person against whom the real burden is enforceable. Presumably, this would include a tenant. A deed of variation or discharge may be registered by the granter of the deed. This is important, especially where the deed is granted by a majority of owners or by a manager where there may be dissenting proprietors who will effectively be included in the definition of grantees.

Duty to disclose identity of owner

70.—A person who has title to enforce a real burden (the "entitled person") may require any person who, at any time, was an owner of the burdened property (the "second person") to disclose to the entitled person—

    (a) the name and address of the owner, for the time being, of such property; or

    (b) (if the second person cannot do that) such other information as the second person has which might enable the entitled person to discover that name and address.

GENERAL NOTE
The party who has title to enforce a real burden may not know the precise identity of the owner of the burdened property as where the property has recently changed hands. This section places an obligation on a previous owner to supply the name and address of the current owner or, failing that, such other information which that party has which might enable the party entitled to enforce to discover the name and address.

PART 6

DEVELOPMENT MANAGEMENT SCHEME

Development management scheme

[1] **71.**—(1) The development management scheme may be applied to any land by registering against the land (in this Part of this Act referred to as "the development") a deed of application granted by, or on behalf of, the owner of the land or, if and in so far as the terms of the order mentioned in subsection (3) below so admit, may be thus applied with such variations as may be specified in the deed; and the scheme shall take effect in relation to the development on the date of registration or, notwithstanding section 3(4) of the 1979 Act (creation of real right or obligation on date of registration etc.)—

    (a) on such later date as may be so specified (the specification being of a fixed date and not, for example, of a date determinable by reference to the occurrence of an event); or

(b) on the date of registration of such other deed as may be so specified,
and different provision for the taking effect of the scheme may be made for
different parts of the development.

(2) The deed of application shall include specification or description of the
matters which the scheme requires shall be specified or described and shall in
any event include—

(a) the meaning, in the scheme, of such expressions as "the development", "scheme property" and "unit";

(b) the name by which any owners' association established by the scheme
is to be known, being a name which either ends with the words
"Owners Association" or begins with those words preceded by the
definite article;

(c) the name and address of the first manager of any association so
established.

(3) In this Act, "the development management scheme" means such
scheme of rules for the management of land as is set out in an order made, in
consequence of this section, under section 104 of the Scotland Act 1998
(c.46) (power to make provision consequential on legislation of, or
scrutinised by, the Scottish Parliament) or, in relation to a particular
development, that scheme as applied to the development.

AMENDMENT
1. This section is not in force to date (March 2005).

GENERAL NOTE
This part of the Act introduces the concept of development management schemes which may
be applied to any land by the registration of a deed of application. The deed of application must
include a specification of matters which the scheme requires along with certain specific
definitions.

Subs.(1)
A development management scheme is applied to land by the registration of a deed of
application granted by or on behalf of the owner of the land. It is a scheme of rules set out by
order of the Secretary of State subject to variations if permitted. The scheme takes effect on the
date of registration or on such later date as may be specified as a fixed date or on the date of
registration of another deed so specified. Different parts of the scheme may take effect at
different times.

Subs.(2)
The application must include specification and description of such matters as the scheme
made under the order requires but must include definitions of "the development", "scheme
property" and "units". The deed of application must also name any owners' association
established by the scheme and that name must include the words "owners association". The
name and address of the first manager of any association must also be given.

Subs.(3)
The basic scheme rules will be set out in an order made under s.104 of the Scotland Act 1998
or the scheme as applied to a particular development. The original Scottish Law Commission
proposals imposed limitations on variation of the scheme. The s.104 order is likely to follow this
pattern.

Application of other provisions of this Act to rules of scheme

[1] **72.**—In so far as the terms of the order mentioned in section 71(3) of this
Act so admit, sections 2, 3, 5, 10 (except subsection (4)(a)), 11, 13, 14, 16, 18,
59 to 61, 67 to 70, 98, 100, 104 and 105 of this Act apply in relation to the
rules of the development management scheme as those sections apply in
relation to community burdens; except that, for the purposes of that
application, in those sections any reference—

(a) to an owner of a benefited property shall be construed as to the
manager of any owners' association established by the scheme;

(b) to a benefited property shall be construed as to a unit of the development in so far as advantaged by those rules;

(c) to a burdened property shall be construed as to a unit of the development in so far as constrained by those rules;

(d) to a community shall be construed as to the development; and

(e) to a constitutive deed shall be construed as to the deed of application.

AMENDMENT

1. This section is not in force to date (March 2005).

GENERAL NOTE

This part of the Act does not indicate in express terms that the rules of the scheme are to be real burdens. However, most of the provisions of the Act relating to real burdens will apply to the rules of the scheme. Section 1 does not apply because the rules are not real burdens. Section 2 does apply, and since that section states that a real burden can only be created as an affirmative, negative or ancillary burden the rules must take on the characteristics of a real burden. Section 4 does not apply because it lays down rules in relation to constitutive deeds, and a scheme is not a constitutive deed as such, although a deed of application is. Section 5 in relation to payments of uncertain amounts in respect of cost does apply. Sections 7, 8 and 9 do not apply. Section 10 does apply with the exception of subs.(4)(a). Sections 11, 13, 14, 16, 18, 54–61, 67–70, 98, 100, 104 and 105 apply. All of these sections apply as they apply to community burdens. Where these sections do apply, then references to the owner of a benefited property shall be construed as to the manager of any owners' association established by the scheme. This places the manager in a very important position in relation to enforcement. A benefited property is construed as a unit of the development so far as advantaged by the rules and the burdened property as one which is constrained by the rules. A community will be construed as the development and the constitutive deed is construed as the deed of application.

Disapplication

[1] **73.**—(1) The development management scheme may be disapplied to the development, or to any part of the development, by an owners' association established by the scheme registering against the development or as the case may be the part, a deed of disapplication granted by that association in accordance with the scheme; and subject to subsection (3) below the disapplication shall take effect—

(a) on the date of registration; or

(b) notwithstanding section 3(4) of the 1979 Act (creation of real right or obligation on date of registration etc.), on such later date as may be specified in the deed (the specification being of a fixed date and not, for example, of a date determinable by reference to the occurrence of an event).

(2) The deed of disapplication may by means of real burdens provide for the future management and regulation—

(a) in the case of disapplication to the development, of the development or of any part of the development; or

(b) in the case of disapplication to a part of the development, of that part or of any part of that part,

and section 4 of this Act shall apply accordingly except that paragraph (b) of subsection (2) of that section shall, for the purposes of this subsection, apply with the substitution, for the reference to the owner of the land which is to be the burdened property, of a reference to the owners' association.

(3) The deed of disapplication shall not, on registration, disapply the development management scheme or impose a real burden unless, after the expiry of the period mentioned in subsection (3) of section 74 of this Act, there is endorsed on the deed (or on an annexation to it referred to in an endorsement on it and identified, on the face of the annexation, as being the annexation so referred to) a certificate executed by a member of the Lands Tribunal, or by their clerk, to the effect that no application for preservation of the scheme has been received under that subsection or that any such application which has been received has been withdrawn; and where more

than one such application has been received the certificate shall relate to both (or as the case may be all) applications.

(4) An owners' association proposing to submit a deed of disapplication granted as mentioned in subsection (1) above for registration shall, before doing so, swear or affirm before a notary public (the deed being endorsed accordingly)—

(a) that section 74 of this Act has been complied with; and

(b) as to the date on which the period mentioned in subsection (3) of that section expires.

(5) Subsection (2)(b) of section 22 of this Act applies in relation to the owners' association and for the purposes of subsection (4) above as it applies in relation to a terminator and for the purposes of subsection (1) of that section.

AMENDMENT

1. This section is not in force to date (March 2005).

GENERAL NOTE

A development management scheme may be disapplied to the development as a whole or any part by an owners' association established by the scheme. The owners' association would register a deed of disapplication in accordance with the scheme. Disapplication would take effect on the date of registration or such later date as specified in the deed which could be a fixed date or one by reference to the occurrence of an event. The deed of disapplication, however, may create real burdens providing for the future management and regulation of a development or the part in respect of which the deed of disapplication applies. Before the deed of disapplication is registered there must be endorsed on the deed, or on an annexation, a certificate executed by members of the Lands Tribunal or their clerk, to the effect that no application for preservation of the scheme has been received in terms of s.74, or where one has been received that it has been withdrawn. An owners' association which is proposing to register a deed of disapplication must swear or affirm that proper intimation has been made. The party making the oath or affirmation would be a person authorised to sign documents on behalf of the owners' association in terms of s.22(2)(b).

Intimation of proposal to register deed of disapplication

¹ **74.**—(1) Where a deed of disapplication is granted as mentioned in section 73(1) of this Act, any proposal to register that deed shall be intimated by the owners' association to every person who is the owner of a unit of the development.

(2) Such intimation to an owner shall be given by sending a copy of the deed, together with a notice stating—

(a) what the effect of registering the deed would be; and

(b) that an owner who has not agreed to the granting of the deed and who wishes to apply to the Lands Tribunal for preservation of the development management scheme must do so by a date specified in the notice (being the date on which the period mentioned in subsection (3) below expires).

(3) A person to whom intimation is given under subsection (2) and who has not so agreed may, during the period of eight weeks beginning with the date by which subsection (1) above has been complied with fully, apply to the Lands Tribunal for preservation of the scheme.

AMENDMENT

1. This section is not in force to date (March 2005).

GENERAL NOTE

Where an owner's association propose to register a deed of disapplication, they must intimate this intention to every person who is the owner of a unit in the development. The owners' association must send a copy of the deed together with a notice stating what the effect of the deed would be and that an owner who does not agree and who wishes to apply to the Lands Tribunal for preservation of the development management scheme must do so by a specified date. The person to whom intimation is given has eight weeks beginning with the date of completed intimation to apply to the Lands Tribunal for preservation.

PART 7

SERVITUDES

Positive servitudes

Creation of positive servitude by writing: deed to be registered

75.—(1) A deed is not effective to create a positive servitude by express provision unless it is registered against both the benefited property and the burdened property.

(2) It shall be no objection to the validity of a positive servitude that, at the time when the deed was registered as mentioned in subsection (1) above, the same person owned the benefited property and the burdened property; but, notwithstanding section 3(4) of the 1979 Act (creation of real right or obligation on date of registration etc.), the servitude shall not be created while that person remains owner of both those properties.

(3) Subsection (1) above—

(a) is subject to section 3(1) of the Prescription and Limitation (Scotland) Act 1973 (c.52) (creation of positive servitude by 20 years' possession following execution of deed); and

(b) does not apply to servitudes such as are mentioned in section 77(1) of this Act.

GENERAL NOTE

Servitudes can be created in a variety of ways. If they are created in writing then the deed will require to be registered against both benefited property and burdened property. This is a change to the law. Servitudes could be created in unregistered documents. There has always been a doubt as to whether or not a servitude was extinguished *confusione* and certainly there has always been a rule that a servitude cannot be created unless there are separate tenements of land in separate ownership. Subsection 2 provides that a positive servitude can be created even where the same person owns the benefited and burdened property, but where that occurs the servitude will be suspended until separation occurs. This is a useful provision and it clarifies the position of general servitudes created in deeds of condition over developments. At the time of the grant of the deed of conditions by the developer, the land is owned by one party. Nevertheless, it has been accepted practice to create servitudes in favour of various plots or units in the development burdening other plots or units in the development. Normally, these would be in respect of pipes, cables, roads etc. Strictly speaking, this was questionable. Subsection (2), however, makes it clear that this can be done. The servitude becomes effective as and when the various units or plots are split off. The requirement that a servitude be created in a registered deed does not apply to servitudes, which have been created by positive prescription following on the grant of a deed, nor does the registration requirement apply to service servitudes in respect of pipes, cables, wires or other enclosed units in terms of s.77(1).

Disapplication of requirement that positive servitude created in writing be of a known type

76.—(1) Any rule of law that requires that a positive servitude be of a type known to the law shall not apply in relation to any servitude created in accordance with section 75(1) of this Act.

(2) Nothing in subsection (1) above permits the creation of a servitude that is repugnant with ownership.

GENERAL NOTE

The view of most academic writers has been that a servitude must be known to the law or at least be a reasonable extension of a known servitude. Difficulties have arisen over such things as servitudes of parking and it has now been held that such a servitude is not recognised by the law of Scotland except perhaps as an adjunct to the servitude of access (*Moncrieff v Jamieson*, 2005 S.L.T. 225). Some of the doubtful servitudes listed by Cusine and Paisley (Cusine and Paisley, *Servitudes and Rights of Way*, Ch.3) may now be regarded as valid. Obvious examples would be servitudes of shooting or fishing, parking, mooring and the like. However, there is a proviso to the effect that it will not be possible to create a servitude which is repugnant with ownership. This presumably means that there must be some limits to the extent by which the servitude actually eats into the normal rights of ownership. An example of a servitude which might be said to be repugnant with ownership would be one which allowed the proprietors of the dominant tenement (benefited property) to have exclusive use of a land comprising the servient tenement (burdened property) without limitation. *Moncrieff v Jamieson* was decided on the basis of the pre November 28, 2004 law. An appeal has been taken to the House of Lords.

Positive servitude of leading pipes etc. over or under land

77.—(1) A right to lead a pipe, cable, wire or other such enclosed unit over or under land for any purpose may be constituted as a positive servitude.

(2) It shall be deemed always to have been competent to constitute a right such as is mentioned in subsection (1) above as a servitude.

GENERAL NOTE

There are countless wayleave agreements (generally with statutory undertakers or providers of services) relating to pipes, cables, sewers, drains, media services and other conductors. There has been doubt as to whether or not these were properly constituted servitudes. There is no doubt that a servitude for a water pipe or a drain is one known to the law. However, the difficulty has often been of identifying a dominant tenement (benefited property), (see *North British Railway Co Ltd v Park Yard Co Ltd* (1898) 25 R (HL) 47). Where a pipe or a cable passes through several properties there may be a succession of burdened and benefited properties and the electricity sub-station, waterworks or sewage works might be said to be the ultimate benefited property. In one unfortunate sheriff court case it was held that a servitude in respect of overhanging cables could not be recognised (*Neill v Scobbie*, 1993 G.W.D. 8–572). This decision has been doubted (Cusine and Paisley, *Servitudes and Rights of Way*, 3.44). This provision makes it clear that a servitude for pipes, cables, wires and other conductors will be recognised as a positive servitude and moreover will be deemed always to have been a proper servitude. The section itself does not remove the requirement for a dominant tenement or benefited property. These types of servitude need not be in a deed which is registered.

Discharge of positive servitude

78.—A positive servitude—

(a) which has been registered against the burdened property; or

(b) which has been noted in, or otherwise appears in, the title sheet of that property,

is discharged by deed only on registration of the deed against the burdened property.

GENERAL NOTE

When a positive servitude has been registered against the burdened property or is noted in the title sheet of that property it can only be discharged by a deed which is also registered. There is no requirement to register the discharge in the title to the benefited property. In terms of s.105 however, the Keeper could alter the title sheet of the benefited property by removing the servitude even where the discharge is recorded in the sasine register. A registered discharge will be required even in cases where a servitude is noted in a title sheet in circumstances where it was constituted by prescription or implied grant as opposed to in a written and registered deed. This section however does not apply to discharges which have been executed before the appointed day (s.119(8)) nor does it prevent a servitude from being extinguished in any other way such as by non-exercise for the period of long negative prescription, acquiescence or destruction of one or more of the properties.

Negative servitudes

Prohibition on creation of negative servitude

79.—On the appointed day it shall cease to be competent to create a negative servitude.

GENERAL NOTE
Negative servitudes exist principally for the protection of amenity. The most common are servitudes which prohibit the obstruction of light or prospect or building above a certain height. The same effect can be achieved by the imposition of a real burden which prohibits building. This section prohibits the creation of negative servitudes on or after the appointed day. After that day obligations this type will require to be created as real burdens in terms of s.2(1)(b).

Transitional

Negative servitudes to become real burdens

80.—(1) A negative servitude shall, on the appointed day, cease to exist as such but shall forthwith become a real burden (such a real burden being, for the purposes of this section, referred to as a "converted servitude").

(2) Subject to subsections (3) and (4) below, a converted servitude shall be extinguished on the expiry of the period of ten years beginning with the appointed day.

(3) If, before the appointed day, a negative servitude was registered against the burdened property or was noted in, or otherwise appeared in, the title sheet of that property the converted servitude shall not be extinguished as mentioned in subsection (2) above.

(4) If, during the period mentioned in subsection (2) above, an owner of the benefited property executes and duly registers, in (or as nearly as may be in) the form contained in schedule 9 to this Act, a notice of converted servitude, the converted servitude shall not be extinguished as mentioned in subsection (2) above (in so far as the burdened property, the benefited property and the converted servitude are, respectively, the burdened property, the benefited property, and the converted servitude identified in the notice of converted servitude).

(5) The notice of converted servitude shall—

(a) identify the land which is the burdened property (or any part of that land);

(b) identify the land which is the benefited property (or any part of that land);

(c) where the person registering the notice does not have a completed title to the benefited property, set out the midcouples linking that person to the person who last had such completed title;

(d) set out the terms of the converted servitude;

(e) include as an annexation the constitutive deed, if any (or a copy of such deed); and

(f) if the land identified for the purposes of paragraph (b) above is not nominated in the constitutive deed, set out the grounds, both factual and legal, for describing that land as a benefited property.

(6) For the purposes of subsection (4) above, a notice is, subject to section 116 of this Act, duly registered only when registered against both properties identified in pursuance of subsection (5)(a) and (b) above.

(7) Subsections (4) and (5) of section 50 of this Act shall apply in respect of a notice of converted servitude as they apply in respect of a notice of preservation.

(8) This section is subject to section 115 of this Act.

GENERAL NOTE
Existing negative servitudes will cease on the appointed day but can become real burdens provided certain procedures are followed.

Subs.(1)
A negative servitude is automatically converted to a real burden on the appointed day. Henceforth it will be referred to as a "converted servitude".

Subs.(2)
A converted servitude is extinguished on the expiry of a 10-year period beginning with the appointed day.

Subs.(3)
The automatic extinguishment after the ten year period does not apply to a negative servitude which was actually registered against the burdened property or was noted in or appeared in the title sheet of that property prior to the appointed day.

Subs.(4)
In the case of non-registered negative servitudes which are converted into negative real burdens the holder of that converted servitude may preserve it by executing and registering a notice in the form contained in Sch.9. Any owner (including a common owner) may register such a notice.

Subs.(5)
This subsection specifies what the notice must contain.

Subs.(6)
The notice must be registered against both the burdened and benefited properties.

Subs.(7)
The requirement that the party registering the notice swear or affirm in terms of s.50 applies.

Subs.(8)
Section 115 sets out a requirement on the owner of the benefited property to send to the owner of the burdened property a copy of the notice and explanatory note where it is reasonably practicable to do so.

Certain real burdens to become positive servitudes
81.—(1) A real burden consisting of a right to enter, or otherwise make use of, the burdened property shall, on the appointed day, cease to exist as such but shall forthwith become a positive servitude.
(2) Subsection (1) above—
(a) is subject to section 17(1) of the 2000 Act (extinction on appointed day of certain rights of superior);
(b) does not apply to real burdens such as are mentioned in section 2(3)(a) of this Act.

GENERAL NOTE
Many real burdens which allow some sort of limited use of other property are in effect positive servitudes. On the appointed day real burdens which consist of a right to enter or make use of burdened property will be converted into positive servitudes. This is the mirror image of the conversion of negative servitudes into negative real burdens. This provision will not apply to feudal burdens which are extinguished by s.17(1) of the 2000 Act. Ancillary real burdens in terms of s.2(3)(a) are not converted into positive servitudes because there is specific provision for these ancillary real burdens.

PART 8

PRE-EMPTION AND REVERSION

Pre-emption

Application and interpretation of sections 83 and 84
82.—Sections 83 and 84 of this Act apply to any subsisting right of pre-emption constituted as a title condition which—
(a) was originally created in favour of a feudal superior; or
(b) was created in a deed executed after 1st September 1974,
and for the purposes of sections 83(1)(a) and 84(1)(b) of this Act the person

last registered as having title to a personal pre-emption burden or rural housing burden shall be taken to be the holder for a right of pre-emption which that burden comprises.

GENERAL NOTE
    This part of the Act applies to existing rights of pre-emption which are constituted as a title condition in favour of an original feudal superior or in another deed executed after September 1, 1974 (the coming into force of the Land Tenure Reform (Scotland) Act 1974). The rules relating to the non-exercise of pre-emption rights were originally contained in s.9 of the Conveyancing Amendment (Scotland) Act 1938 as amended. The basic requirement was for the party whose land was subject to the right of pre-emption to make an offer to the party entitled to the pre-emption. However the practice grew up of simply writing to the party entitled to the pre-emption and asking whether or not it was to be exercised. This part of the Act regularises that informal procedure. The provisions will apply to personal pre-emption burdens or rural housing burdens with the modification that the holder of the personal pre-emption or rural housing burden shall be treated as the person last registered as having title to the pre-emption.

Extinction following pre-sale undertaking

83.—(1) Where, in relation to any burdened property (or, as the case may be, part of such property)—

    (a) the holder of a right of pre-emption to which this section applies gives an undertaking (in the form, or as nearly as may be in the form, contained in schedule 10 to this Act) that, subject to such conditions (if any) as the holder may specify in the undertaking, the holder will not exercise that right during such period as may be so specified;

    (b) a conveyance in implement of the sale of the burdened property (or part) is registered before the end of that period; and

    (c) any conditions specified under paragraph (a) above have been satisfied,

such right shall, on registration of such a conveyance, be extinguished unless the right is constituted as a rural housing burden in which case the title condition shall be taken to have been complied with as respects that sale only.

(2) Any undertaking given under subsection (1) above—

    (a) is binding on the holder of the right of pre-emption; and

    (b) if registered is binding on any successor as holder provided that the undertaking was registered before the successor completed title.

GENERAL NOTE
    The owner of the burdened property which is subject to the pre-emption may obtain an undertaking from the holder of the pre-emption that it will not be exercised for a specific period and (if required) subject to conditions. The holder of the pre-emption will be the owner of the benefited property or in the case of a lease the landlord. There is a statutory form of undertaking set out in Sch.10. If a sale then takes place within the period set out in the undertaking and if any other conditions attached to the undertaking are met the pre-emption is extinguished on registration of the conveyance. If the sale falls through then the pre-emption revives at the expiry of the period contained in the undertaking. It should be noted that these provisions do not apply to pre-emptions created in non-feudal deeds executed prior to September 1, 1974. These pre-emptions are never extinguished even on non-exercise on specific occasions. Apart from this, undertakings given are binding not only on the holder of the right of the pre-emption giving the undertaking but also on successors provided the undertaking is registered before the successor completes title.

Extinction following offer to sell

84.—(1) If in relation to a right of pre-emption to which this section applies—

    (a) an event specified in the constitutive deed as an event on the occurrence of which such right may be exercised occurs; and

    (b) the owner of the burdened property makes, in accordance with subsections (2) to (6) below, an offer to sell that property (or, as the case may be, part of that property) to the holder of such right,

then such right shall, in relation to that property (or part), be extinguished unless it is constituted as a rural housing burden in which case the title condition shall be taken to have been complied with as respects that event only.

(2) An offer shall be in writing and shall comply with section 2 of the Requirements of Writing (Scotland) Act 1995 (c.7) (requirements for formal validity of certain documents).

(3) An offer shall be open for acceptance during whichever is the shorter of—

(a) the period of 21 days, or where the right is constituted as a rural housing burden 42 days, beginning with the day on which the offer is sent;

(b) such number of days beginning with that day as may be specified in the constitutive deed.

(4) An offer shall be made on such terms as may be set out, or provided for, in the constitutive deed; but in so far as no such terms are set out, an offer shall be made on such terms (including any terms so provided for) as are reasonable in the circumstances.

(5) Where—

(a) an offer is sent in accordance with this section; and

(b) the holder of the right does not, within the time allowed by virtue of subsection (3) above for acceptance of the offer, inform (in writing, whether or not transmitted by electronic means) the owner of the burdened property that the holder considers, giving reasons for so considering, that the terms on which the offer is made are unreasonable,

the terms of the offer shall, for the purposes of subsection (4) above, be deemed to be reasonable.

(6) If the holder of a right cannot by reasonable inquiry be identified or found, an offer may be sent to the Extractor of the Court of Session; and for the purposes of this section an offer so sent shall be deemed to have been sent to the holder.

GENERAL NOTE

Section 9 of the Conveyancing Amendment (Scotland) Act 1938 is repealed by Sch.15. Section 75 preserves the old method of dealing with a pre-emption by making an offer but it does not apply to non-feudal deeds executed prior to September 1, 1974.

Subs.(1)

A pre-emption is extinguished where the owner of the burdened property makes an offer to sell the property to the holder of the pre-emption whether or not the offer is accepted unless the pre-emption is a rural housing burden in which case it will continue to be enforceable in the future.

Subs.(2)

The offer must be in writing in terms of s.1(2)(a)(i) of the Requirements of Writing (Scotland) Act 1995 and must be subscribed in terms of s.2 of that Act.

Subs.(3)

The offer lapses if not accepted within 21 days from the date on which it is sent or 42 days in the case of a rural housing pre-emption. The pre-emption right may specify a longer period.

Subs.(4)

Normally, the pre-emption clause will specify the terms and conditions of the offer. In the case of a normal pre-emption clause the requirement will be to offer the property to the holder of the pre-emption at such price and on such terms and conditions as have been offered by a third party. If the pre-emption however does not specify in detail what the terms of the offer shall be then the offer should be on such terms as are reasonable in the circumstances. This is an interesting provision. It seems to close off an argument that the pre-emption is too vague to be enforced.

Subs.(5)

The holder of the pre-emption may object to the terms of the offer but if that party feels that the offer is unreasonable then objection must be taken within 21 days otherwise the offer will be deemed to be reasonable. The holder of the pre-emption would have to state why the offer was unreasonable.

Subs.(6)

Where the holder of the pre-emption right cannot by reasonable enquiry be identified or found the offer may be sent to the Extractor of the Court of Session.

Ending of council's right of pre-emption as respects certain churches

85.—In a scheme framed under subsection (1) of section 22 of the Church of Scotland (Property and Endowments) Act 1925 (c.33) (schemes for the ownership, maintenance and administration of churches etc.), any provision made in accordance with subsection (2)(h) of that section (council's right of pre-emption) shall cease to have effect.

GENERAL NOTE

Local authorities had a right of pre-emption in respect of certain churches where the churches were to be sold. These rights of pre-emption are extinguished, Sch.14 of the Act repeals s.22(2)(h) of the Church of Scotland (Property and Endowments) Act 1925.

Reversion

Reversions under School Sites Act 1841

86.—(1) In a case where—
- (a) land would, under the third proviso to section 2 of the School Sites Act 1841 (4 & 5 Vict. c.38) (the "1841 Act") revert (but for this section) to any person or has so reverted; but
- (b) the person has not, before the day on which this section comes into force, completed title to the land, subsections (2) to (9) below shall (to the extent that subsection (9) admits) apply in place of that proviso and be deemed always to have applied and nothing shall be void or challengeable by virtue of that proviso.

(2) If the circumstances are that a contract of sale of the land has been concluded by, or on behalf of, the education authority, the authority shall pay to the person, where the cessation of use by virtue of which the land would (but for this section) revert, or has reverted, occurred—
- (a) before the day on which this section comes into force, an amount equal to the open market value of the land as at that day;
- (b) on or after that day, an amount equal to the open market value of the land as at the date of cessation less any improvement value as at that date.

(3) If the circumstances are other than is mentioned in subsection (2) above—
- (a) the person may specify an obligation mentioned in paragraph (a), or as the case may be (b), of subsection (4) below and require the authority to comply therewith, which subject to paragraph (b) below the authority shall do;
- (b) the authority may, if the person requires under paragraph (a) above performance of the obligation mentioned in paragraph (a)(i), or as the case may be (b)(i), of that subsection, instead elect to make payment to the person of such amount as is mentioned in paragraph (a)(ii), or as the case may be (b)(ii), of that subsection provided that such election is timeous.

(4) The obligations are, where the cessation of use by virtue of which the ownership of the land would (but for this section) revert, or has reverted, occurred—

(a) before the day on which this section comes into force—
  (i) to convey the land to the person;
  (ii) to make a payment to the person of an amount equal to the open market value of the land as at that day; or
(b) on or after that day—
  (i) on payment by the person of any improvement value as at the date of cessation, to convey the land to the person;
  (ii) to make a payment to the person of an amount equal to the open market value of the land as at the date of cessation less any improvement value as at that date.

(5) Any dispute arising in relation to the assessment of the value for the purposes of this section of any land, buildings or structures may be referred to, and determined by, the Lands Tribunal.

(6) For the purposes of this section—

"education authority" has the meaning given by section 135(1) of the Education (Scotland) Act 1980 (c.44) except that if title to the land has been transferred to any person by any enactment it means that person; and

"improvement value" means such part of the value of the land as is attributable to any building (or other structure) on the land other than any such building (or other structure) erected by or at the expense of—

(a) the person who made the gift, sale or exchange of the land under section 2 of the 1841 Act; or
(b) any predecessor, as owner of such land, of that person.

(7) References in subsection (1) above to the third proviso to section 2 of the 1841 Act shall be construed as including references to that proviso as applied by virtue of any other enactment; and for the purposes of that construction, the reference in paragraph (a) of the definition of "improvement value" in subsection (6) above to the said section 2 shall be construed as a reference to the provision corresponding to that section in such other enactment.

(8) The reference in subsection (3)(b) above to an election being timeous is to its being notified to the person within three months after the requirement in question is made.

(9) Subsections (2) to (8) above do not apply where the person has, before the day on which this section comes into force, accepted an offer of compensation in respect of the land or concluded a contract for, or accepted, a conveyance of the land.

(10) Subsections (1)(b) and (2) of section 67 of this Act shall apply in relation to any proceedings already commenced by virtue of the proviso mentioned in subsection (1)(a) above as they apply in relation to any proceedings already commenced as mentioned in the said subsection (1)(b).

GENERAL NOTE

The School Sites Act 1841 has caused considerable difficulty for local authorities. Basically it applied where land had been conveyed by landowners to education authorities for the building of schools, playgrounds and schoolhouses. Effectively, where a conveyance was subject to the Act on the property ceasing to be a school or schoolhouse it reverted to the estate from which it had been conveyed. The statutory reversion has been held to be effective (see *Hamilton v Grampian Regional Council*, 1995 G.W.D. 8–443; 1996 G.W.D. 5–227). Difficulties arose where local authorities wished to sell surplus educational buildings. Purchasers were wary of accepting a title even with absolute warrandice in circumstances where the Act might apply. The Keeper of the Registers also took a cautious view, excluding indemnity in respect of the Act even in circumstances where the conveyance was not expressly granted in terms of the Act. The effect of the provisions is to convert the rights of reversion which already exist at the time these provisions come in to force (the day after Royal Assent) to rights to limited compensation. This will not apply however where the compensation has already been paid to the reversion holder or the reversioner has in fact completed title prior to the day after Royal Assent.

Subs.(1)

The provisions apply where the person entitled to the reversion has not completed title to the land prior to the day after Royal Assent.

Subs.(2)

If, prior to the day after Royal Assent, the property has ceased to be used for educational purposes, and a contract of sale has been concluded by or on behalf of the education authority, then the authority must pay to the person entitled to the reversion an amount equal to the open-market value of the land as at the day the provision comes into force. However, if the property ceases to be used for educational purposes after this provision comes into force, then the amount to be paid is the open-market value of the land as at the date of cessation of the educational use, less any improvement value as at that date.

Subs.(3)

If the education authority has not sold the property, the holder of the reversion has certain options. The holder may ask the authority to convey the property to him or her in terms of the original reversion or to pay compensation. However, if the holder of the reversion asks for a conveyance rather than compensation the local authority can opt to retain the land and pay compensation. The local authority must indicate which option they are to exercise within three months of the request for a conveyance.

Subs.(4)

Where there has been no sale by the authority if the cessation of the educational purpose occurs before these provisions come into force, then the land is conveyed to the holder of the reversion or compensation based on current open market value is paid without deduction of improvement value. If the cessation occurs after these provisions come into force, improvement value is deducted either by reducing the amount of compensation or by requiring payment from the holder of the reversion of an amount which is equal to the improvement value.

Subs.(5)

The Lands Tribunal has jurisdiction to adjudicate in relation to the assessment of compensation or improvement value.

Subs.(6)

This is a definition section. "Improvement value" is defined as such part of the value of the land as is attributable to any building or other structure other than any building erected by or at the expense of the party who originally gifted or conveyed the land under the 1841 Act or any predecessor as owner of the land of that person.

Subs.(7)

The provisions of the 1841 Act were made applicable in various other statutes. The reforms will apply to these other statutes.

Subs.(8)

The election in subs.(3)(b) must be made within three months.

Subs.(9)

The compensation and reversion provisions do not apply where the person entitled to the reversion has, before the day on which the section comes into force, accepted an offer of compensation in respect of the land, or concluded a contract for or accepted a conveyance of the land in terms of the reversion.

Subs.(10)

Where proceedings have been commenced to enforce the reversion, the provisions of s.67(1)(b) and (2) apply to these proceedings. Section 67 deals with the abolition of rights of irritancy and any proceedings commenced are deemed to be abandoned without further process and without the requirement to pay judicial expenses except in a case where final decree not subject to appeal has been granted prior to the coming into force of the Act.

Right to petition under section 7 of Entail Sites Act 1840

87.—(1) In a case where—

(a) it would be competent but for this section, section 50(1) of the 2000 Act (disentailment on appointed day) and the repeal of the Entail Sites Act 1840 by that Act for a person to apply by petition under section 7 of that Act of 1840 (petition praying to have feu charter or other right or lease declared to be forfeited etc.); but

(b) the person has not, before the day on which this section comes into force, accepted an offer of compensation in respect of the right so to apply,

subsections (2) to (6) and (8) of section 86 of this Act shall, in place of the said section 7 but with the modifications specified in subsection (2) below, apply.

(2) The modifications are that—

(a) for any reference to the education authority there shall be substituted a reference to the parties in whose favour the feu charter or lease was granted, or the successors other than by purchase for value of those parties;

(b) in each of subsections (2) and (4), for the word "revert" there shall be substituted "be forfeit" and for the word "reverted" there shall be substituted "have been forfeit"; and

(c) in subsection (6), for paragraph (a) of the definition of "improvement value" there shall be substituted—

"(a) the person who granted the feu or lease under section 1 of the Entail Sites Act 1840 (3 & 4 Vict. c.48) (grants for sites of churches etc.);".

(3) After such obligations as arise by virtue of this section are met or prescribe, the purposes for which the land in question was feued or leased under the said Act of 1840 need no longer be given effect.

(4) Subsections (1)(b) and (2) of section 67 of this Act shall apply in relation to any application already made by petition as mentioned in subsection (1)(a) above as they apply in relation to any proceedings already commenced as mentioned in the said subsection (1)(b).

GENERAL NOTE

The 2000 Act automatically disentails any remaining entailed land on the appointed day. In terms of s.7 of the Entail Sites Act 1840 restricted areas of land could be conveyed out of entailed estates for public spirited purposes. The heir of entail in possession could reclaim that land if it was not used for these public spirited purposes. This right to reclaim will go when the 2000 Act automatically disentails remaining entailed land. If these parties would have had a right to demand a reversion of the site but for compulsory disentailment then they will have a right to claim using the provisions of s.86. The scope is obviously wider because conveyances under the Entail Sites Act 1840 were not just to education bodies. In many cases the property will have been conveyed to a trust for public trust purposes. Subsection 3(3) provides that the land need no longer be held for the purposes for which the land in question was originally feued or leased under the 1840 Act.

Prescriptive period for obligations arising by virtue of 1841 Act or 1840 Act

88.—In Schedule 1 to the Prescription and Limitation (Scotland) Act 1973 (c.52) (obligations affected by prescriptive periods of five years to which section 6 of that Act applies)—

(a) after sub-paragraph (aa) of paragraph 1 there shall be inserted—

"(ab) to any obligation arising by virtue of a right—

(i) of reversion under the third proviso to section 2 of the School Sites Act 1841 (4 & 5 Vict. c.38) (or of reversion under that proviso as applied by virtue of any other enactment);

(ii) to petition for a declaration of forfeiture under section 7 of the Entail Sites Act 1840 (3 & 4 Vict. c.48);"; and

(b) in paragraph 2—
    (i) in sub-paragraph (e), for the words "or (aa)" there shall be substituted ", (aa) or (ab)"; and
    (ii) after that sub-paragraph there shall be inserted—
        "(ee) so as to extinguish, before the expiry of the continuous period of five years which immediately follows the coming into force of section 88 of the Title Conditions (Scotland) Act 2003 (asp 9) (prescriptive period for obligations arising by virtue of 1841 Act or 1840 Act), an obligation mentioned in sub-paragraph (ab) of paragraph 1 of this Schedule;".

GENERAL NOTE
    The five-year negative prescription will apply to obligations arising in relation to rights of reversion under the School Sites Act 1841 or rights to petition for forfeiture under the Entail Sites Act 1840. This provision comes into effect the day after Royal Assent in respect of the School Sites Act and on the appointed day (November 28, 2004) in respect of the Entail Sites Act. Time which occurs before these provisions come into effect, does not count. If a right is not claimed for five years after the event which lead to its becoming due (*e.g.* a school ceasing to be used as a school) no claim can be made.

Repeal of Reversion Act 1469
    89.—(1) The Reversion Act 1469 (c.3) shall cease to have effect.
    (2) Subsection (1) above shall not affect any right of reversion constituted, before the appointed day, as a real right.

GENERAL NOTE
    The 1469 Act taken together with a Registration Act 1617 allowed reversions to run with the land if registered. The 1469 Act is now repealed subject to the preservation of any rights of reversion which have been constituted as real rights before the appointed day.

PART 9

TITLE CONDITIONS: POWERS OF LANDS TRIBUNAL

Powers of Lands Tribunal as respects title conditions
    90.—(1) Subject to sections 97, 98 and 104 of this Act and to subsections (3) to (5) below, the Lands Tribunal may by order, on the application of—
    (a) an owner of a burdened property or any other person against whom a title condition (or purported title condition) is enforceable (or bears to be enforceable)—
        (i) discharge it, or vary it, in relation to that property; or
        (ii) if the title condition is a real burden or a rule of a development management scheme, determine any question as to its validity, applicability or enforceability or as to how it is to be construed;
    (b) an owner of a benefited property, renew or vary, in relation to that property, a title condition which is—
        (i) a real burden in respect of which intimation of a proposal to execute and register a notice of termination has been given under section 21 of this Act; or
        (ii) a real burden or servitude affected by a proposal to register a conveyance, being a proposal of which notice has been given under section 107(4) of this Act; or
    (c) an owner of a unit in a community, preserve as mentioned in section 34(3) or 37(1) of this Act, a community burden in respect of which intimation of a proposal to register a deed of variation or discharge has been given under section 34(1) or 36(1) of this Act;
    (d) an owner of a unit of the development to which applies a development management scheme in respect of which intimation of

a proposal to register a deed of disapplication has been given under subsection (1) of section 74 of this Act, preserve the scheme;

(e) the owners' association of a development to which applies a development management scheme in respect of which intimation of a proposal to register a conveyance, being a proposal of which notice has been given as mentioned in subsection (b)(ii) above, preserve the scheme;

but where the Lands Tribunal refuse an application under paragraph (b) or (c) above wholly, or an application under paragraph (b) partly, they shall in relation to the benefited property discharge the title condition, wholly or partly, accordingly or as the case may be shall in relation to the units not all of whose owners have granted the deed vary or discharge the community burden accordingly and where they refuse an application under paragraph (d) or (e) above, they shall disapply the development management scheme.

(2) Paragraph (b) of subsection (1) above applies in relation to the application of a holder of a personal real burden as it applies to the application of an owner of a benefited property except that, for the purposes of any application made by virtue of this subsection, the words "in relation to that property" in paragraph (b) shall be disregarded as shall the words "in relation to the benefited property" in what follows paragraph (e) in that subsection.

(3) It shall not be competent to make an application under subsection (1) above in relation to a title condition of a kind specified in schedule 11 to this Act.

(4) It shall not be competent to make an application under subsection (1)(b), (c), (d) or (e) above—

(a) after the renewal date, or as the case may be the date specified by virtue of section 107(6)(d)(ii) of, or the expiry of the period mentioned in section 34(3), 37(1) or 74(3) of, this Act, except with the consent of the terminator or as the case may be of—
  (i) the person proposing to register the conveyance or the deed of variation or discharge, or
  (ii) the owners' association; or

(b) after there has been, in relation to the proposal, endorsement under section 23(1) or, as the case may be, execution of a relevant certificate applied for by virtue of section 107(1)(b), or endorsement under section 37(2) or 73(3), of this Act.

(5) Variation which would impose a new obligation or would result in a property becoming a benefited property shall not be competent on an application—

(a) under subsection (1)(a)(i) above unless the owner of the burdened property consents; or

(b) under subsection (1)(b) above.

¹ (6) Subject to section 97(1) of this Act and to subsections (9) and (10) below, an order discharging or varying a title condition may—

(a) where made under paragraph (a)(i) of subsection (1) above, direct the applicant; or

(b) where made by virtue of the refusal of an application under paragraph (b) or (c) of that subsection, direct the terminator or, as the case may be, the person proposing to register the conveyance or deed of variation or discharge,

to pay to any person who in relation to the title condition was an owner of the benefited property or, where there is no benefited property, to any holder of the title condition, such sum as the Lands Tribunal may think it just to award under one, but not both, of the heads mentioned in subsection (7) below.

(7) The heads are—

[1] (a) a sum to compensate for any substantial loss or disadvantage suffered by, as the case may be—
    (i) the owner, as owner of the benefited property; or
    (ii) the holder of the title condition,
in consequence of the discharge or variation;
(b) a sum to make up for any effect which the title condition produced, at the time when it was created, in reducing the consideration then paid or made payable for the burdened property.

(8) Subject to section 97(1) of this Act and to subsection (11) below, an order discharging, renewing or varying a title condition may impose on the burdened property a new title condition or vary a title condition extant at the time the order is made.

[2](8A) An order disapplying the development management scheme shall, where the deed of disapplication makes such provision as is mentioned in section 73(2) of this Act, impose the real burdens in question.

(9) A direction under subsection (6) above shall be made only if the person directed consents.

(10) Where an application under subsection (1)(b)(ii) above is refused, wholly or partly, any direction under subsection (6) above for payment to that person may be made only if that application was made by virtue of subsection (2) above.

(11) An imposition under subsection (8) above shall be made only if the owner of the burdened property consents.

(12) The jurisdiction conferred by subsection (1) above includes power, in relation to an application under paragraph (a)(ii) only of that subsection, to decline (with reason stated) to proceed to determine the question.

AMENDMENTS
1. As amended by the Title Conditions (Scotland) Act 2003 (Consequential Provisions) Order (SSI 2003/503), Sch.1, para.9 (effective October 22, 2003).
2. Inserted by the Title Conditions (Scotland) Act 2003 (Consequential Provisions) Order (SSI 2003/503), Sch.1, para.9 (effective October 22, 2003) and amended by the Tenements (Scotland) Act 2004 (asp 11), s.25, Sch.4, para.15 (effective October 23, 2004).

GENERAL NOTE
The powers of the Lands Tribunal to vary or discharge title conditions are currently set out in ss.1 and 2 of the Conveyancing and Feudal Reform (Scotland) Act 1970. These Sections are repealed and the jurisdiction of the Tribunal expanded. Under the 1970 provisions a real burden had to be properly constituted and enforceable before the Tribunal had any jurisdiction. The Tribunal could not, for example, declare that a burden was unenforceable because it did not satisfy the rules of constitution or the rules for content. Under the new provisions the Tribunal can decide that a burden in invalid.

Subs.(1)
In terms of the 2003 Act the Tribunal will have to deal with various applications and so the separate jurisdictions of the Tribunal are defined. In the first place, the existing jurisdiction to vary or discharge is reaffirmed in relation to benefited and burdened properties. The provision, however, is extended to "purported" real burdens so the Tribunal will be able to discharge a burden, even although it may consider that the burden is invalid. The Tribunal can also decide if a real burden, including a rule of a development management scheme, is invalid, inapplicable or unenforceable. The Tribunal can also indicate how it is to be construed or interpreted. The second type of jurisdiction relates to applications for renewal of burdens which are affected by the termination procedure, or subject to extinction under s.107(1). This section provides for the extension of real burdens and servitudes where land is acquired by an acquiring authority by agreement. The third jurisdiction will allow the Tribunal to deal with applications to preserve burdens which are under threat of discharge under ss.33 and 35. The Tribunal also has jurisdiction in relation to development management schemes where there is a proposal to register a deed of disapplication under s.74(1).

Subs.(2)

The jurisdiction in relation to preservation notices where the termination procedure is invoked applies to personal real burdens.

Subs.(3)

Title conditions listed in Sch.10 are excluded from the jurisdiction. This was always the case. These include: obligations relating to minerals; obligations created for naval, military or air force purposes; obligations created or imposed for civil aviation purposes or in connection with the use of land as an aerodrome and obligations created in relation to a lease of an agricultural holding; or a holding within the meaning of The Small Landholders (Scotland) Act 1886 to 1931; or a croft.

Subs.(4)

This deals with the various time limits which apply in respect of applications for renewal or preservation.

Subs.(5)

The Tribunal does have, in certain circumstances, the power to impose a new obligation or to vary an obligation that results in property becoming a benefited property. This provision makes it clear that this will not be competent in relation to ordinary applications for discharge or variation without the consent of the owner of the burdened property or in applications for renewal or variation in relation to the termination of provisions.

Subs.(6) and (7)

These subsections deal with compensation. The provisions are the same as under the 1970 Act and presumably the Tribunal will take the same view as it has done in the past (see *Manz v Butter's Trustees*, 1973 S.L.T. (Lands Tr.) 2; *Lothian Development Corporation v County Properties and Developments Ltd*, 1996 S.L.T. 1106).

Subs.(8)

This affirms the power of the Tribunal to impose new title conditions or vary existing conditions at the time any order is made (*see Strathclyde Regional Council v MacTaggart & Mickel Ltd* 1984 S.L.T. (Lands Tr.) 33). Subsection 8 requires the consent of the owner of the burdened property. If that consent cannot be granted the Tribunal may not grant the discharge. Replacement conditions are not competent in applications which are granted on an unopposed basis (s.97(1)). A direction to pay compensation will only be made if the applicant who is to pay the compensation consents. Presumably this provision is to allow such an owner to bow out of the proceedings leaving the real burden intact as opposed to accepting a discharge or variation subject to payment of compensation.

Subs.(8A)

A deed of disapplication of a development management scheme may contain real burdens to regulate future management.

Subs.(9)

Where any application under subs.(1)(b)(ii) is refused wholly or partly any direction to pay compensation under subs.(6) can only be made if the application was one under subs.(2) which relates to personal real burdens.

Subs.(10)

New burdens under subs.(8) can only be imposed if the owner of the burdened property consents.

Subs.(11)

Where the application is simply to determine that a title condition is invalid, inapplicable, unenforceable, or how it is to be interpreted, the Tribunal may decline to deal with the matter because the courts have a concurrent jurisdiction.

Special provision as to variation or discharge of community burdens

91.—(1) Without prejudice to section 90(1)(a)(i) of this Act, an application may be made to the Lands Tribunal under this section by owners of at least one quarter of the units in a community for the variation

("variation" including imposition) or discharge of a community burden as it affects, or as the case may be would affect, all or some of the units in the community.

(2) In the case of an application made by owners of some only of the units in the community, the units affected need not be the units which they own.

(3) Subsections (6), (7) and (9) of section 90 of this Act shall apply in relation to an order made by virtue of subsection (1) above varying or discharging a community burden as they apply to an order under subsection (1)(a)(i) of that section discharging a title condition.

GENERAL NOTE

Clearly, special provision is required in relation to community burdens because a number of people are both benefited and burdened proprietors. Owners of 25 per cent of the units in a community may apply to the Lands Tribunal for a variation or a discharge of a community burden. The Tribunal may vary or discharge a community burden either in relation to all of the community or part of the community. Where the application is made by only some of the owners it does not matter that the burdens which they seek to have discharged or varied affect other units as compensation can be awarded in accordance with the provisions of s.90.

Early application for discharge: restrictive provisions

92.—In the constitutive deed, provision may be made to the effect that there shall be no application under section 90(1)(a)(i) or 91(1) of this Act in respect of a title condition before such date as may be specified in the deed (being a date not more than five years after the creation of the title condition); and if such provision is so made it shall not be competent to make an application under the section in question before that date.

GENERAL NOTE

Under s.2(5) of the 1970 Act an application could not be brought to the Tribunal for a variation and discharge if it related to an obligation which was less than two years old. The new provision is to the effect that the constitutive deed may provide that there can be no application for variation or discharge for a fixed period (not more than five years after creation of the title condition). If there is no such provision, then presumably applications can be made at any time, although the Tribunal will still be wary of granting discharges in respect of recently created burdens (see *Murrayfield Ice Rink v Scottish Rugby Union* 1972, S.L.T. (Lands Tr.) 20; 1973 S.L.T. 99; *Solway Cedar Ltd v Hendry*, 1972 S.L.T. (Lands Tr.) 42; *James Miller and Partners Ltd v Hunt*, 1971 S.L.T. (Lands Tr.) 9).

Notification of application

93.—(1) The Lands Tribunal shall, on receipt of an application under—
  (a) section 90(1)(a) or 91(1) of this Act, give notice of that application to any person who, not being the applicant, appears to them to fall within any of the following descriptions—
    (i) an owner of the burdened property;
    (ii) an owner of any benefited property;
    (iii) a holder of the title condition;
  (b) section 90(1)(b) of this Act, give such notice to any person who appears to them to fall within any of the following descriptions—
    (i) in the case mentioned in sub-paragraph (i) of that provision, the terminator;
    (ii) an owner of the burdened property; or
    (iii) in the case mentioned in sub-paragraph (ii) of that provision, the person proposing to register the conveyance;
  (c) section 90(1)(c) of this Act, give such notice to the person proposing to register the deed of variation or discharge;
  (d) section 90(1)(d) of this Act, give such notice to the owners' association; or
  (e) section 90(1)(e) of this Act, give notice to the person proposing to register the conveyance,
and subject to subsection (2) below shall do so by sending the notice.

(2) Notice under subsection (1) above may be given by advertisement, or by such other method as the Lands Tribunal think fit, if—
- (a) given to a person who cannot, by reasonable inquiry, be identified or found;
- (b) the person to whom it is given, being a person given notice by virtue of paragraph (a)(ii) of that subsection, does not appear to them to have any interest to enforce the title condition; or
- (c) so many people require to be given notice that, in the opinion of the Lands Tribunal, it is not reasonably practicable to send it.

(3) The Lands Tribunal may also give notice of the application, by such means as they think fit, to any other person.

GENERAL NOTE

This section deals with procedure in relation to the notification of the application. The Tribunal must notify interested parties. The meaning of "send" is given in s.124 and notification must be sent to the appropriate party or their agent, where the property is known but the identity of the owner is not known then it may be addressed to the owner or proprietor. "Sent" means being posted, delivered or transmitted by electronic means. Where intimation is posted the article posted should be taken to be sent on the day of posting, and where transmitted by electronic means on the day of transmission.

Subs.(1)

Paragraph (a) deals with an application to discharge or vary burdens or declare them invalid or unenforceable or to interpret them. In such cases the Tribunal must, on receipt of the application, give notice to any person who appears to them to be either an owner of the burdened property, an owner of any benefited property or a holder of the title condition. These provisions also apply to applications under s.91 by proprietors affected by community burdens and to personal burdens where the holder must be notified. Paragraph (b) provides that in applications to renew or vary title conditions which are subject to termination, the application must be notified to the owners of the burdened property and the terminator. When an acquiring authority is involved in terms of s.107(4) intimation is also to be made to the acquiring authority. Paragraph (c) provides that where application is made under s.90(1)(c) notice must be given to the person proposing to register the deed of variation or discharge. Paragraph (d) provides that where the application has been made under s.90(1)(d) intimation must be given to the owners' association. Paragraph (e) provides that where the application is made under s.90(1)(e) notice must be given to the person proposing to register the conveyance.

Subs.(2)

If the person to whom notice must be sent cannot after reasonable enquiry be identified or appears to lack an interest to enforce or intimation is impracticable because of the numbers involved, notification can be given by advertisement or in such a manner as the Tribunal thinks fit.

Subs.(3)

There is a general discretion which allows the Tribunal to give notification to such other people as they think fit. Normally, notification would be to owners.

Content of notice

94.—The Lands Tribunal shall—
- (a) in any notice given by them under section 93 of this Act—
  - (i) summarise or reproduce the application;
  - (ii) set a date (being a date no earlier than twenty-one days after the notice is given) by which representations to them as respects the application may be made;
  - (iii) state the fee which must accompany any such representations; and
  - (iv) in the case of an application for the discharge, renewal or variation of a real burden, or for the preservation of a real burden or development management scheme, state that if the application is not opposed it may be granted without further inquiry; and

(b) in any notice so given (other than by advertisement) in respect of an application under section 90(1)(a) or 91(1) of this Act, also set out the name and address of every person to whom the notice is being sent.

Notification under s.93 must contain a summary or copy of the application and allow a date (no earlier than 21 days after the notice is given) by which representations must be made to the Tribunal. The notice must also state the fee which must accompany representations. In the case of an application for discharge, renewal or variation, or the preservation of a real burden or development management scheme the notice must state that if the application is not opposed it may be granted without further enquiry. Unless the notice is given by advertisement the notice must also state in respect of applications under s.90(1)(a) or 91(1) the name and address of every person to whom the notice is being sent.

Persons entitled to make representations

95.—The persons entitled to make representations as respects an application under section 90(1) or 91(1) of this Act are—
    (a) any person who has title to enforce the title condition;
    (b) any person against whom the title condition is enforceable;
    (c) in the case mentioned in paragraph (b)(ii) or (e) of section 90(1), the person proposing to register the conveyance; and
    (d) in the case mentioned in paragraph (d) of that section, the owners' association and the owner of any unit of the development.

GENERAL NOTE
In general terms, those who are entitled to make representations are persons with a title to enforce the title condition or those against whom the title condition can be enforced. This could include tenants, liferenters, heritable creditors in possession and non-entitled spouses. In the case of applications under s.90(1)(b)(ii) or (e) the person proposing to register the conveyance is also entitled to make representations. In the case of applications under s.90(1)(d) the owners' association and the owner of any unit in the development may make representations.

Representations

96.—(1) Representations made by any person to the Lands Tribunal as respects an application under section 90(1) or 91(1) of this Act shall be in writing and shall comprise a statement of the facts and contentions upon which the person proposes to rely.

(2) For the purposes of this Act, representations are made when they are received by the Lands Tribunal with the requisite fee; and a person sending such representations shall forthwith send a copy of them to the applicant.

(3) Notwithstanding section 94(a)(ii) of this Act, the Lands Tribunal may if they think fit accept representations made after the date set under that section.

GENERAL NOTE
Representations will have to be made in writing and will comprise a statement of facts and arguments. They will require to be sent or transmitted with the appropriate fee. The party sending representations must send a copy of them to the applicant. In so far as the time limit for sending representations is concerned, the Tribunal does retain a discretion to accept late representations.

Granting unopposed application for discharge or renewal of real burden

97.—(1) Subject to subsection (2) below, an unopposed application duly made for—
    (a) the discharge or variation;
    (b) the renewal or variation; or
    (c) the preservation,
of a real burden shall be granted as of right; and as respects an application under paragraph (a) above neither subsection (6)(a) nor subsection (8) of section 90 of this Act shall apply in relation to the order discharging or as the case may be varying the real burden.

(2) Subsection (1) above does not apply as respects an application—

(a) for the discharge or variation of a facility burden;

(b) for the discharge or variation of a service burden; or

(c) under section 91(1) of this Act for the discharge or variation of a community burden imposed on any unit of a sheltered or retirement housing development.

(3) An application is unopposed for the purposes of—

(a) subsection (1)(a) above if, as at the date on which the application falls to be determined, no representations opposing it have been made under section 96 of this Act either by an owner of any benefited property or by a holder of a personal real burden;

(b) subsection (1)(b) above if, as at that date, no representations opposing the application have been made under that section by the terminator or as the case may be the person proposing to register the conveyance; or

(c) subsection (1)(c) above if, as at that date, no representations opposing the application have been made under that section by the person proposing to register the deed of variation or discharge,

or all such representations which have been so made have been withdrawn.

(4) In granting an application under subsection (1)(b) or (c) above, the Lands Tribunal may, as they think fit, order either—

(a) the person who intimated the proposal to execute and register the notice of termination or as the case may be the deed of variation or discharge or the conveyance; or

(b) any other person who succeeded that person as terminator or proposer,

to pay to the applicant a specific sum in respect of the expenses incurred by the applicant or such proportion of those expenses as the Tribunal think fit.

GENERAL NOTE

One of the difficulties of the 1970 provisions was that all applications had to be considered on the merits whether they were opposed or not. This section allows the Tribunal to grant a discharge automatically if the application is not opposed in respect of applications for discharge, renewal or preservation of real burdens. The Tribunal will still require to go through the process of notification or checking that notification has been made. There will be no right to compensation in these cases, nor a right to impose substitute real burdens.

Subs.(1)

Provided that the burden is one over which the Tribunal have jurisdiction the application must be granted if it is unopposed. No orders for compensation or substitute burdens are competent. The same applies to applications for renewal or variation and applications for preservation.

Subs.(2)

The unopposed procedure will not apply in the case of an application for discharge or variation of a facility burden or a service burden or an application for the discharge or variation of a community burden imposed on a unit in a sheltered or retirement housing development.

Subs.(3)

Incompetent representations will not mean that an application is opposed. In the case of a notice to preserve a burden under threat of termination only representations by the terminator will be treated as opposition. If the Tribunal accept representations late then a previously unopposed application will become an opposed application. If representations are withdrawn then the application can proceed as an unopposed application.

Subs.(4)

The Tribunal may award expenses against a terminator or a party who seeks to register a discharge under s.33 or 35, or a conveyance under s.107 where that party does not oppose an application for renewal or preservation under s.90(1)(b) or (c). The reason for this is that such a party's actions have necessitated the application being made by the benefited proprietor to preserve that proprietor's interests.

Granting other applications for variation, discharge, renewal or preservation of title condition

98.—An application for the variation, discharge, renewal or preservation, of a title condition shall, unless it falls to be granted as of right under section 97(1) of this Act, be granted by the Lands Tribunal only if they are satisfied, having regard to the factors set out in section 100 of this Act, that—

(a) except in the case of an application under subsection (3) of section 34 or, in respect of a deed of variation or discharge granted by the owner of an adjacent unit, subsection (1) of section 37 of this Act, it is reasonable to grant the application; or

(b) in such a case, the variation or discharge in question—
¹ (i) is not in the best interests of all the owners (taken as a group) of the units in the community; or
(ii) is unfairly prejudicial to one or more of those owners.

GENERAL NOTE

This section sets out the factors which the Tribunal must consider in relation to any application which is unopposed. The Tribunal must also act reasonably in considering any application. Where an application is made under s.34(3) or in respect of a deed of variation or discharge granted by an owner of an adjacent unit under s.37(1), then the Tribunal must consider whether the variation is in the best interest of the owners of all the units in the community or is unfairly prejudicial to one or more of these owners.

Granting applications as respects development management schemes

99.—(1) An unopposed application for preservation of a development management scheme shall be granted as of right.

(2) An application is unopposed for the purposes of subsection (1) above if, as at the date on which the application falls to be determined, no representations opposing it have been made under section 96 of this Act by the owners' association or, as the case may be, by the person proposing to register the conveyance.

(3) In granting an application under subsection (1) above, the Lands Tribunal may order the owners' association to pay to the applicant a specific sum in respect of the expenses incurred by the applicant or such proportion of those expenses as the Tribunal think fit.

(4) An application for the preservation of a development management scheme shall, unless it falls to be granted as of right under subsection (1) above, be granted by the Lands Tribunal only if they are satisfied, in the case of an application—
¹ (a) under paragraph (d) of section 90(1) of this Act, that the disapplication of the development management scheme or a real burden imposed by the deed of disapplication is not in the best interests of all the owners (taken as a group) of the units of the development or is unfairly prejudicial to one or more of those owners; or

(b) under paragraph (e) of that section, that having regard to the purpose for which the land is being acquired by the person proposing to register the conveyance it is reasonable to grant the application.

Unopposed applications for preservation of a development management scheme shall be granted as of right and provisions apply in relation to the definition of an unopposed application. There is also power to award expenses. In considering an application under s.90(1)(d) the Tribunal must consider whether the disapplication of the development management scheme is in the best interest of all the owners (taken as a group), or is unfairly prejudicial to one or more of these owners. Where there is an application under s.90(1)(d), the Tribunal must have regard to the purpose for which the land is being acquired by the person proposing to register the conveyance and whether in the light of that it is reasonable to grant the application.

Factors to which the Lands Tribunal are to have regard in determining applications etc.

100.—The factors mentioned in section 98 of this Act are—

(a) any change in circumstances since the title condition was created (including, without prejudice to that generality, any change in the character of the benefited property, of the burdened property or of the neighbourhood of the properties);

(b) the extent to which the condition—
  (i) confers benefit on the benefited property; or
  (ii) where there is no benefited property, confers benefit on the public;

(c) the extent to which the condition impedes enjoyment of the burdened property;

(d) if the condition is an obligation to do something, how—
  (i) practicable; or
  (ii) costly,
  it is to comply with the condition;

(e) the length of time which has elapsed since the condition was created;

(f) the purpose of the title condition;

(g) whether in relation to the burdened property there is the consent, or deemed consent, of a planning authority, or the consent of some other regulatory authority, for a use which the condition prevents;

(h) whether the owner of the burdened property is willing to pay compensation;

(i) if the application is under section 90(1)(b)(ii) of this Act, the purpose for which the land is being acquired by the person proposing to register the conveyance; and

(j) any other factor which the Lands Tribunal consider to be material.

Subject to the general principle (where applicable) that the Tribunal must consider the reasonableness of an application the Tribunal must have regard to the various matters set out in this Section. The factors are very similar to the grounds for variation and discharge set out in s.1(3) of the 1970 Act, but there are additional factors which the Tribunal can consider. The Tribunal can look at any number of these factors in coming to a view as to whether it would be reasonable to grant any application. Under the previous legislation there were three grounds. Although applications could be brought under one or more of the grounds, they were separate grounds.

Factor (a)
This is similar to the original ground that the obligation had become unreasonable or inappropriate by reason of a change in the character of the land or the neighbourhood or other circumstances under the 1970 Act. The new factor, however, focuses more on change of circumstances. The Tribunal has considered changes in the character of the land affected and the neighbourhood (see *MacDonald*, 1973 S.L.T. (Lands Tr.) 26; *Bolton v Aberdeen Corporation* 1972 (Lands Tr.) 26; *Manz v Butter's Trustees*, 1973 S.L.T. (Lands Tr.) 2; *Main v Lord Doune*, 1972 S.L.T. (Lands Tr.) 14).

Factor (b)
This factor is similar to the 1970 ground that the obligation had become unduly burdensome compared with the benefit it conferred. This will involve striking a balance in each case (see

Bachoo v George Wimpey & Co Ltd, 1977 S.L.T. (Lands Tr.) 2; *Murrayfield Ice Rink Ltd v Scottish Rugby Union*, 1972 S.L.T. (Lands Tr.) 20).

Factor (c)

This factor is very similar to the third ground under the 1970 Act, namely that the existence of the obligation impedes a reasonable use of the land. This was always regarded as the widest ground; the one which looked forward as opposed to back in relation to the burden (see *Main v Lord Doune*, 1972 S.L.T. (Lands Tr.) 14; *West Lothian Co-op Society Ltd v Ashdale Land & Property Co Ltd*, 1972 S.L.T. (Lands Tr.) 30; *Mercer v Macleod*, 1977 S.L.T. (Lands Tr.) 14). Loss of amenity may be a factor to be considered here (see *Bachoo v George Wimpey & Co Ltd*, 1977 S.L.T. (Lands Tr.) 2).

Factor (d)

If the condition is a positive obligation then the Tribunal may consider how practicable or costly it is to comply with the condition. This is a new factor. It is one which could perhaps be taken together with *Factor (b)*.

Factor (e)

Many burdens may have had greater relevance when they were imposed, but in more modern times present a difficulty with little practical benefit.

Factor (ea)

It may be obvious, particularly in relation to older burdens, that the purpose for which the real burden was created is no longer relevant. This is a factor which could be taken together with *Factor (c)*.

Factor (f)

The Lands Tribunal has always been able to take account of planning permissions or licences in respect of a proposed use (*Main v Lord Doune*, 1972 S.L.T. (Lands Tr.) 14; *Mercer v Macleod*, 1977 S.L.T. (Lands Tr.) 14; *Co-operative Wholesale Society v Ushers Brewery*, 1975 S.L.T. (Lands Tr.) 9). A view taken by the Tribunal has in the past has been that the existence of a permission or licence is only a factor in assessing whether a burden impedes a reasonable use of the land. The Tribunal has in the past taken the view that permissions and licences are granted in the context of the public interest, whereas title conditions are essentially matters of private right.

Factor (fa)

There may be situations where there are genuine issues of amenity and the applicant has attempted to obtain a waiver or a discharge from the benefited proprietor and indeed offered some compensation for any loss of amenity. This factor allows the Tribunal to consider the overall reasonableness of the situation. That is not to say that the Tribunal would force a benefited proprietor to accept a payment where there is a matter of principle at stake. It would, however, allow the Tribunal to deal with matters where it was apparent that the objector or the party making representations was simply exploiting the situation for monetary gain.

Factor (fb)

If the application is under s.90(1)(b)(ii), the Tribunal may consider the purpose for which the land is being acquired. Section 107 provides that where land is acquired by an authority by agreement, and that land could have been acquired by compulsory purchase, then any burden or servitude is extinguished on the registration of the conveyance. However, a benefited proprietor can apply to the Tribunal to have the burden preserved. There may be circumstances where the purpose of the acquisition might not be impeded if the burden were preserved.

Factor (g)

This allows the Tribunal to consider any other factor which they deem to be material to the application. This is a general discretion.

Regulation of applications to Lands Tribunal

101.—The Scottish Ministers may make rules regulating any application under this Act to the Lands Tribunal and may in particular make provision, in those rules, as to the evidence which may be required for such an application.

This allows Scottish Ministers to make rules relating to applications and the evidence which may be required for such applications.

Referral to Lands Tribunal of notice dispute

102.—(1) Any dispute arising in relation to a notice registered under section 50 or 80 of this Act may be referred to the Lands Tribunal; and in determining the dispute the Tribunal may make such order as they think fit discharging or, to such extent as may be specified in the order, restricting the notice in question.

(2) In any referral under subsection (1) above, the burden of proving any disputed question of fact shall be on the person relying on the notice.

(3) An extract of any order made under subsection (1) above may be registered and the order shall take effect as respects third parties on such registration.

GENERAL NOTE
The Lands Tribunal have jurisdiction to resolve disputes relating to s.50 notices (notices of preservation) and s.80 notices (relating to the conversion of negative servitudes to real burdens). The burden of proving a disputed question is on the person relying on the notice. An extract of any order discharging a notice wholly or partially may be registered.

Expenses

103.—(1) The Lands Tribunal may, in determining an application made under this Part of this Act, make such order as to expenses as they think fit but shall have regard, in particular, to the extent to which the application, or any opposition to the application, is successful.

(2) Subsection (1) above is without prejudice to sections 97(4) and 99(3) of this Act.

GENERAL NOTE
The Lands Tribunal will have a discretion in relation to expenses. The Tribunal will have regard to the normal principle that expenses follow success. This is subject to the specific provisions contained in ss.97(4) and 99(3).

Taking effect of orders of Lands Tribunal etc.

104.—(1) The Scottish Ministers may, after consultation with the Scottish Committee of the Council on Tribunals, make rules as to when an order of the Lands Tribunal on an application under section 90(1) or 91(1) of this Act shall take effect.

(2) An order under subsection (1)(a)(i), (b) or (c) of section 90, under subsection (1) of that section on the refusal (wholly or partly as the case may be) of an application under paragraph (b) or (c) of that subsection or under section 91(1) of this Act which has taken effect in accordance with rules made under subsection (1) above may be registered against the burdened property by any person who was a party to the application or who was, under section 95 of this Act, entitled to make representations as respects the application; and on the order being so registered the title condition to which it relates is discharged (wholly or partly), renewed (wholly or partly), imposed, preserved or varied according to the terms of the order.

(3) An order—

(a) which disapplies a development management scheme, whether or not it imposes new burdens, being an order under subsection (1) of section 90 of this Act, or preserves it under paragraph (d) or (e) of that subsection; and

(b) which has taken effect in accordance with rules so made,

may be registered against the units of the development by the owners' association or as the case may be by an owner of a unit of the development or the person proposing to register the conveyance; and on the order being so registered the scheme is disapplied or preserved and the burdens imposed as the case may be.

(4) Any enforceability which the obligation in question has as a contractual obligation shall be unaffected by such an order.

AMENDMENT

1. As amended by the Title Conditions (Scotland) Act 2003 (Consequential Provisions) Order (SSI 2003/503), Sch.1, para.11 (effective October 22, 2003).

GENERAL NOTE

In general terms, orders will come into effect when they are registered and at that point the title condition will be discharged, varied, renewed, or preserved. This provision, however, does not apply to orders declaring a burden to be invalid or unenforceable or interpretative orders in terms of s.90(1)(a)(ii). This may seem an odd exclusion, particularly where a burden appears in the burdens section of a title sheet. Presumably, if the Lands Tribunal declare a burden to be invalid or unenforceable the burdened proprietor will wish the burden removed from the title sheet. The Keeper does, of course, have a discretion to note things on the title sheet and no doubt the order could be noted as opposed to registered. Alternatively, where an order indicates that a burden is wholly invalid the Keeper may accept the order as evidence of this and delete the burden. The reason for the exclusion may be found in subs.3 which provides that any contractual enforceability is to be unaffected by any order of the Tribunal. The Tribunal might presumably declare a burden to be unenforceable because it was not praedial in its nature. However, that might not affect its status as a contractual obligation between the original parties (however, see *Phillips v Lavery* 1962 (Sh. Ct) 57). This section makes special provision for orders disapplying development management schemes. These may be registered against the units of the development by the owners' association or by an owner of a unit.

PART 10

MISCELLANEOUS

Consequential alterations to Land Register

Alterations to Land Register consequential upon registering certain deeds

105.—(1) Subject to subsection (2) below, in registering in the Register of Sasines a document mentioned in subsection (3) below the Keeper of the Registers of Scotland may make such consequential alterations to the Land Register of Scotland as the Keeper considers requisite.

(2) In so registering such a document, or in registering it in the Land Register, by virtue of section 18, 19 or 20 of the 2000 Act or section 4(5), 50, 75 or 80 of this Act, the Keeper shall make such consequential alterations as are mentioned in subsection (1) above.

(3) The documents are—

(a) any decree, deed or other document which varies, discharges, renews, reallots, preserves or imposes a real burden or servitude; and

(b) any deed which comprises a conveyance of part of—

(i) the benefited property; or

(ii) the burdened property.

GENERAL NOTE

The Keeper is entitled to make alterations to the title sheet of any property as a result of the provisions of the 2000 Act and the 2003 Act. This will apply even where one of the titles is in the Sasine Register. If the burdened property is in the Land Register but the benefited property is in the Sasine Register the title sheet of the burdened property can be altered if the Lands Tribunal makes an appropriate order, even although the sasine title to the benefited property will remain the same. The same will apply to documents granted by virtue of certain provisions of the 2000 Act.

Compulsory acquisition of land

Extinction of real burdens and servitudes etc. on compulsory acquisition of land

106.—[1] (1) If land is acquired compulsorily by virtue of a compulsory purchase order to which this section applies then, except in so far as the terms of—

(a) the order; or

(b) the conveyance in implement of such acquisition,

provide otherwise, on registration of the conveyance, any real burden, or servitude, over the land shall be extinguished and any development management scheme applying as respects the land disapplied.

(2) Without prejudice to the generality of the exception in subsection (1) above, such terms as are mentioned in that exception may provide—

(a) for the variation of any of the real burdens or servitudes;

(b) that there shall be such extinction only—

    (i) of certain of the real burdens and servitudes;

    (ii) in relation to certain parts of the burdened property; or

    (iii) in respect of the enforcement rights of the owners of certain of the benefited properties.

(3) If the compulsory purchase order provides for an exception such as is mentioned in subsection (1) above, the conveyance in implement of the acquisition shall not, unless the owners of the benefited properties consent, or as the case may be the owners' association or the holder of any personal real burden consents, be registrable if its terms do not conform in that regard.

(4) Where a personal real burden is extinguished by virtue of subsection (1) above, such person as immediately before the extinction held the right to enforce the burden shall be entitled to receive compensation from the acquiring authority in question for any loss thereby occasioned that person.

[2](4A) This section applies to a compulsory purchase order in respect of which notice is given under–

(a) paragraph 3 of the First Schedule to the Acquisition of Land (Authorisation Procedure) (Scotland) Act 1947 (c.42) on or after the day on which section 109; or

(b) paragraph 2 of Schedule 5 to the Forestry Act 1967 (c. 10) on or after the day on which section 110,

of this Act comes into force.

(5) In this section—

"compulsory purchase order" has the meaning given by section 1(1) of the Acquisition of Land (Authorisation Procedure) (Scotland) Act 1947 (c.42) (procedure for compulsory purchase of land by local authorities etc.) except that it includes a compulsory purchase order made under the Forestry Act 1967 (c.10); and

"conveyance" means—

(a) a—

    (i) disposition;

    (ii) notice of title; or

    (iii) notarial instrument,

which includes a reference to the application of subsection (1) above;

(b) a conveyance in the form set out in Schedule A to the Lands Clauses Consolidation (Scotland) Act 1845 (c.19); or

(c) a general vesting declaration (as defined in paragraph 1(1) of Schedule 15 to the Town and Country Planning (Scotland) Act 1997 (c.8)).

AMENDMENTS
1. As amended by the Title Conditions (Scotland) Act 2003 (Consequential Provisions) Order (SSI 2003/503), Sch.1, para.12 (effective October 22, 2003).
2. Inserted by the Title Conditions (Scotland) Act 2003 (Consequential Provisions) Order (SSI 2003/503), Sch.1, para.12 (effective October 22, 2003).

GENERAL NOTE
There has always been a view that compulsory acquisition of land by general vesting order or statutory conveyance has the effect of extinguishing existing real burdens and servitudes (see *Town Council of Oban v Callander and Oban Railway* (1892) 19 R 912). This section makes it clear that unless the order or the conveyance in implement of the order provides otherwise, then on registration of the conveyance any real burden or servitude over the land acquired is extinguished, and any development management scheme is disapplied. The order or conveyance may provide for the preservation or the variation of any real burdens or servitudes and may provide that only certain real burdens and servitudes are to be extinguished as regards the whole or part of the property. There may also be provision in respect of the enforcement rights of the owners of certain of the benefited properties. Where there are exceptions of this type, the conveyance in implement of the acquisition cannot be registered unless the owners of benefited properties consent, or in the case of a development management scheme, the owners' association consent. In the case of the holder of any personal real burden, the holder would have to consent if the terms of the disposition do not conform with the exceptions or variations of the real burdens contained in the compulsory purchase order. Compensation will be payable to the holders of personal real burdens thus extinguished.

Extinction of real burdens and servitudes etc. where land acquired by agreement

107.—(1) If—
(a) land acquired by a person by agreement could have been so acquired by that person compulsorily by virtue of any enactment; and
(b) the person, having complied with subsection (4) below, registers a conveyance in implement of such acquisition together with a relevant certificate,

then, except in so far as the terms of the conveyance provide otherwise, on such registration any real burden, or servitude, over the land shall be extinguished and any development management scheme applying as respects the land disapplied.

(2) Registration under subsection (1) above shall not vary or extinguish a title condition which is the subject of an application disclosed by the certificate in so far as that title condition—
(a) is constituted in favour of the property of which the applicant is owner; or
(b) is a personal real burden of which the applicant is holder,

or disapply a development management scheme, described in the certificate; but the conveyance may be registered again, together with a further such certificate, under that subsection, the effect of the later registration being determined by reference to the further certificate rather than to the earlier certificate.

(3) Subsection (2) of section 106 of this Act shall apply in relation to the exception in subsection (1) above as it applies in relation to the exception in subsection (1) of that section.

(4) The person proposing to register the conveyance shall, before doing so in accordance with subsection (1)(b) above—
(a) if such registration would extinguish a title condition, give notice to the owner of the benefited property (or in the case of a personal real burden to the holder of that burden); and
(b) if it would disapply a development management scheme, give notice to the owners' association,

of the matters mentioned in subsection (6) below.

(5) Any person to whom notice is given under subsection (4) above may, on or before the date specified by virtue of subsection (6)(d)(ii) below, apply

to the Lands Tribunal for renewal or variation of the title condition or as the case may be preservation of the development management scheme.

(6) The matters are—

(a) a description of the land;

(b) the name and address of the person proposing to register the conveyance;

(c) the fact that, by virtue of this section (and subject to the terms of the conveyance), real burdens and servitudes over the land may be extinguished and any development management scheme disapplied;

(d) that the person given notice—

    (i) may obtain information from the person acquiring the land about any entitlement to compensation; and

    (ii) will require to apply to the Lands Tribunal for Scotland, by a date specified in the notice, if the title condition is to be renewed or varied under paragraph (b) of section 90(1) of this Act or as the case may be the development management scheme preserved under paragraph (e) of that section.

(7) The date so specified may be any date which is not fewer than twenty-one days after the notice is given (intimation by affixing being taken, for the purposes of this subsection, to be given when first the notice is affixed).

(8) Notice under subsection (4)(a) above may be given—

(a) by sending;

(b) by advertisement;

(c) by affixing a conspicuous notice to the burdened property and to—

    (i) in a case where there exists one, and only one, lamp post within one hundred metres of that property, that lamp post; or

    (ii) in a case where there exists more than one lamp post so situated, each of at least two such lamp posts; or

(d) by such other method as the person acquiring the land thinks fit,

and notice under subsection (4)(b) above may be given by sending or by such other means as that person thinks fit.

(9) Subsections (6) and (7) of section 21 of this Act apply in relation to affixing, and to a notice affixed, under subsection (8)(c) above as they apply in relation to affixing, and to a notice affixed, under subsection (2)(b) of that section (the reference in paragraph (a)(ii) of the said subsection (6) to the date specified in the notice as the renewal date being construed as a reference to the date specified by virtue of subsection (6)(d)(ii) above).

(10) In this section—

"conveyance" has the same meaning as in section 106(5) of this Act except that the reference, in paragraph (a) of the definition of that expression in that section, to subsection (1) of that section shall be read as a reference to that subsection of this section and paragraph (c) of that definition shall be disregarded; and

"relevant certificate" means a certificate executed, on or after the date specified by virtue of subsection (6)(d)(ii) above, by a member of the Lands Tribunal, or by their clerk, to the effect that no application in relation to the proposal to register the conveyance has been received under section 90(1)(b)(ii) or (e) of this Act or that any such application which has been received—

(a) has been withdrawn; or

(b) relates, in the case of an application under section 90(1)(b)(ii), (either or both)—

    (i) to one or more but not to all of the title conditions over the land (any title condition to which it relates being described in the certificate);

    (ii) to one or more but not to all (or probably or possibly not to all) of the benefited properties (any benefited property to which it relates being described in the certificate), and where more than one such application has been received the certificate shall relate to both (or as the case may be to all) applications. (11) Any application for a relevant certificate shall be made in the form set out in schedule 12 to this Act.

GENERAL NOTE

Similar provisions in relation to the extinction of real burdens and servitudes apply where land is acquired by agreement if that land could have been acquired by compulsory purchase. The acquiring authority must notify the owner of the benefited property or the holder of a personal real burden or the owners' association where a development management scheme is involved. The time limit for applications to renew burdens is not less than 21 days after notice. Any conveyance must contain a certificate from the Lands Tribunal in relation to any notice or the lack of notices. The certificate would be in similar terms to the certificate under ss.23 and 24 to the effect that no objection had been received timeously or that all objections had been withdrawn, or that the objections related only to particular burdens or were made only by certain of the benefited proprietors. A conveyance in terms of an agreement could be registered without a certificate. The conveyance would be valid but the real burdens or servitudes would not be extinguished. Where the certificate is not obtained until after registration of the conveyance then the conveyance can be reregistered with the certificate.

Amendments

Amendment of Church of Scotland (Property and Endowments) (Amendment) Act 1933

108.—In section 9 of the Church of Scotland (Property and Endowments) (Amendment) Act 1933 (c.44) (right of pre-emption of certain successors in title to persons who granted or disponed without valuable consideration for the erection of a church or manse), after subsection (3) there is added—

"(4) Where part of the lands which adjoin as is mentioned in subsection (3) above are conveyed, then on registration of the conveyance that subsection shall cease to afford a right of pre-emption to any owner of the part conveyed unless in the conveyance it is provided that the subsection shall instead cease to afford such a right to any owner of the part retained (in which case the subsection shall apply accordingly).

(5) The Scottish Ministers may by order made by statutory instrument make provision as to the procedures to be followed for the purposes of subsection (3) above.

(6) Without prejudice to the generality of subsection (5) above, any such order may include provision—

(a) as to how a price is to be fixed; and

(b) for any case where there is at any time, as regards the ground or part, more than one person to whom an opportunity to purchase must be afforded under subsection (3) above.".

GENERAL NOTE

This is a consequential amendment dealing with rights of pre-emption of the successors in title to persons who gifted land for the original church or manse.

Amendment of Acquisition of Land (Authorisation Procedure) (Scotland) Act 1947

109.—(1) The First Schedule to the Acquisition of Land (Authorisation Procedure) (Scotland) Act 1947 (c.42) shall be amended in accordance with the following subsections.

(2) In paragraph 3(b) (which requires a local authority to notify certain persons that a compulsory purchase order is about to be submitted by the authority for confirmation etc.), the existing words from "every owner" to "order", where it first occurs, shall be head (i); and after that head there shall be inserted the following heads—

"(ii) the holder of any personal real burden affecting that land if registration of the conveyance in implement of the order would vary or extinguish the title condition in question;

(iii) the owner of any land which is a benefited property (as defined by section 122(1) of the Title Conditions (Scotland) Act 2003 (asp 9)) in relation to any land comprised in the order if such registration would vary or extinguish the title condition in question; and

(iv) the owners' association of the development in question if a development management scheme applies as respects any land comprised in the order and registration of the conveyance in implement of the order would disapply that scheme,".

¹ (3) After paragraph 3 there shall be inserted—

"(3A) Service of notice under head (ii) or (iii) of paragraph 3(b) above shall be—

(a) by sending (that expression being construed in accordance with section 124 of the said Act of 2003 and as if what was being done was being done under that Act);

(b) by advertisement;

(c) by affixing a conspicuous notice to—

(i) in a case where there exists one, and only one, lamp post which is situated within one hundred metres of that property, that lamp post; or

(ii) in a case where there exists more than one lamp post so situated, each of at least two such lamp posts; or

(d) by such other means as the acquiring authority think fit,

And service of notice under head (iv) of that paragraph shall be by sending (as so construed) or by such other means as the acquiring authority think fit.

(3B) Subsections (6) and (7) of section 21 of the said Act of 2003 apply in relation to affixing, and to a notice affixed, under paragraph 3A(c) above (including that paragraph as it is applied by paragraph 6A below in relation to service of a notice under paragraph 6 below) as they apply in relation to affixing, and to a notice affixed, under subsection (2)(b) of that section (the reference in paragraph (a)(ii) of the said subsection (6) to the date specified in the notice as the renewal date being construed as a reference to the last day of the period specified in the notice given under paragraph 3(b) above) or, as the case may be, paragraph 6 below.".

(4) In paragraph 4 (powers in relation to objectors)—

(a) in sub-paragraph (2), at the beginning there shall be inserted "Subject to sub-paragraph (2A),";

(b) after sub-paragraph (2) there shall be inserted—

"(2A) If the person by whom an objection is made states that he objects as mentioned in sub-paragraph (4)(b) or (c) below, sub-paragraph (2) above shall not apply as respects that objection provided that the acquiring authority give the person a written undertaking that any conveyance in implement of the acquisition will provide that the title condition in question is not varied or extinguished in respect of the enforcement rights of that person or as the case may be that the development management scheme is not disapplied; and any such undertaking shall—

(a) identify the benefited property (if any) and burdened property or as the case may be the development to which the development management scheme applies;

(b) identify the order; and

(c) set out the manner in which the conveyance will fulfil the undertaking.

(2B) The effect, under subsection (1) of section 106 of the Title Conditions (Scotland) Act 2003 (asp 9) (extinction of real burdens and servitudes etc. on compulsory acquisition of land), of registering the conveyance after an undertaking given under sub-paragraph (2A) above has been registered against the burdened property, or as the case may be against the units of the development, shall be subject to the terms of the undertaking irrespective of the terms of the conveyance.

(2C) In sub-paragraphs (2A) and (2B) above, "conveyance" has the same meaning as in subsection (5) of that section.";

(c) in sub-paragraph (4), the existing words from "the grounds thereof" to the end shall be head (a) and after that head there shall be inserted the following heads—

"(b) whether he objects as a person with title to enforce a title condition and, if he does so object, then in that statement to—

   (i) identify the benefited property (if any) and burdened property;

   (ii) identify the title condition (either by setting it out in full or by identifying the constitutive deed, saying where it is registered and giving the date of registration); and

   (iii) if there is a benefited property, describe his connection with it;

(c) whether he objects as owners' association of the development to which a development management scheme applies and, if he does so object, then in that statement to identify—

   (i) the development; and

   (ii) the development management scheme (by identifying the deed of application, saying where it is registered and giving the date of registration).".

[2](4A) In paragraph 6 (which requires an acquiring authority to notify certain persons that a compulsory purchase order has been confirmed) the words "and a copy of the order as confirmed" shall be omitted.

[2](4B) After paragraph 6 there shall be inserted–

"**6A.** Paragraph 3A above applies in relation to service of a notice under paragraph 6 above on any persons on whom notices with respect to the land were required to be served under heads (ii) and (iii) of paragraph 3(b) above as it applies in relation to service of a notice under those heads of the said paragraph 3(b).

6B. Where a notice–

(a) is required by paragraph 6 above to be served on any person mentioned in heads (ii) and (iii) of paragraph 3(b) above and service is by sending as mentioned in paragraph 3A(a) above, the acquiring authority shall send with the notice a copy of the order as confirmed;

(b) is required by the said paragraph 6 to be served on any person mentioned in heads (i) and (iv) of the said paragraph 3(b), the acquiring authority shall serve with the notice a copy of that order.

6C. In paragraph 6B(a) above, the requirement to send a copy of the order shall be construed in accordance with section 124 of the Title Conditions (Scotland) Act 2003 (asp 9) and as if what was being done was being done under that Act.".

[1] (5) After paragraph 6 there is inserted—

"(6D) In this Part, "title condition", "development management scheme" and "personal real burden" have the same meanings as in the Title Conditions (Scotland) Act 2003 (asp 9).".

AMENDMENTS
1. As amended by the Title Conditions (Scotland) Act 2003 (Consequential Provisions) Order (SSI 2003/503), Sch.1, para.13 (effective October 22, 2003).
2. Inserted by the Title Conditions (Scotland) Act 2003 (Consequential Provisions) Order (SSI 2003/503), Sch.1, para.13 (effective October 22, 2003).

GENERAL NOTE

In view of the provisions relating to the extinction of real burdens and conditions on compulsory acquisition, the notification requirements under the Acquisition of Land (Authorisation Procedure) (Scotland) Act 1947 are extended to impose a duty on an acquiring authority, to notify a benefited proprietor or the holder of a personal burden that a compulsory purchase order has been made and is about to be submitted for confirmation. The benefited proprietor or holder of a personal burden who objects will be treated as a statutory objector.

Amendment of Forestry Act 1967

110.—(1) Schedule 5 to the Forestry Act 1967 (c.10) shall be amended in accordance with the following subsections.

[1](2) In paragraph 2 (which provides for notices as respects compulsory purchase orders), after sub-paragraph (1) there shall be inserted—

"(1A) Before making a compulsory purchase order the Scottish Ministers shall give notice of their intention in that regard to—

(a) the holder of any personal real burden affecting the land to which the order relates if registration of the conveyance in implement of the order would vary or extinguish the title condition in question;

(b) the owner of any land which is a benefited property (as defined by section 122(1) of the Title Conditions (Scotland) Act 2003 (asp 9)) in relation to any land comprised in the order if such registration would vary or extinguish the title condition in question; and

(c) the owners' association of the development in question if a development management scheme applies as respects any land comprised in the order and registration of the conveyance in implement of the order would disapply that scheme.

(1B) Notice under sub-paragraph (1A)(a) or (b) above may be given—

(a) by sending (that expression being construed in accordance with section 124 of the said Act of 2003 and as if what was being done was being done under that Act);

(b) by advertisement;

(c) by affixing a conspicuous notice to—

(i) in a case where there exists one, and only one, lamp post which is situated within one hundred metres of that property, that lamp post; or

(ii) in a case where there exists more than one lamp post so situated, each of at least two such lamp posts; or

(d) by such other means as the Scottish Ministers think fit,

and service of notice under sub-paragraph (1A)(c) above shall be by sending (as so construed) or by such other means as the Scottish Ministers think fit.

(1C) Subsections (6) and (7) of section 21 of the said Act of 2003 apply in relation to affixing, and to a notice affixed, under sub-paragraph (1B)(c) above as they apply in relation to affixing, and to a notice affixed, under subsection (2)(b) of that section (the reference in paragraph (a)(ii) of the said subsection (6) to the date specified in the notice as the renewal date being construed as a reference to the last day of the period specified in the notice given under paragraph 2(1)(b) above).".

(3) In each of paragraphs 3(2) and 6, at the beginning, there shall be inserted the words "Subject to paragraph 6B below,"; and in paragraph 4, for the words "paragraph 5" there shall be substituted the words "paragraphs 5 and 6B".

(4) After paragraph 6 there shall be inserted—

"(6A) The Scottish Ministers may require an objector to state in writing whether he objects—

(a) as a person with title to enforce a title condition and if he does so object then in that statement to—
(i) identify the benefited property and burdened property;
(ii) identify the title condition (either by setting it out in full or by identifying the constitutive deed, saying where it is registered and giving the date of registration); and
(iii) describe his connection with the benefited property.

(b) as owners' association and if he does so object then in that statement to identify—
(i) the development; and
(ii) the development management scheme (by identifying the deed of application, saying where it is registered and giving the date of registration).

(6B) If in compliance with paragraph 6A above an objector states that he objects as mentioned in sub-paragraph (a) or (b) of that paragraph, paragraphs 3(2), 4 and 6 above shall not apply as respects that objection provided that the Scottish Ministers give him a written undertaking that any conveyance in implement of the acquisition will provide—

(a) where the objector is as mentioned in paragraph 6A(a) above, that the title condition in question is not varied or extinguished in respect of the enforcement rights of that person, any such undertaking—
(i) identifying the benefited property (if any) and burdened property;
(ii) identifying the order; and
(iii) setting out the manner in which the conveyance will fulfil the undertaking; or

(b) where the objector is as mentioned in paragraph 6A(b) above, that the development management scheme will not be disapplied, any such undertaking—
(i) identifying the development;
(ii) identifying the order; and
(iii) setting out the manner in which the conveyance will fulfil the undertaking.

(6C) The effect, under subsection (1) of section 106 of the Title Conditions (Scotland) Act 2003 (asp 9) (extinction of real burdens and servitudes etc. on compulsory acquisition of land), of registering the conveyance after an undertaking given under paragraph 6B above has been registered against the burdened property, or as the case may be against the units of the development, shall be subject to the terms of the undertaking irrespective of the terms of the conveyance.

(6D) In this Part, "title condition", "development management scheme" and "personal real burden" have the same meanings as in that Act; and in paragraphs 6B and 6C above, "conveyance" has the same meaning as in section 106(5) of that Act.".

AMENDMENTS

1. As amended by the Title Conditions (Scotland) Act 2003 (Consequential Provisions) Order (SSI 2003/503), Sch.1, para.14 (effective October 22, 2003).

GENERAL NOTE
The 1967 Act confers powers of compulsory acquisition but does not actually incorporate the compulsory purchase procedure as set out in the 1947 Act. The amendments in Sch.5 to the 1967 Act bring the procedure into line with the 1947 Act. The amendment in the 2003 Act imposes a duty on Scottish Ministers when making a compulsory purchase order to notify benefited proprietors or holders of personal real burdens of compulsory purchase orders about to be made.

Amendment of Conveyancing and Feudal Reform (Scotland) Act 1970

111.—(1) In section 13 of the Conveyancing and Feudal Reform (Scotland) Act 1970 (c.35) (ranking of standard securities), in subsection (1), for the words from "his present advances" to "to which the security relates" there shall be substituted the following paragraphs—

"(a) the present debt incurred (whenever payable); and
(b) any future debt which, under the contract to which the security relates, he is required to allow the debtor in the security to incur,".

(2) Subsection (1) above does not affect the preference in ranking of the standard security of a creditor if the notice mentioned in the said section 13 was received by that creditor before the day on which this section comes into force.

GENERAL NOTE
One of the problems with standard securities in respect of so-called claw-back burdens was that subsequent securities of which due notice was given might rank in priority because the money secured by the claw-back security was not actually due because the claw-back had not been triggered. The amendment substitutes the word "debt" for the word "advances" in the 1970 Act. A claw-back obligation would be a debt and accordingly this anomaly is removed. This section comes into effect on Royal Assent but it is not retrospective.

Amendment of Land Registration (Scotland) Act 1979

112.—(1) The 1979 Act shall be amended in accordance with the following subsections.

(2) In section 6(1) (duty to make up and maintain title sheet), for paragraph (e) there shall be substituted—

"(e) any subsisting real right pertaining to the interest or subsisting real burden or condition affecting the interest and, where the interest is so affected by virtue of section 18, 18A, 18B, 18C, 19, 20, 27 or 27A of the Abolition of Feudal Tenure etc. (Scotland) Act 2000 (asp 5) or section 4(5), 50, 75 or 80 of the Title Conditions (Scotland) Act 2003 (asp 9), the Keeper shall in the entry identify the benefited property, or as the case may be the dominant tenement, (if any) and any person in whose favour the real burden is constituted;
(ee) any subsisting right to a title condition pertaining to the interest by virtue of section 18, 19 or 20 of that Act of 2000 or 4(5), 50, 75 or 80 of that Act of 2003, the Keeper identifying in the entry the burdened property;".

(3) In section 9 (rectification of Land Register of Scotland), in subsection (3B), the existing words "any provision of the Abolition of Feudal Tenure etc. (Scotland) Act 2000 (asp 5) other than section 4 or 65" shall be paragraph (a); and after that paragraph there shall be inserted the word "; or" and the following paragraph—

"(b) section 49, 50, 58 or 80 of the Title Conditions (Scotland) Act 2003 (asp 9),".

GENERAL NOTE
The Keeper will be allowed to rectify the Land Register, without risk to his indemnity, to take account of the provisions of the 2003 Act. There is a similar provision for feudal burdens in the 2000 Act.

Amendment of Enterprise and New Towns (Scotland) Act 1990

113.—(1) The Enterprise and New Towns (Scotland) Act 1990 (c.35) shall be amended in accordance with the following subsections.

(2) In section 8(6) (powers and duties of Scottish Enterprise or Highlands and Islands Enterprise exercisable on terms and conditions arranged by agreement with person having an interest in land), for the words "section 32(3)" there shall be substituted "section 32".

(3) In section 32 (registration of agreements), for subsection (1) there shall be substituted—

"(1) Scottish Enterprise or Highlands and Islands Enterprise, in exercising the powers and duties conferred on it by this Act, may as respects land which does not belong to it enter into an agreement with any person who has an interest in the land (provided that it is an interest which enables the person to bind the land) for the purpose of restricting or regulating, either permanently or during such period as may be prescribed by the agreement, the development or use of the land; and the agreement may be registered either—

(a) in a case where the land affected by the agreement is registered in the Land Register of Scotland, in that register; or

(b) in any other case, in the appropriate Division of the General Register of Sasines.

(1A) An agreement under subsection (1) above may contain such incidental and consequential provisions (including financial ones) as appear to the body in question to be necessary or expedient for the purposes of the agreement.".

GENERAL NOTE

This section removes the doubt which has surrounded agreements under s.32 of the 1990 Act. That section allowed Scottish Enterprise or Highlands and Islands Enterprise to enter into an agreement which contained obligations which would run with the land. A question had arisen as to whether all those with an interest in the land had to be parties to the agreement including heritable creditors. The amendment here makes it clear that only the owner need enter the agreement. This amendment takes effect on the day after Royal Assent.

Amendment of Abolition of Feudal Tenure etc. (Scotland) Act 2000

114.—(1) The 2000 Act shall be amended in accordance with subsections (2) to (5) below.

(2) After section 18 there shall be inserted—

"Personal pre-emption burdens and personal redemption burden

18A.—(1) Without prejudice to section 18 of this Act, where a feudal estate of *dominium utile* of land is subject to a real burden which comprises a right of pre-emption or redemption and is enforceable by a superior of the feu or would be so enforceable were the person in question to complete title to the *dominium directum* the superior may, before the appointed day, by duly executing and registering against the *dominium utile* a notice in, or as nearly as may be in, the form contained in schedule 5A to this Act, prospectively convert that burden into a personal pre-emption burden or as the case may be into a personal redemption burden.

(2) The notice shall—

(a) set out the title of the superior;

(b) describe, sufficiently to enable identification by reference to the Ordnance Map, the land the *dominium utile* of which is subject to the real burden (or any part of that land);

(c) set out the terms of the real burden; and

    (d) set out the terms of any counter-obligation to the real burden if it is a counter-obligation enforceable against the superior.

(3) Before submitting any notice for registration under this section, the superior shall swear or affirm as is mentioned in subsection (4) of section 18 of this Act.

(4) Subsection (5) of that section applies for the purposes of subsection (3) above as it applies for the purposes of subsection (4) of that section.

(5) If subsections (1) to (3) above are, with subsection (4) of that section, complied with and immediately before the appointed day the real burden is still enforceable by the superior (or his successor) or would be so enforceable, or still so enforceable, were the person in question to complete title to the *dominium directum* then, on that day—

    (a) the real burden shall be converted into a real burden in favour of that person, to be known as a "personal pre-emption burden" or as the case may be as a "personal redemption burden"; and

    (b) the land the *dominium utile* of which was subject to the real burden (or if part only of that land is described in pursuance of subsection (2)(b) above, that part) shall become the servient tenement.

(6) Title to enforce the burden against the land to which the notice relates shall be subject to any such counter-obligation as was set out by virtue of subsection (2)(d) above.

(7) The right to a personal pre-emption burden or personal redemption burden may be assigned or otherwise transferred to any person; and any such assignation or transfer shall take effect on registration.

(8) Where the holder of a personal pre-emption burden or personal redemption burden does not have a completed title—

    (a) title may be completed by the holder registering a notice of title; or

    (b) without completing title, the holder may grant a deed—

        (i) assigning the right to; or

        (ii) discharging, in whole or in part,

The burden; but unless the deed is one to which section 15(3) of the Land Registration (Scotland) Act 1979 (c.33) (circumstances where unnecessary to deduce title) applies, it shall be necessary, in the deed, to deduce title to the burden through the midcouples linking the holder to the person who had the last completed title.

(9) This section is subject to sections 41 and 42 of this Act.

Conversion into economic development burden

    18B.—(1) Without prejudice to section 18 of this Act, where a feudal estate of *dominium utile* of land is subject to a real burden which is imposed for the purpose of promoting economic development and is enforceable by the Scottish Ministers or a local authority, being in either case the superior of the feu, or would be so enforceable were the Scottish Ministers or as the case may be the local authority to complete title to the *dominium directum*, the superior may, before the appointed day, by duly executing and registering against the *dominium utile* a notice in, or as nearly as may be in, the form contained in schedule 5B to this Act, prospectively convert that burden into an economic development burden.

    (2) The notice shall—

    (a) set out the title of the superior;

(b) describe, sufficiently to enable identification by reference to the Ordnance Map, the land the *dominium utile* of which is subject to the real burden (or any part of that land);

(c) set out the terms of the real burden;

(d) set out the terms of any counter-obligation to the real burden if it is a counter-obligation enforceable against the superior; and

(e) state that the burden was imposed for the purpose of promoting economic development and provide information in support of that statement.

(3) If subsections (1) and (2) above are complied with and immediately before the appointed day the real burden is still enforceable by the superior or would be so enforceable were the Scottish Ministers or as the case may be the local authority to complete title to the *dominium directum* then on that day the real burden shall be converted into an economic development burden and on and after that day the Scottish Ministers or, as the case may be, the authority, shall—

(a) have title to enforce the burden against the land to which the notice relates; and

(b) be presumed to have an interest to enforce it.

(4) Title to enforce the burden against the land to which the notice relates shall be subject to any such counter-obligation as was set out by virtue of subsection (2)(d) above.

(5) This section is subject to sections 41 and 42 of this Act.

Conversion into health care burden

18C.—(1) Without prejudice to section 18 of this Act, where a feudal estate of *dominium utile* of land is subject to a real burden which is imposed for the purpose of promoting the provision of facilities for health care and is enforceable by a National Health Service trust or the Scottish Ministers, being in either case the superior of the feu, or would be so enforceable were the trust or as the case may be the Scottish Ministers to complete title to the *dominium directum*, the superior may, before the appointed day, by duly executing and registering against the *dominium utile* a notice in, or as nearly as may be in, the form contained in schedule 5C to this Act, prospectively convert that burden into a health care burden.

(2) The notice shall—

(a) set out the title of the superior;

(b) describe, sufficiently to enable identification by reference to the Ordnance Map, the land the *dominium utile* of which is subject to the real burden (or any part of that land);

(c) set out the terms of the real burden;

(d) set out the terms of any counter-obligation to the real burden if it is a counter-obligation enforceable against the superior; and

(e) state that the burden was imposed for the purpose of promoting the provision of facilities for health care and provide information in support of that statement.

(3) If subsections (1) and (2) are complied with and immediately before the appointed day the real burden is still enforceable by the superior or would be so enforceable were the trust or as the case may be the Scottish Ministers to complete title to the *dominium directum* then on that day the real burden shall be converted into a health care burden and on and after that day the trust or, as the case may be, the Scottish Ministers, shall—

    (a) have title to enforce the burden against the land to which the notice in question relates; and

    (b) be presumed to have an interest to enforce it.

(4) Title to enforce the burden against the land to which the notice relates shall be subject to any such counter-obligation as was set out by virtue of subsection (2)(d) above.

(5) In subsections (1) and (2) above, "facilities for health care" includes facilities ancillary to health care; as for example (but without prejudice to that generality) accommodation for staff employed to provide health care.

(6) This section is subject to sections 41 and 42 of this Act."

(3) After section 27 there shall be inserted—

"Nomination of conservation body or Scottish Ministers to have title to enforce conservation burden

27A.—(1) Where a person other than a conservation body or the Scottish Ministers has the right as superior to enforce a real burden of the class described in section 27(2) of this Act or would have that right were he to complete title to the *dominium directum*, he may, subject to subsection (2) below, before the appointed day nominate for the benefit of the public, by executing and registering against the *dominium utile* of the land subject to the burden a notice in, or as nearly as may be in, the form contained in schedule 8A to this Act, a conservation body or the Scottish Ministers to have title on or after that day to enforce the burden against that land; and, without prejudice to section 27(1) of this Act, any burden as respects which such title to enforce is by virtue of this subsection so obtained shall, on and after the appointed day, be known as a "conservation burden".

(2) Subsection (1) above applies only where the consent of the nominee to being so nominated is obtained—

    (a) in a case where sending a copy of the notice, in compliance with section 41(3) of this Act, is reasonably practicable, before that copy is so sent; and

    (b) in any other case, before the notice is executed.

(3) The notice shall—

    (a) state that the nominee is a conservation body (identifying it) or the Scottish Ministers, as the case may be; and

    (b) do as mentioned in paragraphs (b) to (e) of section 27(3) of this Act.

(4) This section is subject to sections 41 and 42 of this Act except that, in the application of subsection (1)(i) of section 42 for the purposes of this subsection, such discharge as is mentioned in that subsection shall be taken to require the consent of the nominated person."

(4) After section 28 there shall be inserted—

"Effect of section 27A nomination

28A.—If a notice has been executed and registered in accordance with section 27A of this Act and, immediately before the appointed day, the burden to which the notice relates is still enforceable by the nominating person as superior (or by such person as is his successor) or would be so enforceable, or still so enforceable, were the person in question to complete title to the *dominium directum* then, on and after the appointed day, the conservation body or as the case may be the Scottish Ministers shall—

  (a) subject to any counter-obligation, have title to enforce the burden against the land to which the notice in question relates; and

  (b) be presumed to have an interest to enforce that burden."

(5) After section 65 there shall be inserted—

"Sporting rights
65A.—(1) Where a feudal estate of *dominium utile* of land is subject to sporting rights which are enforceable by a superior of the feu or which would be so enforceable were the person in question to complete title to the *dominium directum* the superior may, before the appointed day, by duly executing and registering against the *dominium utile* a notice in, or as nearly as may be in, the form contained in schedule 11A to this Act, prospectively convert those rights into a tenement in land.

  (2) The notice shall—

  (a) set out the title of the superior;

  (b) describe, sufficiently to enable identification by reference to the Ordnance Map, the land the *dominium utile* of which is subject to the sporting rights (or any part of that land);

  (c) describe those rights; and

  (d) set out the terms of any counter-obligation to those rights if it is a counter-obligation enforceable against the superior.

  (3) Before submitting any notice for registration under this section, the superior shall swear or affirm as is mentioned in subsection (4) of section 18 of this Act.

  (4) Subsection (5) of that section applies for the purposes of subsection (3) above as it applies for the purposes of subsection (4) of that section.

  (5) If subsections (1) to (3) above are, with subsection (4) of that section, complied with and immediately before the appointed day the sporting rights are still enforceable by the superior (or his successor) or would be so enforceable, or still so enforceable, were the person in question to complete title to the *dominium directum* then, on that day, the sporting rights shall be converted into a tenement in land.

  (6) No greater, or more exclusive, sporting rights shall be enforceable by virtue of such conversion than were (or would have been) enforceable as mentioned in subsection (5) above.

  (7) Where the *dominium utile* comprises parts each held by a separate vassal, each part shall be taken to be a separate feudal estate of *dominium utile*.

  (8) Where sporting rights become, under subsection (5) above, a tenement in land, the right to enforce those rights shall be subject to any counter-obligation enforceable against the superior immediately before the appointed day; and section 47 of this Act shall apply in relation to any counter-obligation to sporting rights as it applies in relation to any counter-obligation to a real burden.

  (9) In this section, "sporting rights" means a right of fishing or game.

  (10) This section is subject to section 41 of this Act.

  (11) Subsections (1) and (2)(a) of section 43 of this Act apply in relation to a notice submitted for registration under this section as they apply in relation to a notice so submitted under any of the provisions mentioned in those subsections; and paragraph (a) of subsection (3) of that section applies in relation to a determination for the purposes of subsection (5) of this section as it applies in relation to

a determination for the purposes of any of the provisions mentioned in that paragraph.

(12) Subsections (1), (3) and (4) of section 46 of this Act apply in relation to sporting rights extinguished by virtue of section 54 of this Act as they apply in relation to a real burden extinguished by section 17(1)(a) of this Act."

(6) Schedule 13 to this Act, which contains amendments of the 2000 Act consequential upon the provisions of this Act, shall have effect.

GENERAL NOTE

This section introduces six new sections into the Abolition of Feudal Tenure etc. (Scotland) Act 2000. The new Sections are necessary because of the introduction of new types of personal burdens such as personal pre-emptions and personal redemptions, economic development burdens, healthcare burdens and the like. There is also an interesting new section in relation to sporting rights, that may cause some difficulty. It should be borne in mind that these new sections apply to feudal situations. This is an important distinction when one considers the additional provision in respect of sporting rights.

Subs.(2)—new s.18A
Personal pre-emption burdens and personal redemption burdens

Section 18 of the 2000 Act allowed a superior to re-allot a pre-emption or redemption to specific land owned by the superior as a new benefited property. There may be cases of course where the superior does not own any other land. The new s.18A allows a superior to convert a pre-emption or redemption into a personal right, subject to the same provisions in relation to notice, the swearing of oaths and other matters. The right to the personal pre-emption or redemption burden may be assigned and any such assignation takes effect on registration. This indicates the rather odd situation of personal burdens which are not praedial in so far as the benefit is concerned, but yet require registration either of a notice or assignation.

Subs.(2)—new s.18B
Conversion into economic development burden

Economic development burdens in respect of claw-back obligations to local authorities or Scottish Ministers are introduced by s.42A. New s.18B in the 2000 Act will allow Scottish Ministers or a local authority to convert existing feudal burdens into economic development burdens. Again it will not be necessary to re-allot to land. The form of notice is contained in Sch.5B. The local authority or Scottish Ministers will have title to enforce the burden and be presumed to have an interest in it.

Subs.(2)—new s.18C
Conversion into health care burden

This allows a feudal superior (a National Health Service Trust or Scottish Ministers) to convert a burden for the provision of facilities for healthcare into a healthcare burden notwithstanding the fact there is no other land to which the burden can be re-allotted. Provisions are set out for notification and registration. Title and interest are presumed.

Subs.(3)—new s.27A
Nomination of conversation body or Scottish Ministers to have title to enforce conservation burden

The 2000 Act allowed conservation bodies to preserve burdens of a conservation type where these had been created in feudal writs. The new section allows a superior which is not a conservation body to execute and register a notice against the burdened land in terms of Sch.8A to the 2000 Act to the effect that an actual conservation body or Scottish Ministers will have title to enforce the burden. The conservation body or Scottish Ministers who are to take responsibility for enforcement must consent. The existing provisions in relation notice apply.

Subs.(4)—new s.28A
Effect of s.27A nomination

The title and interest of the conservation body or Scottish Ministers taking over the enforcement rights in respect of a conservation burden and the interest to enforce that burden are presumed.

Subs.(5)—new s.65A
Sporting rights

This subsection inserts a new s.65A in relation to sporting rights. This is in many ways an unusual provision. The generally accepted position is that only salmon fishings are capable of ownership. Other fishings and indeed sporting rights of shooting cannot be owned as separate tenements of land (see *Gordon Scottish Land Laws* (2nd ed.) 8–45). These other so-called sporting rights are apparently inseparable from ownership of the land, although they can be leased. Prior to the introduction of the 2000 Act the Scottish Law Commission considered sporting rights and the reservation of these rights in feudal grants. The view of the Commission was that non-exclusive reservations could be treated as real burdens, and accordingly could be re-allotted in terms of s.18 of the 2000 Act. There was, however, considerable doubt as to the classification of the right. It is clear that fishings and shootings cannot be a servitude as such (see Cusine and Paisley, *Servitudes and Rights of Way*, 3.08; *Earl of Galloway v Duke of Bedford* (1902) 4 F 851). Presumably Scottish Ministers took the view that if the effect of abolition of the feudal system was to extinguish rights of fishing and shooting which had been reserved to superiority titles, then there might be a claim under Art.1 of Protocol 1 to the European Convention on Human Rights, especially since no compensation is payable to superiors for the loss of the superiority title. The new section allows a superior to preserve sporting rights if these were enforceable by a superior prior to the appointed day for abolition. The superior must execute and register against the *dominium utile* title a notice in the form contained in Sch.11A. The superior must swear an oath in terms of s.18(4) of the 2000 Act and must give the appropriate intimation. Apparently, if a notice is registered this converts the sporting rights into a tenement in land, something which they would not have been before. The question which arises is whether or not this section elevates so-called sporting rights to ownership rights in other non-feudal situations. Presumably it does not. One could be left therefore with the anomalous situation. Where sporting rights have been reserved to a superiority title and the superior has executed and registered the appropriate notice then the Keeper of the Land Register will have to create a separate title sheet for the sporting rights, even although these were not salmon fishing rights. Presumably, the former superior could then dispone these sporting rights to other parties. However, sporting rights which have been reserved in a disposition will presumably not be capable of separate conveyance but will be merely a personal licence. Presumably, therefore, the Keeper will require some sort of evidence that sporting rights derive from a feudal title and have been appropriately preserved in terms of the new section. It is unfortunate that the new system of land tenure will allow ownership of sporting rights in one sort of case. This section goes against the notion of a unitary concept of ownership. Presumably, however, as a result of this section someone may attempt to argue, given the rather confused nature of the old case law on the subject, that the law has now recognised that sporting rights in general (whether they derive from a feudal title or not) can be regarded as separate tenements of land. The definition of "incorporeal heritable rights" in section 28(1) of the Land Registration (Scotland) Act 1979 is expanded to include sporting rights as defined by s.65A(9). The definition there is simply "a right of fishing or game".

Subs.(1)—new s.65A

The reserved sporting rights must have been enforceable by a superior before the appointed day. If so, the superior can execute and register against the *dominium utile* title a notice in the form of Sch.11A which will convert these rights into a tenement in land.

Subs.(2)—new s.65A

This subsection prescribes what the notice must contain.

Subs.(3)—new s.65A

The superior must swear or affirm in terms of s.18(4) of the 2000 Act before executing and registering a notice.

Subs.(4)—new s.65A

Where the superior by reason of legal disability or incapacity cannot swear or affirm, then a legal representative may swear or affirm and where the superior is not an individual but a corporate or other entity, then any person authorised to sign documents may swear or affirm.

Subs.(5)—new s.65A

This reiterates that on registration of the notice and compliance with the other provisions the sporting rights in so far as they are enforceable are converted into a tenement in land. There is no definition of "tenement in land" in s.110, but the definition of "land" includes heritable property held as a separate tenement. The term "tenement" usually denotes a building divided into flats, but it has been used simply to describe a piece of land especially in relation to servitudes where there is a dominant and servient tenement of land. Perhaps it is because reserved sporting rights appear to have something of the character of a servitude that this rather vague term has been used. It is almost as if the legislators were frightened to use the word "ownership". (For a discussion of separate tenements of land in general see Gordon, *Scottish Land Law* (2nd ed.) Ch.10).

Subs.(6)—new s.65A

Only the sporting rights which have been reserved can be converted. There may of course be general arguments in relation to the terminology used in the reservation. Rights to general fishings which have been reserved to a superior have been upheld, presumably as a pertinent of the superiority (*MacDonald v Farquharson* (1836) 15 S 259). So far as game is concerned, Professor Gordon expresses a doubt that a right to shoot game can actually be reserved to a superior (Gordon, *Scottish Land Law* (2nd ed.) pp.9–12). In the second edition of his text he indicates that the right will go in any event with abolition of the feudal system. This may not now be the case. If, however, there was no enforceable right to take game prior to the coming into effect of this new section, a question must remain. Reservations have been expressed as to the possibility of reserving a right to shoot game to a superiority (*Hemming v Duke of Athole* (1883) 11 R 93 at 97). In that case a reservation of a right to all deer that might be found was restricted to deer which had already been killed and was not interpreted as a right to hunt or stalk.

Subs.(7)—new s.65A

The right to convert will apply even although a *dominium utile* is held by different parties.

Subs.(8)—new s.65A

Where sporting rights become a tenement of land the rights are subject to counter-obligations enforceable against the superior.

Subs.(9)—new s.65A

Sporting rights mean a right of fishing or game.

Subs.(10)—new s.65A

The superior will require to serve notice under s.41 of the 2000 Act to the owner of the servient tenement of the attempt to re-allot.

Subs.(11)—new s.65A

This applies subs.(1) and (2)(a) of s.43 of the 2000 Act to any notices under s.65A. This means that the Keeper of the Registers will not require to determine whether the superior has notified the owner of the *dominium utile*. Nor will the Keeper be required to determine whether, prior to conversion, the superior actually had the ability to enforce the right. No doubt this will mean that the Keeper will not require to make the difficult decisions on interpretation which are almost bound to arise.

Subs.(12)—new s.65A

The Keeper will not require to remove sporting rights which are extinguished by s.54 from the Register unless there is an application for registration or rectification or the Keeper is ordered to remove it. The Keeper also cannot remove sporting rights subject to proceedings before the court or the Lands Tribunal. This will apply when no notice is served to preserve the sporting rights.

Subs.(6)

Schedule 13 contains consequential amendments of the 2000 Act. These amendments come into effect on Royal Assent.

Miscellaneous

Further provision as respects notices of preservation or of converted servitude

115.—(1) This section applies in relation to a notice of preservation or of converted servitude.

(2) Except where it is not reasonably practicable to do so, the owner of the benefited property shall, before executing the notice, send to the owner of the burdened property a copy of—

(a) the notice;
(b) the explanatory note set out in whichever schedule to this Act relates to the notice; and
(c) in the case of a notice of converted servitude, the constitutive deed (if any).
(3) The owner of the benefited property shall, in the notice, state either—
(a) that a copy of the notice has been sent in accordance with subsection (2) above; or
(b) that it was not reasonably practicable for such a notice to be so sent.
(4) However many the benefited or burdened properties may be, if the terms of the real burdens or converted servitudes are set out in a single constitutive deed, execution and registration may be accomplished in a single notice.
(5) The Keeper of the Registers of Scotland shall not be required to determine whether a person submitting a notice for registration has complied with subsection (2) above.
(6) Where—
(a) a notice submitted before the expiry of the period of ten years which commences immediately after the appointed day is rejected by the Keeper; but
(b) a court or the Lands Tribunal then determines that the notice is registrable,
the notice may, if not registered before that expiry, be registered—
(i) within two months after the determination is made; but
(ii) before such date after that expiry as the Scottish Ministers may by order prescribe;
and any notice registered under this subsection shall be treated as if it had been registered before that expiry.
(7) For the purposes of subsection (6) above, the application to the court, or to the Lands Tribunal, which has resulted in the determination shall require to have been made within such period as the Scottish Ministers may by order prescribe.
(8) In subsection (6)(b) above, "court" means Court of Session or sheriff.

GENERAL NOTE
   This section applies to notices of preservation or of converted servitude and sets out what the owner of the benefited property must do before executing the notice. A copy of the notice and explanatory note must be sent to the owner of the burdened property, normally by post. There are further provisions about what is meant by "sending" in s.124. A simple notice will suffice in respect of all real burdens and servitudes. The Keeper does not have to verify that the notice is actually sent to the owner of the burdened property, but an incomplete or inaccurate notice may be rejected by the Keeper. If there is rejection then the applicant can take the matter to the Lands Tribunal or the courts.

Benefited property outwith Scotland
   116.—As respects a real burden or servitude, the benefited property need not be in Scotland; but where it is not then nothing in this Act requires registration against that property.

GENERAL NOTE
   The benefited property can be outwith Scotland, but the burdened property cannot. Where this is the case there is no requirement for dual registration. Registration against the burdened property will suffice.

Pecuniary real burdens
   117.—On and after the day on which this section comes into force, it shall not be competent to create a pecuniary real burden (that is to say, to constitute a heritable security by reservation in a conveyance).

GENERAL NOTE
There has always been a doubt as to whether or not one could reserve a pecuniary real burden in a conveyance. Attempts were made to insert claw-back reservations in respect of ground which was conveyed on a speculative basis. The idea was that if the grantee obtained planning permission, and the value of the land rose, then the granter should be entitled to a monetary payment and this was what was reserved. There was doubts as to whether or not this was an attempt to create a heritable security otherwise than by standard security. Section 117 makes it clear that reservations of burdens of this nature are invalid.

Common interest

118.—On and after the day on which this section comes into force—

(a) it shall not be competent to create a right of common interest; and

(b) no such right shall arise otherwise than by implication of law.

GENERAL NOTE
In general terms common interest arises by operation of the law because of the relationship between particular properties. Thus although a top floor flat proprietor may have no right of ownership (common or otherwise) in the solum or foundations of the tenement the law of common interest would allow that proprietor to prevent operations by the ground floor proprietor which might endanger the stability of the whole tenement. It may be doubted therefore whether a right of common interest can actually be created by express words. If however this was possible then, since a right of common interest is a quite separate right from a right to enforce a real burden or a servitude it would be open to parties to evade the provisions of the 2003 Act. Accordingly, s.118 provides that common interest cannot be created expressly and this section comes into force on Royal Assent to avoid attempts to create quasi-burdens before the appointed day.

PART 11

SAVINGS, TRANSITIONAL AND GENERAL

Savings and transitional provisions etc.

Savings and transitional provisions etc.

119.—(1) Nothing in this Act shall be taken to impair the validity of creating, varying or discharging a real burden by the registering of a deed before the appointed day.

(2) This Act is without prejudice to section 3(1) of the 1979 Act (effect of registration).

(3) The repeal by this Act of section 32 of the Conveyancing (Scotland) Act 1874 (c.94) does not affect the construction of the expression "deed of conditions" provided for in section 122(1) of this Act.

(4) Sections 8 and 14 of this Act do not affect proceedings commenced before the appointed day.

(5) Section 10 of this Act does not apply where a person ceases to be, or becomes, an owner before the appointed day.

(6) Section 16 of this Act does not apply as respects a breach of a real burden which occurs before the appointed day.

(7) Section 61 of this Act does not apply as respects a constitutive deed (or a deed into which the constitutive deed is incorporated) registered before the appointed day except in so far as a real burden the terms of which are set out in the constitutive deed is a community burden.

(8) Sections 75 and 78 of this Act do not apply as respects a deed executed before the appointed day.

(9) [*Repealed by the Tenements (Scotland) Act 2004 (asp 11), s.25, Sch.4, para.18 (effective October 23, 2004)*]

(10) Except where the contrary intention appears, this Act applies to all real burdens, whenever created.

GENERAL NOTE
This section contains savings and transitional provisions. In particular subs.(1) provides that nothing will affect the validity of a deed which is registered before the appointed day. Subsection 2 caters for the case of real burdens in a title sheet of a registered property. Section 3(1) of the Land Registration (Scotland) Act 1979 does not actually require a deed or writing. If the Keeper enters or deletes a real burden then in certain circumstances this may be done without a deed and this would render the Register liable to rectification. Subs.(2) preserves the status quo and allows rectification in the circumstances without a written deed. Subsection (10) is interesting because it provides that except where the contrary intention appears the Act applies to all real burdens whenever created.

General

Requirement for dual registration
120.—A deed which, to be duly registered for the purposes of any provision of this Act, requires to be registered against both a benefited property and a burdened property, shall not be registrable against one only of the properties; nor shall a document which includes but does not wholly consist of such a deed.

GENERAL NOTE
The provisions of the Act require dual registration in the majority of cases. This will particularly apply where new real burdens are being created. If an attempt is made to register against one of the titles only, then the real burden will be ineffective.

Crown application
121.—This Act binds the Crown.

GENERAL NOTE
The Act applies to Crown lands in Scotland including land belonging to Government departments and the private estates of the sovereign and the Prince and Steward of Scotland.

Interpretation
122.—[1] (1) In this Act, unless the context otherwise requires—
"the 1979 Act" means the Land Registration (Scotland) Act 1979 (c.33);
"the 2000 Act" means the Abolition of Feudal Tenure etc. (Scotland) Act 2000 (asp 5);
"affirmative burden" shall be construed in accordance with section 2(2)(a) of this Act;
"ancillary burden" shall be construed in accordance with section 2(4) of this Act;
"appointed day" means the day appointed under section 71 of the 2000 Act;
"benefited property"—
　(a) in relation to a real burden, shall be construed in accordance with section 1(2)(b) of this Act; and
　(b) in relation to a title condition other than a real burden, means the land, or real right in land, to which the right to enforce the title condition is attached;
"burdened property"—
　(a) in relation to a real burden, shall be construed in accordance with section 1(2)(a) of this Act; and
　(b) in relation to a title condition other than a real burden, means the land, or real right in land, which is subject to the title condition;
"community" has the meaning given by section 26(2) of this Act;
"community burdens" shall be construed in accordance with section 25 of this Act;
"conservation body" means any body prescribed by order under subsection (4) of section 38 of this Act;

"conservation burden" shall be construed in accordance with subsection (1) of that section and includes (other than in subsections (1) and (2) of that section) a reference to a real burden the right to enforce which was—
  (a) preserved by virtue of section 27(1) of the 2000 Act (preservation of right to enforce conservation burden); or
  (b) obtained by virtue of section 27A(1) of that Act (nomination of conservation body or Scottish Ministers to have title to enforce conservation burden);

"constitutive deed" is the deed which sets out the terms of a title condition (or of a prospective title condition) but the expression includes any document in which the terms of the title condition in question are varied;

"deed of conditions" means a deed mentioned in section 32 of the Conveyancing (Scotland) Act 1874 (c.94) (importation by reference) and registered before the appointed day having been executed in accordance with that section;

"the development management scheme" has the meaning given by section 71(3) of this Act;

"economic development burden" shall be construed in accordance with subsection (1) of section 45 of this Act and includes (other than in subsections (1) to (3) of that section) a reference to a real burden which was converted under section 18B of the 2000 Act (conversion into economic development burden);

"enactment" includes a local and personal or private Act;

"facility burden" means, subject to subsection (2) below, a real burden which regulates the maintenance, management, reinstatement or use of heritable property which constitutes, and is intended to constitute, a facility of benefit to other land (examples of property which might constitute such a facility being without prejudice to the generality of this definition, set out in subsection (3) below);

"health care burden" shall be construed in accordance with subsection (1) of section 46 of this Act and includes (other than in subsections (1) to (3) of that section) a reference to a real burden which was converted under section 18C of the 2000 Act (conversion into health care burden);

"holder", in relation to a title condition, means the person who has right to the title condition but does not include a person who has title to enforce it only by virtue of any of paragraphs (a), (b) and (c) of section 8(2) of this Act;

"land" includes—
  (a) heritable property, whether corporeal or incorporeal, held as a separate tenement; and
  (b) land covered with water,
but does not include any estate of *dominium directum*;

"Lands Tribunal" means Lands Tribunal for Scotland;

"local authority" means a council constituted under section 2 of the Local Government etc. (Scotland) Act 1994 (c.39);

"maintenance" includes (cognate expressions being construed accordingly)—
  (a) repair or replacement; and
  (b) such demolition, alteration or improvement as is reasonably incidental to maintenance;

"manager", in relation to related properties, means any person (including an owner of one of those properties or a firm) who is authorised (whether by virtue of this Act or otherwise) to act generally, or for such purposes as may be applicable in relation to a particular authorisation, in respect of those properties;

"manager burden" shall be construed in accordance with section 63(1) of this Act;

"maritime burden" shall be construed in accordance with subsection (1) of section 44 of this Act and includes (other than in that subsection) a reference to any real burden in relation to which the Crown has title and interest under section 60(1) of the 2000 Act (preserved right of Crown to maritime burdens);

"midcouple" means such midcouple or link in title as it is competent to specify, under section 5(1) of the Conveyancing (Scotland) Act 1924 (14 & 15 Geo. 5, c.27), in a deduction of title in terms of that Act;

"negative burden" shall be construed in accordance with section 2(2)(b) of this Act;

"notary public" includes, in a case where swearing or affirmation is to take place outwith Scotland, any person duly authorised by the law of the country or territory in question to administer oaths or receive affirmations in that country or territory;

"notice of converted servitude" shall be construed in accordance with section 80(4) and (5) of this Act;

"notice of preservation" shall be construed in accordance with section 50 of this Act;

"notice of termination" shall be construed in accordance with section 20 of this Act;

"owner" shall be construed in accordance with section 123 of this Act;

"personal pre-emption burden" and "personal redemption burden" shall be construed in accordance with section 18A(5) of the 2000 Act;

"personal real burden" shall be construed in accordance with section 1(3) of this Act;

"property" includes unit;

"real burden" has the meaning given by section 1 of this Act except that in construing that section for the purposes of this definition "land" shall be taken to include an estate of *dominium directum*;

"registering", in relation to any document, means registering an interest in land or information relating to an interest in land (being an interest or information for which that document provides) in the Land Register of Scotland or, as the case may be, recording the document in the Register of Sasines (cognate expressions being construed accordingly);

"renewal date" has the meaning given by section 20(4)(d) of this Act;

"road" has the meaning given by section 151(1) of the Roads (Scotland) Act 1984 (c.54) (interpretation);

"rural housing body" means any body prescribed by order under subsection (5) of section 43 of this Act;

"rural housing burden" shall be construed in accordance with subsection (1) of that section and includes a personal pre-emption burden the holder of which is a rural housing body;

"send" shall be construed in accordance with section 124 of this Act (cognate expressions being construed accordingly);

"service burden" means a real burden which relates to the provision of services to land other than the burdened property;

"sheltered or retirement housing development" has the meaning given by section 54(3) of this Act;

"tenement" has the meaning given by section 26 of the Tenements (Scotland) Act 2004 (asp 11); and references to a flat in a tenement shall be construed accordingly;

"terminator" shall be construed in accordance with section 20(2) of this Act;

"title condition" means—

(a) a real burden;

(b) a servitude;

(c) an affirmative obligation imposed, in a servitude, on the person who is in right of the servitude;

(d) a condition in a registrable lease if it is a condition which relates to the land (but not a condition which imposes either an obligation to pay rent or an obligation of relief relating to the payment of rent);

(e) a condition or stipulation—

    (i) imposed under subsection (2) of section 3 of the Registration of Leases (Scotland) Act 1857 (c.26) (assignation of recorded leases) in an assignation which has been duly registered; or

    (ii) contained in a deed registered under subsection (2A) or (5) of that section;

(f) a condition in an agreement entered into under section 7 of the National Trust for Scotland Order Confirmation Act 1938 (c.iv); or

(g) such other condition relating to land as the Scottish Ministers may, for the purposes of this paragraph, prescribe by order;

"unit" means any land which is designed to be held in separate ownership (whether it is so held or not); and

"variation", in relation to a title condition, includes both—

(a) imposition of a new obligation; and

(b) provision that a property becomes a benefited property,

(cognate expressions being construed accordingly).

(2) In so far as it constitutes an obligation to maintain or reinstate which has been assumed—

(a) by a local or other public authority; or

(b) by virtue of any enactment, by a successor body to any such authority,

a real burden is neither—

    (i) a facility burden; nor

    (ii) for the purposes of sections 52 to 54(1) of this Act, to be regarded as imposed as mentioned in any of those sections.

(3) The examples referred to in the definition of "facility burden" in subsection (1) above are—

(a) a common part of a tenement;

(b) a common area for recreation;

(c) a private road;

(d) private sewerage; and

(e) a boundary wall.

AMENDMENT

1. As amended by the Title Conditions (Scotland) Act 2003 (Consequential Provisions) Order (SSI 2003/503), Sch.1, para.15 (effective October 22, 2003) and by the Tenements (Scotland) Act 2004 (asp 11), s.25, Sch.4, para.19 (effective October 23, 2004).

GENERAL NOTE

This is the general interpretation section and many of the interpretations have already been noted. The appointed day was November 28, 2004, the same day on which the feudal system was formally abolished. The definition of land includes heritable property whether corporeal or incorporeal held as a separate tenement. It does not, of course, include the superiority. The definition of the word "maintenance" is always likely to be problematic. Here it is defined as including repair or replacement and such demolition, alteration or improvement as is reasonably incidental to maintenance. The question of improvement is perhaps the most difficult one. One would not replace a burst lead pipe with another lead pipe, but with whatever the modern equivalent was. That would not be improvement as such. However, this would not extend to an operation which changed the character of a property as, *e.g.* where a decision was taken to replace a flat roof with a pitched roof. There will be many awkward situations between these two extremes. What would the position be if, for example, it was proposed to replace old single glazed windows in need of repair with double-glazed units? This definition of maintenance reflects the definition contained in Rule 1.5 of the Tenement Management Scheme (Tenements (Scotland) Act 2004, Sch.1).

The expression "owner"

123.—(1) Subject to subsections (2) and (3) below, in this Act "owner", in relation to any property, means a person who has right to the property whether or not that person has completed title; but if, in relation to the property (or, if the property is held pro indiviso, any pro indiviso share in the property) more than one person comes within that description of owner, then "owner"—

(a) for the purposes of sections 4(2)(b), 6(1)(a), 15, 16, 19, 33(1) and (2) and 35 of this Act, means any person having such right; and

(b) for any other purposes means such person as has most recently acquired such right.

(2) Where a heritable creditor is in lawful possession of security subjects which comprise the property, then "owner"—

(a) for the purposes of the sections mentioned in paragraph (a) of subsection (1) above includes, in addition to any such person as is there mentioned, that heritable creditor; and

(b) for any other purposes (other than of construing section 1 of this Act) means the heritable creditor.

(3) In section 60(1) of this Act, "owner" in relation to any property has the meaning given by subsection (1) above except that, for the purposes of this subsection, in that subsection—

(a) the words "Subject to subsections (2) and (3) below, in this Act" shall be disregarded; and

(b) paragraph (a) shall be construed as if section 60(1) were one of the sections mentioned.

General Note

In the context of this Act the term "owner" means a person who has right to the property whether or not that person has a completed title. Where the property is held *pro indiviso* then "owner" may mean any person having a common right. For a person to have right a disposition would have to have been delivered. Where a heritable creditor is in possession he or she will be the owner in substitution for the debtor except when burdens are being created, varied or discharged where the heritable creditor will simply be treated as one of the owners.

Sending

124.—(1) Where a provision of this Act requires that a thing be sent—

(a) to a person it shall suffice, for the purposes of that provision, that the thing be sent to an agent of the person;

(b) to an owner of property but only the property is known and not the name of the owner, it shall suffice, for the purposes of that provision, that the thing be sent there addressed to "The Owner" (or using some other such expression, as for example "The Proprietor").

(2) Except in subsection (3) below, in this Act any reference to a thing being sent shall be construed as a reference to its being—

(a) posted;

(b) delivered; or

(c) transmitted by electronic means.

(3) For the purposes of any provision of this Act, a thing posted shall be taken to be sent on the day of posting; and a thing transmitted by electronic means, to be sent on the day of transmission.

General Note

Normally, where the Act requires something to be sent then it will be sufficient if it is sent either to the party or that party's solicitor or other agent. If the name of the party or the agent is not known, then it can be addressed to the owner of the property if the property is known. A thing is sent if it is posted, delivered or transmitted by electronic means and a thing posted is taken to be sent on the day of posting. A thing transmitted by electronic means is treated as having been sent on the day of transmission.

References to distance

125.—Where a provision of this Act refers to a property being within a certain distance of another property, the reference is to distance along a horizontal plane, there being disregarded—

(a) the width of any intervening road if of less than twenty metres; and

(b) any pertinent of either property.

GENERAL NOTE

The Act refers to a four-metre distance in various sections. The distance is calculated on a horizontal plain, but disregarding the width of any intervening road if of less than 20 metres and any pertinent of either property. So far as flatted properties are concerned, all flats in the same block will be treated as having no distance between them on a horizontal plain. The vertical distance will be irrelevant. The exclusion of roads of less than 20-metre width, restates the rule for the neighbour notification in planning matters. A pertinent could be a common right in a back green attached to a tenement or block of flats. This can be disregarded so that the four metres measurement would start from the flat and not from the back edge of the common green.

Fees chargeable by Lands Tribunal in relation to functions under this Act

126.—The Scottish Ministers may, after consultation with the Scottish Committee of the Council on Tribunals, make rules as to the fees chargeable by the Lands Tribunal in respect of that tribunal's functions under this Act.

GENERAL NOTE

Scottish Ministers may make rules as to fees chargeable by the Lands Tribunal.

Orders, regulations and rules

127.—(1) Any power of the Scottish Ministers under this Act to make orders, regulations or rules shall be exercisable by statutory instrument; and a statutory instrument containing any such orders, regulations or rules, other than an order under section 128(4) or 129(4), shall be subject to annulment in pursuance of a resolution of the Scottish Parliament.

(2) A statutory instrument containing an order under section 128(4) of this Act shall not be made unless a draft of the instrument has been—

(a) laid before; and

(b) approved by a resolution of,

the Scottish Parliament.

GENERAL NOTE

The power of Scottish Ministers to make orders, regulations or rules will be exercisable by statutory instrument subject to annulment.

Minor and consequential amendments, repeals and power to amend forms

128.—(1) Schedule 14 to this Act, which contains minor amendments and amendments consequential upon the provisions of this Act, shall have effect.

(2) The enactments mentioned in schedule 15 to this Act are repealed to the extent specified.

(3) The Scottish Ministers may by order amend any of schedules—

¹ (a) 1A to 10 and 12 to this Act; and

(b) 1 to 11A to the 2000 Act.

(4) The Scottish Ministers may by order make such incidental, supplemental, consequential, transitional, transitory or saving provision as they consider necessary or expedient for the purposes, or in consequence, of this Act or of any order, regulations or rules made under this Act.

(5) An order under subsection (4) above may amend or repeal any enactment (including any provision of this Act).

AMENDMENT
1. As amended by the Tenements (Scotland) Act 2004 (Consequential Provisions) Order 2004 (SSI 2004/551) art.2, (effective December 22, 2004).

GENERAL NOTE
The minor amendments and repeals are set out in Schs 14 and 15. There are also amendments of the Abolition of Feudal Tenure etc. (Scotland) Act 2000 contained in Sch.13 which are introduced by s.114(6). These latter amendments were necessitated because of the introduction of the new provisions into the 2000 Act. In addition notices are also provided for.

Short title and commencement

129.—(1) This Act may be cited as the Title Conditions (Scotland) Act 2003.

(2) Subject to subsections (3) to (5) below, this Act, except this section, shall come into force on the appointed day.

(3) Sections 63, 66, 67, 86 and 88, except in so far as it inserts a sub-paragraph (ab)(ii) into paragraph 1 of Schedule 1 to the Prescription and Limitation (Scotland) Act 1973 (c.52), Part 9 for the purposes of any application under section 107(5) of this Act, sections 111, 113, 114, 117, 118, 122 to 124, 126, 127, 128(3) to (5), schedules 12 and 13 and, in schedule 14, paragraph 7(1), (3) and (6) come into force on the day after Royal Assent.

(4) There shall come into force on such day as the Scottish Ministers may by order appoint, Parts 3 and 6 and sections 106 to 110; and different days may be so appointed for different provisions.

(5) In so far as—
(a) it relates to paragraph 7(1), (3) and (6) of schedule 14, section 128(1);
(b) it relates to the 2000 Act, section 128(2);
(c) it relates to the 2000 Act, schedule 15;
(d) is necessary for the purposes of Part 3 and section 63, Part 1,
shall come into force on the day after Royal Assent.

GENERAL NOTE
This section sets out when the various provisions will come into effect. The majority of provisions will come into effect on the appointed day which is November 28, 2004. Certain other provisions come into effect on a day to be appointed or on Royal Assent or on the day after Royal Assent.

SCHEDULE 1
(introduced by section 6(2))

FORM IMPORTING TERMS OF TITLE CONDITIONS

There are imported the terms of the title conditions specified in [*refer to the deed of conditions in such terms as shall be sufficient to identify it and specify the register in which it is registered and the date of registration*].

[1] SCHEDULE 1A
(introduced by section 10(2A))

FORM OF NOTICE OF POTENTIAL LIABILITY FOR COSTS

"NOTICE OF POTENTIAL LIABILITY FOR COSTS

This notice gives details of certain maintenance or work carried out, or to be carried out, in relation the property specified in the notice. The effect of the notice is that a person may, on becoming the owner of the property, be liable by virtue of section 10(2A) of the Title Conditions (Scotland) Act 2003 (asp 9) for any outstanding costs relating to the maintenance or work.

Property to which the notice relates:
(see note 1 below)

Description of the maintenance or work to which notice relates:
(see note 2 below)

Person giving notice:
(see note 3 below)

Signature:
(see note 4 below)

Date of signing:"

Notes for completion
(These notes are not part of the notice)

1 Describe the property in a way that is sufficient to identify it. Where the property has a postal address, the description must include that address. Where title to the property has been registered in the Land Register of Scotland, the description must refer to the title number of the property or of the larger subjects of which it forms part. Otherwise, the description should normally refer to and identify a deed recorded in a specified division of the Register of Sasines.
2 Describe the maintenance or work in general terms.
3 Give the name and address of the person applying for registration of the notice ("the applicant") or the applicant's name and the name and address of the applicant's agent.
4 The notice must be signed by or on behalf of the applicant.

AMENDMENT
[1]Inserted by the Tenements (Scotland) Act 2004 (asp 11), s.25, Sch.4, para.20 (effective October 23, 2004) and amended by the Title Conditions (Scotland) Act 2003 (Notice of Potential Liability for Costs) Amendment Order 2004 (SI 2004/552), art.2 (effective December 23, 2004).

SCHEDULE 2
(introduced by section 20(1))

FORM OF NOTICE OF TERMINATION

"NOTICE OF TERMINATION

Name and address of terminator:
(see note for completion 1)

Description of burdened property:
(see note for completion 2)

Terminator's connection with burdened property:
(see note for completion 3)

Terms of real burden(s):
(see note for completion 4)

Extent of termination:
(see note for completion 5)

Renewal date:
(see note for completion 6)

An application to the Lands Tribunal for Scotland for renewal or variation of the real burden(s) must be made by not later than the renewal date.

Persons to whom a copy of the notice sent:
(see note for completion 7)

Date and method of intimation:
(see note for completion 8)

I swear [*or* affirm] that the information contained in this notice is, to the best of my knowledge and belief, true, and that this notice has been duly intimated.

Signature of person so swearing [*or* affirming]:
(see note for completion 9)

Signature of notary public:

Date:

Certificate by Lands Tribunal for Scotland
(see note for completion 10)."

Explanatory note
(This explanation has no legal effect)

This notice, given under section 20(1) of the Title Conditions (Scotland) Act 2003, concerns real burdens which affect a [neighbouring] property (referred to in the notice as the "burdened property"), and is sent to you by the owner of that property or by some other person affected by the burdens. The sender (who is referred to in the notice and in these notes as the "terminator") wishes to free the property of the real burdens listed in the notice. The burdens are more than 100 years old. If you are opposed to the freeing, you can apply to the Lands Tribunal for Scotland for the burdens to be renewed or varied. The address of the Lands Tribunal is [*insert address*] and their telephone number is [*insert telephone number*]. However, you can only apply if you are an owner of a property which, in a legal sense, takes benefit from the burden and which carries enforcement rights or if the burden is a personal real burden. For further guidance you may wish to consult a solicitor or other adviser. [A list of other people who have been sent this notice is given in the notice itself. It is possible to make an application to the Lands Tribunal jointly with other people.] An application to the Lands Tribunal must be made by the renewal date stated in the notice. If no application is made by then, you may lose any right which you may currently hold to enforce the burdens.

Notes for completion of the notice
(These notes have no legal effect)

1 The "terminator" is the person who, at any time, is seeking to terminate the real burden. Where the person who proposes to execute and register the notice of termination and so intimates is not the terminator when the notice comes to be executed, the name and address of the person executing should be appended after the name and address of the person who so intimated.
2 Describe the property in a way that is sufficient to identify it. Where the property has a postal address the description should include that address. Where the title has been registered in the Land Register the description should refer to the title number of the property or of the larger subjects of which the property forms part. Otherwise it should normally refer to and identify a deed recorded in a specified division of the Register of Sasines.
3 Describe the terminator's connection with the burdened property, as for example by identification as owner or tenant or by setting out the midcouple which links (or midcouples which link) the terminator to the person who last had a completed title as owner. Where the circumstances mentioned in note for completion 1 arise, the description should be extended accordingly.
4 Identify the constitutive deed by reference to the appropriate Register, and set out the real burden in full. A single notice may be used for two or more real burdens.
5 If the real burden is wholly to be terminated say so; otherwise describe the extent of termination.
6 Insert the date by which applications for renewal or variation must be made. This can be any date, provided that it is not less than 8 weeks after the last date on which this notice is intimated (intimation by affixing being taken to be given when first the notice is affixed).
7 This notice (and the explanatory note) must be intimated to (a) the owner of any benefited property, (b) the holder of any personal real burden and (c) the owner of the burdened property (or, if the terminator is such an owner, any other owner of that property). Intimation can be by

sending (or delivering) the notice, by affixing a conspicuous notice to the burdened property and also to a lamp post within 100 metres of that property (or to at least two lamp posts if there is more than one within that distance of that property) or by newspaper advertisement. However, affixing or advertisement cannot be used for the owner of a benefited property which lies within 4 metres of the burdened property (disregarding roads less than 20 metres wide) or for the owner of the burdened property or for any such person as is mentioned in paragraph (b) of this note and advertisement cannot be used where affixing can. Where sending or delivery is used, state (i) the name of the person concerned (if known) (ii) the address to which the notice is sent or delivered, and (iii) the address of the benefited (or burdened) property owned by that person, if different from (ii). Since evidence of sending may be required at the time of registration in the Land Register, it is recommended that the notice be sent by recorded delivery or registered post.

8 State the date and method of intimation. By way of example—

    (a) if notices were posted, to the persons listed in the previous note, on 25th March 2003 and advertised in the *Inverness Courier* on 4th April 2003, insert: "(a) Intimation by post on 25th March 2003; (b) Advertisement in the *Inverness Courier* on 4th April 2003."; or

    (b) if on 12th July a notice was posted to the owner of the burdened property and otherwise intimation was given by affixing notices on that date, insert: "(a) Intimation by post on 12th July 2005; (b) Notices affixed to the burdened property and to each of two lamp posts within 100 metres of that property on 12th July 2005.".

The terminator should not swear or affirm, or sign, until the notice has been completed (except for the certificate by the Lands Tribunal for Scotland) and duly intimated. Before signing, the terminator should swear or affirm before a notary public (or, if the notice is being completed outwith Scotland, before a person duly authorised under the local law to administer oaths or receive affirmations) that, to the best of the terminator's knowledge and belief, all the information contained in the notice is true and that the notice has been duly intimated. The notary public should also sign. Swearing or affirming a statement which is known to be false or which is believed not to be true is a criminal offence under the False Oaths (Scotland) Act 1933 (c.20). Normally the terminator should swear or affirm, and sign, personally. If, however, the terminator is legally disabled or incapable (for example because of mental disorder) a legal representative should swear or affirm, and sign. If the terminator is not an individual (for example, if it is a company) a person entitled by law to sign formal documents on its behalf should swear or affirm, and sign.

10 There is to be endorsed before registration the certificate required by section 23(1) of the Title Conditions (Scotland) Act 2003 (asp 9).

SCHEDULE 3
(introduced by section 21(2)(b))

FORM OF AFFIXED NOTICE RELATING TO TERMINATION

"TERMINATION OF REAL BURDEN

This notice is intimation that the person who is described below as terminator wishes to free the property which is described below as the burdened property from a real burden which affects that property. The terminator proposes to register a notice of termination so as to extinguish the real burden. A copy of that notice of termination (which among other things describes the real burden fully) is available from the terminator on request.

Name and address of terminator:
(see note for completion 1)

Description of burdened property:
(see note for completion 2)

The real burden and the extent of termination:
(see note for completion 3)

Renewal date:
(see note for completion 4)

If you wish to apply to the Lands Tribunal for Scotland for renewal or variation of the real burden you must do so by not later than the renewal date. If no application is made by then, you may lose any right which you may currently hold to enforce the burden. For further guidance you may wish to consult a solicitor or other adviser.

Signature of terminator:

Date affixed: ."

Notes for completion of the notice
(These notes have no legal effect)

1 The "terminator" is the person who, at any time, is seeking to terminate the real burden. Give the terminator's name and address (or the terminator's name and the name and address of the terminator's agent).

2 Describe the property in a way that is sufficient to identify it. Where the property has a postal address the description should include that address. Where the title has been registered in the Land Register the description should refer to the title number of the property or of the larger subjects of which the property forms part. Otherwise it should normally refer to and identify a deed recorded in a specified division of the Register of Sasines.

3 Provide briefly a description of the real burden. If the burden is wholly to be terminated say so; otherwise describe the extent of termination.

4 Insert the date by which applications for renewal or variation must be made. This can be any date, provided that it is not less than 8 weeks after the last date on which the notice of termination is intimated (intimation by affixing being taken to be given when first the notice is affixed).

SCHEDULE 4
(introduced by section 34(2)(a))

FORM OF NOTICE OF PROPOSAL TO REGISTER DEED OF VARIATION OR DISCHARGE

"NOTICE OF PROPOSAL TO REGISTER DEED OF VARIATION OR DISCHARGE

Proposer:
(see note for completion 1)

Description of affected unit(s):
(see note for completion 2)

Terms of community burden(s):
(see note for completion 3)

Effect of registration of deed on burden(s):
(see note for completion 4)

An application to the Lands Tribunal for Scotland for preservation of the community burden(s) must be made not later than [*specify the date on which the period mentioned in section 34(3) of this Act expires*].

Signature of proposer:

Date: ."

Explanatory note
(This explanation has no legal effect)

This notice is given under section 34(2)(a) of the Title Conditions (Scotland) Act 2003. The sender (who is referred to in the notice and in these notes as the "proposer") wishes [to free a property of a community burden] *or* [to vary a community burden]. A deed of [discharge] *or* [variation] has already been granted. A copy of the deed in question is attached. If the deed is duly registered the burden will be [discharged] *or* [varied] in relation to the affected unit. If you want to preserve such rights as you may have, you can apply to the Lands Tribunal for Scotland in that regard. The address of the Lands Tribunal is [*insert address*] and their telephone number is [*insert telephone number*]. For further guidance you may wish to consult a solicitor or other adviser. An application to the Lands Tribunal must be made by the date stated in the notice. If no application is made by then, you may lose any right which you may currently hold to enforce the burdens.

Notes for completion of the notice
(These notes have no legal effect)

1 The "proposer" is the person who is seeking to discharge or vary the community burden. Give the proposer's name and address (or the proposer's name and the name and address of the proposer's agent).
2 Describe the unit in a way that is sufficient to identify it. Where the unit has a postal address the description should include that address. Where the title has been registered in the Land Register the description should refer to the title number of the property or of the larger subjects of which the unit forms part. Otherwise it should normally refer to and identify a deed recorded in a specified division of the Register of Sasines.
3 Identify the constitutive deed by reference to the appropriate Register, and set out the community burden in full.
4 State whether the deed is of variation or of discharge. If the community burden is wholly to be discharged say so; otherwise describe the extent of variation or discharge.
5 Intimation is by sending (or delivering) the notice. Since evidence of sending may be required at the time of registration in the Land Register, it is recommended that the notice be sent by recorded delivery or registered post.
6 There is to be endorsed on the deed before registration the certificate required by subsection (2) of section 37 of the Title Conditions (Scotland) Act 2003 (asp 9) (as applied by section 34 of that Act).

SCHEDULE 5
(introduced by section 36(2)(a))

FURTHER FORM OF NOTICE OF PROPOSAL TO REGISTER DEED OF VARIATION OR DISCHARGE OF COMMUNITY BURDEN: SENT VERSION

"NOTICE OF PROPOSAL TO REGISTER DEED OF VARIATION OR DISCHARGE OF COMMUNITY BURDEN

Proposer:
(see note for completion 1)

Description of affected unit:
(see note for completion 2)

Terms of community burden(s):
(see note for completion 3)

Nature of deed:
(see note for completion 4)

An application to the Lands Tribunal for Scotland for preservation of the community burden(s) must be made not later than [*specify the date on which the period mentioned in section 37(1) of this Act expires*].

Signature of proposer:

Date: ."

Explanatory note
(This explanation has no legal effect)

This notice is given under section 36(2)(a) of the Title Conditions (Scotland) Act 2003. The sender (who is referred to in the notice and in these notes as the "proposer") wishes [to free a property of a community burden] *or* [to vary a community burden]. A deed of [discharge] *or* [variation] has already been granted by the owners of adjacent properties and a copy of it is attached. If the deed is duly registered the burden will be [discharged] *or* [varied] in relation to the affected property. If you want to preserve such rights as you may have, you can apply to the Lands Tribunal for Scotland in that regard. The address of the Lands Tribunal is [*insert address*] and their telephone number is [*insert telephone number*]. However, you can only apply if you are an owner of a property which, in a legal sense, takes benefit from the burden and which carries enforcement rights. For further guidance you may wish to consult a solicitor or other adviser. An application to the Lands Tribunal must be made by the date stated in the notice. If no application is made by then, you may lose any right which you may currently hold to enforce the burdens.

Notes for completion of the notice
(These notes have no legal effect)

1 The "proposer" is the person who is seeking to discharge or vary the community burden. Give the proposer's name and address (or the proposer's name and the name and address of the proposer's agent.)
2 Describe the affected unit in a way that is sufficient to identify it. Where the unit has a postal address the description should include that address. Where the title has been registered in the Land Register the description should refer to the title number of the property or of the larger subjects of which the unit forms part. Otherwise it should normally refer to and identify a deed recorded in a specified division of the Register of Sasines.
3 Identify the constitutive deed by reference to the appropriate Register and set out the community burden in full.
4 State whether the deed is of variation or of discharge. If the community burden is wholly to be discharged say so; otherwise describe the extent of variation or discharge.
5 This notice requires to be sent. Since evidence of sending may be required at the time of registration in the Land Register, it is recommended that the notice be sent by recorded delivery or registered post.
6 There is to be endorsed on the deed before registration the certificate required by subsection (2) of section 37 of the Title Conditions (Scotland) Act 2003 (asp 9).

SCHEDULE 6
(introduced by section 36(2)(b))

FURTHER FORM OF NOTICE OF PROPOSAL TO REGISTER DEED OF VARIATION OR DISCHARGE OF COMMUNITY BURDEN: AFFIXED VERSION

"NOTICE OF PROPOSAL TO REGISTER DEED OF VARIATION OR DISCHARGE OF COMMUNITY BURDEN

This notice is intimation that the person who is described below as proposer wishes to vary or discharge a community burden which affects a property described below as the affected unit. The proposer intends to register a deed already granted by certain other owners of units. A copy of the deed in question can be obtained from the proposer on request as can a description of the community burden. If the deed *is* registered the community burden will be varied or discharged in so far as it affects the property.

Proposer:
(see note for completion 1)

Description of affected unit:
(see note for completion 2)

The community burden and the extent of termination:
(see note for completion 3)

An application to the Lands Tribunal for Scotland for preservation of the community burden(s) must be made not later than [*specify the date on which the period mentioned in section 37(1) of this Act expires*]. **If no application is made by then, you may lose any right you may currently hold to enforce the community burden. For further guidance you may wish to consult a solicitor or other adviser.**

Signature of proposer:

Date affixed: ."

Notes for completion of the notice
(These notes have no legal effect)

1 The "proposer" is the person who is seeking to discharge or vary the community burden. Give the proposer's name and address (or the proposer's name and the name and address of the proposer's agent).
2 Describe the affected unit in a way that is sufficient to identify it. Where the unit has a postal address the description should include that address. Where the title has been registered in the Land Register the description should refer to the title number of the property or of the larger subjects of which the unit forms part. Otherwise it should normally refer to and identify a deed recorded in a specified division of the Register of Sasines.
3 Provide a brief description of the community burden. If the burden is wholly to be discharged say so; otherwise describe the extent of variation or discharge.
4 This notice requires to be affixed conspicuously to the affected unit and also to a lamp post within 100 metres of that unit (or to at least two lamp posts if there is more than one within that distance of that unit).
5 There is to be endorsed on the deed before registration the statement required by subsection (2) of section 37 of the Title Conditions (Scotland) Act 2003 (asp 9).

SCHEDULE 7
(introduced by section 50(1))

FORM OF NOTICE OF PRESERVATION

"NOTICE OF PRESERVATION

Name and address of person sending notice:

Description of burdened property:
(see note for completion 1)

Description of benefited property:
(see note for completion 1)

[Links in title:]
(see note for completion 2)

Terms of real burden(s):
(see note for completion 3)

Explanation of why the property described as a benefited property is such a property:
(see note for completion 4)

Service:
(see note for completion 5)

I swear [*or* affirm] that the information contained in this notice is, to the best of my knowledge and belief, true.

Signature of person sending notice:
(see note for completion 6)

Signature of notary public:

Date: .''

Explanatory note for owner of burdened property
(This explanation has no legal effect)

This notice is sent by a person who asserts that the use of your property is affected by the real burden [*or* real burdens] whose terms are described in the notice and that that person is one of the people entitled to the benefit of the real burden [*or* real burdens] and can, if necessary, enforce it [*or* them] against you. In this notice your property (or some part of it) is referred to as the "burdened property" and the property belonging to that person is referred to as the "benefited property". The grounds for the assertion are given in the notice. By section 50 of the Title Conditions (Scotland) Act 2003 (asp 9) that person's rights will be lost unless this notice is registered in the Land Register or Register of Sasines by not later than [*insert date ten years after the appointed day*]. Registration preserves the rights and means that the burden [*or* burdens] can continue to be enforced by that person and by anyone succeeding as owner of that person's property. This notice does not require you to take any action; but if you think there is a mistake in it, or if you wish to challenge it, you are advised to contact your solicitor or other adviser. A notice can be challenged even after it has been registered.

Notes for completion of the notice
(These notes have no legal effect)

1 A single notice may be used for any properties covered by the same constitutive deed. Describe the property in a way that is sufficient to identify it. Where the title has been registered in the Land Register the description should refer to the title number of the property or of the larger subjects of which the property forms part. Otherwise it should normally refer to and identify a deed recorded in a specified division of the Register of Sasines.
2 Include the section "Links in Title" only if the person sending the notice does not have a completed title to the benefited property. Set out the midcouple (or midcouples) linking that person with the person who had the last completed title.
3 A single notice may be used for any real burdens created in the same constitutive deed. Identify the constitutive deed by reference to the appropriate Register, and set out the real burden in full or refer to the deed in such a way as to identify the real burden.
4 Explain the legal and factual grounds on which the land described as a benefited property is a benefited property in relation to the burdened property and the burden described in the notice.
5 Do not complete until a copy of the notice, together with the explanatory note, has been sent (or delivered) to the owner of the burdened property (except in a case where that is not reasonably practicable). Then insert whichever is applicable of the following:
"A copy of this notice has been sent by [*state method and if by post specify whether by recorded delivery, by registered post or by ordinary post*] on [*date*] to the owner of the burdened property at [*address*].''; or
"It has not been reasonably practicable to send a copy of this notice to the owner of the burdened property for the following reason: [*specify the reason*]''.
6 The person sending the notice should not swear or affirm, or sign, until a copy of the notice has been sent (or otherwise) as mentioned in note 5. Before signing, the sender should swear or affirm before a notary public (or, if the notice is being completed outwith Scotland, before a person duly authorised under the local law to administer oaths or receive affirmations) that, to the best of the sender's knowledge and belief, all the information contained in the notice is true. The notary public should also sign. Swearing or affirming a statement which is known to be false or which is believed not to be true is a criminal offence under the False Oaths (Scotland) Act 1933 (c.20). Normally the sender should swear or affirm, and sign, personally. If, however, the sender is legally disabled or incapable (for example because of mental disorder) a legal representative should swear or affirm, and sign. If the sender is not an individual (for example, if it is a company) a person entitled by law to sign formal documents on its behalf should swear or affirm, and sign.

SCHEDULE 8
(introduced by section 55(2))

COMMUNITY CONSULTATION NOTICE

"NOTICE INVITING COMMENTS IN RELATION TO PROPOSAL TO VARY OR DISCHARGE COMMUNITY BURDEN AFFECTING SHELTERED OR RETIREMENT HOUSING

Person to whom comments should be sent:
(see note for completion 1)

Description of development:
(see note for completion 2)

Terms of community burden to be varied or discharged:
(see note for completion 3)

Effect of registration of proposed deed on that burden:
(see note for completion 4)

Date by which any comments are to be made:
(see note for completion 5)

Date of intimation:
(see notes for completion 6)

Signature of a person who proposes to grant the deed:

Date: ."

Explanatory note (This explanation has no legal effect)

This notice, which is sent under section 55 of the Title Conditions (Scotland) Act 2003, concerns a community burden which affects the sheltered or retirement housing development of which your property is part. The sender is intimating to you a proposal to grant a deed of [variation] *or* [discharge] in respect of the burden and invites your comments. If such a deed is granted and duly registered (which cannot be before the date specified, in the notice, as that by which any comments are to be made) the burden [may be varied] *or* [may be discharged] as described in the notice. For further guidance you may wish to consult a solicitor or other adviser.

Notes for completion of the notice
(These notes have no legal effect)

1 This should ordinarily be a person who proposes to grant the deed. Give the person's name and address.
2 Describe the sheltered or retirement housing development in a way that is sufficient to identify it.
3 Set out the community burden in question in full.
4 State whether the proposed deed is of variation or of discharge. If the community burden is wholly to be discharged say so; otherwise describe the extent of variation or discharge.
5 Specify a date no earlier than three weeks after the latest date mentioned in section 55(3) of the Title Conditions (Scotland) Act 2003 (asp 9).
6 Intimation is by sending (or delivering) the notice. Since evidence of sending may be required at the time of registration in the Land Register of any deed granted, it is recommended that the notice be sent by recorded delivery or registered post.

SCHEDULE 9
(introduced by section 80(4))

FORM OF NOTICE OF CONVERTED SERVITUDE

"NOTICE OF CONVERTED SERVITUDE

Name and address of person sending notice:

Description of burdened property:
(see note for completion 1)

Description of benefited property:
(see note for completion 1)

[Links in title:]
(see note for completion 2)

Terms of converted servitude:
(see note for completion 3)

Explanation of why the property described as a benefited property is such a property:
(see note for completion 4)

Service:
(see note for completion 5)

I swear [*or* affirm] that the information contained in this notice is, to the best of my knowledge and belief, true. The constitutive deed [*or A copy of the constitutive deed*] is annexed to the notice.
(see note for completion 6)

Signature of person sending notice:
(see note for completion 7)

Signature of notary public:

Date: ."

Explanatory note for owner of burdened property
(This explanation has no legal effect)

This notice is sent by a person who asserts that the use of your property is affected by a converted servitude which the sender is entitled to enforce. In this notice your property (or some part of it) is referred to as the "burdened property" and the property belonging to the sender is referred to as the "benefited property". The "converted servitude" is a condition which may affect the use of your property. Formerly a servitude, the condition was converted into a real burden by subsection (1) of section 80 of the Title Conditions (Scotland) Act 2003 (asp 9). At the moment the converted servitude is not disclosed against your title on the property registers. By subsection (2) of that section the sender's right will be lost unless this notice is registered in the Land Register of Scotland or the Register of Sasines by not later than [*insert date ten years after the appointed day*]. Registration preserves the right and means that the converted servitude can continue to be enforced by the sender, and by anyone succeeding the sender as owner of that property. This notice does not require you to take any action; but if you think there is a mistake in it, or if you wish to challenge it, you are advised to contact your solicitor or other adviser. A notice can be challenged even after it has been registered.

Notes for completion of the notice
(These notes have no legal effect)

1 A single notice may be used for any properties covered by the same constitutive deed. Describe the property in a way that is sufficient to identify it. Where the title has been registered in the Land Register the description should refer to the title number of the property or of the

larger subjects of which the property forms part. Otherwise it should normally refer to and identify a deed recorded in a specified division of the Register of Sasines.

2 Include the section "Links in Title" only if the person sending the notice does not have a completed title to the benefited property. List the midcouple (or midcouples) linking that person with the person who had the last completed title.

3 A single notice may be used for any converted servitudes created in the same constitutive deed. Set out the converted servitude in full or refer to the constitutive deed in such a way as to identify the servitude. If there is no such deed, explain the factual and legal circumstances in which the servitude was created.

4 Complete this part only if the land described as the benefited property is not nominated as such by the constitutive deed. Explain the legal and factual grounds on which that land is a benefited property in relation to the burdened property and the converted servitude described in the notice.

5 Do not complete until a copy of the notice, together with the constitutive deed and the explanatory note, has been sent (or delivered) to the owner of the burdened property (except in a case where that is not reasonably practicable). Then insert whichever is applicable of the following:

"A copy of this notice has been sent by [*state method and if by post specify whether by recorded delivery, by registered post or by ordinary post*] on [*date*] to the owner of the burdened property at [*address*].""; or

"It has not been reasonably practicable to send a copy of this notice to the owner of the burdened property for the following reason: [*specify the reason*]".

6 Endorse on the constitutive deed (or copy) words to the effect of: "This is the constitutive deed referred to in the notice of converted servitude by [*give name of person sending the notice*] dated [*give date*]." The endorsement need not be signed.

7 The person sending the notice should not swear or affirm, or sign, until a copy of the notice has been sent (or otherwise) as mentioned in note 5. Before signing, the sender should swear or affirm before a notary public (or, if the notice is being completed outwith Scotland, before a person duly authorised under the local law to administer oaths or receive affirmations) that, to the best of the sender's knowledge and belief, all the information contained in the notice is true. The notary public should also sign. Swearing or affirming a statement which is known to be false or which is believed not to be true is a criminal offence under the False Oaths (Scotland) Act 1933 (c.20). Normally the sender should swear or affirm, and sign, personally. If, however, the sender is legally disabled or incapable (for example because of mental disorder) a legal representative should swear or affirm, and sign. If the sender is not an individual (for example, if it is a company) a person entitled by law to sign formal documents on its behalf should swear or affirm, and sign.

SCHEDULE 10

(introduced by section 83(1)(a))

FORM OF UNDERTAKING

"UNDERTAKING NOT TO EXERCISE RIGHT OF PRE-EMPTION"

Property benefited by right of pre-emption:
(see note for completion 1)

Holder of right of pre-emption:
(see note for completion 2)

Property subject to right of pre-emption:
(see note for completion 3)

Deed in which right of pre-emption imposed:
(see note for completion 4)

I hereby undertake that I will not exercise my right of pre-emption in respect of a sale occurring before (*insert date*) [if (*insert any conditions to be satisfied*) – see note for completion 5]

Signature by or on behalf of holder of right of pre-emption:

Signature of witness:

Date: ."

Notes for completion of the undertaking
(These notes have no legal effect)

1 Describe the property in a way that is sufficient to enable it to be identified. Where the title has been registered in the Land Register the description should refer to the title number. Otherwise it should normally refer to and identify a deed recorded in a specified division of the Register of Sasines. Where the right of pre-emption is a personal pre-emption burden or rural housing burden, insert (only) "Personal pre-emption burden" *or* "Rural housing burden".
2 Insert the holder's name and address. The holder is the owner of the benefited property or, in the case of a personal pre-emption burden or rural housing burden, the person in whose favour the burden is constituted. (The person last registered as having title to such a burden is taken to be the holder of the right of pre-emption which the burden comprises.)
3 Describe the property in a way that is sufficient to enable it to be identified. Where the title has been registered in the Land Register the description should refer to the title number. Otherwise it should normally refer to and identify a deed recorded in a specified division of the Register of Sasines. If part only of the burdened property is to be sold, describe that part only.
4 Give the name of the deed and the particulars of its registration or recording.
5 Insert any conditions concerning the type of sale in respect of which the right of pre-emption will not be exercised (for example, "if the consideration for the sale is £100,000 or more").

SCHEDULE 11
(introduced by section 90(3))

TITLE CONDITIONS NOT SUBJECT TO DISCHARGE BY LANDS TRIBUNAL

1 An obligation, however constituted, relating to the right to work minerals or to any ancillary rights in relation to minerals ("minerals" and "ancillary rights" having the same meanings as in the Mines (Working Facilities and Support) Act 1966 (c.4)).
2 In so far as enforceable by or on behalf of—
  (a) the Crown, an obligation created or imposed for naval, military or air force purposes; or
  (b) the Crown or any public or international authority, an obligation created or imposed—
      (i) for civil aviation purposes; or
      (ii) in connection with the use of land as an aerodrome.
3 An obligation created or imposed in or in relation to a lease of—
  (a) an agricultural holding (as defined in section 1(1) of the Agricultural Holdings (Scotland) Act 1991 (c.55));
  (b) a holding (within the meaning of the Small Landholders (Scotland) Acts 1886 to 1931); or
  (c) a croft (within the meaning of the Crofters (Scotland) Act 1993 (c.44)).

SCHEDULE 12
(introduced by section 107(11))

FORM OF APPLICATION FOR RELEVANT CERTIFICATE

"APPLICATION BY ACQUIRING AUTHORITY FOR RELEVANT CERTIFICATE

Acquiring authority:

Description of land acquired:
(see note for completion 1)

Proposed effect of registering conveyance:
(see note for completion 2)

Date and method of intimation:
(see note for completion 3)

Date by which any application to Lands Tribunal must be made:
(see note for completion 4)

Signature:
(see note for completion 5)

Date: ."

Notes for completion of the application
(These notes have no legal effect)

1 Give the postal address if there is one, then describe the land in a way that is sufficient to enable the Keeper to identify it by reference to the Ordnance Map. Where the title to the land has been registered in the Land Register the description should refer to the title number of the land or the larger subjects of which the land forms part. Otherwise it should normally refer to and identify a deed recorded in a specified division of the Register of Sasines.
2 If it is proposed that all real burdens and servitudes be extinguished, and any development management scheme disapplied, say so. If the terms of the conveyance are to provide otherwise, annex a copy of the draft conveyance to the application.
3 Intimation can be by sending, by advertisement or by such other method as the acquiring authority thinks fit.
4 Specify a date no fewer than 21 days after the date of intimation.
5 The signature is to be that of a person entitled by law to sign formal documents on behalf of the acquiring authority.

SCHEDULE 13
(introduced by section 114(6))

AMENDMENT OF ABOLITION OF FEUDAL TENURE ETC. (SCOTLAND) ACT 2000

1 The 2000 Act shall be amended in accordance with the following paragraphs.
2 In section 17 (extinction of superior's rights)—
    (a) in subsection (1), after the word—
        (i) "18" there shall be inserted "to 18C";
       (ii) "27," there shall be inserted "27A,";
      (iii) "28," there shall be inserted "28A,"; and
      (iv) "Act" there shall be inserted "and to sections 52 to 56 (which make provision as to common schemes, facility burdens and service burdens) and 63 (which makes provision as to manager burdens) of the Title Conditions (Scotland) Act 2003 (asp 9)",
and at the end of paragraph (b) there shall be added other than in that person's capacity as owner of land or as holder of a conservation burden, health care burden or economic development burden; and
    (b) in subsection (3), after paragraph (a) there shall be inserted—
      "(aa) a right of enforcement held by virtue of any of the provisions mentioned in subsection (1) above;".
3 In section 18 (reallotment of real burden by nomination of new dominant tenement)—
    (a) in subsection (1), at the beginning there shall be inserted "Without prejudice to sections 18A to 18C of this Act,";
    (b) in subsection (6), at the beginning there shall be inserted "Subject to subsection (6A) below,";
    (c) after subsection (6) there shall be inserted—
      "(6A) Such compliance as is mentioned in subsection (6) above shall not be effective to preserve any right to enforce a manager burden ("manager burden" being construed in accordance with section 63(1) of the Title Conditions (Scotland) Act 2003 (asp 9))."; and
    (d) in subsection (7)(b)(i), after the word "right" there shall be inserted "(other than any sporting rights, as defined by section 65A(9) of this Act)".
4. In section 20 (reallotment of real burden by order of Lands Tribunal)—

249

(a) in subsection (1), the words from "within" to "ends" are repealed; and

(b) in subsection (7)—

 (i) in paragraph (a), for the words "substantial loss or disadvantage to the applicant as owner (taking him to be such)" there shall be substituted "material detriment to the value or enjoyment of the applicant's ownership (taking him to have ownership)"; and

 (ii) paragraph (b), and the word "or" which immediately precedes that paragraph, are repealed.

5 In section 25 (counter-obligations on reallotment)—

(a) for the words ", 20 or 23" there shall be substituted "or 20";

(b) after the word "Act" there shall be inserted the words "or under section 56 or 63 of the Title Conditions (Scotland) Act 2003 (asp 9) (which make provision, respectively, as to facility burdens and service burdens and as to manager burdens)"; and

(c) for the words from "(as the case may be)" to the end there shall be substituted "reallotment is effected".

6 In section 27 (notice preserving right to enforce conservation burden)—

(a) in subsection (1), after the words "Act; and" there shall be inserted ", without prejudice to section 27A(1) of this Act,"; and

(b) in subsection (3)(a), for the words "26 of this Act" there shall be substituted "38 of the Title Conditions (Scotland) Act 2003 (asp 9) (which makes provision generally as respects conservation burdens)".

7 In section 42 (further provision as respects certain sections of that Act which relate to real burdens)—

(a) in each of subsections (1)(a), (3) and (4)(a), after the word—

 (i) "18," there shall be inserted "18A, 18B, 18C,"; and

 (ii) "27" there shall be inserted ", 27A"; and

(b) at the end there shall be added—

 "(5) Nothing in this Part requires registration against land prospectively nominated as a dominant tenement but outwith Scotland.".

8 In section 43 (notices and agreements under certain sections: extent of Keeper's duty)—

(a) in each of subsections (1) and (2)(a), after the word—

 (i) "18," there shall be inserted "18A, 18B, 18C,"; and

 (ii) "27" there shall be inserted ", 27A";

(b) in subsection (2), after paragraph (b) there shall be inserted—

 "(bb) section 18B or 18C of this Act, the Keeper shall not be required to determine whether—

  (i) the requirements of subsection (1) of the section are satisfied: or

  (ii) the statement made in pursuance of subsection (2)(e) of the section in question is correct;" " and

(c) in subsection (3)(a), after—

 (i) the words "18(6)," there shall be inserted "18A(5), 18B(3), 18C(3),"; and

 (ii) the word "28" there shall be inserted ", 28A".

9 In section 46(2) (discretion of Keeper in relation to entries in title sheet), for the word "enforceable" there shall be substituted "subsisting".

10 In section 49 (interpretation of Part 4)—

(a) in the definition of "conservation body", for the words "under section 26(1) of this Act" there shall be substituted "by order under section 38(4) of the Title Conditions (Scotland) Act 2003 (asp 9)";

(b) in the definition of "conservation burden", for the words "section 27(1)" there shall be substituted "sections 27(1) and 27A(1)";

(c) after the definition of "development value burden" and "development value" there shall be inserted—

 " "economic development burden" shall be construed in accordance with section 18B(3) of this Act;

 "health care burden" shall be construed in accordance with section 18C(3) of this Act;

 "local authority" means a council constituted under section 2 of the Local Government etc. (Scotland) Act 1994 (c.39);";

(d) after the definition of "notary public" there shall be inserted—

 " "personal pre-emption burden" and "personal redemption burden" shall be construed in accordance with section 18A(5) of this Act"; and

    (e) in the definition of "real burden", at the end of paragraph (b) there shall be added "or sporting rights (as defined by section 65A(9) of this Act)".

11 In section 54 (extinction of superior's rights and obligations *qua* superior)—

    (a) in subsection (1)—

        (i) for the words "section 60(1)" there shall be substituted "sections 60(1) and 65A"; and

        (ii) after the words "*qua* superior" there shall be inserted "(including, without prejudice to that generality, sporting rights as defined by subsection (9) of that section 65A)"; and

    (b) in subsection (3), after paragraph (a) there shall be inserted—

    "(aa) a right of enforcement held by virtue of of section 13, 33, 60(1) or 65A of this Act;".

12 In section 56 (extinction etc. of certain payments analogous to feuduty)—

    (a) in subsection (1), for the words "land obligation" there shall be substituted "title condition"; and

    (b) for subsection (3) there shall be substituted—

    "(3) The definition of "title condition" in section 122(1) of the Title Conditions (Scotland) Act 2003 (asp 9) shall apply for the purposes of this section as that definition applies for the purposes of that Act.".

13 In section 73 (feudal terms in enactments and documents: construction after abolition of feudal system)—

    (a) in subsection (1)—

        (i) in each of paragraphs (a), (b) and (c), at the end, there shall be added "before that day";

        (ii) the word "or" which immediately follows paragraph (b) is repealed; and

        (iii) for the words "before the appointed day, then" there shall be substituted "; or

        (d) in the Land Register of Scotland or in—

            (i) a land certificate;

            (ii) a charge certificate; or

            (iii) an office copy,

        Issued, whether or not before that day, under the Land Registration (Scotland) Act 1979 (c.33),

  then";

    (b) in subsection (2)—

        (i) the existing words "in any document executed before that day" shall become paragraph (a);

        (ii) after that paragraph there shall be inserted the word "or" and the following paragraph—

        "(b) in the Land Register of Scotland or in any certificate or copy such as is mentioned in subsection (1)(d) above (whenever issued),"; and

        (iii) for the words "19, 20, 23, 28 or, as the case may be, 60 of this Act" there shall be substituted "18A, 18B, 18C, 19, 20, 28, 28A or 60 of this Act or section 56 of the Title Conditions (Scotland) Act 2003 (asp 9) (facility burdens and service burdens)"; and

    (c) after subsection (2) there shall be added—

    "(2A) In construing, after the appointed day and in relation to a right enforceable on or after that day, a document, or entry in the Land Register, which—

        (a) sets out the terms of a real burden; and

        (b) is not a document or entry references in which require to be construed as mentioned in subsection (2) above,

any provision of the document or entry to the effect that a person other than the person entitled to enforce the burden may waive compliance with, or mitigate or otherwise vary a condition of, the burden shall be disregarded.".

14 In section 75 (saving for contractual rights) the existing words become subsection (1) and after that subsection there is added—

    "(2) In construing the expression "parties to the grant" in subsection (1) above, any enactment or rule of law whereby investiture is deemed renewed when the parties change shall be disregarded.".

15 In section 77 (short title and commencement)—

    (a) in subsection (2)(a), for the words "63 to" there shall be substituted "64, 65,"; and

    (b) in subsection (4)(a), for the words "and 47 to 49" there shall be substituted ", 47 to 49, 63 and 65A".

16 After schedule 5 there shall be inserted—

"SCHEDULE 5A
(introduced by section 18A(1))

FORM OF NOTICE PROSPECTIVELY CONVERTING REAL BURDEN INTO PERSONAL PRE-EMPTION BURDEN OR PERSONAL REDEMPTION BURDEN

"NOTICE PROSPECTIVELY CONVERTING REAL BURDEN INTO PERSONAL PRE-EMPTION BURDEN OR PERSONAL REDEMPTION BURDEN

Superior:
(see note for completion 1)

Description of land which is to be servient tenement:
(see note for completion 2)

Terms of real burden:
(see note for completion 3)

Any counter obligation:
(see note for completion 3)

Title to the superiority:
(see note for completion 4)

Service:
(see note for completion 5)

I swear [or affirm] that the information contained in the notice is, to the best of my knowledge and belief, true.

Signature of superior:
(see note for completion 6)

Signature of notary public:

Date: ."

Explanatory Note
(This explanation has no legal effect)

This notice is sent by your feudal superior. In this notice your property (or some part of it) is referred to (prospectively) as the "servient tenement". By this notice the feudal superior asserts that at present your property is subject to a right of pre-emption [or of redemption] enforceable by him and claims the right to continue to enforce it not as superior but in a personal capacity. The notice, if it is registered in the Land Register or Register of Sasines under section 18A of the Abolition of Feudal Tenure etc. (Scotland) Act 2000, will allow him to enforce the right after the feudal system is abolished (which will be shortly). If you think that there is a mistake in this notice or if you wish to challenge it, you are advised to contact your solicitor or other adviser.

Notes for completion of the notice
(These notes have no legal effect)

1 Insert name and address of superior.
2 Describe the land in a way that is sufficient to enable the Keeper to identify it by reference to the Ordnance Map. Where the title to the land has been registered in the Land Register the description should refer to the title number of the land or of the larger subjects of which the land forms part. Otherwise it should normally refer to and identify a deed recorded in a specified division of the Register of Sasines.
3 Specify by reference to the appropriate Register the deed or deeds in which the real burden

or counter-obligation was imposed. Set out the real burden or counter-obligation in full or refer to the deed in such a way as to identify the real burden or counter-obligation.

4 Where the title has been registered in the Land Register of Scotland and the superior is—

(a) registered as proprietor, specify the title number;

(b) not so registered, specify the title number and set out the midcouples or links between the person last registered and the superior so as sufficiently to identify them.

Where the title has not been registered in the Land Register and the superior—

(a) has a recorded title, specify by reference to the Register of Sasines the deed constituting the immediate title;

(b) does not have a recorded title, either—

(i) specify by reference to the Register of Sasines the deed constituting the immediate title of the person with the last recorded title and set out the midcouples or links between that person and the superior so as sufficiently to identify them; or

(ii) if there is no such deed, specify the nature of the superior's title.

5 Do not complete until a copy of the notice has been sent to the owner of the prospective servient tenement (except in a case where this is not reasonably practicable). Then insert whichever is applicable of the following:

"The superior has sent a copy of this notice by [*specify whether by recorded delivery or registered post or by ordinary post*] on [*date of posting*] to the owner of the prospective servient tenement at [*state address*]."; or

"It has not been reasonably practicable to send a copy of this notice to the owner of the prospective servient tenement for the following reason: [*specify the reason*]".

6 The superior should not swear or affirm, or sign, until a copy of the notice has been sent (or otherwise) as mentioned in note 5. Before signing, the superior should swear or affirm before a notary public (or, if the notice is being completed outwith Scotland, before a person duly authorised under the local law to administer oaths or receive affirmations) that, to the best of the superior's knowledge and belief, all the information contained in the notice is true. The notary public should also sign. Swearing or affirming a statement which is known to be false or which is believed not to be true is a criminal offence under the False Oaths (Scotland) Act 1933. Normally the superior should swear or affirm, and sign, personally. If, however, the superior is legally disabled or incapable (for example, because of mental disorder) his legal representative should swear or affirm and sign. If the superior is not an individual (for example, if it is a company) a person entitled by law to sign formal documents on its behalf should swear or affirm and sign.

SCHEDULE 5B

(introduced by section 18B(1))

FORM OF NOTICE PROSPECTIVELY CONVERTING REAL BURDEN INTO ECONOMIC DEVELOPMENT BURDEN

"NOTICE PROSPECTIVELY CONVERTING REAL BURDEN INTO ECONOMIC DEVELOPMENT BURDEN

Superior:
(see note for completion 1)

Description of land which is to be servient tenement:
(see note for completion 2)

Terms of real burden:
(see note for completion 3)

Statement that purpose was to promote economic development:
(with supporting evidence: see note for completion 3)

Any counter obligation:
(see note for completion 3)

Title to the superiority:
(see note for completion 4)

Service:
(see note for completion 5)

Signature on behalf of superior:

Date: ."

Explanatory Note
(This explanation has no legal effect)

This notice is sent by your feudal superior; that is to say by [the Scottish Ministers] *or* [*specify local authority*]. By this notice the feudal superior asserts that at present your property is subject to a real burden enforceable by the superior and claims both the right to continue to enforce it, not as superior but in a personal capacity, and that the real burden is for the purpose of promoting economic development. The notice, if it is registered in the Land Register or Register of Sasines under section 18B of the Abolition of Feudal Tenure etc. (Scotland) Act 2000, will allow the superior to enforce that right after the feudal system is abolished (which will be shortly). If you think that there is a mistake in this notice or if you wish to challenge it, you are advised to contact your solicitor or other adviser.
Notes for completion of the notice
(These notes have no legal effect)

1 Insert "the Scottish Ministers" or as the case may be the name and address of the local authority.
2 Describe the land in a way that is sufficient to enable the Keeper to identify it by reference to the Ordnance Map. Where the title to the land has been registered in the Land Register the description should refer to the title number of the land or of the larger subjects of which the land forms part. Otherwise it should normally refer to and identify a deed recorded in a specified division of the Register of Sasines.
3 Specify by reference to the appropriate Register the deed or deeds in which the real burden or counter-obligation was imposed. Set out the terms of the real burden, or as the case may be the terms of the counter-obligation, in full or refer to the deed in such a way as to identify the real burden or counter-obligation. Provide the statement specified and set out any information which supports it.
4 Where the title has been registered in the Land Register of Scotland and the superior is—
    (a) registered as proprietor, specify the title number;
    (b) not so registered, specify the title number and set out the midcouples or links between the person last registered and the superior so as sufficiently to identify them.
Where the title has not been registered in the Land Register and the superior—
    (a) has a recorded title, specify by reference to the Register of Sasines the deed constituting the immediate title;
    (b) does not have a recorded title, either—
        (i) specify by reference to the Register of Sasines the deed constituting the immediate title of the person with the last recorded title and set out the midcouples or links between that person and the superior so as sufficiently to identify them; or
        (ii) if there is no such deed, specify the nature of the superior's title.
5 Do not complete until a copy of the notice has been sent to the owner of the prospective servient tenement (except in a case where such sending is not reasonably practicable). Then insert whichever is applicable of the following:
    "The superior has sent a copy of this notice by [*specify whether by recorded delivery or registered post or by ordinary post*] on [*date of posting*] to the owner of the prospective servient tenement at [*state address*]."; or
    "It has not been reasonably practicable to send a copy of this notice to the owner of the prospective servient tenement and the reason is that: [*specify the reason*]."

SCHEDULE 5C
(introduced by section 18C(1))

FORM OF NOTICE PROSPECTIVELY CONVERTING REAL BURDEN INTO HEALTH CARE BURDEN

"NOTICE PROSPECTIVELY CONVERTING REAL BURDEN INTO HEALTH CARE BURDEN

Superior:
(see note for completion 1)

Description of land which is to be servient tenement:
(see note for completion 2)

Terms of real burden:
(see note for completion 3)

Statement that purpose was to promote the provision of facilities for health care:
(with supporting evidence: see note for completion 3)

Any counter obligation:
(see note for completion 3)

Title to the superiority:
(see note for completion 4)

Service:
(see note for completion 5)

Signature on behalf of superior:

Date: ."

Explanatory Note
(This explanation has no legal effect)

This notice is sent by your feudal superior; that is to say by [the Scottish Ministers] *or* [*specify National Health Service trust*]. By this notice the feudal superior asserts that at present your property is subject to a real burden enforceable by the superior and claims both the right to continue to enforce it, not as superior but in a personal capacity, and that the real burden is for the purpose of promoting the provision of facilites for health care. The notice, if it is registered in the Land Register or Register of Sasines under section 18C of the Abolition of Feudal Tenure etc. (Scotland) Act 2000, will allow the superior to enforce that right after the feudal system is abolished (which will be shortly). If you think that there is a mistake in this notice or if you wish to challenge it, you are advised to contact your solicitor or other adviser.

Notes for completion of the notice
(These notes have no legal effect)

1 Insert "the Scottish Ministers" or as the case may be the name and address of the National Health Service trust.
2 Describe the land in a way that is sufficient to enable the Keeper to identify it by reference to the Ordnance Map. Where the title to the land has been registered in the Land Register the description should refer to the title number of the land or of the larger subjects of which the land forms part. Otherwise it should normally refer to and identify a deed recorded in a specified division of the Register of Sasines.
3 Specify by reference to the appropriate Register the deed or deeds in which the real burden or counter-obligation was imposed. Set out the terms of the real burden, or or as the case may be the terms of the counter-obligation, in full or refer to the deed in such a way as to

identify the real burden or counter-obligation. Provide the statement specified and set out any information which supports it.

4 Where the title has been registered in the Land Register of Scotland and the superior is—

(a) registered as proprietor, specify the title number;

(b) not so registered, specify the title number and set out the midcouples or links between the person last registered and the superior so as sufficiently to identify them.

Where the title has not been registered in the Land Register and the superior—

(a) has a recorded title, specify by reference to the Register of Sasines the deed constituting the immediate title;

(b) does not have a recorded title, either—

    (i) specify by reference to the Register of Sasines the deed constituting the immediate title of the person with the last recorded title and set out the midcouples or links between that person and the superior so as sufficiently to identify them; or

    (ii) if there is no such deed, specify the nature of the superior's title.

5 Do not complete until a copy of the notice has been sent to the owner of the prospective servient tenement (except in a case where such sending is not reasonably practicable). Then insert whichever is applicable of the following:

"The superior has sent a copy of this notice by [*specify whether by recorded delivery or registered post or by ordinary post*] on [*date of posting*] to the owner of the prospective servient tenement at [*state address*]."; or

"It has not been reasonably practicable to send a copy of this notice to the owner of the prospective servient tenement and the reason is that: [*specify the reason*].".".

17 In schedule 8 (form of notice preserving conservation body's or Scottish Ministers' right to real burden), for note 1 of the notes for completion of the notice there shall be substituted—

"1 In the case of a conservation body, insert the year and number of the relevant statutory instrument and the name and address of that body.".".

18 After schedule 8 there shall be inserted—

"SCHEDULE 8A

(introduced by section 27A(1))

FORM OF NOTICE NOMINATING CONSERVATION BODY OR SCOTTISH MINISTERS TO HAVE TITLE TO ENFORCE REAL BURDEN

"NOTICE NOMINATING CONSERVATION BODY OR SCOTTISH MINISTERS TO HAVE TITLE TO ENFORCE REAL BURDEN

Superior:

Nominee (being a conservation body or the Scottish Ministers):
(see note for completion 1)

Description of land subject to the real burden:
(see note for completion 2)

Terms of real burden:
(see note for completion 3)

Any counter-obligation:
(see note for completion 3)

Title to the superiority:
(see notes for completion 4 and 5)

Service:
(see note for completion 6)

Signature of superior:
(see note for completion 7)

Signature of consenting nominee:
(see note for completion 8)

Signature of superior's witness:

Name and address of witness:

Signature of nominee's witness:

Name and address of witness:

Date: .''

Explanatory note
(This explanation has no legal effect)

This notice is sent by your feudal superior. At present the use of your property is subject to certain burdens and conditions enforceable by the feudal superior. The feudal system is shortly to be abolished. The feudal superior intends to nominate a conservation body or the Scottish Ministers to have title to enforce certain of those burdens (referred to prospectively as "conservation burdens") when he ceases to have such title. These are burdens which have been imposed in the public interest for the preservation or protection either of architectural or historic characteristics of land or of some other special characteristic of land derived from the flora, fauna or general appearance of the land. By virtue of this notice the nominee would have the right to enforce a conservation burden in the capacity of conservation body or of the Scottish Ministers, as the case may be. The notice, if it is registered in the Land Register of Scotland or recorded in the Register of Sasines under section 27A of the Abolition of Feudal Tenure etc. (Scotland) Act 2000, will allow the burden to be so enforced after the feudal system has been abolished. If you think there is a mistake in this notice or if you wish to challenge it, you are advised to consult your solicitor or other adviser.

Notes for completion of the notice
(These notes have no legal effect)

1 In the case of a conservation body, insert the year and number of the relevant statutory instrument and the name and address of that body.
2 Describe the land in a way that is sufficient to enable the Keeper to identify it by reference to the Ordnance Map. Where the title to the land has been registered in the Land Register the description should refer to the title number of the land or of the larger subjects of which the land forms part. Otherwise it should normally refer to and identify a deed recorded in a specified division of the Register of Sasines.
3 Specify by reference to the appropriate Register the deed or deeds in which the real burden or counter-obligation was imposed. Set out the real burden or counter-obligation in full or refer to the deed in such a way as to identify the real burden or counter-obligation.
4 Where the title has been registered in the Land Register of Scotland and the superior is—
    (a) infeft, specify the title number;
    (b) uninfeft, specify the title number and set out the midcouples or links between the person last infeft and the superior so as sufficiently to identify them.
5 Where the title has not been registered in the Land Register and the superior—
    (a) has a recorded title, specify by reference to the Register of Sasines the deed constituting the immediate title;
    (b) does not have a recorded title, either—
        (i) specify by reference to the Register of Sasines the deed constituting the immediate title of the person last infeft and set out the midcouples or links between the person last infeft and the superior so as sufficiently to identify them; or
        (ii) if there is no such deed, specify the nature of the superior's title.
6 Do not complete until a copy of the notice has been sent to the owner of the land subject to the burden (except in a case where this is not reasonably practicable). Then insert whichever is applicable of the following:
    "The superior has sent a copy of this notice by [*specify whether by recorded delivery or registered post or by ordinary post*] on [*date of posting*] to the owner of the land subject to the real burden at [*state address*]."; or

"It has not been reasonably practicable to send a copy of this notice to the owner of the land subject to the real burden for the following reason: [*specify the reason*]."
7 The notice should not be signed by the superior until a copy of it has been sent (or otherwise) as mentioned in note 6.
8 The nominee should sign, so as to indicate consent, before that copy is sent (or otherwise) as so mentioned.".

19 After schedule 11 there shall be inserted—

"SCHEDULE 11A
(introduced by section 65A(1))

FORM OF NOTICE PROSPECTIVELY CONVERTING SPORTING RIGHTS INTO TENEMENT IN LAND

"NOTICE PROSPECTIVELY CONVERTING SPORTING RIGHTS INTO TENEMENT IN LAND

Superior:
(see note for completion 1)

Description of land subject to sporting rights:
(see note for completion 2)

Description of sporting rights:
(see note for completion 3)

Any counter-obligation:
(see note for completion 3)

Title to the superiority:
(see note for completion 4)

Service:
(see note for completion 5)

I swear [*or* affirm] that the information contained in this notice is, to the best of my knowledge and belief, true.

Signature of superior:
(see note for completion 6)

Signature of notary public:

Date: ."

Explanatory note
(This explanation has no legal effect)

This notice is sent by your feudal superior. By it the feudal superior asserts that at present your property is subject to certain sporting rights (that is to say, to rights of fishing or game) enforceable by him as superior and he seeks to continue to enjoy those rights on a different basis: that is to say, as a tenement in land. The notice, if it is registered in the Land Register of Scotland or recorded in the Register of Sasines under section 65A of the Abolition of Feudal Tenure etc. (Scotland) Act 2000, will have that effect when (shortly) the feudal system is abolished. If you think there is a mistake in this notice or if you wish to challenge it, you are advised to consult your solicitor or other adviser.

Notes for completion of the notice
(These notes have no legal effect)

1 Insert name and address of superior.

2 Describe the land in a way that is sufficient to enable the Keeper to identify it by reference to the Ordnance Map. Where the title to the land has been registered in the Land Register the description should refer to the title number of the land or of the larger subjects of which the land forms part. Otherwise it should normally refer to and identify a deed recorded in a specified division of the Register of Sasines.

3 Specify by reference to the appropriate Register the deed or deeds in which the sporting rights were reserved or the counter-obligation was imposed. Describe the sporting rights or set out the counter-obligation in full or refer to the deed in such a way as to identify those rights or that counter-obligation.

4 Where the title has been registered in the Land Register of Scotland and the superior is—

   (a) infeft, specify the title number;
   (b) uninfeft, specify the title number and set out the midcouples or links between the person last infeft and the superior so as sufficiently to identify them.

Where the title has not been registered in the Land Register and the superior—

   (a) has a recorded title, specify by reference to the Register of Sasines the deed constituting the immediate title;
   (b) does not have a recorded title, either—

      (i) specify by reference to the Register of Sasines the deed constituting the immediate title of the person last infeft and set out the midcouples or links between the person last infeft and the superior so as sufficiently to identify them; or
      (ii) if there is no such deed, specify the nature of the superior's title.

5 Do not complete until a copy of the notice has been sent to the owner of the land subject to the sporting rights (except in a case where this is not reasonably practicable). Then insert whichever is applicable of the following:

   "The superior has sent a copy of this notice by [*specify whether by recorded delivery or registered post or by ordinary post*] on [*date of posting*] to the owner of the land subject to the sporting rights at [*state address*]".; or

   "It has not been reasonably practicable to send a copy of this notice to the owner of the land subject to the sporting rights for the following reason: [*specify the reason*]".

6 The notice should not be signed by the superior until a copy of it has been sent (or otherwise) as mentioned in note 5. Before signing, the superior should swear or affirm before a notary public (or, if the notice is being completed outwith Scotland, before a person duly authorised under the local law to administer oaths or receive affirmations) that, to the best of the superior's knowledge and belief, all the information contained in the notice is true. The notary public should also sign. Swearing or affirming a statement which is known to be false or which is believed not to be true is a criminal offence under the False Oaths (Scotland) Act 1933. Normally the superior should swear or affirm, and sign, personally. If, however, the superior is legally disabled or incapable (for example, because of mental disorder) his legal representative should swear or affirm and sign. If the superior is not an individual (for example, if it is a company) a person entitled by law to sign formal documents on its behalf should swear or affirm and sign.".

20 In schedule 12 (minor and consequential amendments), in paragraph 9(17), for the word "offences" there shall be substituted "offices".

SCHEDULE 14
(introduced by section 128(1))

MINOR AND CONSEQUENTIAL AMENDMENTS

Registration of Leases (Scotland) Act 1857 (c.26)

1—(1) Section 3 of the Registration of Leases (Scotland) Act 1857 (assignation of recorded, or registered, leases etc.) shall be amended in accordance with this paragraph.

(2) In subsection (2)—

   (a) the existing words "to impose conditions and make stipulations" shall become paragraph (i); and
   (b) after that paragraph there shall be inserted the word "or" and the following paragraph—

      "(ii) to import such conditions and stipulations,".

(3) After subsection (2) there shall be inserted—

"(2A) Any person entitled to grant an assignation under this section may—

    (a)   execute a deed containing such conditions, or stipulations, as may be specified in an assignation under subsection (2) above; and

    (b)   register such conditions and stipulations in the Land Register of Scotland or, as the case may be, record the deed in the Register of Sasines,

    and, subject to subsection (2C) below, on such registration or, as the case may be, recording such conditions and stipulations shall be effectual.

(2B) "Import" in subsection (2)(ii) above means to import into itself from a deed of conditions ("deed of conditions" having the meaning given by section 122(1) of the Title Conditions (Scotland) Act 2003 (asp 9)) the terms of the conditions or stipulations; and importation in or as nearly as may be in the form set out in schedule 1 to that Act (but with the modification that for the references in that form to the terms of the title conditions there are substituted references to the terms of the conditions or stipulations) shall suffice in that regard.

(2C) Where, notwithstanding section 3(4) of the Land Registration (Scotland) Act 1979 (c.33) (creation of real right or obligation on date of registration etc.), a deed provides for the postponement of effectiveness of any conditions or, as the case may be, stipulations to—

    (a)   a date specified in that deed (the specification being of a fixed date and not, for example, of a date determinable by reference to the occurrence of an event); or

    (b)   the date of—

        (i)   registration of an interest in land under; or

        (ii) recording of,

some other deed so specified,

the conditions, or stipulations, shall take effect in accordance with such provision.".

(4) In subsection (3), after the word "(2)" there shall be inserted "or (2A)".

(5) In subsection (4), after the word "assignation"—

    (a)   where it first occurs, there shall be inserted ", or as the case may be in a deed such as is mentioned in subsection (2A) above,"; and

    (b)   where it secondly occurs, there shall be inserted ", or as the case may be the deed,".

Titles to Land Consolidation (Scotland) Act 1868 (c.101)

2 In section 138 of the Titles to Land Consolidation (Scotland) Act 1868 (use in any deed of short clauses of consent to registration), for the words "forms Nos. 1 and 2" there shall be substituted "form No.1".

Conveyancing (Scotland) Act 1924 (c.27)

3—(1) The Conveyancing (Scotland) Act 1924 shall be amended in accordance with this paragraph.

(2) In section 8(5) (application of Schedule D to the Act), for the words "Schedule H of the Conveyancing (Scotland) Act 1874" there shall be substituted "schedule 1 to the Title Conditions (Scotland) Act 2003 (asp 9)".

(3) In section 40(2) (powers of creditor), after the word "conditions" there shall be inserted "(whether or not by creating a real burden)".

Conveyancing and Feudal Reform (Scotland) Act 1970 (c.35)

4—(1) The Conveyancing and Feudal Reform (Scotland) Act 1970 shall be amended in accordance with this paragraph.

(2) In section 9 (which introduces the standard security)—

    (a)   after subsection (2A) there shall be inserted—

        "(2B) It shall not be competent to grant a standard security over a personal pre-emption burden or personal redemption burden (both within the meaning of Part 4 of the Abolition of Feudal Tenure etc. (Scotland) Act 2000 (asp 5).";; and

    (b)   in subsection (8)(b), for the definition of "interest in land" there shall be substituted—

        ""real right in land" means any such right, other than ownership or a real burden, which is capable of being held separately and to which a title may be recorded in the Register of Sasines;".

(3) In section 19 (calling-up of standard security), in subsection (4), for the words "infeft in" there shall be substituted "having title to".

(4) In section 19A(1) (notice to occupier of calling up), for the words "an interest" there shall be substituted "land or a real right".

(5) In section 24(3) (application by creditor for remedies on default), for the words "an interest" there shall be substituted "land or a real right".

Prescription and Limitation (Scotland) Act 1973 (c.52)

5—(1) The Prescription and Limitation (Scotland) Act 1973 shall be amended in accordance with this paragraph.

(2) In section 1 (prescriptive period in relation to real rights in land), in subsection (3), after the word "to", where it fourthly occurs, there shall be inserted "real burdens,".

(3) In Schedule 1 (obligations affected by prescriptive periods of five years under section 6 of the Act)—

(a) in paragraph 1(a)(vii), for the words "land obligation" there shall be substituted "title condition"; and

(b) for paragraph 4 there shall be substituted—

"4 In this Schedule, "title condition" shall be construed in accordance with section 122(1) of the Title Conditions (Scotland) Act 2003 (asp 9).".

(4) In Schedule 3 (rights and obligations which are imprescriptible for certain purposes of the Act), in sub-paragraph (h), for the word "interest" there shall be substituted "real right".

Land Tenure Reform (Scotland) Act 1974 (c.38)

6—In section 2 of the Land Tenure Reform (Scotland) Act 1974 (prohibition of new ground annuals and other periodical payments from land)—

(a) in subsection (1), for the words "land obligation" there shall be substituted "title condition"; and

(b) after subsection (2) there shall be added—

"(3) In subsection (1) above, "title condition" has the meaning given by section 122(1) of the Title Conditions (Scotland) Act 2003 (asp 9).".

Land Registration (Scotland) Act 1979 (c.33)

7—(1) The 1979 Act shall be amended in accordance with this paragraph.

(2) In each of sections 2(6) (interpretation) and 3(1) (effect of registration), for the words "sections 17, 18 and" there shall be substituted "section".

(3) In section 3(6) (special provision as respects completion of title)—

(a) for the words "an uninfeft proprietor" there shall be substituted "an unregistered holder";

(b) for the words "the uninfeft proprietor" there shall be substituted "him";

(c) for the word "infeft" there shall be substituted "registered as entitled to the interest"; and

(d) for the words from "section 4" to "land", where it secondly occurs, there shall be substituted "—

(a) section 4 of the Conveyancing (Scotland) Act 1924 (c.27);

(b) section 18A(8)(a) of the Abolition of Feudal Tenure etc. (Scotland) Act 2000 (asp 5); and

(c) section 41(a) of the Title Conditions (Scotland) Act 2003 (asp 9),

(each of which relate to completion of title) shall be of no effect in relation to such an interest in land.".

(4) In section 6 (the title sheet), at the end there is added—

"(6) In subsections (1)(e) and (2) above, "condition" includes a servitude created by a deed registered in accordance with section 75(1) of the Title Conditions (Scotland) Act 2003 (asp 9) and a rule of a development management scheme ("development management scheme" being construed in accordance with section 71 of that Act).".

(5) In section 12 (indemnity in respect of loss)—

(a) in subsection (3), after paragraph (g) there shall be inserted—

"(gg) the loss arises from inability to enforce sporting rights converted into a tenement in land by virtue of section 65A of the Abolition of Feudal Tenure etc. (Scotland) Act 2000 (asp 5), unless the Keeper expressly assumes responsibility for the enforceability of those rights;"; and

(b) at the end there is added—

"(5) In subsection (3)(g) above, "condition" includes a rule of a development management scheme ("development management scheme" being construed in accordance with section 71 of the Title Conditions (Scotland) Act 2003 (asp 9)).".

(6) In section 15 (simplification of deeds relating to registered interests), for subsection (3) there shall be substituted—

"(3) It shall not be necessary, in any deed relating to a registered interest in land, to deduce title if evidence of sufficient midcouples or links between the unregistered holder and the person last registered as entitled to the interest are produced to the Keeper on registration in respect of that interest in land.".

(7) In section 28(1) (interpretation)—

   (a) in the definition of "incorporeal heritable right"—

       (i) the existing words "a right to salmon fishings" shall become paragraph (a);

       (ii) after that paragraph there shall be inserted the word "; or" and the following paragraph—

          "(b) sporting rights (as defined by section 65A(9) of the Abolition of Feudal Tenure etc. (Scotland) Act 2000 (asp 5));"; and

   (b) in paragraph (d) of the definition of "overriding interest", for the words "a servitude" there shall be substituted "any servitude which was not created by registration in accordance with section 75(1) of the Title Conditions (Scotland) Act 2003 (asp 9)".

Ancient Monuments and Archaeological Areas Act 1979 (c.46)

8—In section 17 of the Ancient Monuments and Archaeological Areas Act 1979 (agreements concerning ancient monuments and land in their vicinity), for subsection (7) there shall be substituted—

   "(7) Section 84 of the Law of Property Act 1925 (c.20) (power of Lands Tribunal to discharge or modify restrictive covenant) shall not apply to an agreement under this section.".

Health and Social Services and Social Security Adjudications Act 1983 (c.41)

9—In section 23 of the Health and Social Services and Social Security Adjudications Act 1983 (arrears of contributions secured over interest in land in Scotland)—

   (a) in subsection (1)(b)—

       (i) after the word "Scotland" (and within the parentheses) there shall be inserted " "an interest in land" meaning land or,"; and

       (ii) after the words "1970" (and within the parentheses) there shall be inserted ", a real right in land"; and

   (b) for subsection (4) there shall be substituted—

   "(4) Where an interest in land (as defined in subsection (1)(b) above) over which a charging order is made is an interest to which the debtor does not have a completed title, the order shall be as valid as if the debtor had such title.".

Further and Higher Education (Scotland) Act 1992 (c.37)

10—In Schedule 3 to the Further and Higher Education (Scotland) Act 1992 (transfer and apportionment of property)—

   (a) in paragraph 1—

       (i) in each of sub-paragraphs (2) and (3), for the words "land obligations" there shall be substituted "title conditions"; and

       (ii) for sub-paragraph (5) there shall be substituted—

       "(5) In this Schedule, "title conditions" has the meaning given by section 122(1) of the Title Conditions (Scotland) Act 2003 (asp 9)."; and

   (b) in paragraph 4(6), for the words "land obligations" there shall be substituted "title conditions".

Crofters (Scotland) Act 1993 (c.44)

11—In section 16(6) of the Crofters (Scotland) Act 1993 (provisions relating to conveyance), for the words "land obligations as defined in section 1(2) of the Conveyancing and Feudal Reform (Scotland) Act 1970" there shall be substituted "title conditions, within the meaning given by section 122(1) of the Title Conditions (Scotland) Act 2003 (asp 9),".

Standards in Scotland's Schools etc. Act 2000 (asp 6)

12—In section 58(1) of the Standards in Scotland's Schools etc. Act 2000 (interpretation), in the definition of "land", for the words "land obligations (as defined in section 2(6) of the Conveyancing and Feudal Reform (Scotland) Act 1970 (c.35)" there shall be substituted "title conditions, within the meaning given by section 122(1) of the Title Conditions (Scotland) Act 2003 (asp 9)".

13—In each of sections 1(1) (application to suspend enforcement of standard security) and 4(4) (notices to proprietors and occupiers) of the Mortgage Rights (Scotland) Act 2001, for the words "an interest" there shall be substituted "land or a real right".

SCHEDULE 15
(introduced by section 128)

REPEALS

Enactment	Extent of repeal
Registration Act 1617 (c.16) (Act of the Parliaments of Scotland)	The words from "It is", where they first occur, to "improving"; and the words from "It is", where they thirdly occur, to "sufficient".
Redemptions Act 1661 (c.247) (Act of the Parliaments of Scotland)	The whole Act.
Registration of Leases (Scotland) Act 1857 (c.26)	Section 3(5).
Conveyancing (Scotland) Act 1874 (c.94)	Section 32. Schedule H.
Conveyancing (Scotland) Act 1924 (c.27)	Section 9. Section 40(3). In Schedule B, in Form No 1, the words "there are"; and the words from "and have entered" to "and others which affect the land or any part thereof". Schedule E. In Schedule O, the words "with a warrant of registration".
Church of Scotland (Property and Endowments) Act 1925 (c.33)	Section 22(2)(h).
Church of Scotland (Property and Endowments) (Amendment) Act 1933 (c.44)	In section 9(3), the words from "at such price" to the end.
Conveyancing Amendment (Scotland) Act 1938 (c.24)	Section 9.
Conveyancing and Feudal Reform (Scotland) Act 1970 (c.35)	Sections 1, 2 and 7. In section 53(4), the definition of "prescribed". Schedule 1.
Land Tenure Reform (Scotland) Act 1974 (c.38)	In section 19, the words "and section 2(4) of the said Act of 1970" and "in both of those provisions,".
Land Registration (Scotland) Act 1979 (c.33)	In section 15(2), paragraph (a); and the words "; and (b)" immediately following that paragraph. Sections 17 and 18.
Aviation Security Act 1982 (c.36)	In Schedule 1, in paragraph 5(b), the words "to a feuduty or ground annual or".
Housing (Scotland) Act 1987 (c.26)	Section 72(7).

Aviation and Maritime Security Act 1990 (c.31)	In Schedule 2, in paragraph 5(b), the words "to a feuduty or ground annual or".
Enterprise and New Towns (Scotland) Act 1990 (c.35)	In section 32(3), the words "as is mentioned in section 8(6) of this Act".
Further and Higher Education (Scotland) Act 1992 (c.37)	In Schedule 3, in paragraph 2(3), the words ", feuduties, stipend".
Requirements of Writing (Scotland) Act 1995 (c.7)	Section 13(2).
Abolition of Feudal Tenure etc. (Scotland) Act 2000 (asp 5)	In section 17(1), the words "23,". Section 20(8)(b) and (c). Section 23. In section 24, the words "and 23". Section 26. In section 28, the words "Subject to section 31 of this Act,". Sections 29 to 32. In section 46(1), the words "or 20(8)(b) or (c)". In section 49, in the definition of "real burden", paragraph (a)(iii). Section 60(2). In section 77, in subsection (2), the words "Subject to subsection (4)(c) and (d) below,"; and in subsection (4), paragraphs (c) and (d) and the words from "but" to the end. In schedule 8, in the explanatory note, the words "or that a conservation body shall enforce those burdens on their behalf". In schedule 12, paragraphs 2 and 7(6); in paragraph 9, in sub-paragraph (4)(d)(ii), the word "shall" and sub-paragraphs (8) and (21); paragraphs 15(8), 16(2)(a), 18(3) and 30(2), (3), (5), (6)(d)(ii) and (22); and, in paragraph 39, head (c) of sub-paragraph (3) (and the word "and" immediately preceding that head) and sub-paragraph (6). Schedule 13 in so far as it relates to section 32 of and Schedule H to the Conveyancing (Scotland) Act 1874; to section 9 of the Conveyancing (Scotland) Act 1924; to section 22(2)(h) of the Church of Scotland (Property and Endowments) Act 1925; to section 2 of and Schedule 1 to the Conveyancing and Feudal Reform (Scotland) Act 1970; and to sections 3(6) and 15(2)(a) of the Land Registration (Scotland) Act 1979.

TENEMENTS (SCOTLAND) ACT 2004

(asp 11)

CONTENTS

The Bill for this Act of the Scottish Parliament was passed by the Parliament on 16th September 2004 and received Royal Assent on 22nd October 2004

An Act of the Scottish Parliament to make provision about the boundaries and pertinents of properties comprised in tenements and for the regulation of the rights and duties of the owners of properties comprised in tenements; to make minor amendments of the Title Conditions (Scotland) Act 2003 (asp 9); and for connected purposes.

INTRODUCTION AND GENERAL NOTE

The Tenements (Scotland) Act 2004 received Royal Assent on October 22, 2004. The main provisions of the Act came into effect on November 28, 2004. In many other jurisdictions there are extensive statutory codes relating to flatted properties and condominiums. The Scottish law of the tenement was largely set out in the 19th century although tenements existed in Scotland as early as the 16th century. It has long been recognised that the existing common law of the tenement is largely unworkable relying as it does on the law of common interest and treating the tenement as a series of arbitrary pieces. Thus the owner of the top flat owns the roof and the roof void subject to the common interest of the others in the tenement. (*Taylor v Dunlop* (1872) 11 R 25; *Sanderson's Trustees v Yule* (1897) 25 R 211). The interaction of the law of the tenement and the law of common interest has meant that the owner of the top flat has an obligation to maintain the roof so as to provide shelter for the lower flats. In many cases however the common law of the tenement is altered by specific provision in the title deeds. The normal title regime is to make structural parts of the tenement such as the roof, foundations, solum, passages and stairs, outside walls and pipes, drains and other services common. However the law of common property has its own difficulties the main one being that each common owner has a right to a voice in any decision relating to the common property. It is true that where a repair is absolutely essential any one common owner can insist on it being done but deciding what repairs are essential and what might be regarded as more routine has always been difficult (see *Rafique v Amin*, 1997 S.L.T. 1385). There is no doubt that a badly managed tenement is almost bound to be a poorly repaired tenement.

Although the 2004 Act is the last of three significant pieces of property law legislation (the Abolition of Feudal Tenure etc (Scotland) Act 2000 and the Title Conditions (Scotland) Act 2003 are the other two), the Scottish Law Commission published a discussion paper on the law of the tenement as early as 1990 (discussion paper No. 91 (1990)). A report followed in 1998 (Scot Law Com No. 162) and in March 2003 the Scottish Executive published a consultation paper. Responses were sought by July and in September 2003 these were published. On January 30, 2004 the Tenements (Scotland) Bill was presented to the Scottish Parliament.

The Act has 34 sections and 4 schedules. Sections 1–3 deal with the legal boundaries in a tenement and the ancillary pertinent rights which attach to each unit. Section 4 contains the provisions relating to the tenement management scheme and schedule 1 contains the rules of the scheme. Sections 5 and 6 provide for applications to the sheriff in relation to the annulment of decisions and the resolution of disputes. Sections 7–10 contain provisions which replace the existing common law rules of common interest with statutory obligations of support and shelter. Sections 11–17 contain provisions in relation to costs, liabilities and rights of access. Section 18 imposes an obligation on the owners of units to insure their properties. Section 19 contains a statutory provision in relation to the installation of service pipes, cables and other equipment. One of the difficulties which has arisen in the past relates to the site of demolished tenements and abandoned or partially abandoned tenemental property. Sections 20–23 contain provisions which will allow the majority of owners of units in a tenement to deal with demolition, use and disposal of the site or building. Section 24 creates a liability to a non-owner for certain damage costs. Sections 25–34 are miscellaneous, general and interpretation sections. There are several amendments to the Title Conditions (Scotland) Act 2003 which are contained in Schedule 4. The most important of these is an amendment to section 53 of the 2003 Act which has proved almost impossible to interpret. Where related properties are subject to a common scheme in terms of section 53 it will not now be necessary to identify all the benefited properties subject to the common scheme nor will dual registration against the titles of both burdened and benefited properties be necessary. Schedule 1 contains the tenement management scheme as applied by section 4. Schedule 2 contains the forms of notice for potential liability for costs. The fact that a new owner might be liable for costs incurred during a previous party's time of ownership caused difficulty and was subject to a late amendment requiring notice of a potential liability to be registered. Schedule 3 contains provisions in relation to applications for power to sell sites of former tenements or abandoned tenements. Schedule 4 contains amendments to the Title Conditions (Scotland) Act 2003.

Boundaries and pertinents

Determination of boundaries and pertinents

1.—(1) Except in so far as any different boundaries or pertinents are constituted by virtue of the title to the tenement, or any enactment, the boundaries and pertinents of sectors of a tenement shall be determined in accordance with sections 2 and 3 of this Act.

(2) In this Act, "title to the tenement" means—

(a) any conveyance, or reservation, of property which affects—
    (i) the tenement; or
    (ii) any sector in the tenement; and
(b) where an interest in—
    (i) the tenement; or
    (ii) any sector in the tenement,

has been registered in the Land Register of Scotland, the title sheet of that interest.

GENERAL NOTE

The approach taken in the Act in relation to ownership is to retain the common law. At first glance this may seem odd. A more radical approach would have meant, for example, that all parts of a tenement would be declared to be common property. Where the titles did not themselves alter the common law that would have resulted in a substantial re-distribution of ownership within the tenement. Some parties would have lost property rights and others would have gained property rights. It was felt that there could be a significant risk of a challenge under Article 1 of Protocol 1 of the European Convention on Human Rights. Accordingly sections 1 to 3 of the 2004 Act effectively re-state the common law rules of ownership with clarification. The radical change comes with the statutory maintenance obligations which are no longer tied to ownership.

Subs.(1)

Where the title provides for ownership to be split in a particular way then the title will rule. The new provisions only apply where the title is silent or deficient.

Subs.(2)

Title to a tenement is defined as any conveyance or reservation of property which affects the tenement or any sector in the tenement or the title sheet of any interest in the tenement or any such sector.

Tenement boundaries

2.—(1) Subject to subsections (3) to (7) below, the boundary between any two contiguous sectors is the median of the structure that separates them; and a sector—

(a) extends in any direction to such a boundary; or
(b) if it does not first meet such a boundary—
    (i) extends to and includes the solum or any structure which is an outer surface of
    the tenement building; or
    (ii) extends to the boundary that separates the sector from a contiguous building which is not part of the tenement building.

(2) For the purposes of subsection (1) above, where the structure separating two contiguous sectors is or includes something (as for example, but without prejudice to the generality of this subsection, a door or window) which wholly or mainly serves only one of those sectors, the thing is in its entire thickness part of that sector.

(3) A top flat extends to and includes the roof over that flat.

(4) A bottom flat extends to and includes the solum under that flat.

(5) A close extends to and includes the roof over, and the solum under, the close.

(6) Where a sector includes the solum (or any part of it) the sector shall also include, subject to subsection (7) below, the airspace above the tenement building and directly over the solum (or part).

(7) Where the roof of the tenement building slopes, a sector which includes the roof (or any part of it) shall also include the airspace above the slope of the roof (or part) up to the level of the highest point of the roof.

GENERAL NOTE

This section is a re-statement of the existing law of the tenement. Middle lines are in general the boundaries between flats. The Act uses the term "sector" which is defined as meaning a flat, any close or lift or any other three dimensional space not comprehended by a flat, close or lift (s.29(1)).

Subs.(1)

The boundary between any two contiguous sectors is the middle line of the structure that separates them. Where the boundary is an external part of the building such as an exterior wall or foundations and the solum then the whole wall or solum adjacent or subjacent to that flat or sector will be within the ownership of that flat or sector.

Subs.(2)

Doors or windows or other features which wholly or mainly serve one of the sectors such as a door in a close leading to a flat are owned exclusively by the flat or other sector which is served by that feature.

Subs.(3)

Where the titles are silent the top flat extends to and includes the roof over the flat. The words "extends to" necessarily imply that where the titles are silent any attic or roof space will also pertain to the top flat. Subs (7) contains special provision in relation to sloping roofs.

Subs.(4)

If the titles are silent the bottom flat extends to and includes the solum under that flat. This necessarily implies that any foundations will also be within the ownership of the bottom flat.

Subs.(5)

A close is defined as a connected passage, stairs and landings within a tenement building which together constitute a common access to two or more of the flats (s.29(1)). A close, as defined, extends to include the roof over and the solum under the close. A close is a sector of the tenement and accordingly where a flat wall bounds with a close and the close is common the boundary will be the middle line. If the titles are silent concerning ownership of the close then it will become a common pertinent (s.3(1)(a)).

Subs.(6)

Subject to the special provisions in subs (7) airspace above the tenement building will go with ownership of the solum or share in the solum if it is in common ownership.

Subs.(7)

There have always been problems concerning dormer windows. Even where the titles are silent and existing common law therefore implies that ownership of the roof pertains to the top flat the throwing out of a dormer presents problems if the airspace above the roof is in the ownership of the ground flat. Accordingly there is a specific provision to the effect that where the roof of a tenement building slopes a sector such as a top flat which includes the roof or any part of the roof also includes the triangle of airspace above the slope of the roof up to the highest point of the roof which would normally be the ridge. This will allow an owner of the top flat who owns the roof to throw out a dormer in that triangle of airspace. If the titles provide that the roof is common then the normal rules of common property will apply and the owner of the top flat will not be able to throw out a dormer or otherwise interfere with the roof without the consent of all the common owners. This would be an interference with the common roof. If the roof is common the triangle of airspace is also common.

Pertinents

3.—(1) Subject to subsection (2) below, there shall attach to each of the flats, as a pertinent, a right of common property in (and in the whole of) the following parts of a tenement—
 (a) a close;
 (b) a lift by means of which access can be obtained to more than one of the flats.
 (2) If a close or lift does not afford a means of access to a flat then there shall not attach to that flat, as a pertinent, a right of common property in the close or, as the case may be, lift.
 (3) Any land (other than the solum of the tenement building) pertaining to a tenement shall attach as a pertinent to the bottom flat most nearly adjacent to the land (or part of the land); but this subsection shall not apply to any part which constitutes a path, outside stair or other way affording access to any sector other than that flat.
 (4) If a tenement includes any part (such as, for example, a path, outside stair, fire escape, rhone, pipe, flue, conduit, cable, tank or chimney stack) that does not fall within subsection (1) or (3) above and that part—
 (a) wholly serves one flat, then it shall attach as a pertinent to that flat;
 (b) serves two or more flats, then there shall attach to each of the flats served, as a pertinent, a right of common property in (and in the whole of) the part.
 (5) For the purposes of this section, references to rights of common property being attached to flats as pertinents are references to there attaching to each flat equal rights of common property; except that where the common property is a chimney stack the share allocated to a flat shall be determined in direct accordance with the ratio which the number of flues serving it in the stack bears to the total number of flues in the stack.

GENERAL NOTE

 Although the Act leaves common law of the tenement intact so far as rights of exclusive ownership are concerned where the titles are silent the Bill provides that certain pertinents will attach to each unit. The law of pertinents has been described as both confused and confusing (Halliday, *Conveyancing Law and Practice* (2nd ed.) 33–38). The law of pertinents is clarified so far as tenemental property is concerned. Pertinents are defined and created as common property. The scheme of the Act is to apply a service test. Whether something is a commonly owned pertinent will depend on whether or not the pertinent can be said to benefit or service more than one flat. The Scottish Law Commission proposed that each flat would have an equal share in all those parts of the tenement which served that flat. This would include common passages and stairs, pipes, cables, drains and other services.

Subs.(1)

 Each flat has a right of common property, as a pertinent, in any close or any lift by means of which access can be obtained to more than one of these flats. The definition of a close as including stairs and landings should be borne in mind.

Subs.(2)

If the close or lift does not afford a means of access to a particular flat then that flat does not have the benefit of this pertinent. If should be borne in mind of course that the provisions in relation to pertinents only apply where the titles are silent. It may be that the titles will provide, for example, that a lift is to be common property notwithstanding the fact that the ground floor proprietors will never use it.

Subs.(3)

The Scottish Law Commission recommended that the common law position relating to garden ground should prevail so in the absence of any specific provision in the titles such ground will be owned by the ground floor flat or flats except where any part of the ground constitutes a path, outside stair or other means of owning access to any other sector other than the ground flat.

Subs (4)

The service test is applied to paths, outside stairs and other services which are not common pertinents to all flats. Such parts may be exclusive to a particular flat in which case they will attach to that flat and that flat alone. If these parts serve two or more flats then they attach to the flats which are served.

Subs.(5)

Where the statutory provisions apply and a pertinent attaches to a particular flat as a right of common property then the share of common property applying to each flat is deemed to be an equal share with the other flats. The only exception to this is where the common property is a chimney stack in which case the share allocated to a flat is determined in accordance with the ratio which is the number of flues serving that flat in the stack bears to the total number of flues in the stack.

Tenement Management Scheme

Application of the Tenement Management Scheme

4.—(1) The Tenement Management Scheme (referred to in this section as "the Scheme"), which is set out in schedule 1 to this Act, shall apply in relation to a tenement to the extent provided by the following provisions of this section.

(2) The Scheme shall not apply in any period during which the development management scheme applies to the tenement by virtue of section 71 of the Title Conditions (Scotland) Act 2003 (asp 9).

(3) The provisions of rule 1 of the Scheme shall apply, so far as relevant, for the purpose of interpreting any other provision of the Scheme which applies to the tenement.

(4) Rule 2 of the Scheme shall apply unless—

(a) a tenement burden provides procedures for the making of decisions by the owners; and

(b) the same such procedures apply as respects each flat.

(5) The provisions of rule 3 of the Scheme shall apply to the extent that there is no tenement burden enabling the owners to make scheme decisions on any matter on which a scheme decision may be made by them under that rule.

(6) Rule 4 of the Scheme shall apply in relation to any scheme costs incurred in relation to any part of the tenement unless a tenement burden provides that the entire liability for those scheme costs (in so far as liability for those costs is not to be met by someone other than an owner) is to be met by one or more of the owners.

(7) The provisions of rule 5 of the Scheme shall apply to the extent that there is no tenement burden making provision as to the liability of the owners in the circumstances covered by the provisions of that rule.

(8) The provisions of rule 6 of the Scheme shall apply to the extent that there is no tenement burden making provision as to the effect of any procedural irregularity in the making of a scheme decision on—

   (a) the validity of the decision; or

   (b) the liability of any owner affected by the decision.

   (9) Rule 7 of the Scheme shall apply to the extent that there is no tenement burden making provision—

   (a) for an owner to instruct or carry out any emergency work as defined in that rule; or

   (b) as to the liability of the owners for the cost of any emergency work as so defined.

   (10) The provisions of—

   (a) rule 8; and

   (b) subject to subsection (11) below, rule 9,

of the Scheme shall apply, so far as relevant, for the purpose of supplementing any other provision of the Scheme which applies to the tenement.

   (11) The provisions of rule 9 are subject to any different provision in any tenement burden.

   (12) The Scottish Ministers may by order substitute for the sums for the time being specified in rule 3.3 of the Scheme such other sums as appear to them to be justified by a change in the value of money appearing to them to have occurred since the last occasion on which the sums were fixed.

   (13) Where some but not all of the provisions of the Scheme apply, references in the Scheme to "the scheme" shall be read as references only to those provisions of the Scheme which apply.

   (14) In this section, "scheme costs" and "scheme decision" have the same meanings as they have in the Scheme.

GENERAL NOTE

   This section has to be read with tenement management scheme set out in Sched. 1. When the legislation was being drafted it was thought appropriate to have a statutory management scheme for tenemental property. Originally the Scottish Law Commission recommended that the norm should be that the majority could make decisions through the scheme. The Commission thought the scheme should apply only to existing buildings and that future buildings should be governed either by the development management scheme provided for in the Title Conditions (Scotland) Act 2003 or by a separate scheme drawn up in each case by the sellers or developers of the new building. The Act however applies the tenement management scheme to all tenemental properties (s.4(1)) except those to which the development management scheme applies (s.4(2)). The scheme itself contains eight rules which provide for a system of maintenance and management. Essentially this is a fall-back scheme where either provisions in the title deeds do not exist or are in some way defective or lacking. The Title Conditions (Scotland) Act 2003 contains detailed provisions relating to community burdens and these burdens can provide for managers meetings and maintenance. In the case of tenemental properties however the Tenements (Scotland) Act 2004 will apply and sections 28(1)(a) and (d) and (2)(a), 29 and 31 of the 2003 Act will not apply where the community consists of one tenement (Title Conditions (Scotland) Act 2003, s.31A).

Subs.(1)

   The scheme applies to all tenements to the extent provided in s.4.

Subs.(2)

   The scheme does not apply during any period where a development management scheme applies.

Subs.(3)

   Rule 1 contains the definitions which apply in the scheme. Of particular importance are the definitions of scheme property and scheme decisions. Rule 1 also contains the all important definition of "maintenance".

Subs.(4)

   Rule 2 sets out the procedure for making scheme decisions and it applies unless there is an existing scheme in the title for making decisions and that scheme can work because it applies to each flat. If there is no scheme or the scheme in the deeds does not apply to every flat then the management procedure set out in rule 2 will apply.

Subs.(5)

Rule 3 sets out the matters on which a scheme decisions may be made. Rule 3 only applies where there is no tenement burden which enables owners to make scheme decisions. Title deeds of tenemental properties may contain general obligations of maintenance and repair but may not specify in detail what type of decision may be taken. Rule 3 will fill this gap.

Subs.(6)

Apart from the special conditions set out in rule 5 liability for scheme costs is apportioned in terms of rule 4. The provisions in rule 4 however only apply where there is no burden in the title which deals with apportionment. In some cases there is inconsistency in the titles and the burdens do not provide for the entire liability to be met by one or more of the owners. In some cases one finds, after an examination of all the split writs, that only seven eighths of the liability has been dealt with. In such cases rule 4 will apply.

Subs.(7)

Rule 5 deals with certain special cases relating to scheme costs. Rule 5 applies only to the extent that there is no burden in the titles which makes provision for liability of the owners in such cases.

Subs.(8)

Rule 6 provides that any procedural irregularity in making a scheme decision will not affect the validity of the decision. However rule 6 only applies to the extent that there is no tenement burden which makes provision as to the effect of such a procedural irregularity.

Subs.(9)

Rule 7 deals with emergency work and provides that any owner may instruct or carry out emergency work and costs will to be dealt with as scheme costs. Rule 7 only applies to the extent there is no burden in the title which makes provision for emergency work as defined in rule 7 or as to liability of owners for the cost of such emergency work. The definition of emergency work in rule 7 is work which, before a scheme decision can be obtained, requires to be carried out to scheme property to prevent damage to any part of the tenement or in the interests of health or safety.

Subs.(10)

Rule 8 relates to enforcement and provides generally that a scheme decision is binding on all owners and their successors and also can be enforced by any owner or third party authorised by an owner. The provisions of rules 8 and 9 apply so far as relevant for the purposes of supplementing other provisions of the scheme which apply.

Subs.(11)

The provisions of rule 9 (which relates to notices to owners) are subject to any different provisions in any title burden.

Subs.(12)

Scottish Ministers may change the monetary limits specified in 3.3 to take account of inflation.

Subs.(13)

In some cases only some provisions of the scheme will apply in which case the scheme will be construed accordingly.

Subs.(14)

The terms "scheme costs" and "scheme decisions" have the same meanings as are set out in the rules.

Resolution of disputes

Application to sheriff for annulment of certain decisions

5.—(1) Where a decision is made by the owners in accordance with the management scheme which applies as respects the tenement (except where that management scheme is the development management scheme), an owner mentioned in subsection (2) below may, by summary application, apply to the sheriff for an order annulling the decision.

(2) That owner is—

(a) any owner who, at the time the decision referred to in subsection (1) above was made, was not in favour of the decision; or

(b) any new owner, that is to say, any person who was not an owner at that time but who has since become an owner.

(3) For the purposes of any such application, the defender shall be all the other owners.

(4) An application under subsection (1) above shall be made—

(a) in a case where the decision was made at a meeting attended by the owner making the application, not later than 28 days after the date of that meeting; or

(b) in any other case, not later than 28 days after the date on which notice of the making of the decision was given to the owner for the time being of the flat in question.

(5) The sheriff may, if satisfied that the decision—

(a) is not in the best interests of all (or both) the owners taken as a group; or

(b) is unfairly prejudicial to one or more of the owners,

make an order annulling the decision (in whole or in part).

(6) Where such an application is made as respects a decision to carry out maintenance, improvements or alterations, the sheriff shall, in considering whether to make an order under subsection (5) above, have regard to—

(a) the age of the property which is to be maintained, improved or, as the case may be, altered;

(b) its condition;

(c) the likely cost of any such maintenance, improvements or alterations; and

(d) the reasonableness of that cost.

(7) Where the sheriff makes an order under subsection (5) above annulling a decision (in whole or in part), the sheriff may make such other, consequential, order as the sheriff thinks fit (as, for example, an order as respects the liability of owners for any costs already incurred).

(8) A party may not later than fourteen days after the date of—

(a) an order under subsection (5) above; or

(b) an interlocutor dismissing such an application,

appeal to the Court of Session on a point of law.

(9) A decision of the Court of Session on an appeal under subsection (8) above shall be final.

(10) Where an owner is entitled to make an application under subsection (1) above in relation to any decision, no step shall be taken to implement that decision unless—

(a) the period specified in subsection (4) above within which such an application is to be made has expired without such an application having been made and notified to the owners; or

(b) where such an application has been so made and notified—

(i) the application has been disposed of and either the period specified in subsection (8) above within which an appeal against the sheriff's decision may be made has expired without such an appeal having been made or such an appeal has been made and disposed of; or

(ii) the application has been abandoned.

(11) Subsection (10) above does not apply to a decision relating to work which requires to be carried out urgently.

GENERAL NOTE

The whole point of the legislation and the tenement management scheme is to remove areas of dispute. However the Act does provide a method of resolution by application to the sheriff. These provisions apply not just to tenements governed by the statutory tenement management scheme but also to tenements governed by their own scheme as contained in the title deeds.

Subs.(1)

Procedure will be by summary application to the sheriff for an order annulling a decision.

Subs.(2)

Owners who are not in favour of the decision or were not owners at the time the decision was made can make the application.

Subs.(3)

In any application the defenders will be the other owners. This will include owners who were in favour of the decision as well as other dissenters.

Subs.(4)

If the owner making the application was present at the meeting when the decision was taken then the application must be made not later that 28 days after the date of the meeting. In other cases the application must be made not later that 28 days from the date notification of the decision was made to that owner.

Subs.(5)

The sheriff may annul the decision in whole or in part if satisfied that the decision is not in the best interests of all or both the owners taken as a group or is unfairly prejudicial to one or more of the owners.

Subs.(6)

Guidance is given as to the issues which the sheriff must consider before coming to a view. The sheriff must consider the age of the property, its condition, the cost involved and the reasonableness of that cost where the application is made in relation to a decision to carry out maintenance, improvements or alterations.

Subs.(7)

The sheriff may make consequential orders as well as an annulment order including an order relating to the liability of owners for costs already incurred.

Subs.(8)

An appeal against an annulment order or a refusal to grant such an order lies to the Court of Session but only on a point of law.

Subs.(9)

A decision of the Court of Session on an appeal is final

Subs.(10)

Where this kind of decision has been taken no step can be taken to implement that decision until such time as the 28 day period for making application to the sheriff for annulment has expired. Where an application to annul has been made and notified no step can be taken to implement the scheme decision until the application has disposed of and the 14 day period for lodging appeal to the Court of Session on a point of law has expired. Where an appeal to the Court of Session has been made no steps can be taken to implement the scheme decision until the appeal has been disposed of. Where an application has been made to sheriff but has been abandoned the scheme decision can be implemented.

Subs.(11)

The provisions relating to the non-implementation of scheme decisions pending applications or appeals do not apply to the decision relating to work which has to be carried out urgently as an emergency repair.

Application to sheriff for order resolving certain disputes

6.—(1) Any owner may by summary application apply to the sheriff for an order relating to any matter concerning the operation of—
  (a) the management scheme which applies as respects the tenement (except where that management scheme is the development management scheme); or
  (b) any provision of this Act in its application as respects the tenement.
  (2) Where an application is made under subsection (1) above the sheriff may, subject to such conditions (if any) as the sheriff thinks fit—
  (a) grant the order craved; or
  (b) make such other order under this section as the sheriff considers necessary or expedient.
  (3) A party may not later than fourteen days after the date of—
  (a) an order under subsection (2) above; or
  (b) an interlocutor dismissing such an application,
appeal to the Court of Session on a point of law.
  (4) A decision of the Court of Session on an appeal under subsection (3) above shall be final.

GENERAL NOTE

In addition to the specific jurisdiction of the sheriff in relation to scheme decisions there is provision for an application to be made to resolve disputes relating to the operation of the tenement management scheme or the Act. The provisions here are general and no guidance is given to the sheriff.

Subs.(1)

Applications can relate to the operation of any management scheme which applies as regards the tenement whether or not this is the statutory scheme or a scheme imposed in the title deeds. An application cannot be made however where the development management scheme under the Title Conditions (Scotland) Act 2003 is in operation. An application can also be made in relation to any provision of the Act. There is no guidance as to what sort of order can be applied for so presumably there is wide discretion.

Subs.(2)

The sheriff may grant the order craved or refuse it or make another order if he or she considers it necessary or expedient.

Subs.(3)

Appeal lies to the Court of Session on a point of the law.

Subs.(4)

The decision of the Court of Session is final.

Support and shelter

Abolition as respects tenements of common law rules of common interest

7.—Any rule of law relating to common interest shall, to the extent that it applies as respects a tenement, cease to have effect; but nothing in this section shall affect the operation of any such rule of law in its application to a question affecting both a tenement and—
  (a) some other building or former building (whether or not a tenement); or
  (b) any land not pertaining to the tenement.

GENERAL NOTE
The previous common law of the tenement relied heavily on the principles of common interest. Although the top most proprietor owned the roof void and the roof his or her right of ownership was limited by the common interest of the other proprietors in the tenement. Accordingly the topmost proprietor had to maintain the roof so as to provide shelter. Similarly the owner of the ground flat could do nothing to the foundations or solum which might affect the structural integrity of the whole building because his or her right of ownership in the solum and foundations was limited by the common interest of all the other proprietors in the tenement. The statutory provisions of the Act and the tenement management scheme replace the existing rules of common interest as they apply to tenements. Common interest will continue to apply in relation to questions affecting a tenement and another building or former building such as adjoining tenement or relating to any land which does not actually pertain to the tenement.

Duty to maintain so as to provide support and shelter etc.

8.—(1) Subject to subsection (2) below, the owner of any part of a tenement building, being a part that provides, or is intended to provide, support or shelter to any other part, shall maintain the supporting or sheltering part so as to ensure that it provides support or shelter.

(2) An owner shall not by virtue of subsection (1) above be obliged to maintain any part of a tenement building if it would not be reasonable to do so, having regard to all the circumstances (and including, in particular, the age of the tenement building, its condition and the likely cost of any maintenance).

(3) The duty imposed by subsection (1) above on an owner of a part of a tenement building may be enforced by any other such owner who is, or would be, directly affected by any breach of the duty.

(4) Where two or more persons own any such part of a tenement building as is referred to in subsection (1) above in common, any of them may, without the need for the agreement of the others, do anything that is necessary for the purpose of complying with the duty imposed by that subsection.

GENERAL NOTE

Common law entitled an owner within a tenement to rights of support, shelter, light and the right to use chimney vents. These were not rights of property but real rights or interests in the property of other parties. Ss. 8 and 9 of the Bill deal with the duty to provide support and shelter and introduce a prohibition against interference with these rights.

Subs.(1)

The owner of any part of a building which supports or is intended to support or shelter another part must maintain the supporting or sheltering part.

Subs.(2)

There may be situations where the obligation to maintain support or shelter is unreasonable having regard to the age of the building, its condition and the likely cost of such maintenance. Presumably therefore where a ruinous tenement property has been abandoned by all the owners bar one recalcitrant owner that remaining owner cannot insist on the upper floor proprietors carrying out expensive repairs to provide shelter for him or her. There may of course be provisions in the title which are more specific and may be enforceable. The provisions of the Act merely replace the law of common interest.

Subs.(3)

Any affected owners may enforce where they are affected by any breach of the duty to provide support and shelter.

Subs.(4)

In many cases the part of the tenement providing support of shelter may be owned in common such as the foundations or the roof. In such a case any one common owner can carry out works necessary to comply with the obligation.

Prohibition on interference with support or shelter etc.

9.—(1) No owner or occupier of any part of a tenement shall be entitled to do anything in relation to that part which would, or would be reasonably likely to, impair to a material extent—

(a) the support or shelter provided to any part of the tenement building; or

(b) the natural light enjoyed by any part of the tenement building.

(2) The prohibition imposed by subsection (1) above on an owner or occupier of a part of a tenement may be enforced by any other such owner who is, or would be, directly affected by any breach of the prohibition.

GENERAL NOTE

There is a counter-balancing obligation on the owner or occupiers of parts of the tenement not to do anything which might impair to a material extent support or shelter or natural light. It should be noted that this prohibition applies not just to the owners of parts of the tenement providing support, shelter or light but to occupiers such as tenants. However the prohibition can only be enforced by other owners directly affected by the breach.

Recovery of costs incurred by virtue of section 8

10.—Where—

(a) by virtue of section 8 of this Act an owner carries out maintenance to any part of a tenement; and

(b) the management scheme which applies as respects the tenement provides for the maintenance of that part,

the owner shall be entitled to recover from any other owner any share of the cost of the maintenance for which that other owner would have been liable had the maintenance been carried out by virtue of the management scheme in question.

GENERAL NOTE

There will be cases where an owner or owners of parts of the tenement require to carry out work in order to fulfil their obligations to provide support or shelter. If the management scheme which applies to the tenement provides for maintenance of that particular part then the owner or owners can recover the share of the costs from the other owners despite the fact that the work may have been carried out in implementation of this statutory obligation. The management scheme can either be the statutory scheme or a scheme contained in the title.

Repairs: costs and access

Determination of when an owner's liability for certain costs arises

11.—(1) An owner is liable for any relevant costs (other than accumulating relevant costs) arising from a scheme decision from the date when the scheme decision to incur those costs is made.

(2) For the purposes of subsection (1) above, a scheme decision is, in relation to an owner, taken to be made on—

(a) where the decision is made at a meeting, the date of the meeting; or

(b) in any other case, the date on which notice of the making of the decision is given to the owner.

(3) An owner is liable for any relevant costs arising from any emergency work from the date on which the work is instructed.

(4) An owner is liable for any relevant costs of the kind mentioned in rule 4.1(d) of the Tenement Management Scheme from the date of any statutory notice requiring the carrying out of the work to which those costs relate.

(5) An owner is liable for any accumulating relevant costs (such as the cost of an insurance premium) on a daily basis.

(6) Except where subsection (1) above applies in relation to the costs, an owner is liable for any relevant costs arising from work instructed by a manager from the date on which the work is instructed.

(7) An owner is liable in accordance with section 10 of this Act for any relevant costs arising from maintenance carried out by virtue of section 8 of this Act from the date on which the maintenance is completed.

(8) An owner is liable for any relevant costs other than those to which subsections (1) to (7) above apply from—

(a) such date; or

(b) the occurrence of such event,

as may be stipulated as the date on, or event in, which the costs become due.

(9) For the purposes of this section and section 12 of this Act, "relevant costs" means, as respects a flat—

(a) the share of any costs for which the owner is liable by virtue of the management scheme which applies as respects the tenement (except where that management scheme is the development management scheme); and

(b) any costs for which the owner is liable by virtue of this Act.

(10) In this section, "emergency work", "manager" and "scheme decision" have the same meanings as they have in the Tenement Management Scheme.

GENERAL NOTE

This section sets out the time when liability arises in respect of costs. Costs for which owners are liable are stated to be "relevant costs" which mean as respects any flat or unit in the tenement any share of costs for which the owner is liable by virtue of the tenement management scheme or by virtue of any burden in the title or by virtue of the Act (subs. 9).

Subs.(1)

Liability arises from the date when the scheme decision to incur the costs is made except in the case of accumulating relevant costs.

Subs.(2)

A decision is treated as having been taken either at the date of the meeting at which the decision was made or in other cases on the date on which notice of the making of the decision is given to the owner.

Subs.(3)

Where works are carried out as an emergency liability arises on the date when the work is instructed irrespective of any meetings or notification.

Subs.(4)

Where repairs are carried out as the result of a statutory notice then liability arises from the date of the statutory notice which requires the work to be carried out.

Subs.(5)

Owners are liable for accruing costs such as insurance premiums on a daily basis.

Subs.(6)

Where a manager instructs work then unless the work arises as a result of a scheme decision liability arises on the date when the work is instructed by the manager.

Subs.(7)

Where work is carried out in implementation of the statutory obligation of support and shelter it can be charged back to other owners in terms of whatever management scheme applies and liability arises in respect of these other owners from the date in which the maintenance is completed.

Subs.(8)

There may be costs which arise which are not relevant costs. In such cases liability arises on whatever date or on the occurrence of whatever event is stipulated as the date when costs become due.

Subs.(9)

Relevant costs mean as respects any flat the share of costs which arise by virtue of any management scheme except the development management scheme and any costs which arise by virtue of the Act.

Subs.(10)

The terms "emergency work", "manager" and "scheme decision" have the same meanings as they have in the statutory tenement management scheme contained in Sched.1.

Liability of owner and successors for certain costs

12.—(1) Any owner who is liable for any relevant costs shall not, by virtue only of ceasing to be such an owner, cease to be liable for those costs.

(2) Subject to subsection (3) below, where a person becomes an owner (any such person being referred to in this section as a "new owner"), that person shall be severally liable with any former owner of the flat for any relevant costs for which the former owner is liable.

(3) A new owner shall be liable as mentioned in subsection (2) above for relevant costs relating to any maintenance or work (other than local authority work) carried out before the acquisition date only if—

(a) notice of the maintenance or work—

    (i) in, or as near as may be in, the form set out in schedule 2 to this Act; and

    (ii) containing the information required by the notes for completion set out in that
schedule,

(such a notice being referred to in this section and section 13 of this Act as a "notice of potential liability for costs") was registered in relation to the new owner's flat at least 14 days before the acquisition date; and

(b) the notice had not expired before the acquisition date.

(4) In subsection (3) above—

"acquisition date" means the date on which the new owner acquired right to the flat; and

"local authority work" means work carried out by a local authority by virtue of any enactment.

(5) Where a new owner pays any relevant costs for which a former owner of the flat is liable, the new owner may recover the amount so paid from the former owner.

(6) This section applies as respects any relevant costs for which an owner becomes liable on or after the day on which this section comes into force.

GENERAL NOTE

Liability of successors for arrears of common charges proved to be the most controversial aspect of this Bill. Originally the successor of an owner was severally liable with the former owner for relevant costs. Relevant costs are, as respects any flat or unit in a tenement, any share of any costs for which the owner is liable by virtue of the tenement management scheme, by virtue of a real burden in the title or by virtue of the Act (s.11(9)). The new provision is to the effect that a successor owner will only be liable if a notice of potential liability for costs is registered at least 14 days before the acquisition date.

Subs.(1)

Although liability may transmit in certain circumstances an owner who has been liable for relevant costs does not cease to be liable simply because that person ceases to be owner.

Subs.(2)

Subject to the requirement to register a notice a successor is liable severally with the former owner for costs.

Subs.(3)

A new owner is only liable if a notice of the maintenance of the work in the form of Schedule 2 and containing information required by the notes to Schedule 2 was registered in respect of the flat at least 14 days before the acquisition date and the notice has not expired before the acquisition date. "Acquisition date" is rather oddly defined as the date on which the new owner acquired right to the flat. Where the work is being carried out by a local authority by virtue of any enactment the notice procedure is inapplicable. Presumably a new owner does not acquire right to a flat until that person's title is registered, missives only giving rise to a personal right between seller and purchaser and delivery of a deed having no effect. (*Burnett's Tr. v Grainger* [2004] UKHL 8). The provision will be altered by statutory instrument so that it covers work still to be carried out.

Subs.(5)

Primary liability still remains with the former owner and there is a right of relief in favour of the successor owner.

Subs.(6)

The provisions of the section only apply in respect of relevant costs for which an owner becomes liable after the coming into force of the section.

Notice of potential liability for costs: further provision

13.—(1) A notice of potential liability for costs—
(a) may be registered in relation to a flat only on the application of—
(i) the owner of the flat;
(ii) the owner of any other flat in the same tenement; or
(iii) any manager (within the meaning of the Tenement Management Scheme) of the tenement; and
(b) shall not be registered unless it is signed by or on behalf of the applicant.
(2) A notice of potential liability for costs may be registered—
(a) in relation to more than one flat in respect of the same maintenance or work; and
(b) in relation to any one flat, in respect of different maintenance or work.
(3) A notice of potential liability for costs expires at the end of the period of 3 years beginning with the date of its registration, unless the notice is renewed by being registered again before the end of that period.
(4) This section applies to a renewed notice of potential liability for costs as it applies to any other such notice.
(5) The Keeper of the Registers of Scotland shall not be required to investigate or determine whether the information contained in any notice of potential liability for costs submitted for registration is accurate.
(6) The Scottish Ministers may by order amend schedule 2 to this Act.
(7) In section 12 of the Land Registration (Scotland) Act 1979 (c.33), in subsection (3) (which specifies losses for which there is no entitlement to be indemnified by the Keeper under that section), after paragraph (p) there shall be added—
"(q) the loss arises in consequence of an inaccuracy in any information contained in a notice of potential liability for costs registered in pursuance of—
(i) section 10(2A)(a) or 10A(3) of the Title Conditions (Scotland) Act 2003 (asp 9); or
(ii) section 12(3)(a) or 13(3) of the Tenements (Scotland) Act 2004 (asp 11)."

GENERAL NOTE

This section contains formal provision in relation to the notice for potential liability for costs setting out who may register.

Subs.(1)

Only the owner of the flat concerned or the owner of any other flat in the same tenement or any manager may register a notice of potential liability for costs. The notice must be signed by or on behalf of the applicant.

Subs.(2)

In some cases more than one proprietor may be in arrears with payment of the costs. In such a case other owners or the manager may register against all flats concerned. Similarly there may be different kinds of maintenance or work unpaid for in respect of different flats.

Subs.(3)

The notice of potential liability ceases to have effect at the end of 3 years from the date of registration. Presumably what this means is that if the new owner has not paid within that period then he cannot be pursued after the expiry date. However a former owner or other owners may renew the notice by registering again before the end of the period.

Subs.(4)

The provisions of the section will apply to a renewed notice.

Subs.(5)

The Keeper will require to take notices at face value and will have no obligation to investigate.

Subs.(6)

Scottish Ministers may alter the form of notice by order.

Subs.(7)

Since the Keeper will not investigate the validity or otherwise of a notice he will have no liability to pay indemnity to any party if the loss arises because of an inaccuracy in any information contained in the notice.

Former owner's right to recover costs

14.—An owner who is entitled, by virtue of the Tenement Management Scheme or any other provision of this Act, to recover any costs or a share of any costs from any other owner shall not, by virtue only of ceasing to be an owner, cease to be entitled to recover those costs or that share.

GENERAL NOTE

Where an owner is entitled to relief from another owner in respect of costs or a share of costs then that right of relief will remain enforceable after the recovering owner ceases to be an owner. Presumably therefore it will not transmit in favour of a new owner.

Prescriptive period for costs to which section 12 relates

15. In Schedule 1 to the Prescription and Limitation (Scotland) Act 1973 (c.52) (obligations affected by prescriptive periods of five years to which section 6 of that Act applies)—

    (a) after paragraph 1(ab) there shall be inserted—

        "(ac) to any obligation to pay a sum of money by way of costs to which section 12 of the Tenements (Scotland) Act 2004 (asp 11) applies;"; and

    (b) in paragraph 2(e), for the words "or (ab)" there shall be substituted ", (ab) or (ac)".

GENERAL NOTE

The five year prescription will apply to any obligation to pay money under s.12. This will apply whether the money is due by a former owner or a successor owner.

Common property: disapplication of common law right of recovery

16. Any rule of law which enables an owner of common property to recover the cost of necessary maintenance from the other owners of the property shall not apply in relation to any common property in a tenement where the maintenance of that property is provided for in the management scheme which applies as respects the tenement.

<small>GENERAL NOTE</small>
The statutory provisions replace any common law rule under the law of common property which entitles a common owner to recover a share of the cost of maintenance.

Access for maintenance and other purposes

17.—(1) Where an owner gives reasonable notice to the owner or occupier of any other part of the tenement that access is required to, or through, that part for any of the purposes mentioned in subsection (3) below, the person given notice shall, subject to subsection (5) below, allow access for that purpose.

(2) Without prejudice to subsection (1) above, where the development management scheme applies, notice under that subsection may be given by any owners' association established by the scheme to the owner or occupier of any part of the tenement.

(3) The purposes are—

(a) carrying out maintenance or other work by virtue of the management scheme which applies as respects the tenement;

(b) carrying out maintenance to any part of the tenement owned (whether solely or in common) by the person requiring access;

(c) carrying out an inspection to determine whether it is necessary to carry out maintenance;

(d) determining whether the owner of the part is fulfilling the duty imposed by section 8(1) of this Act;

(e) determining whether the owner or occupier of the part is complying with the prohibition imposed by section 9(1) of this Act;

(f) doing anything which the owner giving notice is entitled to do by virtue of section 19(1) of this Act;

(g) where floor area is relevant for the purposes of determining any liability of owners, measuring floor area; and

(h) where a power of sale order has been granted in relation to the tenement building or its site, doing anything necessary for the purpose of or in connection with any sale in pursuance of the order (other than complying with paragraph 4(3) of schedule 3 to this Act).

(4) Reasonable notice need not be given as mentioned in subsection (1) above where access is required for the purpose specified in subsection (3)(a) above and the maintenance or other work requires to be carried out urgently.

(5) An owner or occupier may refuse to allow—

(a) access under subsection (1) above; or

(b) such access at a particular time,

if, having regard to all the circumstances (and, in particular, whether the requirement for access is reasonable), it is reasonable to refuse access.

(6) Where access is allowed under subsection (1) above for any purpose, such right of access may be exercised by—

(a) the owner who or owners' association which gave notice that access was required; or

(b) such person as the owner or, as the case may be, owners' association may authorize for the purpose (any such person being referred to in this section as an "authorised person").

(7) Where an authorised person acting in accordance with subsection (6) above is liable by virtue of any enactment or rule of law for damage caused to any part of a tenement, the owner who or owners' association which authorised that person shall be severally liable with the authorised person for the cost of remedying the damage; but an owner or, as the case may be,

owners' association making any payment as respects that cost shall have a right of relief against the authorised person.

(8) Where access is allowed under subsection (1) above for any purpose, the owner who or owners' association which gave notice that access was required (referred to as the "accessing owner or association") shall, so far as reasonably practicable, ensure that the part of the tenement to or through which access is allowed is left substantially in no worse a condition than that which it was in when access was taken.

(9) If the accessing owner or association fails to comply with the duty in subsection (8) above, the owner of the part to or through which access is allowed may—

(a) carry out, or arrange for the carrying out of, such work as is reasonably necessary to restore the part so that it is substantially in no worse a condition than that which it was in when access was taken; and

(b) recover from the accessing owner or association any expenses reasonably incurred in doing so.

GENERAL NOTE

Statutory rights of access will apply where an owner requires access for certain purposes. To exercise these rights of access the owner must give reasonable notice to the owner or occupier of the part to which access is to be taken.

Subs.(1)

Where reasonable notice is given by one owner to another owner or occupier then that other party must allow access subject to the provisions of *Subs. (5)*.

Subs.(2)

Where the development management scheme under the Title Conditions (Scotland) Act 2003 applies notice can be given by any owners' association established by the scheme to an owner or occupier of any part of the tenement.

Subs.(3)

This sub-section lists the purposes for which the statutory right of access may be exercised. Maintenance and inspection are the obvious purposes but there are other more unusual purposes such as determining any liability by measuring the floor area and doing anything necessary for the purposes of a sale of a tenement or its site where a power of sale order has been granted.

Subs.(4)

Reasonable notice does not require to be given in the case of access for carrying out maintenance work by virtue of the management scheme set out in the title deeds or under the statutory tenement management scheme where maintenance or work requires to be carried out urgently.

Subs.(5)

An owner occupier may refuse to allow access or specify a particular time if it is reasonable to do so.

Subs.(6)

Where access is allowed the right of access may be exercised by the owner or owners' association giving notice or an authorised person. Presumably a tradesman with some sort of authorisation or a factor or surveyor would be entitled to access.

Subs.(7)

Where an authorised person is liable for damage caused to any part of the tenement as a result of taking access then although it may be the authorised person who is primarily liable the owner who authorised that person or the owners' association concerned are severally liable with the authorised person for the cost.

Subs.(8)

Where access is taken there is an obligation to ensure that the part of the tenement over which access is taken is left substantially in no worse condition.

Subs.(9)

If there is damage caused through the exercise of the access right then the owner who has suffered the damage can carry out remedial work and recover the cost from the owner taking or authorising the access.

Insurance

Obligation of owner to insure

18.—(1) It shall be the duty of each owner to effect and keep in force a contract of insurance against the prescribed risks for the reinstatement value of that owner's flat and any part of the tenement building attaching to that flat as a pertinent.

(2) The duty imposed by subsection (1) above may be satisfied, in whole or in part, by way of a common policy of insurance arranged for the entire tenement building.

(3) The Scottish Ministers may by order prescribe risks against which an owner shall require to insure (in this section referred to as the "prescribed risks").

(4) Where, whether because of the location of the tenement or otherwise, an owner—

(a) having made reasonable efforts to do so, is unable to obtain insurance against a particular prescribed risk; or

(b) would be able to obtain such insurance but only at a cost which is unreasonably high, the duty imposed by subsection (1) above shall not require an owner to insure against that particular risk.

(5) Any owner may by notice in writing request the owner of any other flat in the tenement to produce evidence of—

(a) the policy in respect of any contract of insurance which the owner of that other flat is required to have or to effect; and

(b) payment of the premium for any such policy,

and not later than 14 days after that notice is given the recipient shall produce to the owner giving the notice the evidence requested.

(6) The duty imposed by subsection (1) above on an owner may be enforced by any other owner.

GENERAL NOTE

Quite apart from any obligation in the title to maintain insurance or indeed a scheme decision to maintain common insurance there is a statutory duty placed on the owner of each flat to insure.

Subs.(1)

Each owner must insure his or her flat against prescribed risks for re-instatement value. The insurance must cover the flat and any part of the tenement building attaching to the flat as a pertinent. It should be borne in mind that the definition of flat includes not just a dwellinghouse but any other premises in a tenement building (s.29(1)).

Subs.(2)

The duty to insure may be satisfied in whole or in part by way of a common policy covering the whole tenement. Common policies are often the best way of effecting insurance. Individuals may have their own ideas as to re-instatement value and if the whole building is destroyed by fire there may not be adequate cover if everything is left to individual insurance.

Subs.(3)

Scottish Ministers may by order list the prescribed risks. Presumably the risks may alter from time to time.

Subs.(4)

There may be cases where, for one reason or another, it is difficult to obtain insurance against a particular prescribed risk. Where this occurs or where such insurance can only be obtained at an unreasonably high cost there will be no duty to insure against that particular risk. It might be for example that there would be difficulty in obtaining flood insurance where the tenement is beside a river which has flooded in the past.

Subs.(5)

An obligation to insure is only of value if everyone implements it. Accordingly any owner may by written notice request the owner of any other flat to produce evidence of insurance and payment of the premium where the insurance is on an individual basis. The recipient of the notice must produce the evidence within 14 days.

Subs.(6)

The duty to insure can be enforced by any other owner. There is no requirement that a majority are involved.

Installation of service pipes etc.

Installation of service pipes etc.

19.—(1) Subject to subsections (2) and (3) below and to section 17 of this Act, an owner shall be entitled—

(a) to lead through any part of the tenement such pipe, cable or other equipment; and

(b) to fix to any part of the tenement, and keep there, such equipment,

as is necessary for the provision to that owner's flat of such service or services as the Scottish Ministers may by regulations prescribe.

(2) The right conferred by subsection (1) above is exercisable only in accordance with such procedure as the Scottish Ministers may by regulations prescribe; and different procedures may be so prescribed in relation to different services.

(3) An owner is not entitled by virtue of subsection (1) above to lead anything through or fix anything to any part which is wholly within another owner's flat.

(4) This section is without prejudice to any obligation imposed by virtue of any enactment relating to—

(a) planning;

(b) building; or

(c) any service prescribed under subsection (1) above.

GENERAL NOTE

Difficulties have sometimes been encountered in relation to the myriad of pipes, cables, satellite dishes, aerials and other equipment which modern living seems to require where these services require to pass through other parts of a tenement. While it would probably be accepted that the affixation of gutters and downpipes to a common wall is an ordinary use of common property there could conceivably be arguments over satellite dishes, air conditioning units, flues and the like although these are ever more common nowadays. This section was introduced late on in the bill's progress and Scottish Ministers have still to prescribe a range of services in respect of which conductors or equipment can be led or fixed. An owner will be entitled to lead pipes, cables or equipment through any part of the tenement and also to fix equipment on any part of the tenement. However the right cannot be exercised over any part of the tenement which is wholly within another owner's flat and can only be exercised in accordance with such procedure as may be prescribed by Scottish Ministers. Different procedures may be prescribed in relation to different services. The statutory right is without prejudice to any other obligation to obtain planning or building warrant. It will be interesting to see just what services Scottish Ministers regard as appropriate for modern flat living.

Demolition and abandonment of tenement building

Demolition of tenement building not to affect ownership

20.—(1) The demolition of a tenement building shall not alone effect any change as respects any right of ownership.

(2) In particular, the fact that, as a consequence of demolition of a tenement building, any land pertaining to the building no longer serves, or affords access to, any flat or other sector shall not alone effect any change of ownership of the land as a pertinent.

GENERAL NOTE

Ownership of tenemental property is rather odd. The proprietor of a third floor flat essentially has exclusive ownership of a slice of airspace. The same applies when the tenement is being demolished although just how one would pinpoint the slice of airspace with accuracy is difficult to see. Demolition however does not change ownership as such. If therefore the land itself is no longer required as support for a third floor flat that does not mean that the ownership rights have changed.

Cost of demolishing tenement building

21.—(1) Except where a tenement burden otherwise provides, the cost of demolishing a tenement building shall, subject to subsection (2) below, be shared equally among all (or both) the flats in the tenement, and each owner is liable accordingly.

(2) Where the floor area of the largest (or larger) flat in the tenement is more than one and a half times that of the smallest (or smaller) flat the owner of each flat shall be liable to contribute towards the cost of demolition of the tenement building in the proportion which the floor area of that owner's flat bears to the total floor area of all (or both) the flats.

(3) An owner is liable under this section for the cost of demolishing a tenement building—

(a) in the case where the owner agrees to the proposal that the tenement building be demolished, from the date of the agreement; or

(b) in any other case, from the date on which the carrying out of the demolition is instructed.

(4) This section applies as respects the demolition of part of a tenement building as it applies as respects the demolition of an entire tenement building but with any reference to a flat in the tenement being construed as a reference to a flat in the part.

(5) In this section references to flats in a tenement include references to flats which were comprehended by the tenement before its demolition.

(6) This section is subject to section 123 of the Housing (Scotland) Act 1987 (c.26) (which makes provision as respects demolition of buildings in pursuance of local authority demolition orders and recovery of expenses by local authorities etc.).

GENERAL NOTE

It would perhaps be unusual to find a provision in a tenemental title which dealt with the apportionment of the costs of demolition. There may well be provision for dealing with the cost of maintenance and repair but that is a different matter. Unless there is a tenement burden which deals with the costs of demolition the cost is severally shared equally among all flats. The definition of flat should be borne in mind as including units which are not domestic dwellinghouses.

Subs.(1)

This sets out the general rule of equal sharing.

Subs.(2)

Where there are large discrepancies in the size of flats floor area will be relevant and the share will not be equal.

Subs.(3)

Where there has been an agreement liability for the cost of demolition arises from the date of that agreement but in other cases from the date when demolition is instructed.

Subs.(4)

The provisions apply in relation to partial demolition as well as total demolition.

Subs.(5)

For the avoidance of doubt a reference to flats in a tenement will include references to the airspace taken up by former flats after demolition.

Subs.(6)

The statutory provisions do not affect liabilities to third parties such as local authorities. Section 123 of the Housing (Scotland) Act 1987 makes provision in respect of demolition of buildings in pursuit of local authority demolition orders and the recovery of expenses by local authorities. In such cases the local authority can recover from the owners in such proportions as the owners may agree. A local authority can place a charging order on the property.

Use and disposal of site where tenement building demolished

22.—(1) This section applies where a tenement building is demolished and after the demolition two or more flats which were comprehended by the tenement building before its demolition (any such flat being referred to in this section as a "former flat") are owned by different persons.

(2) Except in so far as—

(a) the owners of all (or both) the former flats otherwise agree; or

(b) those owners are subject to a requirement (whether imposed by a tenement burden or otherwise) to erect a building on the site or to rebuild the tenement, no owner may build on, or otherwise develop, the site.

(3) Except where the owners have agreed, or are required, to build on or develop the site as mentioned in paragraphs (a) and (b) of subsection (2) above, any owner of a former flat shall be entitled to apply for power to sell the entire site in accordance with schedule 3.

(4) Except where a tenement burden otherwise provides, the net proceeds of any sale in pursuance of subsection (3) above shall, subject to subsection (5) below, be shared equally among all (or both) the former flats and the owner of each former flat shall be entitled to the share allocated to that flat.

(5) Where—

(a) evidence of the floor area of each of the former flats is readily available; and

(b) the floor area of the largest (or larger) former flat was more than one and a half times that of the smallest (or smaller) former flat,

the net proceeds of any sale shall be shared among (or between) the flats in the proportion which the floor area of each flat bore to the total floor area of all (or both) the flats and the owner of each former flat shall be entitled to the share allocated to that flat.

(6) The prohibition imposed by subsection (2) above on an owner of a former flat may be enforced by any other such owner.

(7) In subsections (4) and (5) above, "net proceeds of any sale" means the proceeds of the sale less any expenses properly incurred in connection with the sale.

(8) In this section references to the site are references to the solum of the tenement building that occupied the site together with the airspace that is directly above the solum and any land pertaining, as a means of access, to the tenement building immediately before its demolition.

GENERAL NOTE

There are a number of sites which are effectively sterilised because all previous flat owners cannot be traced. Where they all have a common right in the solum a valid conveyance cannot be granted unless all sign. This section applies where a tenement building is demolished and there is difficulty in disposal of the site.

Subs.(1)

Where two or more flats are owned by different persons then disposal of the site is facilitated.

Subs.(2)

The owners of all or both the former flats may agree to re-instate or there may be a requirement in the title to re-instate. If neither of these alternatives apply no one owner can build on or develop the site.

Subs.(3)

If there is no agreement or obligation to rebuild then any owner of a former flat can apply to the court for power to sell the entire site in accordance with Schedule 3.

Subs.(4)

Subject to anything in the title the net proceeds of sale of the site will generally be shared equally among the owners of the former flats.

Subs.(5)

Where there is a large difference in the size of flats the floor area will regulate the shares of sale proceeds.

Subs.(6)

Any owner can prevent another owner from attempting to sell if that other owner has not gone through the statutory procedure.

Subs.(7)

The expenses of sale properly incurred will be deducted before the net proceeds are struck.

Subs.(8)

The site includes that part of the land occupied by the building together with the airspace directly above it and any other land pertaining as a means of access to the tenement building before demolition. The definition of tenement includes land pertaining thereto.

Sale of abandoned tenement building

23.—(1) Where—
 (a) because of its poor condition a tenement building has been entirely unoccupied by any owner or person authorised by an owner for a period of more than six months; and
 (b) it is unlikely that any such owner or other person will occupy any part of the tenement building,
any owner shall be entitled to apply for power to sell the tenement building in accordance with schedule 3.

 (2) Subsections (4) and (5) of section 22 of this Act shall apply as respects a sale in pursuance of subsection (1) above as those subsections apply as respects a sale in pursuance of subsection (3) of that section.

 (3) In this section any reference to a tenement building includes a reference to its solum and any land pertaining, as a means of access, to the tenement building.

GENERAL NOTE

This section only applies where a tenement building has been entirely unoccupied. Accordingly it will not apply while someone still occupies even one flat. The provisions will only apply where the building has been entirely unoccupied because of its poor condition for a period of more than six months and it is unlikely that any owner will in the future occupy any part of the tenement building. Accordingly this section will not apply where a tenement building in poor condition is being refurbished, the owners temporarily rehoused and the refurbishment takes more than six months. Any owner will be entitled to apply for power to sell in accordance with Sched. 3 and the provisions of subss (4) and (5) of s.22 apply in respect of any such sale.

The provisions apply not just to the tenement building but to the solum and any land used as an access. It should be borne in mind that the definition of a tenement includes the solum and any other land pertaining thereto so it is the whole site which would be subject to the order.

Liability for certain costs

Liability to non owner for certain damage costs

24.—(1) Where—

(a) any part of a tenement is damaged as the result of the fault of any person (that person being in this subsection referred to as "A"); and

(b) the management scheme which applies as respects the tenement makes provision for the maintenance of that part,

any owner of a flat in the tenement (that owner being in this subsection referred to as "B") who is required by virtue of that provision to contribute to any extent to the cost of maintenance of the damaged part but who at the time when the damage was done was not an owner of the part shall be treated, for the purpose of determining whether A is liable to B as respects the cost of maintenance arising from the damage, as having been such an owner at that time.

(2) In this section "fault" means any wrongful act, breach of statutory duty or negligent act or omission which gives rise to liability in damages.

GENERAL NOTE

Where any part of a tenement is damaged as a result of the fault of any person and the management scheme which applies to the tenement makes provision for maintenance of that part any other owner of a flat in the tenement who is required to contribute to the cost of maintenance of the damaged part who at the time when the damage was done was not an owner of the damaged part will be deemed to be an owner for the purposes of determining liability between the owner damaging the part and the party causing the damage. Fault means any wrongful act, breach of statutory duty or negligent act or omission. This provision covers the case where there is an obligation to maintain without actual ownership of the part maintained.

Miscellaneous and general

Amendments of Title Conditions (Scotland) Act 2003

25. The Title Conditions (Scotland) Act 2003 (asp 9) shall be amended in accordance with schedule 4.

GENERAL NOTE

The Act contains certain amendments of the Title Conditions (Scotland) Act 2003 as set out in Schedule 4.

Meaning of "tenement"

26.—(1) In this Act, "tenement" means a building or a part of a building which comprises two related flats which, or more than two such flats at least two of which—

(a) are, or are designed to be, in separate ownership; and

(b) are divided from each other horizontally,

and, except where the context otherwise requires, includes the solum and any other land pertaining to that building or, as the case may be, part of the building; and the expression "tenement building" shall be construed accordingly.

(2) In determining whether flats comprised in a building or part of a building are related for the purposes of subsection (1), regard shall be had, among other things, to—

(a) the title to the tenement; and

(b) any tenement burdens,

treating the building or part for that purpose as if it were a tenement.

The definition of a tenement is wide enough to include not just a tenement or block of flats but a sub-divided villa. The definition includes not just the building itself but the solum on which the building rests and any other land which pertains to the building. It must comprise at least two related flats which are designed to be in separate ownership and divided from each other horizontally. The requirement for horizontal as opposed to vertical division excludes a semi-detached or terraced property from the definition. Whether the flats can be said to be related will depend primarily on physical juxtaposition but regard is to be had to the title of the tenement and tenement burdens which treat the building or part of the building as if it were a tenement. A flat is defined as including any premises whether or not used or intended to be used for residential purposes and whether or not on the one floor (s.29(1)). Accordingly commercial premises such as shops and offices are included.

Meaning of "management scheme"

27. References in this Act to the management scheme which applies as respects any tenement are references to—

(a) if the Tenement Management Scheme applies in its entirety as respects the tenement, that Scheme;

(b) if the development management scheme applies as respects the tenement, that scheme; or

(c) in any other case, any tenement burdens relating to maintenance, management or improvement of the tenement together with any provisions of the Tenement Management Scheme which apply as respects the tenement.

GENERAL NOTE
There are references to the management scheme applying to a particular tenement throughout the Act. This can mean the tenement management scheme in Schedule 1 to the Act where it applies in its entirety. Alternatively it may mean the development management scheme in terms of the Title Conditions (Scotland) Act 2003 where that applies to the tenement. In any other case the scheme will be as set out in the title deeds where there are tenement burdens relating to maintenance, management or improvement of the tenement together with any of the provisions of the statutory tenement management scheme which apply where there are gaps in the title scheme.

Meaning of "owner", determination of liability etc.

28.—(1) In this Act, references to "owner" without further qualification are, in relation to any tenement, references to the owner of a flat in the tenement.

(2) Subject to subsection (3) below, in this Act "owner" means, in relation to a flat in a tenement, a person who has right to the flat whether or not that person has completed title; but if, in relation to the flat (or, if the flat is held *pro indiviso*, any *pro indiviso* share in it) more than one person comes within that description of owner, then "owner" means such person as has most recently acquired such right.

(3) Where a heritable security has been granted over a flat and the heritable creditor has entered into lawful possession, "owner" means the heritable creditor in possession of the flat.

(4) Subject to subsection (5) below, if two or more persons own a flat in common, any reference in this Act to an owner is a reference to both or, as the case may be, all of them.

(5) Any reference to an owner in sections 5(1) and (2), 6(1), 8(3), 9, 10, 12 to 14, 17(1), (6) and (7), 18(5) and (6), 19, 22, 23 and 24 of, and schedule 3 to, this Act shall be construed as a reference to any person who owns a flat either solely or in common with another.

(6) Subsections (2) to (5) above apply to references in this Act to the owner of a part of a tenement as they apply to references to the owner of a flat, but as if references in them to a flat were to the part of the tenement.

(7) Where two or more persons own a flat in common—

(a) they are severally liable for the performance of any obligation imposed by virtue of this Act on the owner of that flat; and

(b) as between (or among) themselves they are liable in the proportions in which they own the flat.

GENERAL NOTE

The term owner is used throughout the Act. An owner is a person who has right to a flat whether or not that person has a completed title. If more than one person comes within the description of owner then owner means such person as has most recently acquired the right. Where a heritable security has been granted and the heritable creditor has entered into lawful possession the term owner will include the heritable creditor in possession. It should be noted that a heritable creditor who calls up evicts and then exercises the power of sale is not deemed to be in possession even although that creditor may have a set of keys. If two or more people own a flat in common then the term applies to both or all of these parties. In relation to certain rights conferred on owners one common owner can exercise the rights without consulting his or her fellow common owners. In so far as obligations are concerned where two or more people own a flat then they are jointly and severally liable for any costs but as between or among themselves they are liable in the proportions in which they own the flat concerned.

Interpretation

29.—(1) In this Act, unless the content otherwise requires—

"chimney stack" does not include flue or chimney pot;

"close" means a connected passage, stairs and landings within a tenement building which together constitute a common access to two or more of the flats;

"demolition" includes destruction and cognate expressions shall be construed accordingly; and demolition may occur on one occasion or over any period of time;

"the development management scheme" has the meaning given by section 71(3) of the Title Conditions (Scotland) Act 2003 (asp 9);

"door" includes its frame;

"flat" includes any premises whether or not—

    (a) used or intended to be used for residential purposes; or

    (b) on the one floor;

"lift" includes its shaft and operating machinery;

"local authority" means a council constituted under section 2 of the Local Government etc. (Scotland) Act 1994 (c.39);

"owner" shall be construed in accordance with section 28 of this Act;

"power of sale order" means an order granted under paragraph 1 of schedule 3 to this Act;

"register", in relation to a notice of potential liability for costs or power of sale order, means register the information contained in the notice or order in the Land Register of Scotland or, as appropriate, record the notice or order in the Register of Sasines, and "registered" and other related expressions shall be construed accordingly;

"sector" means—

    (a) a flat;

    (b) any close or lift; or

    (c) any other three dimensional space not comprehended by a flat, close or lift,

and the tenement building shall be taken to be entirely divided into sectors;

"solum" means the ground on which a building is erected;

"tenement" shall be construed in accordance with section 26 of this Act;

"tenement burden" means, in relation to a tenement, any real burden (within the meaning of the Title Conditions (Scotland) Act 2003 (asp 9)) which affects—

    (a) the tenement; or

    (b) any sector in the tenement;

"Tenement Management Scheme" means the scheme set out in schedule 1 to this Act;

"title to the tenement" shall be construed in accordance with section 1(2) of this Act; and "window" includes its frame.

(2) The floor area of a flat is calculated for the purposes of this Act by measuring the total floor area (including the area occupied by any internal wall or other internal dividing structure) within its boundaries; but no account shall be taken of any pertinents or any of the following parts of a flat—

(a) a balcony; and

(b) except where it is used for any purpose other than storage, a loft or basement.

GENERAL NOTE

This section contains the general definitions. The more important definitions occur in specific sections. A tenement is construed in accordance with s.26 and an owner in accordance with s.28. Commercial properties are included within the definition of a flat and a sector in the tenement can mean a flat, any close or lift or any other three dimensional space not comprehended by a flat, close or lift. Frames are included in the definition of doors and windows and shafts and operating machinery are included in the definition of lift. Where floor area has to be calculated then it is calculated by measuring the total floor area including the area occupied by an internal wall or other internal dividing structure within the boundaries of the flat. No account however is taken of any of the pertinents of a flat nor of any balcony or loft or basement unless the loft or basement is used for a purpose other than storage.

Giving of notice to owners

30.—(1) Any notice which is to be given to an owner under or in connection with this Act (other than under or in connection with the Tenement Management Scheme) may be given in writing by sending the notice to—

(a) the owner; or

(b) the owner's agent.

(2) The reference in subsection (1) above to sending a notice is to its being—

(a) posted;

(b) delivered; or

(c) transmitted by electronic means.

(3) Where an owner cannot by reasonable inquiry be identified or found, a notice shall be taken for the purposes of subsection (1)(a) above to be sent to the owner if it is posted or delivered to the owner's flat addressed to "The Owner" or using some similar expression such as "The Proprietor".

(4) For the purposes of this Act—

(a) a notice posted shall be taken to be given on the day of posting; and

(b) a notice transmitted by electronic means shall be taken to be given on the day of transmission.

GENERAL NOTE

The tenement management scheme contains its own provisions in relation to notices under the scheme (rule 9). Other notices which require to be given in terms of the Act may be given in writing by sending the notice to the owner or the owner's agent. A notice may be posted, delivered or transmitted by electronic means. Where the notice is posted it is taken to be given on the day of posting and where it is transmitted by electronic means it is taken to be given on the day of transmission. Presumably where it is delivered it is simply treated as being given when delivered. Where an owner cannot by reasonable enquiry be identified or found then it may be posted or delivered to the owner's flat addressed simply to "the owner" or "the proprietor" or some other similar title.

Ancillary provision

31.—(1) The Scottish Ministers may by order make such incidental, supplemental, consequential, transitional, transitory or saving provision as they consider necessary or expedient for the purposes, or in consequence, of this Act.

(2) An order under this section may modify any enactment (including this Act), instrument or document.

GENERAL NOTE
This type of clause is colloquially referred to as a "Henry VIII clause". Effectively it gives Scottish Ministers complete discretion to amend the Act by statutory order without the need to pass amending legislation.

Orders and regulations

32.—(1) Any power of the Scottish Ministers to make orders or regulations under this Act shall be exercisable by statutory instrument.

(2) A statutory instrument containing an order or regulations under this Act (except an order under section 34(2) or, where subsection (3) applies, section 31) shall be subject to annulment in pursuance of a resolution of the Scottish Parliament.

(3) Where an order under section 31 contains provisions which add to, replace or omit any part of the text of an Act, the order shall not be made unless a draft of the statutory instrument containing the order has been laid before, and approved by a resolution of, the Parliament.

GENERAL NOTE
An order of Scottish Ministers will be made by statutory instrument generally subject to annulment procedure. Where the order is to amend the Act or any other Act a draft of the statutory instrument must be laid before and approved by the Scottish Parliament.

Crown application

33.—This Act, except section 18, binds the Crown.

GENERAL NOTE
The Act binds the Crown apart from section 18 which relates to insurance. The Crown is not under any obligation to insure its own property.

Short title and commencement

34.—(1) This Act may be cited as the Tenements (Scotland) Act 2004.

(2) This Act (other than this section, section 25 and schedule 4) shall come into force on such day as the Scottish Ministers may by order appoint; and different days may be appointed for different purposes.

(3) Section 25 and schedule 4 shall come into force on the day after Royal Assent.

GENERAL NOTE
Generally speaking the Act came into force on 28th November 2004 apart from the amendments to the Title Conditions (Scotland) Act 2003 which came into force on Royal Assent.

SCHEDULE 1

(introduced by section 4)

TENEMENT MANAGEMENT SCHEME

RULE 1—SCOPE AND INTERPRETATION

1.1 Scope of scheme
This scheme provides for the management and maintenance of the scheme property of a tenement.

1.2 Meaning of "scheme property"

For the purposes of this scheme, "scheme property" means, in relation to a tenement, all or any of the following—

    (a) any part of the tenement that is the common property of two or more of the owners,

    (b) any part of the tenement (not being common property of the type mentioned in paragraph (a) above) the maintenance of which, or the cost of maintaining which, is, by virtue of a tenement burden, the responsibility of two or more of the owners,

    (c) with the exceptions mentioned in rule 1.3, the following parts of the tenement building (so far as not scheme property by virtue of paragraph (a) or (b) above)—

        (i) the ground on which it is built,

        (ii) its foundations,

        (iii) its external walls,

        (iv) its roof (including any rafter or other structure supporting the roof),

        (v) if it is separated from another building by a gable wall, the part of the gable wall that is part of the tenement building, and

        (vi) any wall (not being one falling within the preceding sub-paragraphs), beam or column that is load bearing.

1.3 Parts not included in rule 1.2(c)

The following parts of a tenement building are the exceptions referred to in rule 1.2(c)—

    (a) any extension which forms part of only one flat,

    (b) any—

        (i) door,

        (ii) window,

        (iii) skylight,

        (iv) vent, or

        (v) other opening,

    which serves only one flat,

    (c) any chimney stack or chimney flue.

1.4 Meaning of "scheme decision"

A decision is a "scheme decision" for the purposes of this scheme if it is made in accordance with—

    (a) rule 2, or

    (b) where that rule does not apply, the tenement burden or burdens providing the procedure for the making of decisions by the owners.

1.5 Other definitions

In this scheme—

    "maintenance" includes repairs and replacement, cleaning, painting and other routine works, gardening, the day to day running of a tenement and the reinstatement of a part (but not most) of the tenement building, but does not include demolition, alteration or improvement unless reasonably incidental to the maintenance,

    "manager" means, in relation to a tenement, a person appointed (whether or not by virtue of rule 3.1(c)(i)) to manage the tenement, and

    "scheme costs" has the meaning given by rule 4.1.

1.6 Rights of co owners

If a flat is owned by two or more persons, then one of them may do anything that the owner is by virtue of this scheme entitled to do.

GENERAL NOTE

The Act does not alter the common law of the tenement to any great extent so far as property rights are concerned. The majority of tenemental titles do alter the common law position. The common law position is unsatisfactory in relation to maintenance of vital parts of the tenement such as the roof and foundations. Accordingly the tenement management scheme defines those parts of the tenement as "scheme property". There is no alteration in property rights. The concept of scheme property is a purely artificial one for the purposes of the management and maintenance of those parts of the tenement. Scheme property includes any property which by the title is made common property of two or more persons or in relation to which the cost of maintenance is by virtue of a real burden the responsibility of two or more of the owners.

However even where there is no right of common property nor any obligation of common maintenance the following are deemed to be scheme property no matter what the title says:

(a) the ground on which the tenement is built
(b) the foundations
(c) the external walls
(d) the roof including any rafter or other structure supporting the roof
(e) part of a mutual gable wall separating the tenement from another building
(f) any other wall, beam or column that is load bearing.

To avoid confusion certain parts of the tenement are not scheme property. These are any extension which forms part of one flat or any door, window, skylight, vent or other opening which serves only one flat. The chimneystack or chimney flue is not scheme property despite the fact that it is sited on the roof. A scheme decision is one which is made in accordance with rule 2 or in accordance with a real burden contained in the tenemental title which deals with procedure for making decisions. Of some significance is the definition of maintenance. A difficulty is sometimes caused where some proprietors wish to carry out maintenance which involves some element of improvement. There is of course a distinction between carrying out a repair and renewing some particular part of the tenement. In some cases a repair is uneconomic and renewal is the only sensible course of action. For this reason the definition of maintenance is wider than the dictionary definition. It includes replacement, cleaning, painting and other routine works such as gardening. It also includes re-instatement of a part but not most of the tenement building. It does not however include demolition, alteration and improvement unless reasonably incidental to the maintenance. This is probably as good a definition as one can hope for. That is not to say there will not be disputes in the future. One can see an argument for example that if lead piping fractures then it should not be repaired but be replaced by copper or some other up-to-date material. However one would not say that painting could include the commissioning of a mural on a gable end. Each case will obviously depend on its own circumstances. Where a flat is owned by two or more people then the rights of an owner will apply to both in terms of the scheme.

RULE 2—PROCEDURE FOR MAKING SCHEME DECISIONS

2.1 Making scheme decisions

Any decision to be made by the owners shall be made in accordance with the following provisions of this rule.

2.2 Allocation and exercise of votes

Except as mentioned in rule 2.3, for the purpose of voting on any proposed scheme decision one vote is allocated as respects each flat, and any right to vote is exercisable by the owner of that flat or by someone nominated by the owner to vote as respects the flat.

2.3 Qualification on allocation of votes

No vote is allocated as respects a flat if—

(a) the scheme decision relates to the maintenance of scheme property, and
(b) the owner of that flat is not liable for maintenance of, or the cost of maintaining, the property concerned.

2.4 Exercise of vote where two or more persons own flat

If a flat is owned by two or more persons the vote allocated as respects that flat may be exercised in relation to any proposal by either (or any) of them, but if those persons disagree as to how the vote should be cast then the vote is not to be counted unless—

(a) where one of those persons owns more than a half share of the flat, the vote is exercised by that person, or
(b) in any other case, the vote is the agreed vote of those who together own more than a half share of the flat.

2.5 Decision by majority

A scheme decision is made by majority vote of all the votes allocated.

2.6 Notice of meeting

If any owner wishes to call a meeting of the owners with a view to making a scheme decision at that meeting that owner must give the other owners at least 48 hours' notice of the date and time of the meeting, its purpose and the place where it is to be held.

2.7 Consultation of owners if scheme decision not made at meeting

If an owner wishes to propose that a scheme decision be made but does not wish to call a meeting for the purpose that owner must instead—

(a) unless it is impracticable to do so (whether because of absence of any owner or for other good reason) consult on the proposal each of the other owners of flats as respects which votes are allocated, and

(b) count the votes cast by them.

2.8 Consultation where two or more persons own flat

For the purposes of rule 2.7, the requirement to consult each owner is satisfied as respects any flat which is owned by more than one person if one of those persons is consulted.

2.9 Notification of scheme decisions

A scheme decision must, as soon as practicable, be notified—

(a) if it was made at a meeting, to all the owners who were not present when the decision was made, by such person as may be nominated for the purpose by the persons who made the decision, or

(b) in any other case, to each of the other owners, by the owner who proposed that the decision be made.

2.10 Case where decision may be annulled by notice

Any owner (or owners) who did not vote in favour of a scheme decision to carry out, or authorise, maintenance to scheme property and who would be liable for not less than 75 per cent. of the scheme costs arising from that decision may, within the time mentioned in rule 2.11, annul that decision by giving notice that the decision is annulled to each of the other owners.

2.11 Time limits for rule 2.10

The time within which a notice under rule 2.10 must be given is—

(a) if the scheme decision was made at a meeting attended by the owner (or any of the owners), not later than 21 days after the date of that meeting, or

(b) in any other case, not later than 21 days after the date on which notification of the making of the decision was given to the owner or owners (that date being, where notification was given to owners on different dates, the date on which it was given to the last of them).

GENERAL NOTE

Rule 2 does not apply where a tenement burden provides procedures for the making of decisions by owners provided that these procedures apply to every flat in the tenement. In some cases the burdens in all the titles are inconsistent. If the management scheme is the same in every title then it will apply and rule 2 will not apply. However if there is no management scheme or if it does not apply to all flats then rule 2 will apply to every flat. Basically decisions are taken by majority counting one vote for each flat. If a decision on maintenance has to be taken in respect of a particular part of the tenement then only owners who have an obligation to maintain that part will be entitled to vote. Where a flat is owned in common either common owner can vote provided that they both agree. If there is disagreement then there will be no vote for that flat unless an owner or owners own more than one half share in which case they will be entitled to cast the vote. Decisions may be taken either at a formal meeting properly called or by consultation. A scheme decision must be notified. If any owner or owners together would be liable for 75% or more of the costs arising from the decision and they were not in favour of it then they may annul the decision by giving notice to each of the other owners. Such notification must be given not later than 21 days after the date of the meeting or if the decision was taken by consultation, 21 days after notification of the decision was given.

RULE 3—MATTERS ON WHICH SCHEME DECISIONS MAY BE MADE

3.1 Basic scheme decisions

The owners may make a scheme decision on any of the following matters—

(a) to carry out maintenance to scheme property,

(b) to arrange for an inspection of scheme property to determine whether or to what extent it is necessary to carry out maintenance to the property,

(c) except where a power conferred by a manager burden (within the meaning of the Title Conditions (Scotland) Act 2003 (asp 9)) is exercisable in relation to the tenement—

    (i) to appoint on such terms as they may determine a person (who may be an owner or a firm) to manage the tenement,

    (ii) to dismiss any manager,

(d) to delegate to a manager power to exercise such of their powers as they may specify, including, without prejudice to that generality, any power to decide to carry out maintenance and to instruct it,

(e) to arrange for the tenement a common policy of insurance complying with section 18 of this Act and against such other risks (if any) as the owners may determine and to determine on an equitable basis the liability of each owner to contribute to the premium,

(f) to install a system enabling entry to the tenement to be controlled from each flat,

(g) to determine that an owner is not required to pay a share (or some part of a share) of such scheme costs as may be specified by them,

(h) to authorise any maintenance of scheme property already carried out,

(i) to modify or revoke any scheme decision.

3.2 Scheme decisions relating to maintenance

If the owners make a scheme decision to carry out maintenance to scheme property or if a manager decides, by virtue of a scheme decision, that maintenance needs to be carried out to scheme property, the owners may make a scheme decision on any of the following matters—

(a) to appoint on such terms as they may determine a person (who may be an owner or a firm) to manage the carrying out of the maintenance,

(b) to instruct or arrange for the carrying out of the maintenance,

(c) subject to rule 3.3, to require each owner to deposit—

    (i) by such date as they may decide (being a date not less than 28 days after the requirement is made of that owner), and

    (ii) with such person as they may nominate for the purpose, a sum of money (being a sum not exceeding that owner's apportioned share of a reasonable estimate of the cost of the maintenance),

(d) to take such other steps as are necessary to ensure that the maintenance is carried out to a satisfactory standard and completed in good time.

3.3 Scheme decisions under rule 3.2(c) requiring deposits exceeding certain amounts

A requirement, in pursuance of a scheme decision under rule 3.2(c), that each owner deposit a sum of money—

(a) exceeding £100, or

(b) of £100 or less where the aggregate of that sum taken together with any other sum or sums required (otherwise than by a previous notice under this rule) in the preceding 12 months to be deposited by each owner by virtue any scheme decision under rule 3.2(c) exceeds £200,

shall be made by written notice to each owner and shall require the sum to be deposited into such account (the "maintenance account") as the owners may nominate for the purpose.

3.4 Provision supplementary to rule 3.3

Where a requirement is, or is to be, made in accordance with rule 3.3—

(a) the owners may make a scheme decision authorising a manager or at least two other persons (whether or not owners) to operate the maintenance account on behalf of the owners,

(b) there must be contained in or attached to the notice to be given under rule 3.3 a note comprising a summary of the nature and extent of the maintenance to be carried out together with the following information—

    (i) the estimated cost of carrying out that maintenance,

    (ii) why the estimate is considered a reasonable estimate,

    (iii) how the sum required from the owner in question and the apportionment among the owners have been arrived at,

    (iv) what the apportioned shares of the other owners are,

    (v) the date on which the decision to carry out the maintenance was made and the names of those by whom it was made,

    (vi) a timetable for the carrying out of the maintenance, including the dates by which it is proposed the maintenance will be commenced and completed,

    (vii) the location and number of the maintenance account, and

    (viii) the names and addresses of the persons who will be authorised to operate hat account on behalf of the owners,

(c) the maintenance account to be nominated under rule 3.3 must be a bank or building society account which is interest bearing, and the authority of at least two persons or of a manager on whom has been conferred the right to give authority, must be required for any payment from it,

(d) if a modification or revocation under rule 3.1(i) affects the information contained in the notice or the note referred to in paragraph (b) above, the information must be sent again, modified accordingly, to the owners,

(e) an owner is entitled to inspect, at any reasonable time, any tender received in connection with the maintenance to be carried out,

(f) the notice to be given under rule 3.3 may specify a date as a refund date for the purposes of paragraph (g)(i) below,

(g) if—

    (i) the maintenance is not commenced by—

        (A) where the notice under rule 3.3 specifies a refund date, that date, or

        (B) where that notice does not specify such a date, the twenty-eighth day after the proposed date for its commencement as specified in the notice by virtue of paragraph (b)(vi) above, and

    (ii) a depositor demands, by written notice, from the persons authorised under paragraph (a) above repayment (with accrued interest) of such sum as has been deposited by that person in compliance with the scheme decision under rule 3.2(c),

    the depositor is entitled to be repaid accordingly, except that no requirement to make repayment in compliance with a notice under sub-paragraph (ii) arises if the persons so authorised do not receive that notice before the maintenance is commenced,

(h) such sums as are held in the maintenance account by virtue of rule 3.3 are held in trust for all the depositors, for the purpose of being used by the persons authorised to make payments from the account as payment for the maintenance,

(i) any sums held in the maintenance account after all sums payable in respect of the maintenance carried out have been paid shall be shared among the depositors—

    (i) by repaying each depositor, with any accrued interest and after deduction of that person's apportioned share of the actual cost of the maintenance, the sum which the person deposited, or

    (ii) in such other way as the depositors agree in writing.

3.5 Scheme decisions under rule 3.1(g): votes of persons standing to benefit not to be counted

A vote in favour of a scheme decision under rule 3.1(g) is not to be counted if—

  (a) the owner exercising the vote, or

  (b) where the vote is exercised by a person nominated by an owner—

    (i) that person, or

    (ii) the owner who nominated that person,

    is the owner or an owner who, by virtue of the decision, would not be required to pay as mentioned in that rule.

GENERAL NOTE

The provisions of Rule 3 only apply to the extent that there is no tenement burden in the titles enabling the owners to make scheme decisions on any matter on which a scheme decision may be made under rule 3. The title deeds of tenemental properties may contain general obligations of maintenance and repair but may not specify in detail what type of decisions may be taken. Rule 3 will fill this gap. The matters on which a scheme decision may be taken are listed and they cover most issues which are likely to arise. Once a decision has been taken then it can be carried through by the appointment of a factor or manager or simply by the instruction of the work. Deposits may be required to provide some sort of float to pay for the cost. There are detailed provisions in relation to the holding of such deposits. If deposits are required then information must be given to the owners in relation to the nature and extent of the maintenance to be carried out and the estimated cost as well as the shares apportioned to each owner. There are detailed provisions as to how a bank account containing a float or sinking fund is to be operated. If it is proposed to make a decision authorising maintenance of scheme property already carried out by an owner then that owner cannot vote.

RULE 4—SCHEME COSTS: LIABILITY AND APPORTIONMENT

4.1 Meaning of "scheme costs"

Except in so far as rule 5 applies, this rule provides for the apportionment of liability among the owners for any of the following costs—

(a) any costs arising from any maintenance or inspection of scheme property where the maintenance or inspection is in pursuance of, or authorised by, a scheme decision,

(b) any remuneration payable to a person appointed to manage the carrying out of such maintenance as is mentioned in paragraph (a),

(c) running costs relating to any scheme property (other than costs incurred solely for the benefit of one flat),

(d) any costs recoverable by a local authority in respect of work relating to any scheme property carried out by them by virtue of any enactment,

(e) any remuneration payable to any manager,

(f) the cost of any common insurance to cover the tenement,

(g) the cost of installing a system enabling entry to the tenement to be controlled from each flat,

(h) any costs relating to the calculation of the floor area of any flat, where such calculation is necessary for the purpose of determining the share of any other costs for which each owner is liable,

(i) any other costs relating to the management of scheme property,

and a reference in this scheme to "scheme costs" is a reference to any of the costs mentioned in paragraphs (a) to (i).

4.2 Maintenance and running costs

Except as provided in rule 4.3, if any scheme costs mentioned in rule 4.1(a) to (d) relate to—

(a) the scheme property mentioned in rule 1.2(a), then those costs are shared among the owners in the proportions in which the owners share ownership of that property,

(b) the scheme property mentioned in rule 1.2(b) or (c), then—

(i) in any case where the floor area of the largest (or larger) flat is more than one and a half times that of the smallest (or smaller) flat, each owner is liable to contribute towards those costs in the proportion which the floor area of that owner's flat bears to the total floor area of all (or both) the flats,

(ii) in any other case, those costs are shared equally among the flats,

and each owner is liable accordingly.

4.3 Scheme costs relating to roof over the close

Where—

(a) any scheme costs mentioned in rule 4.1(a) to (d) relate to the roof over the close, and

(b) that roof is common property by virtue of section 3(1)(a) of this Act,

then, despite the fact that the roof is scheme property mentioned in rule 1.2(a), paragraph (b) of rule 4.2 shall apply for the purpose of apportioning liability for those costs.

4.4 Insurance premium

Any scheme costs mentioned in rule 4.1(f) are shared among the flats—

(a) where the costs relate to common insurance arranged by virtue of rule 3.1(e), in such proportions as may be determined by the owners by virtue of that rule, or

(b) where the costs relate to common insurance arranged by virtue of a tenement burden, equally,

and each owner is liable accordingly.

4.5 Other scheme costs

Any scheme costs mentioned in rule 4.1(e), (g), (h) or (i) are shared equally among the flats, and each owner is liable accordingly.

GENERAL NOTE

Apart from the special conditions set out in rule 5 liability is apportioned in accordance with rule 4. There is an extensive definition of scheme costs. These cover maintenance, inspection, factorial and management charges, costs in respect of local authority work, common insurance premiums and the cost of installing a secure entry system. Where the scheme costs relate to scheme property which is owned in common in terms of the title then the costs are shared among the owners in the proportions in which they share ownership of that common property. If the scheme costs relate to scheme property which is not owned in common but must be maintained in terms of the title deeds by two or more owners or is scheme property within the meaning of rule 1.2(c) then scheme costs are shared among the owners. The proportions due by each will depend on whether or not the various flats or other units are roughly of equal size. In any case where the floor area of the largest or larger flat or unit is more than one and half times that of the smallest or smaller flat or unit each owner is liable to contribute in proportion to floor area. In other cases where the flats or units are roughly the same the costs will be shared equally. Where the part of the tenement in question is the roof over the close and that is common property by virtue of being a pertinent it will be treated for the purposes of apportionment of the scheme costs as scheme property. So far as insurance premiums are concerned where the costs relate to a common insurance then the premium will be shared as may be determined by the owners in terms of the scheme decision in favour of common insurance under rule 3.1(e). Where however the common insurance has been taken out in terms of a real burden in the title then the cost is shared equally. Any other scheme costs relating to the remuneration of a factor or manager, the cost of installing a secure entry system, the cost of calculating the floor area and any other costs are shared equally.

RULE 5—REDISTRIBUTION OF SHARE OF COSTS

Where an owner is liable for a share of any scheme costs but—
   (a) a scheme decision has been made determining that the share (or a portion of it) should not be paid by that owner, or
   (b) the share cannot be recovered for some other reason such as that—
        (i) the estate of that owner has been sequestrated, or
        (ii) that owner cannot, by reasonable inquiry, be identified or found,
then that share must be paid by the other owners who are liable for a share of the same costs (the share being divided equally among the flats of those other owners), but where paragraph (b) applies that owner is liable to each of those other owners for the amount paid by each of them.

GENERAL NOTE
   One of the most difficult problems which arises in relation to maintenance of tenemental properties is the situation which arises where a particular owner cannot or will not pay his or her share. Rule 5 provides that a scheme decision can be made to the effect that a share due by a particular owner shall not be paid by that owner. This is perhaps an unlikely scenario. The rule goes on to provide however that where a share cannot be recovered for some other reason such as bankruptcy or the disappearance of an owner then that share simply falls to be paid by the other owners who are liable. The share is divided equally among the remaining owners who have a right of relief against the defaulting owner for what that may be worth.

RULE 6—PROCEDURAL IRREGULARITIES

6.1 Validity of scheme decisions
   Any procedural irregularity in the making of a scheme decision does not affect the validity of the decision.

6.2 Liability for scheme costs where procedural irregularity
   If any owner is directly affected by a procedural irregularity in the making of a scheme decision and that owner—
   (a) was not aware that any scheme costs relating to that decision were being incurred, or
   (b) on becoming aware as mentioned in paragraph (a), immediately objected to the incurring of those costs,
that owner is not liable for any such costs (whether incurred before or after the date of objection), and, for the purposes of determining the share of those scheme costs due by each of the other owners, that owner is left out of account.

GENERAL NOTE
   In general terms procedural irregularities will not affect the validity of a scheme decision. However this is qualified by the sub-rule which provides that any owner who is directly affected by a procedural irregularity will have no liability for scheme costs, if that owner was not aware that any scheme costs relating to that decision were being incurred or on becoming so aware

immediately objected. In such a case the owner is not liable for the costs whether incurred before or after the date of objection and these costs will simply have to be shared among the other owners.

RULE 7—EMERGENCY WORK

7.1 Power to instruct or carry out
Any owner may instruct or carry out emergency work.

7.2 Liability for cost
The owners are liable for the cost of any emergency work instructed or carried out as if the cost of that work were scheme costs mentioned in rule 4.1(a).

7.3 Meaning of "emergency work"
For the purposes of this rule, "emergency work" means work which, before a scheme decision can be obtained, requires to be carried out to scheme property—
    (a) to prevent damage to any part of the tenement, or
    (b) in the interests of health or safety.

GENERAL NOTE
There is no requirement for meetings or consultation in relation to scheme decisions if work requires to be carried out as a matter of emergency and any owner can carry out such work. Owners are liable for the cost of such work as if they were scheme costs under rule 4.1(a) which refers to maintenance or inspection costs relating to scheme property. Emergency work is defined as work which has to be carried out to prevent damage to any part of the tenement or in the interests of health or safety.

RULE 8—ENFORCEMENT

8.1 Scheme binding on owners
This scheme binds the owners.

8.2 Scheme decision to be binding
A scheme decision is binding on the owners and their successors as owners.

8.3 Enforceability of scheme decisions
Any obligation imposed by this scheme or arising from a scheme decision may be enforced by any owner.

8.4 Enforcement by third party
Any person authorised in writing for the purpose by the owner or owners concerned may—
    (a) enforce an obligation such as is mentioned in rule 8.3 on behalf of one or more owners, and
    (b) in doing so, may bring any claim or action in that person's own name.

GENERAL NOTE
Between or among owners the tenement management scheme is binding on all and any scheme decision binds the owners and their successors. One should bear in mind here the provisions of sections 12 and 13 of the Act in relation to the notice procedure. In terms of section 12 a successor owner is not liable unless a notice potential liability for costs has been registered at least 14 days before the acquisition of the property. The definition of relevant costs can be found in s.11(9) of the Act and these costs would include any costs incurred in terms of the tenement management scheme. Rule 8 however refers to decisions as opposed to costs whereas sections 12 and 13 relate to costs. Presumably therefore what rule 8 means is that a new owner will not be entitled to object to a decision which has already been taken but may not be liable for the costs of any work carried out as a result of that decision unless a notice has been registered. It should also be borne in mind that s.12(3) refers at the moment only to work which has been actually carried out before the acquisition date whereas rule 8 could refer to a decision to carry out work in the future well beyond the acquisition date. It is likely this will be amended by statutory instrument. It would seem therefore that the combined effect of ss.12 and 13 and rule 8 will be that a future owner will be liable for the costs of maintenance instructed under a

scheme decision made before acquisition unless the work has been carried out prior to acquisition and no notice of potential liability for costs has been registered 14 days before the acquisition date. The acquisition date is defined in s.12(4) as the date on which the new owner acquired right to the flat. Presumably in the light of the decision of the House of Lords in *Burnett's Trustee v Grainger* ([2004] UKHL 8) the new owner does not acquire right to the flat until registration of title.

RULE 9—GIVING OF NOTICE

9.1 Giving of notice
Any notice which requires to be given to an owner under or in connection with this scheme may be given in writing by sending the notice to—
    (a) the owner, or
    (b) the owner's agent.

9.2 Methods of "sending" for the purposes of rule 9.1
The reference in rule 9.1 to sending a notice is to its being—
    (a) posted,
    (b) delivered, or
    (c) transmitted by electronic means.

9.3 Giving of notice to owner where owner's name is not known
Where an owner cannot by reasonable inquiry be identified or found, a notice shall be taken for the purposes of rule 9.1(a) to be sent to the owner if it is posted or delivered to the owner's flat addressed to "The Owner" or using some other similar expression such as "The Proprietor".

9.4 Day on which notice is to be taken to be given
For the purposes of this scheme—
    (a) a notice posted shall be taken to be given on the day of posting, and
    (b) a notice transmitted by electronic means shall be taken to be given on the day of transmission.

GENERAL NOTE
Any notice under the tenement management scheme may be given in writing by sending the notice to the owner or the owner's agent. Notice is sent if it is posted, delivered or transmitted by electronic means. A notice is taken as having been given on the day of posting or on the day of electronic transmission. Where the notice is delivered presumably it is given on delivery. Where an owner cannot be found then the notice can be addressed to "the owner" or "the proprietor" and simply posted or delivered to the flat in question.

¹SCHEDULE 2

(introduced by section 12(3))

FORM OF NOTICE OF POTENTIAL LIABILITY FOR COSTS

"NOTICE OF POTENTIAL LIABILITY FOR COSTS

This notice gives details of certain maintenance or work carried out, or to be carried out, in relation to the flat specified in the notice. The effect of the notice is that a person may, on becoming the owner of the flat, be liable by virtue of section 12(3) of the Tenements (Scotland) Act 2004 (asp 11) for any outstanding costs relating to the maintenance or work.

Flat to which notice relates:
(see note 1 below)

Description of the maintenance or work to which notice relates:
(see note 2 below)

Person giving notice:
(see note 3 below)

Signature:
(see note 4 below)

Date of signing:"

Notes for completion

(These notes are not part of the notice)

1   Describe the flat in a way that is sufficient to identify it. Where the flat has a postal address, the description must include that address. Where title to the flat has been registered in the Land Register of Scotland, the description must refer to the title number of the flat or of the larger subjects of which it forms part. Otherwise, the description should normally refer to and identify a deed recorded in a specified division of the Register of Sasines.

2   Describe the maintenance or work in general terms.

3   Give the name and address of the person applying for registration of the notice ("the applicant") or the applicant's name and the name and address of the applicant's agent.

4   The notice must be signed by or on behalf of the applicant.

AMENDMENT NOTE

1 As amended by the Tenements (Scotland) Act 2004 (Notice of Potential Liability for Costs) Amendment Order 2004 (SSI 2004/490), art.2 (effective December 6, 2004).

SCHEDULE 3

(introduced by sections 22(3) and 23(1))

SALE UNDER SECTION 22(3) OR 23(1)

Application to sheriff for power to sell

1.—(1) Where an owner is entitled to apply—

(a) under section 22(3), for power to sell the site; or

(b) under section 23(1), for power to sell the tenement building,

the owner may make a summary application to the sheriff seeking an order (referred to in this Act as a "power of sale order") conferring such power on the owner.

(2) The site or tenement building in relation to which an application or order is made under sub-paragraph (1) is referred to in this schedule as the "sale subjects".

(3) An owner making an application under sub-paragraph (1) shall give notice of it to each of the other owners of the sale subjects.

(4) The sheriff shall, on an application under sub-paragraph (1)—

(a) grant the power of sale order sought unless satisfied that to do so would—

(i)   not be in the best interests of all (or both) the owners taken as a group; or

(ii) be unfairly prejudicial to one or more of the owners; and

(b) if a power of sale order has previously been granted in respect of the same sale subjects, revoke that previous order.

(5) A power of sale order shall contain—

(a) the name and address of the owner in whose favour it is granted;

(b) the postal address of each flat or, as the case may be, former flat comprised in the sale subjects to which the order relates; and

(c) a sufficient conveyancing description of each of those flats or former flats.

(6) A description of a flat or former flat is a sufficient conveyancing description for the purposes of sub-paragraph (5)(c) if—

(a) where the interest of the proprietor of the land comprising the flat or former flat has been registered in the Land Register of Scotland, the description refers to the number of the title sheet of that interest; or

(b) in relation to any other flat or former flat, the description is by reference to a deed recorded in the Register of Sasines.

(7) An application under sub-paragraph (1) shall state the applicant's conclusions as to—

(a) which of subsections (4) and (5) of section 22 applies for the purpose of determining how the net proceeds of any sale of the sale subjects in pursuance of a power of sale order are to be shared among the owners of those subjects; and

   (b) if subsection (5) of that section is stated as applying for that purpose—

      (i) the floor area of each of the flats or former flats comprised in the sale subjects; and

     (ii) the proportion of the net proceeds of sale allocated to that flat.

Appeal against grant or refusal of power of sale order

  2.—(1) A party may, not later than 14 days after the date of—

   (a) making of a power of sale order; or

   (b) an interlocutor refusing an application for such an order,

appeal to the Court of Session on a point of law.

  (2) The decision of the Court of Session on any such appeal shall be final.

Registration of power of sale order

  3.—(1) A power of sale order has no effect—

   (a) unless it is registered within the period of 14 days after the relevant day; and

   (b) until the beginning of the forty-second day after the day on which it is so registered.

  (2) In sub-paragraph (1)(a) above, "the relevant day" means, in relation to a power of sale order—

   (a) the last day of the period of 14 days within which an appeal against the order may be lodged under paragraph 2(1) of this schedule; or

   (b) if such an appeal is duly lodged, the day on which the appeal is abandoned or determined.

Exercise of power of sale

  4.—(1) An owner in whose favour a power of sale order is granted may exercise the power conferred by the order by private bargain or by exposure to sale.

  (2) However, in either case, the owner shall—

   (a) advertise the sale; and

   (b) take all reasonable steps to ensure that the price at which the sale subjects are sold is the best that can reasonably be obtained.

  (3) In advertising the sale in pursuance of sub-paragraph (2)(a) above, the owner shall, in particular, ensure that there is placed and maintained on the sale subjects a conspicuous sign—

   (a) advertising the fact that the sale subjects are for sale; and

   (b) giving the name and contact details of the owner or of any agent acting on the owner's behalf in connection with the sale.

  (4) So far as may be necessary for the purpose of complying with sub-paragraph (3) above, the owner or any person authorised by the owner shall be entitled to enter any part of the sale subjects not owned, or not owned exclusively, by that owner.

Distribution of proceeds of sale

  5.—(1) An owner selling the sale subjects (referred to in this paragraph as the "selling owner") shall, within seven days of completion of the sale—

   (a) calculate each owner's share; and

   (b) apply that share in accordance with sub-paragraph (2) below.

  (2) An owner's share shall be applied—

   (a) first, to repay any amounts due under any heritable security affecting that owner's flat or former flat;

   (b) next, to defray any expenses properly incurred in complying with paragraph (a) above; and

   (c) finally, to pay to the owner the remainder (if any) of that owner's share.

  (3) If there is more than one heritable security affecting an owner's flat or former flat, the owner's share shall be applied under paragraph (2)(a) above in relation to each security in the order in which they rank.

  (4) If any owner cannot by reasonable inquiry be identified or found, the selling owner shall consign the remainder of that owner's share in the sheriff court.

  (5) On paying to another owner the remainder of that owner's share, the selling owner shall also give to that other owner—

   (a) a written statement showing—

      (i) the amount of that owner's share and of the remainder of it; and

     (ii) how that share and remainder were calculated; and

   (b) evidence of—

(i) the total amount of the proceeds of sale; and

(ii) any expenses properly incurred in connection with the sale and in complying with sub-paragraph (2)(a) above.

(6) In this paragraph—

"remainder", in relation to an owner's share, means the amount of that share remaining after complying with sub-paragraph (2)(a) and (b) above;

"share", in relation to an owner, means the share of the net proceeds of sale to which that owner is entitled in accordance with subsection (4) or, as the case may be, subsection (5) of section 22.

Automatic discharge of heritable securities

6. Where—

(a) an owner—

(i) sells the sale subjects in pursuance of a power of sale order; and

(ii) grants a disposition of those subjects to the purchaser or the purchaser's nominee; and

(b) that disposition is duly registered in the Land Register of Scotland or recorded in the Register of Sasines,

all heritable securities affecting the sale subjects or any part of them shall, by virtue of this paragraph, be to that extent discharged.

General Note

This schedule sets out the procedure which must be followed where there is an application to the sheriff for a power to sell the site of a demolished tenement or abandoned tenement. The procedure is by way of summary application seeking a power of sale order. Notice must be given to other owners and the sheriff must grant the power of sale unless satisfied that this would not be in the interests of all or both the owners as a group or alternatively would be unfairly prejudicial to one or more of the owners. A power of sale can be revoked on summary application. A power of sale order must contain the appropriate details including a sufficient conveyancing description of each of the flats or former flats. If title to a flat has been registered then the title number will be appropriate. Otherwise there must be a reference to a description contained in a deed recorded in the Register of Sasines. The application must contain averments as to how the proceeds of sale will be divided in accordance with the statutory provisions. Appeal lies to the Court of Session on a point of law but no further. The power of sale order must be registered within 14 days and has no effect until the expiry of the 42nd day after registration. If an appeal is taken to the Court of Session the 14 day period does not start until the appeal is abandoned or determined. Once the power of sale order takes effect the owner in whose favour it is granted may sell by private bargain or public auction. There is however an obligation to advertise and take all reasonable steps to ensure that the price is the best that can be reasonably obtained. There is a specific obligation to place and maintain a for sale sign on the subject giving the name and contact details of the party selling or any agent. These provisions are similar to the provisions which set out the obligation of a heritable creditor selling security subjects (Conveyancing and Feudal Reform (Scotland) Act 1970, s.25; see *Dick v Clydesdale Bank Plc* 1991 S.L.T. 678). The party who has exercised the power of sale is subject to strict statutory obligations in relation to the calculation and disbursement of each owner's share. Any heritable securities must be cleared first then expenses of the sale. Only then can the net proceeds of sale be distributed. If an owner cannot be traced then the sum due can be consigned in the Sheriff Court. There is no need however for any discharges of heritable securities. Once the disposition in favour of the purchaser is duly registered all heritable securities are discharged. There is no suggestion that this automatic discharge is in any way conditional on the selling owner actually paying off the securities. Accordingly heritable creditors may find themselves in a position of having to take less than the sum due. There does not appear to be any requirement on the owner applying for the power of sale to obtain the consent of the holders of heritable securities.

SCHEDULE 4

(introduced by section 25)

Amendments of Title Conditions (Scotland) Act 2003

1. The Title Conditions (Scotland) Act 2003 (asp 9) shall be amended as follows.

2. In section 3(8) (waiver, mitigation and variation of real burdens), for "the holder" there shall be substituted "a holder".

3. In section 4 (creation of real burdens), in subsection (7), after "sections" there shall be inserted "53(3A),".

4. In section 10 (affirmative burdens: continuing liability of former owner)—

(a) in subsection (2), at the beginning there shall be inserted "Subject to subsection (2A) below,";

(b) after subsection (2) there shall be inserted—

"(2A) A new owner shall be liable as mentioned in subsection (2) above for any relevant obligation consisting of an obligation to pay a share of costs relating to maintenance or work (other than local authority work) carried out before the acquisition date only if—

(a) notice of the maintenance or work—

(i) in, or as near as may be in, the form set out in schedule 1A to this Act; and

(ii) containing the information required by the notes for completion set out in that schedule,

(such a notice being referred to in this section and section 10A of this Act as a "notice of potential liability for costs") was registered in relation to the burdened property at least 14 days before the acquisition date; and

(b) the notice had not expired before the acquisition date.

(2B) In subsection (2A) above—

"acquisition date" means the date on which the new owner acquired right to the burdened property; and

"local authority work" means work carried out by a local authority by virtue of any enactment."; and

(c) at the end there shall be added—

"(5) This section does not apply in any case where section 12 of the Tenements (Scotland) Act 2004 (asp 11) applies.".

5. After section 10 there shall be inserted—

"10A Notice of potential liability for costs: further provision

(1) A notice of potential liability for costs—

(a) may be registered in relation to burdened property only on the application of—

(i) an owner of the burdened property;

(ii) an owner of the benefited property; or

(iii) any manager; and

(b) shall not be registered unless it is signed by or on behalf of the applicant.

(2) A notice of potential liability for costs may be registered—

(a) in relation to more than one burdened property in respect of the same maintenance or work; and

(b) in relation to any one burdened property, in respect of different maintenance or work.

(3) A notice of potential liability for costs expires at the end of the period of 3 years beginning with the date of its registration, unless it is renewed by being registered again before the end of that period.

(4) This section applies to a renewed notice of potential liability for costs as it applies to any other such notice.

(5) The Keeper of the Registers of Scotland shall not be required to investigate or determine whether the information contained in any notice of potential liability for costs submitted for registration is accurate.

(6) The Scottish Ministers may by order amend schedule 1A to this Act."

6. In section 11 (affirmative burdens: shared liability), after subsection (3) there shall be inserted—

"(3A) For the purposes of subsection (3) above, the floor area of a flat is calculated by measuring the total floor area (including the area occupied by any internal wall or other internal dividing structure) within its boundaries; but no account shall be taken of any pertinents or any of the following parts of a flat—

(a) a balcony; and

(b) except where it is used for any purpose other than storage, a loft or basement.".

7. In section 25 (definition of the expression "community burdens"), in subsection (1)(a), for "four" there shall be substituted "two".

8. In section 29 (power of majority to instruct common maintenance)—

(a) in subsection (2)—
  (i) in paragraph (b)—
    (A) for the words from the beginning to "that" where it first occurs there shall be substituted "subject to subsection (3A) below, require each"; and
    (B) for sub-paragraph (ii) there shall be substituted—
      "(ii) with such person as they may nominate for the purpose," ; and
  (ii) paragraph (c) shall be omitted;
(b) after subsection (3) there shall be inserted—
  "(3A) A requirement under subsection (2)(b) above that each owner deposit a sum of money—
    (a) exceeding £163;100; or
    (b) of £163;100 or less where the aggregate of that sum taken together with any other sum or sums required (otherwise than by a previous notice under this subsection) in the preceding 12 months to be deposited under that subsection by each owner exceeds £163;200,
  shall be made by written notice to each owner and shall require the sum to be deposited into such account (the "maintenance account") as the owners may nominate for the purpose.
  (3B) The owners may authorise a manager or at least two other persons (whether or not owners) to operate the maintenance account on their behalf.";
(c) in subsection (4), for "(2)(b)" there shall be substituted "(3A)";
(d) after subsection (6) there shall be inserted—
  "(6A) The notice given under subsection (2)(b) above may specify a date as a refund date for the purposes of subsection (7)(b)(i) below.";
(e) in subsection (7)(b)—
  (i) in sub-paragraph (i), for "the fourteenth" there shall be substituted
  "—
    (A) where the notice under subsection (2)(b) above specifies a refund date, that date; or
    (B) where that notice does not specify such a date, the twenty-eighth";
  (ii) in sub-paragraph (ii), for "(4)(h)" there shall be substituted "(3B)";
(f) after subsection (7) there shall be inserted—
  "(7A) A former owner who, before ceasing to be an owner, deposited sums in compliance with a requirement under subsection (2)(b) above, shall have the same entitlement as an owner has under subsection (7)(b) above.";
(g) in subsection (8), for "(2)(b)" there shall be substituted "(3A)"; and
(h) after subsection (9) there shall be inserted—
  "(10) The Scottish Ministers may by order substitute for the sums for the time being specified in subsection (3A) above such other sums as appear to them to be justified by a change in the value of money appearing to them to have occurred since the last occasion on which the sums were fixed.".

9. After section 31 there shall be inserted—
"31A Disapplication of provisions of sections 28, 29 and 31 in certain cases
(1) Sections 28(1)(a) and (d) and (2)(a), 29 and 31 of this Act shall not apply in relation to
a community consisting of one tenement.
(2) Sections 28(1)(a) and (d) and 31 of this Act shall not apply to a community in any period during which the development management scheme applies to the community.".

10. In section 33 (majority etc. variation and discharge of community burdens)—
(a) in subsection (1)(b), the words "where no such provision is made," shall be omitted; and
(b) in subsection (2)(a), at the beginning there shall be inserted "where no such provision as is mentioned in subsection (1)(a) above is made,".

11. In section 35 (variation and discharge of community burdens by owners of adjacent units), in subsection (1), the words "in a case where no such provision as is mentioned in section 33(1)(a) of this Act is made" shall be omitted.

12. In section 43 (rural housing burdens)—
(a) in subsection (1), after "burden" where it first occurs there shall be inserted "over rural land"; and
(b) in subsection (6), for "on rural land or to provide rural" there shall be substituted "or".

13. In section 45 (economic development burdens), subsection (6) shall be omitted.

14. In section 53 (common schemes: related properties), after subsection (3) there shall be inserted—

> "(3A) Section 4 of this Act shall apply in relation to any real burden to which subsection (1) above applies as if—
>> (a) in subsection (2), paragraph (c)(ii);
>> (b) subsection (4); and
>> (c) in subsection (5), the words from "and" to the end,
> were omitted."

15. In section 90 (powers of Lands Tribunals as respects title conditions), in subsection (8A), for "application" there shall be substituted "disapplication".

16. In section 98 (granting certain applications for variation, discharge, renewal or preservation of title conditions), in paragraph (b)(i), for the words "the owners of all" there shall be substituted "all the owners (taken as a group) of".

17. In section 99 (granting applications as respects development management schemes), in subsection (4)(a), for the words "the owners" there shall be substituted "all the owners (taken as a group)".

18. In section 119 (savings and transitional provision etc.), subsection (9) shall be omitted.

19. In section 122(1) (interpretation)—
  (a) the definition of "flat" shall be omitted;
  (b) after the definition of "Lands Tribunal" there shall be inserted—
>> " "local authority" means a council constituted under section 2 of the Local Government etc. (Scotland) Act 1994 (c.39);"; and
  (c) for the definition of "tenement" there shall be substituted—
>> " "tenement" has the meaning given by section 26 of the Tenements (Scotland) Act 2004 (asp 11); and references to a flat in a tenement shall be construed accordingly;".

20. After schedule 1 there shall be inserted—

"SCHEDULE 1A

(introduced by section 10(2A))

Form of notice of potential liability for costs

"Notice of potential liability for costs

This notice gives details of certain maintenance or work carried out in relation the property specified in the notice. The effect of the notice is that a person may, on becoming the owner of the property, be liable by virtue of section 10(2A) of the Title Conditions (Scotland) Act 2003 (asp 9) for any outstanding costs relating to the maintenance or work.

Property to which the notice relates:
(see note 1 below)

Description of the maintenance or work to which notice relates:
(see note 2 below)

Person giving notice:
(see note 3 below)

Signature:
(see note 4 below)

Date of signing:"

Notes for completion

(These notes are not part of the notice)

1   Describe the property in a way that is sufficient to identify it. Where the property has a postal address, the description must include that address. Where title to the property has been registered in the Land Register of Scotland, the description must

refer to the title number of the property or of the larger subjects of which it forms part. Otherwise, the description should normally refer to and identify a deed recorded in a specified division of the Register of Sasines.

2   Describe the maintenance or work in general terms.

3   Give the name and address of the person applying for registration of the notice ("the applicant") or the applicant's name and the name and address of the applicant's agent.

4   The notice must be signed by or on behalf of the applicant."

GENERAL NOTE

Schedule 4 contains various amendments to the Title Conditions (Scotland) Act 2003. The procedure applicable to tenements for the registration of a notice of potential liability for costs is applied to non-tenemental burdens. The provisions of s.11 in relation to shared liability are modified introducing the definition of a floor area of a flat. Section 25 of the Title Conditions (Scotland) Act 2003 is amended in relation to the definition of community burdens. The original provision was that there had to be a common scheme on four or more units. This is reduced to two or more units. The provisions of ss.28, 29 and 31 of the 2003 Act will not apply to communities which consist of one tenement. The considerable difficulty which faced local authorities in relation to the interpretation of the original s.53 of the Title Conditions (Scotland) Act 2003 has been removed. Where there is a common scheme and there are related properties then it will not be necessary to identify all the benefited properties nor to effect dual registration. If further properties are sold from an estate subject to the same burdens as were imposed in prior feus then the new properties will effectively become part of a rolling community and will on registration of the disposition become both burdened and benefited property without further identification or specification.

INDEX

[all references are to page number]